Playful Early Childhood Care and Education

Lorayne Excell

Vivien Linington

(editors)

JUTA

Playful Early Childhood Care and Education

Juta and Company (Pty) Ltd
First Floor, Sunclare Building, 21 Dreyer Street, Claremont, 7708
Cape Town, South Africa

www.juta.co.za

© 2020 Juta and Company (Pty) Ltd

ISBN 978 1 48512 586 0

All rights reserved. No part of this publication may be reproduced or transmitted in any form or by any means, electronic or mechanical, including photocopying, recording, or any information storage or retrieval system, without prior permission in writing from the publisher. Subject to any applicable licensing terms and conditions in the case of electronically supplied publications, a person may engage in fair dealing with a copy of this publication for his or her personal or private use, or his or her research or private study. See Section 12(1)*(a)* of the Copyright Act 98 of 1978.

Project Manager: Deoni Conradie
Editor: Wendy Priilaid
Cover designer: Genevieve Simpson
Indexer: Adami Geldenhuys
Typesetter: Elinye Ithuba DTP Solutions

Typeset in 10.5pt Bembo Std

The author and the publisher believe on the strength of due diligence exercised that this work does not contain any material that is the subject of copyright held by another person. In the alternative, they believe that any protected pre-existing material that may be comprised in it has been used with appropriate authority or has been used in circumstances that make such use permissible under the law.

Contents

About the Editors xiv

Chapter 1: Early childhood care and education 1

1.1 Introduction.. 1
    1.1.1 The changing landscape... 2
    1.1.2 Terminology in the context of this book........................ 2

1.2. What is early childhood care and education?............................. 3

1.3 The importance of early childhood care and education 4

1.4 The multifaceted relationship between care and nurturing and growth, development and learning in young children 7
    1.4.1 Why is it important to provide quality ECCE services?.. 7

1.5 Looking at the past to make sense of the present 8
    1.5.1 The years before democracy 8
    1.5.2 The shift from pre-primary to early childhood development: An uneasy name change 9
    1.5.3 A new focus: the shift from ECD to ECCE.................... 14

1.6 ECCE provisioning: different settings for young children........... 16
    1.6.1 Home visiting 16
    1.6.2 Playgroups 17
    1.6.3 Toy libraries 18
    1.6.4 Community-based informal childcare 18
    1.6.5 Formal/centre-based services for children from birth to six years 19

1.7 Career pathways for teachers in the ECCE birth to four to five years phase.. 20

1.8 Summary 20

References... 21

Chapter 2:   Who is the young child? Constructions of children and childhood.................................... 25

2.1   Introduction 25
2.2   Shifts in our understandings of children and childhood 25
2.3   Differing constructions of childhood 27
     2.3.1   The historical child 27
     2.3.2   The sociological child 30
     2.3.3   African perspective... 32
2.4   The psychological perspective – the developing child 35
2.5   The being, belonging and becoming child............................... 39
     2.5.1   The being child... 39
     2.5.2   The belonging child 39
     2.5.3   The becoming child 40
2.6   Summary 40
References.. 41

Chapter 3:   A lens on development: a pathway of change 43

3.1   Introduction.. 43
3.2   Informing developmental theories and theorists: how young children develop and learn 44
     3.2.1   Maturation theory... 44
     3.2.2   Behaviourist theory 46
     3.2.3   Psychodynamic theory 47
     3.2.4   Cognitive theory: constructivism and sociocultural theory... 50
     3.2.5   Early childhood and neuroscience................................. 54
3.3   Developmental domains 56
3.4   Factors that influence overall wellbeing of young children, ie growth, development and learning 104
3.5   Summary 107
References.. 108

Chapter 4: Professional spaces: reimagining the role of the teacher **110**

4.1 Introduction.. 110
4.2 Who are today's early childhood teachers?............................... 110
    4.2.1 Characteristics of an ECCE professional educator........... 112
    4.2.2 The role of emotional intelligence 113
    4.2.3 Professional ethics 115
    4.2.4 The core value of inclusion 118
    4.2.5 The role of reflection in becoming a professional 121
4.3 Summary 122
References 122

Chapter 5: I am because we are: the role of community in the development and learning of the young child **125**

5.1 Introduction.. 125
5.2 Parents and community involvement and partnerships 126
    5.2.1 Parent involvement and partnerships 127
    5.2.2 Community involvement.. 131
5.3 Continuous communication and meaningful involvement with relevant stakeholders... 132
5.4 How the learning environment can build a community of children 135
5.5 Playroom assistants and volunteers in the birth to four-year-old centre 137
5.6 Referrals to services for support and enrichment..................... 138
5.7 Summary 141
References 141

Chapter 6: Playful pedagogies: creating playful spaces and places **143**

6.1 Introduction 143
6.2 Why play?... 144
6.3 What is play?.. 147

6.4	Theoretical underpinnings of play	148
	6.4.1 Piaget	148
	6.4.2 Vygotsky	149
	6.4.3 Sigmund Freud	149
	6.4.4 Erikson	149
	6.4.5 Other theorists	149
	6.4.6 Playful pedagogies	151
6.5	Underpinning principles and characteristics of play	155
6.6	Classification of play	156
6.7	Types of play	157
	6.7.1 Functional play	158
	6.7.2 Construction play	158
	6.7.3 Manipulative play	159
	6.7.4 Socio-dramatic play (fantasy, pretend play, make-believe play)	160
	6.7.5 Games with rules	161
	6.7.6 Implications for care, teaching and learning and the role of the teacher	162
6.8	Problematising play	164
6.9	Summary	165
References		165

Chapter 7: A creative and responsive curriculum for early childhood care and education 169

7.1	Introduction	169
7.2	What is a curriculum?	170
	7.2.1 Why a specialised curriculum for young children?	171
	7.2.2 The South African National Curriculum Framework	171
	7.2.3 The child and the NCF	172
7.3	Play, learning, teaching and the early childhood curriculum	177
	7.3.1 Understanding learning	178
	7.3.2 Understanding teaching: a playful pedagogic perspective (see chapters 6 and 8)	179
7.4	Implementing a play-based curriculum	181
	7.4.1 Holistic development and wellbeing	182

		7.4.2	A culturally responsive, inclusive and integrated curriculum	182

	7.4.3	Language as a tool for learning in a stimulating learning environment	182
	7.4.4	Responsive and caring adults who interact meaningfully with young children	183
	7.4.5	Learning through play	183
7.5	Realising the curriculum		184
	7.5.1	Creating playful learning spaces	184
	7.5.2	Creating the social and emotional environment	186
7.6	The intellectual environment		186
7.7	The temporal environment: use of time in the ECCE setting		187
	7.7.1	Routines	187
	7.7.2	Teacher-guided activities	188
	7.7.3	Child-initiated activities (free play)	191
7.8	Summary		193
References			193

Chapter 8: Supporting playful teaching and learning: a pedagogy of possibilities ... 199

8.1	Introduction		199
8.2	Playful teaching approaches		200
8.3	Promoting a playful approach in the implementation of general teaching strategies		201
	8.3.1	Demonstrating	201
	8.3.2	Describing	202
	8.3.3.	Encouraging, praising and giving feedback	203
	8.3.4	Facilitating and suggesting	205
	8.3.5	Telling and instructing	207
	8.3.6	Listening	208
	8.3.8	Positioning of people and equipment	211
	Positioning people		211
	8.3.9	Grouping	212
	8.3.10	Supervision	213
	8.3.10	Supervision	220

		8.3.11 Questioning...	214
		8.3.12 Singing and rhyme (see chapters 11 and 12)	216
8.4	Some additional strategies		216
	8.4.1	Scaffolding	216
	8.4.2	Co-construction of knowledge	217
	8.4.3	Documenting	219
	8.4.4	Empowering	220
8.5	Summary		222
References			223

Chapter 9: Nurturing care: a pathway to health 224

9.1	Introduction..		224
9.2	Key legislation in South Africa for the provision of safe and healthy childcare		224
9.3	The rationale for a health and safety policy framework for childcare		226
9.4	Health and safety policies in ECCE centres		227
	9.4.1.	Environmental hygiene issues	227
	9.4.2	Personal hygiene	231
	9.4.3	Nutrition, food and feeding practices	233
9.5	Rest and sleep..		240
9.6	Safety..		242
	Specific staff concerns		244
9.7 Preventative health care			250
	9.7.1	Children who become sick during the day	251
	9.7.2	Conditions that do not normally require exclusion	252
	9.7.3	Conditions where children should be excluded from group childcare	252
	9.7.4	Prevention of communicable diseases in the ECCE centre	254
	9.7.5	Medication administration in ECCE settings...................	255
9.8	Health education		256
9.9	Summary		257
References			257

Chapter 10: Building social and emotional wellbeing............. 259

10.1 Introduction.. 259
10.2 Unpacking terms... 260
    10.2.1 Emotional development... 260
    10.2.2 Personal development... 260
    10.2.3 Social development 260
10.3 Developing emotional understanding: exploring children's feelings 261
    10.3.1 Emotions frequently expressed by young children 262
    10.3.2 Strategies to deal with children's anxieties and fears 263
10.4 Personal development... 264
10.5 Developing social relationships 266
10.6 Theoretical perspectives... 268
10.7 Supporting children's emotional, social and personal development 269
    10.7.1 Helping children settle into the ECCE centre 270
10.8 Understanding and managing the social world 271
    10.8.1 Learning about social behaviour..................................... 272
    10.8.2 Conflict management 273
    10.8.3 Childhood friendships 276
    10.8.4 Dealing with grief 276
    10.8.5 Disruptive behaviours... 278
    10.8.6 Some specific behavioural problems 281
    10.8.7 Managing discriminatory behaviours and language 284
    10.8.8 Managing sexual behaviour 285
10.9 Self-regulatory behaviours 287
10.10 Summary 287
References... 287

Chapter 11: Creativity in early childhood............................ 289

11.1 Introduction 289
11.2 Exploring the meaning of creativity.. 290
    11.2.1 Teachers of young children should nurture their creativity.. 290
    11.2.2 The importance of creative learning............................... 291

11.3	The role of the creative in learning and development	291
	11.3.1 Physical development	292
	11.3.2 Coordinating gross and fine motor skills	293
	11.3.3 Perceptual motor development	294
	Understanding the role of the senses	302
	11.3.4 Sensory motor integration	303
11.4	Arts activities and creative development in early childhood	304
11.5	Music	305
	11.5.1 The role of music in the holistic development of the young child	305
	11.5.2 Music implementation	311
11.6	Setting up music and dance activities to promote creative learning opportunities in early childhood	317
11.7	Drama and imaginative play	319
	11.7.1 Books, stories, rhymes and poems	320
	11.7.2 Setting up drama and imaginative play activities to promote creative learning opportunities in early childhood	321
11.8	Visual art	325
	11.8.1 Scribbling stage	325
	11.8.2 Pre-schematic stage	326
	11.8.3 Setting up visual art activities to promote creative learning opportunities in early childhood	329
	11.8.4 Media suggestions for visual art projects	334
	11.8.5 Suggestions for parents in relation to the creative development of their young children	336
11.9	Summary	337
References		339

Chapter 12 : From babbles to books: literacy and the young child **344**

12.1	Introduction	344
12.2	Exploring early literacy	345
12.3	Literacy development	347
	12.3.1 The holistic nature of early literacy development	349

12.4	Strategies to promote early literacy development in the young child..	355
	12.4.1 The role of picture books	355
	12.4.3 Activities to enhance early writing	361
12.5	Technology and early literacy	362
12.6	Assessment and early intervention..	363
	12.6.1 Physical factors	369
	12.6.2 Emotional factors	370
	12.6.3 Social factors	370
12.7	Language diversity and multilingualism	371
12.8	Summary	374
References..		374

Chapter 13: Opening the doors of learning: a playful approach to understanding the world and nurturing an inquisitive mind 378

13.1	Introduction	378
13.2	How to support children's investigations through a playful pedagogical approach	379
13.3	Implementing STEM and STEAM	381
13.4	Exploring early mathematics..	382
	13.4.1 Learning about number concept..................................	384
	13.4.2 Patterns, functions and algebra	386
	13.4.3 Shape and space	386
	13.4.4 Measurement and data handling	387
	13.4.5 Integrating mathematical activities into the young child's day	388
13.5	Science and the young child	391
	13.5.1 Playful science	392
	13.5.2 Places and spaces for doing science	393
	13.5.3 The role of the teacher...	396
13.6	Technology	397
13.7	Exploring the social sciences..	400
	13.7.1 Social studies content in ECCE	400
	13.7.2 Embracing playful pedagogy: a useful approach to introducing the social sciences	403

13.8	Some concluding thoughts about social studies	405
13.9	Summary	407
References		407

Chapter 14: Responsive spaces: observation and assessment in a democratic context ... 409

14.1	Introduction	409
14.2	What is assessment?	410
14.3	Collecting evidence: assessment strategies	412
	14.3.1 Observation	412
	14.3.2 Other assessment strategies: portfolio	418
14.4	Identification, assessment, intervention and referral of young children with diverse needs	420
	14.4.1 Early identification and assessment	420
	14.4.2 Red flags for development from birth to four years	422
14.5	Reflecting on assessment	430
14.6	Reporting assessment data	430
14.7	Summary	431
References		432

Chapter 15: ECD policy in practice ... 434

15.1	Introduction	434
15.2	The legislative and policy framework for ECCE in South Africa	435
	15.2.1 National Development Plan 2030	435
	15.2.2 Children's Act 38 of 2005	435
	15.2.3 National Integrated Early Childhood Development (NIECD) Policy, 2015	436
	15.2.4 National Early Learning and Development Standards (NELDS) for children from birth to four years (2009)	437
	15.2.5 National Curriculum Framework (NCF) birth to four years (2015)	437
15.3	Roles of different departments and levels of government	438

15.4	Policy and legislative requirements for ECCE service providers and teachers	439
	15.4.1 Registration requirements	440
	15.4.2 Legal requirements for ECCE services operating on a for-profit and non-profit basis	445
	15.4.3 Funding for ECD services and programmes	445
15.5	Managing an ECCE centre	446
	15.5.1 Centre policies and operations	446
	15.5.2 Personnel and human resource development	447
	15.5.3 Financial and asset management	447
	15.5.4 Programme planning and evaluation	448
	15.5.5 Marketing and public relations	448
	15.5.6 Family partnerships	448
15.6	ECCE services as hubs for supporting broader early childhood development needs	449
15.7	Future policy directions	451
15.8	Summary	451
	References	452
Glossary		**455**
Index		**463**

About the Editors

Lorayne Excell co-ordinated early childhood development and, before retiring, headed the Foundation Studies Division at the Wits School of Education. She is currently employed as a Visiting Researcher at the Wits School of Education, specifically to develop the new ECCE qualification. Her specialisation and research interests are in early childhood education. Dr Excell has worked extensively with Vivien Linington over the last 20 years teaching Grade R and other ECD practitioners, researching the early childhood education field and actively promoting what is now termed the 'pedagogy of play'.

Vivien Linington is involved in student development at the Wits School of Education and Varsity College. Her two fields of interest are early childhood education and educational theory. Together with Lorayne Excell, she has researched and published in areas such as social justice, professional teacher development, the importance of high-quality early childhood education as well as the central role of play. She continues to play a central role in this field.

Chapter 1

Early childhood care and education

Lorayne Excell, Vivien Linington,
Jane Sethusha and Linda Biersteker

There can be no keener revelation of a society's soul than the way in which it treats its children (**Nelson Mandela**).

In this chapter we consider

- what is meant by the term 'early childhood care and education' (ECCE), and explain the importance of quality care and stimulation for all children even before birth
- critically reflect on the multifaceted relationship between the following two domains – care and nurturing; and growth, development and learning in young children
- the history of early childhood education in South Africa, and the historical shifts that have led to current policies and the introduction of formal qualifications for the care and education young children from birth onwards
- different settings for young children and how these came about, and critically reflect on the effectiveness of different ECCE settings
- reflect on possible career pathways for teachers working in this phase of education.

1.1 INTRODUCTION

The care and education of babies, toddlers and young children has entered an exciting phase in the South African landscape. While ECCE still remains a marginalised phase of education, there are many indicators that point to substantial growth and expansion in the overall field, as well as to increasing economic, social and political support for early childhood care and education (DHET, 2017).

A variety of different terminology is used when talking about this phase of education. Last-century terms such as 'nursery school', 'crèche', 'preschool', 'early learning', 'pre-primary', 'play group', 'educare', and a host of others abounded both within South Africa and internationally. In the 1990s, the term 'early childhood development' (ECD) was introduced (RSA, 1996a). This term was understood differently by different people and, from a South African policy perspective, referred to children aged from birth to nine years.

In reality, however, ECD has come to mean the care and education of children aged from birth to four/five years (ie before they enter the Grade R year). Progressive legislation, especially the introduction of the Minimum Qualification Requirements for Teachers in Early Childhood Care and Education (DHET, 2017), has opened new possibilities for the phase.

In this chapter we will explore these possibilities and some of the reasons why ECCE has captured the imagination of political leaders as well as civil society.

1.1.1 The changing landscape

These new insights and understandings of ECCE and their importance in ensuring the optimal growth, development, learning and wellbeing of all children have many different origins. Contributions from alternative disciplines such as anthropology and sociology have challenged traditional early childhood theories and practices that emanated from the discipline of developmental psychology. In addition, there has been a growing movement from the African continent and elsewhere that has questioned why alternative philosophies and practices such as indigenous knowledge systems are not considered. The decolonising discourse and a growing realisation of the value of indigenous knowledge in early education have added momentum to the debate. These new perspectives will be reflected throughout this book, while at the same time the principles that continue to underpin quality early learning (and have been followed over the centuries) will inform its structure and content.

Specific themes will be woven throughout the book and foregrounded in certain chapters. . These themes include:

- a focus on social reform which acknowledges equity and social justice across the curriculum and the necessity of ensuring all ECCE practice is culturally responsive and contextually relevant
- the understanding that all children are important and unique, and the recognition that they are competent and capable within their own right, and that all of them have a right to be heard; in other words, they have agency
- foregrounding the place of playful learning and teaching in early education
- professionalism, which includes becoming a critically reflective teacher who acknowledges the parent as the child's primary educator and the value of partnerships between home and school.

1.1.2 Terminology in the context of this book

Given that a new era is beginning, we are also going to introduce some changes in terminology in this book. We will refer to all places that offer childcare and education as ECCE centres. We will, however, still make mention of the home and unique ECCE situations such as a toy library. Given new perspectives and understandings of ECCE, we are also not going to conform to gender stereotyping. When writing about children, we will use the terms she/he, her/his interchangeably. We will do the same for adults, be they parents, teachers or other community members, rather than being gender specific.

As we have indicated above, there is a wide range of people who might be the child's primary caregiver. These could be parents, members of the extended family, other community members and even older siblings. To make this book 'less wordy', we will, in the majority of instances, use the term 'parent' in an inclusive way to refer to any primary caregiver of the child. Similarly, while acknowledging that babies, toddlers and young children are unique in their own right, we will use the term 'children' or ''young children to refer to all children from birth to five. An exception to this, of course, will be where we focus on a particular age group.

This book should be of interest to anyone who cares for and educates children from birth to age five (before they enter Grade R). With these thoughts in mind, we will now explore what is meant by the term 'ECCE', how we in South Africa have arrived at our current situation and explore some career possibilities for those adults who undertake the new qualifications that are being introduced.

1.2. WHAT IS EARLY CHILDHOOD CARE AND EDUCATION?

Early childhood signifies a period of expansive growth, development and learning which is most rapid in the early years of life from conception to age five. These early years of development and learning are critical for providing a firm foundation in cognitive, language and motor development, as well as social, emotional, regulatory and moral development (Fauth & Thompson, 2009). ECCE encompasses a variety of activities and programmes that focus on holistic development, wellbeing and learning of young children from conception until age four or five (until they commence Grade R).

ECCE as a discipline focuses on the following:
- Holistic development – physical, cognitive (including language), creative, social, emotional and moral, many aspects of which will be influenced by the socioeconomic and cultural context
- Understanding the connections and relationship between growth, development and learning
- Understanding the roles and responsibilities of parents, teachers and others who interact with the young child
- Understanding the environmental, biological, social and cultural influences on growth, development and learning (Fink & Rockers, 2014).

ECCE benefits society in the sense that young children learn from the start and are also prepared for future learning by acquiring the skills, knowledge and opportunities to thrive later in life. In short, children exposed to effective and quality EECE programmes and activities become better prepared for formal schooling and lifelong learning. Early childhood programmes focus on play as the most important approach for development and learning. Play is key because it affords children an opportunity to engage in a range of educational and social activities, which fosters effective learning (Department of Social Development, 2015).

1.3 THE IMPORTANCE OF EARLY CHILDHOOD CARE AND EDUCATION

Research in South Africa and internationally indicates that the early years are critical for development (Bakken, Brown & Downing, 2017; Wood & Hedges, 2016; Jones et al, 2016). The stages from birth to seven years signify an extremely important phase of rapid physical, cognitive, emotional, social and moral growth and development and learning. This is a period when young children acquire concepts, skills and attitudes that lay the foundation for lifelong learning (Bakken et al, 2017). Such holistic development includes the acquisition of language and perceptual-motor skills. These skills are necessary for successful learning, including learning to read and write, the acquisition of emergent numeracy concepts and skills, problem-solving skills, enthusiasm in learning, and the formation and sustenance of relationships.

Challenges are created in later years if opportunities to learn and develop in early childhood are missed, thus it can be said that effective investments in the early years are crucial for human development. Investing in early childhood education, care and development is one of the best investments a country can make to boost economic growth, promote peaceful and sustainable societies, and eliminate extreme poverty and inequality (Yoshikawa & Kabay, 2015). Poor diets are leading to alarming levels of child malnutrition worldwide, causing millions of children to be stunted, overweight or lacking essential vitamins and nutrients. Overall, one-third of children under the age of five are not growing well because they are not eating well (UNICEF, 2019). Furthermore, it is important for governments to adopt a strategy of investing in early child development in order to meet the Millennium Development Goals (Lomazzi, Borisch & Laaser, 2014) for poverty reduction, education and health.

It is during these early years that the morals and values required to build a peaceful, prosperous and democratic society are acquired. Such values include respect for human rights, appreciation of diversity, anti-bias, tolerance and justice. History has shown that democracy is open to challenge. It is therefore important that ECCE plays its role in laying the foundations for strengthening this form of inclusive governance by giving its young citizens the requisite skills, attitudes and values for future participation.

Democracy is aligned with the Bill of Rights. The Bill of Rights in South Africa (RSA, 1996b) stipulates that every child and young person has rights, no matter who they are or where they live, and it is the responsibility of government to protect, respect and fulfil them.

Section 28 of the Bill of Rights of the Constitution of the Republic of South Africa outlines that every child has a right to the following:

- Basic nutrition
- Shelter
- Health care and social services
- Protection from maltreatment, neglect, abuse or degradation.

While it is not specific to children, the Constitution also guarantees the right to education (RSA, 1996b).

As children grow, they need to be guided towards the understanding that rights are accompanied by responsibilities. This is a process.

Try this out

Consider the following rights of children and decide on the appropriate responsibility by completing the column on the right. The first one has been done for you.

Rights	Responsibilities
I have the right to be heard	I have the responsibility to listen to others
I have the right to good health care, especially when I am sick	
I have the right to go to school and learn	
I have the right to be loved and protected from harm	
I have the right to belong, even if I am different from most other people	

Something to consider

Quality ECCE programme will respect these rights and set the basis for lifelong learning through the monitoring of a child's safety, health and nutrition status during this critical period of development (Yoshikawa & Kabay, 2015). In addition, young children require stimulating, nurturing and stable relationships with adults, parents and other caregivers. It remains the responsibility of ECCE teachers and parents to ensure that children are provided with quality interactive opportunities to learn and develop as it is these interactions, behaviours and teaching practices that contribute towards and influence children's development as well as their successful entry into formal schooling. Quality opportunities also include providing a rich learning environment with age and developmentally appropriate and culturally responsive resources, and making effective decisions in creative and appropriate ways (Yoshikawa & Kabay, 2015).

Find out more

Not providing children with relevant experiences and opportunities to learn is detrimental to their holistic development and learning and can result in a widening achievement gap prior to children even beginning Grade R (Jacob & Ludwig, 2009). This must be borne in mind when working with children in disadvantaged contexts, particularly where communities are poverty-stricken (Garcia & Frede, 2010). ECCE cannot be 'one size (way) fits all'.

Vulnerable children, especially in deep rural contexts and previously disadvantaged areas, frequently require extensive opportunities to learn and develop, and often have limited access to these opportunities. In these situations, therefore, the provision of opportunities to nurture healthy development and early learning becomes extremely important. It is also important for adults working in these situations to carefully consider how to improve strategies used to support children at varying levels of development and competency. Every child, regardless of their background, should be given the best possible opportunities for learning and development.

Reflection

How can an ECCE teacher provide quality learning opportunities for all children under the age of five years?

Did you consider that teachers could use strategies such as implementing a flexible curriculum and adapting activities to suit the context, age and stage of development of each child? (See chapters 6, 7 and 8.) They could also, of course, implement the curriculum flexibly. Teachers must also track children's progress, and at the same time respond open-endedly to various basic care needs of the children and the families they serve. All these tasks require a teacher who has a detailed knowledge of child development and learning, in addition to skills, and attitudes that are adaptable.

1.4 THE MULTIFACETED RELATIONSHIP BETWEEN CARE AND NURTURING AND GROWTH, DEVELOPMENT AND LEARNING IN YOUNG CHILDREN

Nurturing and care refer to the provision by parents and other adults of a safe and stable environment that ensures children's good health and nutrition, and protection from harm and threats. This should also provide opportunities for early learning through interactions that are emotionally supportive and responsive (Burger, 2010). Nurturing and care are based on the premise that a good start in life increases the chances for success. Nurturing and caring adults should be responsible for ensuring that children' physical, social-emotional and cognitive growth and development and learning are at the heart of quality child care. Children learn from daily interactions with their caregivers, therefore it is important that relationships between them are nurtured, individualised, responsive and predictable. Nurturing and care starts at birth, and caregivers need in particular to understand how to respond to individual children's social and emotional needs. In addition, adults require training in facilitating the play-based and exploratory approaches that serve as the basis for successful learning and development. Regardless of the type of ECCE centre or setting (such as childcare centres, family–child care homes, ECD centres and crèches), they should all be places where nurturing staff provide an environment rich in language and stimulating activities guided by quality early childhood programmes. Such a caring and stimulating environment will allow children to reach their optimal potential and guarantee a strong foundation for future health, positive behaviour and successful learning.

ECCE is a discipline and therefore knowledge and insight of practitioners regarding child development is crucial. Teachers are required to have passion for the work that they do, sensitivity towards the needs of children, a positive attitude towards caring for children and, most importantly, love for children. Specialised continuous education is required for teachers in order to expand their knowledge.

1.4.1 Why is it important to provide quality ECCE services?

ECCE services provide education and care to children in the temporary absence of their parents or adult caregivers (Department of Social Development, 2015). Such services require a holistic approach and consideration for the importance of health, nutrition, education, psychosocial and other basic needs within the context of the family and the community (Munthali, Mvula & Silo, 2014).

In South Africa, the Department of Social Development is entrusted with the responsibility of ensuring that opportunities and conditions are created for the optimum development and learning of all children and their families through the provision and support of appropriate services (Department of Social Development, 2015). Quality ECCE ensures that disadvantaged children and those with disabilities are not marginalised, and that their development and learning needs are not ignored. Such children need to be accommodated in ECCE services, and teachers must provide appropriate activities and programmes that meet their specific needs.

ECCE services are an important support system within the community. Community members, parents and all other family structures should complement the services provided at ECCE centres. Close collaboration between stakeholders is required in order to address children's holistic needs (see Chapters 5 and 9).

1.5 LOOKING AT THE PAST TO MAKE SENSE OF THE PRESENT

Within the South African context, the preschool movement (the years before children begin formal schooling) has experienced enormous development, and is predominantly based on theories and practices that originated in England and Europe. Informing ideas were drawn from the German educationist Froebel, who founded the kindergarten (or 'children's garden'); the McMillan sisters, who began the open-air nursery school in England; and Robert Owen, a philanthropic factory owner who opened the British Infant School. They all offered some form of play-based learning which in turn influenced early childhood education in South Africa.

Although the aims and focus of each approach may have been different, they all shared similar philosophies about the nature of learning and development in young children. These ideas (which in turn have been passed down since the time of the ancient Greeks) still continue to inform practice, with play as a consistent and crucial thread running through all them. And despite different understandings of play, early childhood theorists and educationists continue to acknowledge its importance in early learning and development (Pound, 2014).

1.5.1 The years before democracy

Early childhood education started from humble beginnings in 1930 when the Johannesburg Medical Officer of Health opened the first nursery school in Fordsburg (a suburb in Johannesburg), specifically for indigent (poor) white children (Hallett, 1972). From the outset, there was little government support for the nursery school movement, and it was through the endeavours of civil society that their numbers slowly increased. Given the political context of the time, the limited services on offer were predominately for white children, and minimal training was available for white women. In fact, in 1948 when the Nationalist government came to power, they wrote in their Education Manifesto that parents should not palm their childcare and parenting responsibilities off onto the state (NEPI, 1992). There were very few services available for other population groups.

The Education Act of 1967 made pre-primary education (as it was then named) a provincial competence. A three-year (and later a four-year) Pre-Primary Diploma was introduced at colleges of education. Depending on provincial decisions, some white pre-primary schools were then either fully or partially subsidised. Other pre-primary schools were independent but had to register with the relevant education department. In certain provinces, for example the Cape Province, a limited pre-primary service and training for teachers was offered to coloured people and in Natal to Indians, with fewer opportunities made available to black people. For a time, the Soweto College of Education offered some pre-primary qualifications, as did some of the teacher training colleges in the homelands. A small number of crèches (subsidised by the Department of Social Welfare) were opened for black children. However, preschool provisioning and training were extremely limited for the majority of the population.

It thus fell to civil society and what has become known as non-governmental and non-profit organisations (NGOs and NPOs respectively) to fill the gap. From the early 1970s onward a number of organisations opened their doors to provide training for people working with babies and young children. In some cases, services have also been offered to children. During the dark days of apartheid, if it had not been for the NGO movement most of the population would not have had access to any early childhood preschool services, and this has continued to play a pivotal role in keeping the early childhood debate on the table.

1.5.2 The shift from pre-primary to early childhood development: An uneasy name change

The advent of democracy brought sweeping educational change to all phases of education when the Schools Act of 1996 was promulgated (RSA, 1996a), and a new phase of education was introduced. The period from birth to nine years of age was called early childhood development (ECD). According to Seleti (2009), in the South African context ECD refers to a comprehensive approach to policies and programmes for children from birth to nine years of age, with the active participation of their parents and caregivers. Its purpose is to protect the child's rights to develop her full cognitive, emotional, social and physical potential. The South African Schools Act of 1996 defines ECD as a process of emotional, cognitive, sensory, spiritual, moral, physical, social and communication development of children from birth to school-going age (RSA, 1996a).

Within this broad ECD sphere, the junior primary phase was renamed the Foundation Phase and what had previously been a three-year phase of formal schooling was extended by a year. This additional year was seen as a bridging year and is known as the reception year or Grade R. It was envisaged that Grade R would become a compulsory school year by 2019, but this has not happened.

The introduction of the Grade R year has had unforeseen consequences for the ECD phase, some of which are described in the following sections.

1.5.2.1 The changing ECD focus

Despite ECD being conceptualised as being from birth to age nine, the focus was predominantly on the Foundation Phase. The introduction of the Grade R year was slow to materialise. When White Paper 5 on Early Childhood Development (DoE, 2001) was introduced, the emphasis was on the roll-out of the Grade R year, and the preceding years were given scant attention. There was a minimal budget, little capacity and a lack of expertise for the pre-Grade R years as the focus was on qualifying Grade R practitioners. What little ECD training was offered fell to the NGOs. The majority of ECD practitioners were and remain un- or underqualified.

15.2.2 The change to the school admission age

Prior to the passing of the Education Act in 1996, Grade R had been the final year of preschool education. The school admission age was six – children had to start Grade 1 in the year they were turning seven. This has not changed, but following a Constitutional Court ruling in 2001 children can now begin Grade 1 at age five, provided that they turn six before 30 June of their Grade 1 year. This in effect lowered the entry age for Grade R to four and a half years. A consequence of the Constitutional Court's ruling was a subtle but negative shift in the age cohort of children covered by ECD services. There appeared to be a move to place a number of children aged four and a half into Grade R, regardless of their developmental level. At the same time, the focus for preschool education was shifted from birth to four years, whereas it had previously been birth to five years, turning six. There is still considerable debate about the pedagogical soundness of this situation, as it is now uncertain whether the needs of the five-year-old are adequately met. A possible solution lies in the National Development Plan 2030 that has proposed a second preschool year. It is envisaged that this year would precede Grade R and could in theory address the age group three and a half to four, turning five. This proposal is currently under review.

1.5.2.3 Change of the government department responsible for ECD provisioning

Initially, post-1996 early childhood education was the responsibility of the Department of Education. However, in the early 2000s, when a greater emphasis was placed on the implementation of the Grade R year, government took the decision to relocate the responsibility and control for the ECD sector (the years before Grade R) to the Department of Social Development (DSD). Though there is talk that ECD will once again become the responsibility of the Department of Basic Education (DBE), at the time of writing the DSD remains the lead organisation (Ilifa Labantwana, 2017).

1.5.2.4 Changes to teacher qualification structures

The publication of the Committee on Teacher Education Policy (South Africa (COTEP) document in 2001 restructured the framework for teacher qualifications. Part of this restructuring was to withdraw the existing formal qualifications for pre-primary teachers, which meant that there were now no formally recognised qualifications for teachers of young children. The resultant gap was filled mainly by the NGO sector, which offered a variety of non-formal qualifications. These qualifications, which are now registered on the National Qualifications Framework (NQF), ranged between NQF levels 2 and 5. There are very few organisations which offer NQF level 5 or 6 qualifications. When one considers that a matric qualification is at NQF level 4 and a formal teaching qualification (Bachelor of Education) is an NQF level 7, ECD qualifications are not ranked very highly. They are vocational and occupational in nature, and do not allow the holder to register with the South African Council for Educators (SACE). Consequently, ECD practitioners currently have little status, are poorly remunerated and have a dismal career pathway. This dearth in formal qualifications for the ECD sector has only recently been addressed when in 2017 the Department of Higher Education and Training (DHET) published the Policy on Minimum Requirements for Programmes Leading to Qualifications in Higher Education for Early Childhood Development Educators. These new qualifications comprise a higher certificate in ECCE, an NQF level 6 diploma and an NQF level 7 degree in ECCE. It is envisaged that the introduction of these qualifications will assist towards the greater professionalisation of the sector, which is now being called ECCE.

Something to consider

The ECCE journey has been a tumultuous (chaotic) one. Given that care and nurturing as well as appropriate stimulation and education are equally important in quality ECCE provisioning, the importance of a multidisciplinary, interdepartmental approach to administer service provisioning has been recognised for a long time. Three key departments were identified – those of [Basic] Education (DBE), Social Development (DSD) and Health (DoH) – and certain roles specific to each one were assigned. For instance, improving quality through practitioner training and curriculum development was delegated to all three collectively, but increasing access and improving quality to Grade R (and lower age cohorts), for example, were the responsibility of the DBE and the DSD only (DBE, 2016). In addition, the different key ECD departments (the DBE, the DSD and the DoH) developed a number of documents and policies relating to their ECD roles, and provided guidelines for managing the children and the specific age cohort for which they were responsible. In reality, however, many different departments and stakeholders all had some ECD input prior to the development of the National Integrated ECD Policy (DSD, 2015). Some examples are given in Table 1.1.

Table 1.1 ECD input prior to the development of the National Integrated ECD Policy

Department	Age cohort	Chief areas of concern	Policies
Social Development	Birth to five years	Social grants; subsidies; site registration	White Paper on Social Development 1997; Children's Act 38 of 2005 and as amended 2007 and 2010; The National Integrated Early Childhood Development Policy, 2015
Department of [Basic] Education	Birth to nine years	Curriculum development and implementation; early stimulation; teacher qualifications; learning and teaching resources	The South African Schools Act, 1996; The National ECD Pilot project, 2001; ECD White Paper, 2001; The National Early Learning Development Standards, 2007; The National Curriculum Framework, 2015

Department	Age cohort	Chief areas of concern	Policies
Health	Prenatal to nine years	Maternal and childcare; primary health care; HIV and AIDS interventions; Health Sector Strategic Framework	Integrated Management of Childhood Diseases; School Health Policy; Integrated Plan for Children affected and infected by HIV and AIDS; Road to Health booklet
Home Affairs	Birth +	Birth registration	
Women and Children		New National Policy Investigation, 1992	
Some other stakeholders			
Ilifa Labantwana	Prenatal to four years	Essential package – which looks as child health, welfare, stimulation	
UNICEF	Prenatal to four years	Provides support for many ECD initiatives and policy development by various government departments	

SOURCE: SELETI (2009)

Relevant polices are discussed in Chapter 15.

Despite a number of excellent policies, the country is struggling to implement them successfully. South Africa remains a country where quality ECCE is sorely lacking despite many different forms of ECD provisioning being available (see section 1.6). According to 2016 figures presented by the DBE, there were 5.3 million children aged from birth to four years, of which 43.2% lived in rural areas and 56.8% in urban areas. Of these children, 71.9% were exposed to some form of ECD, with this percentage rising to 80.4% in the two to four year age group (DBE, 2016). This could take the form of visits to a toy library, attendance at an ECCE centre or visits to a playgroup-type situation. Most playgroup programmes are offered at least two days a week or more. However, we know that access to ECCE does not necessarily guarantee quality.

1.5.3 A new focus: the shift from ECD to ECCE

In the last decade, there has been increasing evidence, both international and national, on the importance of quality experiences in the first five years to ensure children's optimal growth, development and learning. Evidence is drawn from a variety of sources. The work on neurogenesis (the process by which new neurons are formed in the brain) has provided concrete evidence on how quality care and stimulation from conception onwards encourages the development of neurones and neural plasticity in young children, thus enabling and enhancing later learning opportunities for young children (see Chapter 3). These studies also recognise the importance of windows of opportunity for learning, which are recognised times when children are more ready to acquire certain skills and concepts. It is now accepted that the first five years are essential for the acquisition of basic skills and concepts (see section 3.2.5). In South Africa these results have also been verified by the Diagnostic Review (DR) (Richter et al, 2012).

Find out more

This review is based on 112 relevant policy documents, evaluations and studies, as well as consultations with ECD practitioners, civil society, researchers and government officials at national, provincial and local levels.

Key policy findings from the Diagnostic Review are as follows:
- A broader definition of ECD programmes than is currently in the Children's Act is needed to cover all aspects of children's development from conception to the Foundation Phase of schooling.
- Using this broader definition, many elements of comprehensive ECD support and services are already in place, and some are performing well. These include some aspects of basic services provision, citizenship (birth registration), social security, health care for women and children, ECCE, and preparation for formal schooling. Improvements in access and quality must continue to be sought in all areas.
- There are important gaps, notably support for parenting, the prevention of stunting among young children, safe and affordable child care for very young children and other families needing assistance, and planned rapid expansion ECCE and provision of services to the most at-need families, including children with disabilities. (Richter et al, 2012: 1)
- This Review recommended that the key ECD strategies should be: (i) to deliver comprehensive services to young children, using all opportunities of contact with families; to extend ECCE through home- and community-based programmes, beginning with the poorest communities not reached by current services; (ii) to ensure food security and adequate

daily nutrition for the youngest children to avert the lifelong damaging effects of stunting; (iii) to launch well-designed high-profile parent support programmes through media campaigns, community activities and services that acknowledge and reinforce the importance of positive parenting for young children.
- ECD services require strong and coordinated intersectoral vision, commitment and action. The current coordination structures are not working adequately (Richter et al, 2012: 1–2).

Interested readers can go to the following website for further details on the Review: https://www.dpme.gov.za/keyfocusareas/evaluationsSite/Evaluations/Diagnostic%20Review%20of%20Early%20Childhood%20Development.pdf

This Review as a whole identified many obstacles faced by especially vulnerable children in realising their optimal potential. Obstacles include poverty, malnutrition, disease, neglect and violence, to name a few. It is also known that vulnerable children are the ones least likely to receive quality ECCE (Richter et al; 2012; Ilifa Labantwana, 2013).

There is obviously huge concern in South Africa about the plight of young, vulnerable children (Berry, Dawes & Biersteker, 2013; Ilifa Labantwana, 2013). An important project aimed at addressing some of these concerns was launched in 2013. Called The Essential Package, and informed by the Diagnostic Review (Richter et al, 2012), it is a series of continuous interventions aimed at the family, which is recognised as the primary level of support. It has identified a range of ECD services considered essential for vulnerable children including health, welfare and education as well as promoting human rights. For readers who would like to explore this package in more detail consult the website: http://www.ilifalabantwana.co.za

Many studies throughout the Western world and some in South Africa point to the importance of quality care and stimulation in ensuring that children reach their optimal growth, development and learning potential (Siraj-Blatchford & Woodhead, 2009; Siraj- Blatchford, 2009; Bruce, 2015). These studies also identify the teacher as being pivotal to the ECCE project, and show that well-qualified teachers do make a difference. It has also been shown that vulnerable children will benefit the most from quality ECCE. Research has shown that these children, when immersed in quality learning environments, show more learning gains than those from more privileged families.

All these studies have led to a shift in government thinking as we have already noted. In 2013, the National Development Plan highlighted ECD as a priority area. This has had important consequences for the phase. The DHET has recently introduced formal teacher education qualifications for those wishing to teach young children (DHET, 2017). Among other qualifications, the DHET has introduced a higher certificate, a diploma and a degree in ECCE. The possibility of introducing a compulsory pre-Grade R year by

2030 is also being discussed, but as yet there is no firm decision (Kotze, 2015. President Ramaphosa in his 2019 State of the Nation Address (SONA) made two important announcements in relation to ECCE:

1. The DBE will take over the responsibility for ECD centres from the DSD.
2. The government will push ahead towards the implementation of two years of compulsory ECD for all children before they enter Grade 1 (Ramaphosa, 2019).

These exciting initiatives certainly offer new opportunities to all those working in the ECCE phase, as well as for different type of ECCE provisioning.

1.6 ECCE PROVISIONING: DIFFERENT SETTINGS FOR YOUNG CHILDREN

Young children under school-going age receive ECCE services in a variety of different settings. These include nurseries or preschools, ECD centres/crèches, playgroups and day mothers, as well as home-visiting programmes and toy libraries. ECD centres/crèches are the most common service, reaching approximately 20% of young children in 2016 (Statistics South Africa, 2017). In response to a scarcity of ECCE services, especially for poor children, various types of less-formal services are offered, mostly by the non-governmental sector. Some of these receive DSD funding.

There are two main types of delivery:
1. Home-visiting programmes
2. Group sessions, such as community playgroups.

Interventions often include combinations of these approaches, with some group activities accompanying a home-visiting approach or some home visits supporting a group activity.

1.6.1 Home visiting

Home visiting is a strategy for supporting parents and promoting the growth and development of young children, including their school readiness (Rao et al, 2014). In South Africa there are several kinds of home-visiting services in which trained community members visit vulnerable households where children do not attend preschool. The programme usually has an educational component for primary caregiver and/or child, psychosocial and practical support to the caregiver (eg accessing documents, grants and services). Evidence is that these programmes can be very effective for promoting health, safety and positive parenting, but that in order to effectively improve children's educational outcomes they need to be long term (at least a year) and frequent (Rao et al,

2014). The Turkish Early Education Project had significant long-term positive effects on children's cognitive skills, social relations and school adjustment compared with those of control peers, even seven years after the end of the intervention. This was a two-year programme with weekly participation, a one-on-one visit in week one and a group meeting every second week (Kagitcibasi et al, 2009).

South African ECD policy promotes home visits by health workers for carers of children under three years to support health, nutrition and responsive caregiving.

1.6.2 Playgroups

Community playgroups bring children together, with or without their parents, for a group educational experience. Caregivers may participate in them or have a separate educational session while the children are busy. Some of these playgroups are offered by mobile units fitted out with educational equipment that visit remote villages and children on farms. It is common for playgroups to be offered for shorter hours than a preschool – three to four hours twice or three times a week. Playgroups are usually established by NGOs who train community members to facilitate them, supply basic play materials and may contribute a stipend to the facilitators as the service is often free in poor communities.

Find out more

Research on the effectiveness of playgroups is inconclusive because they take so many forms and focus on different goals. For example, many focus on improving parenting practice or providing a social play experience but very few studies have investigated the effectiveness of playgroups in improving the school readiness of children. However, there is evidence from Northern Ireland (Turner, 1974) that children who participated in a playgroup for three hours a day, five days per week had significantly higher vocabulary and cognitive scores than non-attending children from the same community. A low-income country experimental study in Cambodia found that playgroup children had better developmental outcomes than those who had not participated in a programme, and had the same performance as those who attended a five session per week home-based preschools, though children attending higher-quality government schools performed best. A recent Ugandan study (Centre for Basic Research, 2017) assessed the extent to which attendance in home learning groups run by parent educators three days a week for three hours a day and including a parent education component, improved learning in the Foundation Phase. Children performed somewhat higher on numeracy and literacy tests in Grade 3 than those who had not attended a programme. Playgroups that have sessions more frequently and are delivered by well-trained facilitators with a curriculum related to the abilities needed for learning at school are more likely to be successful.

1.6.3 Toy libraries

Toy libraries may target children or also involve caregivers. These include special-needs-focused libraries where parents receive specific instruction on how to support their children's development. There are many toy libraries for children in disadvantaged communities to help them to develop the physical and cognitive skills needed for formal learning and to encourage interactive play. Some toy libraries offer a 'drop-in' experience to expose children attending other services such as preschools and playgroups to a greater range of equipment and materials, while some offer a lending service where parents may borrow toys and books.

1.6.4 Community-based informal childcare

Childminding or day-mother care for fewer than six children at home is a common informal form of childcare in areas where there are employment opportunities for women. Childminders tend to have mixed age groups and may also provide after care for school-age children for part of the day. If it is of sufficient quality, this convenient, flexible family-style care is especially beneficial for infants and toddlers. It needs to be distinguished from larger group programmes offered from homes, converted garages, etc, that could be classified as home-based ECD centres or crèches. Because care of fewer than six children is not regulated by the Children's Act (RSA, 2005), little is known about the extent and quality of this form of care. In countries such as the UK, the US and Australia, this is a common form of provision carefully regulated by local authorities. There is limited research on the effectiveness of childminding, and findings are mixed. However, studies do point to the importance of quality (Ang, Brooker & Stephen, 2017).

> **Find out more**
>
> The *Hogares Comunitarios* (Community Day Care Programme) is an example of a large-scale state-subsidised urban programme delivered in two countries (Colombia and Guatemala) and targeting children aged up to six years of working women in poor communities. Children participate in a structured daily programme (either for the whole or part of the day) and basic equipment, training and oversight are provided, as well as a strong health and nutrition component. Children who had participated in **Hogares** for more than 16 months showed modest but significant improvements in receptive language, mathematical reasoning, general knowledge and verbal ability compared to those who did not have access to the programme (Bernal & Fernandez, 2013).

1.6.5 Formal/centre-based services for children from birth to six years

This is the most prevalent form of provision and comprises the following:
- Pre-primary/nursery schools that provide for children from three to five or six years of age (recently some pre-primary and nursery schools have admitted younger children)
- ECD centres/crèches that provide for children from birth to five years.

Pre-primary or nursery schools have an educational focus and usually offer a part-day programme. Societal change has led to many previously part-time programmes being extended to include after care and other forms of full-day provision.

ECD centres or crèches provide full day care with or without an educational component, and are the main form of provision. In the past, these offered custodial care for children of working mothers but it is now a Children's Act requirement that an educational component is offered (RSA, 2005). These centres may be private businesses or services run by NGOs, religious organisations, communities and, less commonly, some employers (eg universities, hospitals, some factories and financial institutions). A limited number of public ECD centres are run by municipalities, such as the City of Tshwane. All centres have to be registered (RSA, 1996). (Registration will be discussed in Chapter 15.)

An extensive body of research shows that high-quality ECD centre programmes have positive effects on child development and can narrow the achievement gap between children from low-income families and their more advantaged peers in the preschool years (Raikes et al, 2017). Some studies indicate that these benefits endure into the primary years of school, while others show that they fade for a variety of possible reasons, particularly when delivered at a scale and quality that is difficult to maintain (Lipsey, Farran & Hofer, 2015). Very high-quality, intensive and long-duration programmes for poor children, such as the Perry Preschool and the Abecedarian, have been found to have long-term effects (Heckman et al, 2010). The Perry Preschool Project included two years of high-quality preschool for three- and four-year-old children delivered by graduate teachers – one for each six children. This was supplemented by weekly home visits to mother and child. The Abecedarian Project which was for children aged from three months to the year before school, included a high-quality, centre-based early-care programmes, with one carer to three children, plus an intensive home-visiting programme along with social and medical services, and nutritional supplements. The effects are significantly greater for lower-income children than for their wealthier counterparts (Dahl & Lochner, 2005). This is not surprising as it is well known that the home environment contributes substantially to children's chances of school success. Children from better-off homes have greater access to the types of resources and stimulation at home that prepares them for school than poorer children do. This means that it is urgent to prioritise increasing access to good quality ECCE programmes for the poorest children.

1.7 CAREER PATHWAYS FOR TEACHERS IN THE ECCE BIRTH TO FOUR TO FIVE YEARS PHASE

The diploma in Early Childhood Care and Education, and the Bachelor of Education in Early Childhood Care and Education degree to which we have already referred prepare teachers with focused knowledge and skills related to the care and education of children from birth to four years of age. Policy provides that this can take place in a range of ECCE settings including preschools, ECD centres, playgroups and parenting programmes.

ECCE in South Africa is expanding and formalising, and while there is currently a limited range of career pathways for teachers working with children prior to school-going age, there will be increasing opportunities as we progress towards realisation of the National Development Plan 2030 (National Planning Commission, 2013). Currently, ECCE teaching opportunities are not available in the public sector but with the addition of a second pre-primary year to be known as the Pre-Grade R year (National Planning Commission, 2013) currently in the planning phase, this will change but is likely to take some time. Other opportunities include the following:

- Au pair
- Teacher of a birth to age four class in a private or community-based preschool or ECCE centre
- Principal of a private or community-based preschool or ECCE centre
- Lecturer or practical work supervisor in ECCE at a technical and vocational education and training (TVET) college or university, in a private or NGO training institution providing training at NQF level 4 or 5 (certificate) at level 6 (diploma) and at degree level 7 (BEd). Lecturing short ECCE courses is also a possibility
- Programme manager in an ECCE service organisation including parenting organisations, toy libraries and playgroups
- Official responsible for ECCE in provincial or local government services.
- At a university level, an ECCE graduate could move in to postgraduate studies involving research and policy development.

1.8 SUMMARY

In this chapter, we have explored the current status of ECCE provisioning in South Africa. We briefly explained the historical shifts that have influenced ECCE policy and led to the introduction of formal qualifications in early childhood education. We have examined what is meant by the term 'early childhood care and education' (ECCE) and interrogated the relationship between the care and nurturing of young children and early education. Consideration has also been given to different settings for young children and the efficacy of these has been critiqued. We have also suggested possible career pathways for teachers working in this phase of education based on the new qualifications framework. The next chapter will consider the current constructions of children in a rapidly developing field of study.

REFERENCES

Ang, L, Brooker, E & Stephen, C. 2017. A review of the research on childminding: Understanding children's experiences in home-based childcare settings. *Early Childhood Education Journal,* 45(2): 261–270.

Bakken, L, Brown, N & Downing, B. 2017. Early childhood education: The long-term benefits. *Journal of Research in Childhood Education,* 31(2): 255–269.

Bernal, I & Fernandez, C. 2013. Subsidized childcare and child development in Colombia: Effects of *Hogares Comunitarios de Bienestar* as a function of timing and length of exposure. *Social Science and Medicine,* 97: *241–249.*

Berry, L, Dawes, A & Biersteker, L. 2013. Getting the basics right: An essential package of services and support for ECD, in Berry, L, Biersteker, L, Dawes, A, Lake, L & Smith, C. *Child gauge.* Cape Town. University of Cape Town & The Children's Institute.

Bruce, T. 2015. *Early childhood education.* 5th ed. London: Hodder & Stoughton.

Centre for Basic Research. 2017. *Testing theories in families' involvement in children's basic education: Towards a generalizable approach.* http://www.cbr.ug/

Burger, K. 2010. How does early childhood care and education affect cognitive development? An international review of the effects of early interventions for children from different social backgrounds. *Early Childhood Research Quarterly,* 25: 140–165.

Dahl, G & Lochner, L. 2005. *The impact of family income on child achievement.* NBER Working Paper No 11279. Cambridge, MA: National Bureau of Economic Research.

Department of Basic Education (DBE). 2016. *Early childhood development implementation: DBE & social development briefing.* Pretoria: DBE. https://pmg.org.za/committee-meeting/23202/ (Accessed 25 July 2018).

Department of Social Development (DSD). 2014. *Audit of Early Childhood Development (ECD) Centres National Report.* http://www.dsd.gov.za/index2.php?option=com_docman&task=doc_view&gid=608&Itemid=39 (Accessed 6 April 2017).

Department of Social Development (DSD). 2015. *National Integrated Early Childhood Development Policy.* https://www.google.co.za/webhp?sourceid=chrome-instant&rlz=1C1CAFA_enZA657ZA657&ion=1&espv=2&ie=UTF-8#q=Guidelines+for+Early+Childhood+Development+Services.+2006.+Department+of+Social+Development:+Pretoria (Accessed 6 April 2017).

Department of Education (DoE). 2001. *Education White Paper 5 on early childhood development. Meeting the challenges of early childhood education.* Pretoria.

Department of Higher Education and Training (DHET). 2017. *Policy on minimum requirements for programmes leading to qualifications in Higher Education for Early Childhood Development Educators.* Pretoria.

Ebrahim, HB. 2010. Mapping historical shifts in early care and education. *South African Journal of Education*, 48: 119–135.

Fauth, B & Thompson, M. 2009. *Young children's well-being. Domains and contexts of development from birth to age 8.* London: National Children's Bureau.

Fink, G & Rockers, PC. 2014. Childhood growth, schooling, and cognitive development: Further evidence from the Young Lives study. *American Journal of Clinical Nutrition,* 100(1): 182–188.

Garcia, EE & Frede, EC (eds). 2010. *Young English language learners: Current research and emerging directions for practice and policy.* New York: Teachers College Press.

Hallett, J. 1972. *Looking back – fifty years of growth, change and development.* Johannesburg: Central Rand Association of Early Childhood Educare.

Heckman, JJ, Moon, SH, Pinto, R, Savelyev, P & Yavitz, A. 2010. *The rate of return to the High/Scope Perry Preschool Program.* NBER Working Paper Series, DP no 4533(4533): 1–62.

Ilifa Labantwana. 2013. *The essential package. Early childhood services and support.* Cape Town.

Ilifa Labantwana. 2017. *Development to basic education.* Cape Town: The Policy Post. https://ilifalabantwana.co.za/ecd-to-move-from-department-of-social-development-to-basic-education (Accessed 24 July 2018).

Jacob, B & Ludwig, J. 2009. Improving educational outcomes for poor children. *Focus,* Fall, 26(2): 56–61.

Kagitcibasi, C, Sunar, D, Bekman, S, Baydar, N & Cemalcilar, Z. 2009. Continuing effects of early enrichment in adult life: The Turkish Early Enrichment Project 22 years later. *Journal of Applied Developmental Psychology*, 30(6): 764–779.

Kotzé, J. 2015. Rethinking pre-grade RESEP Policy Brief. *Research on Socio Economic Policy Brief.* Department of Economics: Stellenbosch University.

Jones, SM, Zaslow, M, Darling-Churchill, KE & Halle, TG. 2016. Key conceptual and measurement issues that emerge from the special issue papers on early childhood social and emotional development. *Journal of Applied Developmental Psychology*, 45: 1–7.

Lipsey, MW, Farran, DC & Hofer, KG. 2015. *A randomized control trial of a statewide voluntary prekindergarten program on children's skills and behaviors through third grade.* Research Report, Peabody Research Institute.

Lomazzi, M, Borisch, B & Laaser, U. 2014. The Millennium Development Goals: Experiences, achievements and what's next. *Glob Health Action,* 7: 23695. http://dx.doi.org/10.1111/10.3402/gha.v7.23695

Munthali, A, Mvula, P & Silo, L. 2014. Early childhood development: The role of community based childcare centres in Malawi. *Springer Plus,* 3: 305. 10.1186/2193-1801-3-305.

NEPI (National Education Policy Investigation). 1992. *Early childhood care. Report of the NEPI Education Research Group.* Cape Town: Oxford University Press.

National Planning Commission. 2013. *National Development Plan 2030. Our future: Make it work.* Pretoria: National Planning Commission. https://www.google.co.za/search?q=National+Development+programme+2030&rlz=1C1CAFA_enZA657ZA657&oq=National+Development+programme+2030&aqs=chrome..69i57.16935j0j4&sourceid=chrome&ie=UTF-8 (Accessed 6 April 2017).

Pound, L. 2014. *How children learn: Educational theories and approaches – from Comenius the father of modern education to giants such as Piaget, Vygotsky and Malaguzzi.* London: Practical Preschool Books.

Raikes, A, Britto, PR, Yoshikawa, H & Iruka, I. 2017. Children, youth and developmental science in the 2015–2030 Global Sustainable Development Goals. *Social Policy Report,* 30(3).

Ramaphosa, C. 2019. *State of the Nation Address.* 7 February. https://www.google.com/search?q=sona+2019&rlz=1C1CAFA_enZA657ZA657&oq=SONA+2019&aqs=chrome.0.0j69i6012j0l3.8136j0j7&sourceid=chrome&ie=UTF-8 (Accessed 10 February 2019).

Rao, N, Sun, J, Wong, JMS, Weekes, BIP, Shaeffer, S, Young, M, Bray, M, Chen, E & Lee, D. 2014. *Early childhood development and cognitive development in developing countries: A rigorous literature review.* London: Department for International Development.

Rao, N, Sun, J, Pearson, V, Pearson, E, Liu, H, Constas, MA, Engle, PL. 2012. Is something better than nothing? An evaluation of early childhood programs in Cambodia. *Child Development,* 83(3): 864–876.

Republic of South Africa. 1996a. The South African Schools Act 84 of 1996. Pretoria: Government Printer.

The Republic of South Africa. 1996b. The Constitution of the Republic of South Africa. Pretoria: Government Printer.

Republic of South Africa. 2005. The Children's Act 38 of 2005. Consolidated Regulations pertaining to the Children's Act, 2005. Government Notice no R261. Pretoria: *Government Gazette,* 1 April 2010, no 33076.

Richter, L, Biersteker, L, Burns, J, Desmond, C, Feza, N, Harrison D, Martin, P, Saloojee, H & Slemming, W. 2012. *Diagnostic review of early childhood development*. Pretoria: Human Science Research Council (HSRC).

Seleti, J. 2009. *Early childhood development in South Africa. Policy and practice*. Presentation for the World Bank Technical Workshop of the Africa ECCE Initiative. 26–28 October, Zanzibar. https://www.google.com/search?q=Seleti+ECD+presentation&rlz=1C1CAFA_enZA657ZA657&oq=Seleti+ECD+presentation&aqs=chrome..69i57.8098j0j7&sourceid=chrome&ie=UTF-8 (Accessed 25 July 2018).

Siraj-Blatchford, I. 2007. *Effective leadership in the early years sector: The ELEYS Study*. University of London: Institute of Education.

Siraj-Blatchford, I. 2009. Quality teaching in the early years, in Anning, A, Cullen, J & Fleer, M (eds). *Early childhood education: Society and culture*. London: SAGE: 147–157.

Siraj-Blatchford, I & Woodhead, M (eds). 2009. *Effective early childhood programmes*. Milton Keynes: The Open University.

Statistics South Africa. 2017. *Education Series Volume IV: Early childhood development in South Africa, 2016*. Pretoria: Statistics South Africa.

Turner, IF. 1974. Cognitive effects of playgroup attendance. *The Irish Journal of Education/Iris Eireannach an Oideachais*: 30–35.

UNICEF. 2019. *The state of the world's children 2019*. New York. Outreach@unicef.org (Accessed 23 October 2019).

Wood, E & Hedges, H. 2016. Curriculum in early childhood education: Critical about content, coherence, and control. *The Curriculum Journal*, 27(3): 387–405. ISSN 0958-5176.

Yoshikawa, H & Kabay, SB. 2014. The evidence base on early childhood care and education in global contexts. *Global Monitoring Report on Education for All*. Paris: UNESCO.

Chapter 2
Who is the young child? Constructions of children and childhood

Lorayne Excell and Vivien Linington

> **In this chapter we consider:**
> - the shifts in how we view children and childhood
> - different theoretical perspectives used to understand child and childhood, and how these impact our understanding of children
> - how these theoretical perspectives have led to alternative constructions of child and childhood, including the concepts of the child as being, belonging and becoming.

2.1 INTRODUCTION

Views on children and childhood have undergone major shifts in recent years. One of these is away from the once predominant view that in early childhood development (ECD) one could talk about a universal child. The emergence of a strong focus on sociocultural, economic, historical and other factors has led researchers to now explore the concepts of 'children' and 'childhood' through multiple lenses. In this chapter, we set out and evaluate alternative perspectives on children and childhood, and how the principles underlying these perspectives impact practice.

2.2 SHIFTS IN OUR UNDERSTANDINGS OF CHILDREN AND CHILDHOOD

We can all remember being a child. However, we all had very different types of childhoods. Today we realise that it is very difficult to talk about a universal child (one type) and a specific type of childhood. There is an increasing realisation that childhood is a social construction. There is no definition of childhood that holds true for all cultures (McDowall Clark, 2010).

Try this out

On a piece of paper, write down your understandings of child and childhood. Start each sentence with 'I believe a child is …' and then 'I believe childhood is …'

Now compare what you have written to that of a few colleagues/fellow students (if possible from different cultural orientations). Compare the similarities and differences between each person's understandings. If you think about the different responses that you will undoubtedly get, you will start to realise that understandings of child and childhood are a social as well as a cultural construct. These understandings will differ according to each individual person's context and cultural background. The differing interpretations have led to (and continue to lead to) many debates and contestations (differing of opinions). The result has been a shift in the meaning of childhood, how we view children, and new interpretations of appropriate early childhood practice.

This shift has influenced the start of a new discipline 'the sociology of childhood'. Understandings of early childhood are no longer predominantly informed by developmental psychology where the focus was on the development of the individual child. Traditionally, development, according to Piaget and other developmental psychologists, unfolds naturally and universally (all in the same way). From this traditional perspective 'children's behaviour and social skills will inevitably follow on from biological and physical growth' (Wyness, 2006: 123). Little attention is given to the socialisation process a child undergoes.

The sociology of childhood as a social and cultural construct considers the child in a wider context with a particular focus on the influence of the historical background, culture and interdependent (mutually supportive) relationships that change as the child grows and develops. In other words, the child's overall growth, development and behaviour are influenced by social and cultural factors as well as developmental aspects.

Thus to understand children and childhood in today's society, we consider multiple perspectives. We cannot look at childhood from only a psychological or a sociological perspective – we have to consider many different understandings. This idea of both/and as opposed to either/or perspectives is becoming more important as the formerly predominant view of the universal child is increasingly interrogated (questioned). To unpack this multifaceted (complex) understanding of child and childhood, we will explore some of today's different constructions or perspectives on child and childhood. We will then explore current understandings of child development and some of the factors affecting development. To conclude, we will discuss the interdependent nature of differing perspectives and how quality early childhood practice draws on this interdependency.

2.3 DIFFERING CONSTRUCTIONS OF CHILDHOOD

According to Mc Dowall Clark (2010), the concept of childhood is relatively new. New approaches, such as post-structural approaches, which have been influenced by the work of Michel Foucault, have opened new ways of exploring our understandings of child and childhood (Aubrey, 2017). One of the questions that has sparked considerable debate is whose voice is more powerful and should therefore be given the most recognition. Is it the adult, the child or the theorist? The assumption that the adult is all powerful and knowing is therefore being challenged. The voice of the child is being increasingly recognised. As a result, children's opinions now count. As we have already said, childhood is understood as a social construct, and the socialisation of the child is influenced by culture, context and diversity. The debate to which we have referred has led to a number of different constructions of children, which we will now consider. At the outset we note how understandings of children have changed over time (the historical perspective) and how these are often culturally based. We then explore the notion of the child from a sociological perspective and childhood from the traditional African perspective. We conclude by contrasting these understandings with the once-dominant notion of the child from a developmental perspective.

Something to consider

When you were a child, were you allowed to offer your opinion on matters affecting you? In other words, were you given voice? If so, in which discussions were you allowed to participate? Were there some from which you were excluded? Elaborate.

2.3.1 The historical child

As we have already said, childhood is a relatively modern idea. Aries, (1962), writing from a European perspective, argues that in the Middle Ages (about 500 years ago) children were seen as underdeveloped adults; they were not treated differently to adults nor thought to need any particular care and concern because of their young age (McDowall Clark, 2010). Adults made little emotional investment in their children because of the high infant mortality (death) rates. Children wore the same type of clothing and undertook similar activities to adults. They learnt about life by participating in it. There was no concept of development as we know it today.

It was only during the 17th century that children started to receive different types of recognition. In 1692, a well-known educationist, John Locke (1632–1714), suggested that when children were born their mind was a blank slate or *tabula rasa*. He suggested the importance of moulding (shaping) children from an early age through reasoning rather than punishment to develop self-control and sound morality. These are some of the first recorded ideas of children being viewed differently to adults. The rising middle class began to pay more attention to the view that children were different from adults and needed particular care.

During the 18th century, an intellectual movement known as the Enlightenment or the Age of Reason spread across Europe. People promoted the idea that young children should be considered in their own right. Enlightenment thinkers rejected irrational superstitions such as the belief that evil spirits or tiny demons hid between the leaves of lettuces and cabbage. These spirits could enter anyone who swallowed them, making the person ill (Maitland, nd). The idea that man was a rational, thinking being began to take hold.

According to McDowall Clark (2010), many of the principles that are central to democratic practice, such as equality and liberty, began to be formulated during the Enlightenment. A new view of children – as innocent rather than ignorant – began to develop. Jean Jacques Rousseau (1712–1778), a well-known supporter of the Enlightenment movement, suggested that man is born good but corrupted by society. Rousseau emphasised the importance of learning through nature, and suggested that teachers should follow the young child's interests because this was how children learned what they needed to know. However, meaningful education was suggested for boys; girls received a much more limited education – to prepare them to become suitable wives! Sadly in some parts of the world this notion that girls do not need a good education still exists.

Many of Rousseau's ideas that influenced later educationists can still be seen to have an impact on early childhood education. Pestalozzi (1746–1827) incorporated some of Rousseau's ideas when he established his first school for young children. These ideas included the importance of children learning through movement, being active learners, having concrete learning experiences, and the value of nature and the outdoor environment to ensure stimulating learning opportunities. Pestalozzi went on to influence the German educationist, Friedrick Froebel (1782–1852), the father of the kindergarten (children's garden) (Bruce, 2012). In Froebel's kindergarten, play was a crucial part of any early childhood experience. In fact Froebel suggested that children should only begin formal education when they turned seven.

The onset of industrialisation shattered (destroyed) the idea of children being innocent and having the freedom to grow up in relative tranquillity. The Industrial Revolution that began in the late 1700s was a period of major social, cultural and economic change in the Western world. The growth of different industries began to replace what had, until then, been a more rural, agricultural lifestyle. Both adults and children were employed as workers in mills and factories, and children no longer worked alongside their parents as part of the family unit (McDowall Clark, 2010). Child labour was cheap, and children, because of their size, were able to do a number of tasks more easily than adults, hence they became a valuable economic commodity.

Industrialisation and the subsequent urbanisation meant that many families no longer had their own food-producing land, and this led to a host of new problem, including poverty. By the 19th century, the enormous gap between rich and poor was very evident. Social reformers questioned how conditions for poor children could be improved. Young children (before they were old enough to be employed to work as child labourers) were left unattended as their parents worked long hours. These children were generally neglected; there was little control over their behaviour, and discipline was poor (McDowall Clark, 2010). The [English] government's solution was to introduce compulsory schooling, which was introduced in 1880, even if for only a few years until children were old enough to join the workforce.

This idea of schooling, especially for more disadvantaged communities, was also extended to the very young child, and the nursery school movement began in England. Initially the aim was to provide indigent (poor) children with some health care, basic nutritional needs and some stimulation. Movement and play-based learning was considered to be essential to support early learning. These ideas, influenced by Froebel, spread to the US and later, in the early 1900s, to South Africa.

Find out more

As time allocated to schooling gradually increased, the idea that children were ignorant, innocent and dependent beings was reinforced (Hendrick, 1997). By the 20th century this deficit (negative) concept of children was well entrenched. Scientific study, particularly the new and growing field of psychology, spawned new theories of development (McDowall Clark, 2010). The idea that there were 'norms' that described what might be expected of children was accepted, and developmental milestones for children from birth upwards were set. These milestones, which were standardised on Western middle-class children, continue to inform assessment standards in the early childhood phase today.

Reflection

Do you think that there is a problem with this form of assessment? Have you considered that such assessments could and have been increasingly criticised for ignoring contextual and cultural features and thereby reinforcing the idea of a universal child? Using a universal lens on childhood means that all children are expected to show the same behaviours at the same ages.

With the limitations apparent in the notion of a universal child, a new field of study rapidly grew, namely the sociology of early childhood.

2.3.2 The sociological child

Sociology is the study of society and human social interaction. It examines 'why we do things, the way we do things, what are the reasons for doing specific things or engaging in specific activities and adopting certain behaviours' (Ferrante et al, 2016: 3). A useful way to study early childhood is through the lens of relational sociology, which focuses on how children see themselves in relation to other people, both younger and older. These other people are usually parents, teachers and other significant adults, as well as peers with whom they are friendly, and siblings.

Young children are born into interdependent relationships that may already exist between parents, and between parents and other children. To grow as a social being, young children need to learn from their elders and other significant people in their lives. These learnings are historically and culturally shaped, and influenced by time, space and aspects of power. The notion of power affects society at every level. For example, in an ECD centre the owner has more power over decisions taken than a general assistant usually has. Adults, for example, have power over children and this can be used positively or negatively.

Something to consider

How do power relationships influence decision making in your early childhood care and education (ECCE) centre? Are decisions about childcare and children's stimulation taken collaboratively? Is it a consultative process between you and the parent and you and the head teacher? Or do you sometimes feel that you have little or no say in the decisions made? Likewise, are children's interests and choices considered when planning the daily programme? Another example of power relationships is when we consider developmental norms and whether or not children's abilities align (are in keeping) with these norms. For instance, can a child be assessed as being developmentally delayed because they cannot cut along at straight line at age 3 when they have never practised this skill before because there is no pair of scissors in the home? In this case, the reason for not being able to cut on a straight line is probably a socioeconomic or cultural factor and not because of physiological (biological) factors and points yet again to the importance of context and sociocultural issues when trying to understand a particular issue.

2.3.2.1 *Sociocultural context*

All children grow within specific sociocultural contexts. Culture refers to the ideas, customs and social behaviour of a particular people or society. A sociocultural approach focuses on how values, beliefs, skills and traditions are transmitted to the next generation. A child is embedded in the family and culture of his community and a number of aspects of his development are therefore culturally specific (Gordon & Browne, 2017).

A sociocultural approach draws on the work of the Russian psychologist Vygotsky (1978), who argued that we become ourselves through others. In short, culture and family influences impact the development of the whole child. As Rutgers (2015) points out, Vygotsky held the view that children develop within their social world and that interactions with peers and elders are important in fostering (encouraging) higher levels of cognitive and social development.

Wyness (2012) also points to the importance of environmental factors when he argues that the environment plays an influential role in pushing the child along the developmental pathway. Families, of course, are an integral (essential) part of this environment. Each family will prioritise certain skills and values and beliefs, for example vocabulary development, cooperation with siblings, self-care and independence. In each sociocultural context, therefore, there will be similarities and differences that will inform the unique role that a child plays in the family.

Something to consider

As a teacher you create your own sociocultural context, and the children for whom you are responsible will be part of this context. Is there a 'fit', you must ask yourself, between each child's home and ECCE context? Is there an emphasis on similar roles, attitudes and values? Are the literacy practices similar? Or are the two contexts – the home and the (ECCE) setting – a mismatch? For instance, what is important in one context, for example turn-taking, may be considered irrelevant in the other. Perhaps a home belief is that 'children should be seen and not heard', while in the ECCE context the child's active participation in decision making is encouraged. These differing views about the role of the child could fan conflict between the ECCE centre and the home.

2.3.2.2 The child as an active participant

The new sociology of childhood stresses the importance of children as active participants in the making of decisions that affect them. Morgan (in Wyness, 2006: 56) makes a distinction between 'being in' and 'doing' family life in relation to debates about agency within family. Agency, if you recall, refers to children who are given an opportunity to express their opinions and choices in family and other decision-making issues. In so doing, they influence and shape their everyday life (Markstrom & Hallden, 2009). In short, agency is the capacity of individuals to act independently and to make their own free choices. The distinction between 'being in' and 'doing' is, we argue, equally applicable to 'being in' and 'doing' in ECCE centres where children should also be encouraged to use their agency by making choices and giving input to decisions affecting them.

Morgan's distinction associates 'being in' with a passive notion of family (and we would add ECCE) life. When children are not given opportunities to express themselves, they drift into or conform to pre-given roles and responsibilities, and are in fact rendered voiceless and have no agency. Morgan further contends that 'being in' families aligns with the conventional status of children as dependants whose role in the family group is barely noticeable.

'Doing', on the other hand, implies a more active involvement in choosing, creating and changing how one participates in the family or ECCE situation. 'Doing' life challenges passivity. It illustrates the different ways in which children can be active within families and ECCE centres (Morgan, in Wyness, 2006). They could, for instance, negotiate familiar routines, like choosing which shirt to wear or toy to play with or book to listen to. They do not have to be passive recipients of care; for example, babies should be allowed to try to feed themselves when they show a desire to do so. In an ECCE centre, children should be given suitable responsibilities, such as helping to fetch the plastic mugs at snack time.

To summarise, a child who has agency 'does' life, therefore it is important that adults listen to children as this forms an important part of understanding what they are feeling and experiencing. A child from a sociological perspective should be valued and respected for who they are now rather than for whom they will become in the future. Today, childhood is viewed as an important space where children's own opinions and feelings about what happens in their lives have value.

We will now consider another particular perspective the constructions of children and childhood through an African lens.

2.3.3 African perspective

As we have repeatedly mentioned, many of the dominant theories on child development and learning offer a predominately Western or European perspective on childhood. Though many of the claims put forward by these theories appear to be valid regardless of race, colour or creed, theory has to be revisited to take into account different competing perspectives. One of these is exploring constructions of children and childhood from an African perspective. We do not claim to be able to accurately represent the cultural beliefs and child-rearing practices of the many different groups of people who live in South Africa, but we do offer some thoughts drawn from eminent African philosophers and educationists on constructions of children and childhood.

Try this out

Think about your own cultural beliefs and practices. Can you identify specific practices in your culture that might differ from other cultural practices? Consider, for example, different child-rearing practices and attendant norms and values. Are pregnant woman given particular considerations? Are there specific post-natal practices? What about the naming of children – how are names chosen and why that specific name? Is there a particular child-naming ceremony? Do these names change as the child grows older? Are there particular sleeping arrangements, for example babies co-sleeping with parents? What are the approaches to feeding children? Are certain types of foods avoided or encouraged? Why? How are toddlers potty trained? What is the approach to supervising and looking after young children? Is it the mother's responsibility or does this task fall to older siblings? What, if any, tasks are young children expected to do around the home?

Reflection

You may be able to think of many more culturally specific practices. Share your ideas with your colleagues and start thinking about how these different practices might impact early childhood care and education? Do your cultural practices conflict with the cultural practices of others? If conflict does occur, how might it be resolved in an ECCE setting?

2.3.3.1 Theorising early care and education and the young African child

As noted by Pence and Nsamenang (2008), African ECD has not been sufficiently theorised. Penn (2005) claims that Western ECD approaches do not consider culture, context and diversity, specifically from an African perspective. We are only now recognising the need for a local, indigenous, community-sensitive approach to child development, learning and wellbeing.

Child-rearing practices within traditional African philosophical thought should provide a political and social space for children to develop and to perpetuate the cultural legacies of their ancestors (Boakye-Boaten, 2010). In indigenous African societies, children are educated through taking part in family life and being immersed in their traditional customs and values. Spiritual values stem from religious rituals and practices. These values lay the foundation for the respectful governance of the community and the love, respect and obedience which the children are expected to show their parents and elders. Moral and ethical codes of behaviours as well as social relationships are taught to children by the elders through traditional tales and myths. Children in traditional African culture are perceived to be human beings in need of help and direction (Boakye-Boaten, 2010). It is the responsibility of the society to ensure the protection and proper socialisation of children while simultaneously respecting them. This resonates with the African proverb that 'it takes a village to raise a child'.

According to Boakye-Boaten (2010), the social construction of children has two distinctly different elements. The biological element sees children as vulnerable beings in need of protection and nurturing. The sociological element prescribes social functions and relationships for all family members. Fathers are the providers of the family, and mothers are the nurturers (Boakye-Boaten, 2010). Children in traditional Africa philosophy have a fundamental role as future insurance for their families.

Something to consider

According to Nsamenang and Lamb (1994) and Boakye-Boaten (2010), tension exists between traditional African education ideas and practices, and more contemporary approaches. They claim that traditional child-rearing practices often sit uneasily with expectations of the more economically privileged African families who want their young children to have a Western education, including access to well-resourced schools, experienced teachers, smaller class sizes, an authentic curriculum and engaging pedagogies. Many other African families are now making similar demands.

Find out more

Aubrey (2017) states that within South Africa today there is a very distinctive political and socio-economic climate with competing discourses (conversations) specifically around indigenous knowledge and decolonisation. In other words, topics like indigenous knowledge and decolonisation are hotly debated. An example of an indigenous African practice is the carrying of a baby on the mother's back. In the West, a baby is more likely to be placed in a stroller. What do you believe are the benefits and limitations of these two approaches?

Reflection

The picture that has emerged thus far is complex and contradictory. It has brought together a range of different beliefs and practices drawn from the fields of biological determinism and sociology. A social construct is man-made, crafted from age-old norms, values, beliefs and attitudes. Biological determinism is based on developmental theory, for example babies babble before they start to form words. As Walsh (2005) claims, 'development is necessary but not sufficient.' It is the sociology of childhood that takes culture and context into account and begins to address the 'not sufficient' element. However, we cannot discard the 'necessary' developmental element. We will now briefly unpack the developmental perspectives and return to development in more depth in the next chapter.

2.4 THE PSYCHOLOGICAL PERSPECTIVE – THE DEVELOPING CHILD

We have already discussed how understandings of children and childhood are continually shifting as new research and arguments appear. This shift also applies to the field of child development, which has been predominately influenced by the field of developmental psychology. Initially, child development was confined to tracking changes in children's growth and development, and one of the most influential theorists was Gesell, a maturational theorist. He and other theorists such as Mary Sheridan observed and recorded norms or standards for different aspects of children's growth and development. These developmental norms which continue to influence early childhood education are now applicable to all the developmental domains (areas). They provide milestones (signposts or markers) that guide theory and practice. Researchers have explored specific aspects of the developmental domains in an attempt to show how changes in development and learning occur. Table 2.1 presents an overview of theories of child development and learning, which will be explored in more depth in Chapter 3.

Table 2.1 Overview of theories of child development and learning

Theory and theorists	Provides explanation of change in the following developmental areas:	Important features of theory
Behaviourists – Skinner, Watson	Behaviour Cognition Language Physical and motor	Learning through external environmental stimulus Classical conditioning – stimulus response approach Examples: child listens to the teacher, is successful and gets a star as a reward; through practice and repetition, child acquires skills, like riding a bicycle
Social learning theory – Bandura	Cognition Social and emotional Physical and motor	Learns through imitation and role modelling Examples: child observes adult behaviour and acts similarly; child observes teacher hopping and then is asked to hop in the same way

Theory and theorists	Provides explanation of change in the following developmental areas:	Important features of theory
Constructivist – Piaget	Cognition Moral	Development leads learning Children are active sensorimotor learners Example: children learn through exploration and discovery Play is important
Social constructivist – Vygotsky	Cognition Language Affective	Learning leads development Zone of proximal development Language and social interaction pivotal for learning Play, specifically socio-dramatic play, is important in learning Cultural tools, for example language, mediates the child's learning, suggesting, for example, how to complete the puzzle
Psychosexual – Freud	Affective – personal and emotional	The young child has three main phases of development: oral (birth to one year), anal (ages one to three years) and phallic, where the focus is on the genitals (ages three to six years) Behaviour is controlled by id, ego and superego

Theory and theorists	Provides explanation of change in the following developmental areas:	Important features of theory
Psychosocial – Erikson	Affective – social and emotional	Series of stages which ideally are successfully resolved before moving on to following stage Example: if a baby's needs are met, she learns to trust and can then move with confidence to the next stage of development, which is to start gaining autonomy
Moral development – Kohlberg	Cognitive Moral	Outlines stages of moral development (understandings of right or wrong)
Attachment theory – Bowlby, Ainsworth, Brazelton	Emotional Social	Early attachment to primary caregiver essential for positive emotional development and the building of social relationships Example: caring, nurturing relationships with primary caregiver allows child to interact positively with others. Often the negative effects of poor attachment in infancy will only become noticeable during later childhood or even in adulthood

➡

Theory and theorists	Provides explanation of change in the following developmental areas:	Important features of theory
Theory of needs – Maslow	Cognitive, Social, Emotional } Self-actualisation	There is a hierarchy of human needs. Basic needs, which are physiological, come first, then safety and belonging needs, then self-esteem, and at the top, when all other needs are met, self-actualisation is achieved Example: a child who receives adequate food, water and security can then progress to having the need for belonging met
Normative/maturational theory – Gesell, Sheridan	Cognitive Language Social Emotional Physical and motor areas	Identifies a series of age/stage norms for all aspects of development Milestones established for each specific stage/age of development
Ecological theory – Bronfenbrenner	All areas of development and learning influenced by environmental factors and culture	Individuals are viewed within their culture, and their specific environmental contexts are taken into account when reviewing development and learning. This theory explores in ever-widening circles how the immediate environment (home, the ECCE centre, school, etc, and more distant factors such as politics and the economy) affects a child's life experience, including his learning

SOURCES: ADAPTED FROM CHARLESWORTH (2017); GORDON & BROWNE (2017)

> **Something to consider**
>
> To date, we have discussed the following concepts of child and childhood from different perspectives:
> - The historical perspective
> - The sociological perspective
> - The African perspective
> - The psychological perspective.

We will now consider a fifth perspective that could be regarded as an alternative way of theorising early childhood. This perspective considers the being, belonging and becoming child.

2.5 THE BEING, BELONGING AND BECOMING CHILD

This perspective is cross-disciplinary. Drawing on sociology and cross-cultural studies, the focus moves to the different ways that children collectively become more experienced and accomplished members of society (Wyness, 2012). It talks specifically to the notion of the belonging and being child. The sociological lens has led to a new understanding of the developmental perspective, and the child viewed through a developmental lens is called the becoming child. These constructions have informed an innovative inclusive, culturally responsive practice that underpins, for example, the current Australian early childhood curriculum. Consult the following website if you want to read further about this curriculum: https://www.education.gov.au/early-years-learning-framework-0

We will now look at each individual construction.

2.5.1 The being child

This child is situated in the present. She is acknowledged and respected for what she can do at this time. She is a competent, capable child. Sociocultural theory, which underpins this image of child, suggests that she will be an active participant in her environment and make her own, reasoned choices. She is a child who has voice and agency. Supportive, responsive adults provide an enabling environment and give her the space to co-construct her own knowledge and reach her potential.

2.5.2 The belonging child

This construction is underpinned by human rights theory. The child is in a respectful environment where tolerance and equity are key. This child is accepted for who he is. His right to be a child is endorsed and he is immersed in an appropriate play-based programme where he feels physically and emotionally safe. In such a loving and secure environment, supported by responsive adults, he develops a strong sense of self and eventually a strong self-concept.

2.5.3 The becoming child

In this image of child, the child is always striving for something more. He is in a constant state of development. He must learn this, develop that. Consequently there is little acceptance of the child for who he currently is and for his current competencies. There is always another milestone for him to reach. This can become a deficit approach if we expect the child to reach certain milestones before he is developmentally ready to do so.

Something to consider

Good ECCE practice does not put a child in one category and ignore the other two. All three constructions should be interwoven so that a child is seen as being, becoming and belonging as opposed to one or the other. We accept the child and recognise his competencies (recognition of the being child). Through respectful responsive interactions (acknowledging the belonging child), we encourage children to explore their environment. We challenge children, support co-construction of knowledge and so encourage them to attain new skills and concepts appropriate for their age and stage of development (the becoming child). In this way we establish a safe, culturally and contextually supportive environment that supports the child's holistic development, learning and wellbeing.

Reflection

What is your current understanding of child? Would you place a child in one of the three categories or support a blend of all three? Give reasons for your choice.

2.6 SUMMARY

Current understandings on children and childhood have hopefully caused you to reflect on traditional understandings which have proved to be problematic in the 21st century. Critiques of a purely developmental approach to childhood have been unpacked to show that the long-held notion of a universal child is no longer valid. It cannot account for the social, economic, historical, cultural and other factors, as well as specific child-rearing practices that influence the growth, development and learning of young children.

In the next chapter we will, as indicated, look in more depth at the developmental perspective, or what has been called the becoming child. We will elaborate on our argument that developmental knowledge is necessary although not, to draw on the ideas of Walsh (2005), sufficient.

REFERENCES

Aries, P. 1962, *Centuries of childhood*. New York: Vintage Books.

Aubrey, C. 2017. Sources of inequality in South African. Early child development services. *South African Journal of Childhood Education*, 7(1). https://sajce.co.za/index.php/sajce/article/view/450/461 (Accessed 4 June 2018).

Boakye-Boaten, A. 2010. Changes in the concept of childhood: Implications on children in Ghana. *The Journal of International Social Research*, 3(10): Winter.

Bruce, T. 2012. *Early childhood practice. Froebel today.* London: SAGE.

Charlesworth, R. 2017. *Understanding child development.* Boston, MA: Wadsworth.

Empson, JM & Nabuzoka, D. 2004. *Atypical child development in context.* Hampshire: Macmillan.

Ferrante, J, Seedat-Khan, M, Kaziboni, A & Uys, T. 2016. The sociological imagination, in Seedat-Khan, M, Jansen, ZL & Smith, R (eds). *Sociology: A South African perspective.* Andover, UK: Cengage.

Gabriel, N. 2017. *The sociology of early childhood. Critical perspectives.* London: SAGE.

Gordon, AM & Browne, KW. 2017. *Beginnings and beyond. Foundations in early childhood education.* Boston, MA: Cengage Learning.

Hendrick, J. 1997. *The whole child.* New York: Macmillan.

Keenan, T, Evans, S & Crowley, K. 2016. *An introduction to child development.* 3rd ed. Los Angeles: SAGE.

Maitland, K. nd. *Ten historical superstitions we carry on today.* https://www.historyextra.com/period/medieval/historical-superstitions-why-friday-13th-unlucky-kiss-under-mistletoe/ (Accessed 24 October 2019).

Markstrom, A & Hallden, G. 2009. *Children's strategies for agency in preschool.* National Children's Bureau. https://onlinelibrary.wiley.com/doi/full/10.1111/j.1099-0860.2008.00161.x (Accessed 24 October 2019).

McDowall Clark, R. 2010. *Childhood in society for the early years.* London: SAGE.

Neaum, S. 2016. *Child development for early years students and practitioners.* 3rd ed. Los Angeles: SAGE.

Nsamenang, AB & Lamb, ME. 1994. Socialization of Nso children in the Bamenda Grassfields of northwest Cameroon, in Greenmailed, PM & Cocking, RR (eds). *Cross-cultural roots of minority child development.* Hillsdale, NJ: Erlbaum.

Pence, A & Nsamenang, B. 2008. A case for early childhood education in sub-Saharan Africa. Early childhood development, in Garcia, M & Evans, J. *Beyond quality in early childhood education.* New York: UNICEF.

Penn, H. 2005. *Unequal childhoods.* London: Routledge.

Rutgers, L. 2015. Guiding principles of Grade R curriculum, teaching and learning, in Excell L & Linington, V (eds). *Teaching Grade R.* Cape Town: Juta.

Sharma, A & Cockerill, H. 2014. *Mary Sheridan's from birth to five years. Children's developmental progress.* London: Routledge.

Walsh, D. 2005. Development theory and early childhood education: Necessary but not sufficient, in Yelland, N (ed). *Critical issues in early childhood education.* Berkshire: Open University Press.

Wyness, M. 2006. *Childhood and society. An introduction to the sociology of childhood.* Hampshire: Macmillan.

Wyness, M. 2012. *Childhood and society.* 2nd ed. Hampshire: Macmillan.

Chapter 3
A lens on development: a pathway of change

Lorayne Excell and Vivien Linington

In this chapter we consider:

- some theoretical perspectives framing developmental approaches and their implications for teaching
- the concept of holistic development, developmental domains, and reflect on their implications for practice
- developmental milestones from birth to five years, and their implication for practice
- factors that influence growth and development from birth through to age five
- key messages supporting growth, development, learning and wellbeing

3.1 INTRODUCTION

As we outlined in Chapter 2, we now realise that there are different disciplines as well as theoretical perspectives that inform teaching and learning in the early years, thus the underpinning theoretical approach is eclectic (varied). In Chapter 2 we explored some alternative theoretical perspectives that highlight the importance of taking each child's context and cultural background into account. We suggested adopting an approach where we consider teaching and learning through three different lenses, namely the being, belonging and becoming child. In this chapter we will further explore aspects of the becoming child, which draws on the developmental perspective. We will examine some of the important informing developmental theorists as well as interrogate the notion of developmental domains. We will also present some milestones of development and explore their implications for practice.

3.2 INFORMING DEVELOPMENTAL THEORIES AND THEORISTS: HOW YOUNG CHILDREN DEVELOP AND LEARN

As we have mentioned in Chapter 2, there are a number of important theorists who have influenced our understandings of how children develop and learn. We will briefly outline some of them, and explore the implications of these theories for growth and development as well as teaching and learning.

3.2.1 Maturation theory

Maturation theory, which was primarily responsible for articulating milestones for motor (physical) development, has given rise to certain principles of development that have been refined over the years (Neaum, 2016).

- *Child development occurs in a predictable sequence*
  - Development occurs from head to toe (cephalo–caudal) – children walk before they run, and run before they gallop; and develop from the midline outwards (ie from proximal to distal). To better understand the meaning of proximal–distal, study Figure 3.1. The child is standing with her arms down and the palms of the hand facing outwards. You can see that the little finger is closer to the midline than the thumb. Children therefore first develop an ulnar grasp (little finger) then a palmar grasp (middle of the hand) before refining their pincer grasp (thumb and forefinger)

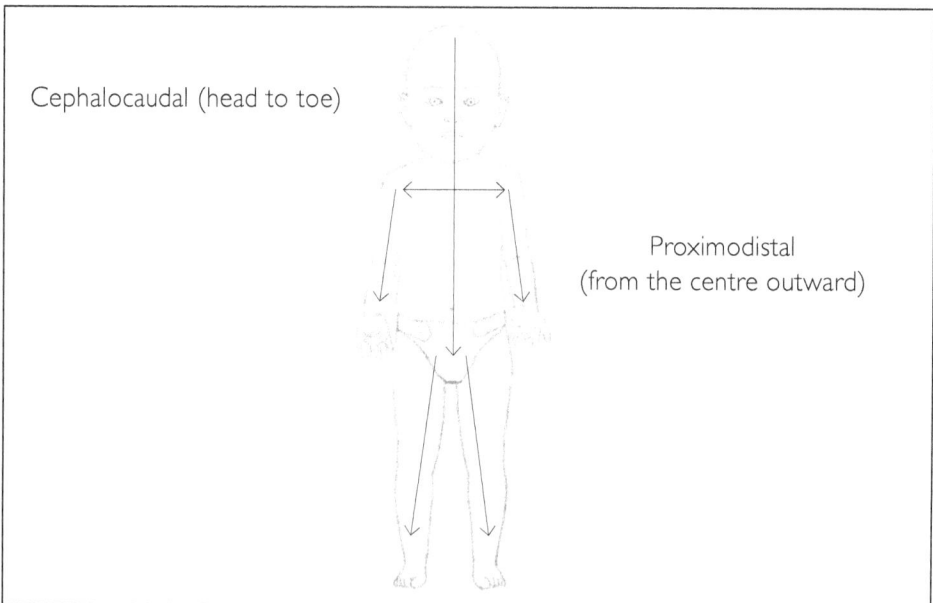

Figure 3.1 A diagrammatic representation of cephalo–caudal and proximal–distal development

- Children follow a similar same pattern of development but the rate differs. Children first gain head control, then sit, crawl and walk. With language they coo, gurgle and babble in single sounds ('ah', 'ga') before double babbling ('ba-ba', 'da-da') begins. According to Empson and Nabuzoka (2004), the social emotional domains show a greater variation than the physical ones. This variation is to be expected because children's development is influenced by many different factors that are both contextual and cultural. Even though average ages for milestone acquisition are given, the rate can differ quite markedly (see table of milestones (Table 3.4) for examples). For example, the average age of walking is 13 months, but we all know of children who walk before nine months or only begin walking nearer the age of two.
- Development occurs from the simple to the complex (whole hand grasp is eventually refined to a pincer grasp); and from the general to the specific; for example, emotion is first shown by whole body movement, which is eventually replaced by appropriate verbal responses.

- *Development is cumulative*
  - Development begins at conception and continues throughout life. Each stage builds on previous ones. For example, babbling is a forerunner of speech. Give children sufficient time and opportunities to practise each skill and to consolidate it to ensure they have a sound foundation before moving on to the next stage. Stimulating free play where choice and self-activity is valued will afford children these types of opportunities.
  - Also think of children with special learning needs. These children are also competent, but may, however, require more time and additional experiences to master specific skills. If the stages and ages of development are applied in a rigid way, such children will be disadvantaged. Before observations of milestones are interpreted, make sure to consider adequately all additional factors, for example any illnesses the child might have had. Chronic middle ear infections could negatively impact language acquisition as hearing might be distorted because of fluid in the middle ear.

Something to consider

Some of these milestones have been set out in the National Early Learning Development Standards (NELDS), which was published by the Department of Basic Education (DBE) in 2009. Download this document from the following website: https://www.unicef.org/southafrica/resources_16275.html

Read though the NELDS document and compare what is written there with the table of milestones given in Table 3.4.

3.2.1.1 Implications for care, teaching and learning

Development milestones are guidelines. They provide markers for each child's growth and development, but remember that each child is unique – there is no such thing as a 'universal child'. The guidelines inform and guide observations and assessments of children, but they must be carefully interpreted. In addition to valuable information about each child, they also provide a lens through which teachers can evaluate their own practice.

Reflection

Ask yourself critical questions such as: 'How is the learning environment responsive to the children's abilities and needs?' and 'Are the activities sufficiently stimulating or are they too challenging?' Discuss. Your responses will inform how you vary and adapt children's learning experiences to provide rich learning opportunities. The question of learning is considered by behaviourist theory.

3.2.2 Behaviourist theory

This theory is influenced by John Locke's idea that children are born as an 'empty slate' or what Locke termed a *tabula rasa*. Well-known behaviourists include Pavlov, Watson, Skinner and Bandura, who later modified his approach. Behaviourism focuses on observable behaviour and describes learning as the acquisition of new behaviour (Pritchard, 2005). This method of learning is called conditioning, and is controlled through the implementation of rewards (positive reinforcement) or withholding something the child enjoys (negative reinforcement). Positive reinforcement is anything that could strengthen and lead to a particular type of behaviour being adopted. Negative reinforcement, on the other hand, should lead to the decline of undesirable behaviour.

There are two types of reinforcers: social reinforcers, which include attention, praise, a hug, or smile, and non-social reinforcers, which include tokens, stars, gifts, stickers and food (Gordon & Browne, 2017). For example, we reward good behaviour – children who take part in the tidying-up routine receive a gold star. We discourage undesirable behaviour – children who throw sand while playing in the sandpit are not allowed to play there for the remainder of the week.

Something to consider

We often use behaviourist principles when interacting with babies and young children. Think of your own practice and try to identify at least two occasions when you have used positive reinforcement and two occasions when you have used negative reinforcement. Was there, on reflection, possibly a better way to manage the child's behaviour?

3.2.2.2 A further dimension to behaviourism: social learning theory

Albert Bandura refined and adapted behaviourism to describe what is called social learning theory. He was interested in observing how children acquire socialisation skills or, in other words, internalise the rules of society and conform to them. According to this theory, children learn the rules through role modelling and imitation. Bandura suggested that children are most likely to learn the rules of social behaviour through positive interactions with role models such as parents, teachers and peers. Social learning theory suggests that in general these role models are warm, kind, empathic and affectionate.

3.2.2.3 Implications for care, teaching and learning

Bandura was interested in studying how children acquired aggressive behaviour, and stated that much of their learning occurs though observing others. This finding has significant implications for teachers and parents of young children. Think, for example, how your behaviour influences the children in your care. Do you perhaps unintentionally teach them how to behave aggressively because you shout at them, or even smack them, or because they see you fighting with another adult? What happens when children are allowed to view aggressive behaviour on television? To what extent do they emulate (copy) these actions even in play?

We know that quality early childhood care and education (ECCE) is largely dependent upon warm, responsive relationships and interactions between adults and young children. Social reinforcers such as a smile, a word of praise or a hug should be used often when interacting with young children. This can also happen in socio-dramatic play where characters such as Superman and Batman always support the side of right.

3.2.3 Psychodynamic theory

Where the behaviourists suggest that behaviour has an external trigger (the environment), the psychodynamic theorists contended that emotional development and hence personality stem from internal factors (factors within ourselves) (Hardman, 2012). Often, we are not aware of what these factors are – they come from our unconscious mind. This theory suggested that people have three basic drives: a survival instinct, a sexual instinct and a drive for destructiveness (Gordon & Browne, 2017). We will briefly explore two psychodynamic theories.

3.2.3.1 Psychosexual theory of development

Sigmund Freud proposed that children go through a series of psychosexual stages that lead to the development of the adult personality. He describes the stages of childhood psychosexual development as shown in Table 3.1.

Table 3.1 Freudian stages of psychosexual development

Age	Stage	Description
Birth–1/2 years	Oral	Mouth (sucking, biting, eating, teething) is source of pleasure
1/2–3 years	Anal	Bowel movement is a source of pleasure; toilet training
3–6 years	Phallic	Genitals are source of pleasure; identification of sex/gender role; development of conscience (see 3.2.4.2 on self-regulatory behaviour)
6–12 years	Latent	Sexual forces are dormant
12–18 years	Genital	Genitals are source of pleasure

SOURCE: ADAPTED FROM GORDON & BROWNE (2017)

Freud contends that 'each stage has its own area of pleasure and crisis between the child and parent. How the child experiences these crises or conflicts determines basic personality and behaviour patterns' (Gordon & Browne, 2017: 102). In each stage, the sensual satisfaction associated with each body part is linked to a major challenge for that age. For example, in toddlers, biting or thumb sucking can lead to conflict between parent and child, as can playing 'doctor doctor' in the younger child. Each stage brings its own challenges and possible conflict with adult/parents.

- *Implications for care, teaching and learning*

How the child experiences these conflicts (in other words, how adults manage them), determines basic personality and behaviour patterns. To enhance optimal development and learning, the theory suggests that children's behaviours are managed in a warm, responsive manner that is respectful to all concerned, but specifically to the children. Children should not be humiliated because they are, for example, still sucking a dummy or because they are playing with their genitalia. Gently redirect their behaviour and encourage them to do something else, such as to play with blocks or in the fantasy corner.

3.2.3.2 Psychosocial development theory

Erik Erikson was influenced by Freud and expanded on psychodynamic theory to develop a theory of psychosocial development. He proposed that children pass through a series of stages, each growing from the previous one. Each stage is critical for the development of an important aspect of the personality.

Erikson described eight stages of development (see Table 3.2), each of which is represented by a specific developmental crisis or challenge. Each stage is structured along a continuum, which allows for a possible positive resolution (best scenario) of the stage or a negative resolution (worst scenario). A positive resolution is represented by the emergence of a specific emotional strength or learning disposition (characteristic) and allows for a smooth transition to the following stage. A negative resolution can lead to a young child feeling guilty about becoming independent (Hardman, 2012).

When children succeed, they develop confidence and are better able to tackle the next set of developmental crises. Erikson called this struggle in dealing with competing urges an 'identity crisis', which helps answer the question: 'Who am I' (Gordon & Browne, 2017).

Table 3.2 Erikson's psychosocial theory

Stage	Age	Developmental crisis/challenge	Strength/quality that emerges through successful resolution
Stage 1	Birth	Trust versus mistrust	Hope
Stage 2	Toddler	Autonomy versus shame and doubt	Willpower
Stage 3	Early childhood	Initiative versus guilt	Purpose
Stage 4	Primary school	Competence (industry) versus inferiority	Competence
Stage 5	Adolescence	Search for identity versus role confusion	Fidelity (loyalty)
Stage 6	Young adulthood	Intimacy (love and friendship) versus isolation (loneliness)	Love
Stage 7	Middle age	Generativity (caring for the next generation) versus stagnation	Care
Stage 8	Old age	Integrity (honour) versus despair	Wisdom

- *Implications for care, teaching and learning*

For ECCE teachers, the first three stages are crucial. In, for example, stage 1, if babies have their needs met in an efficient, friendly and responsive way, they begin to develop a sense of trust in the world through their interactions with the significant adults in their environment. They perceive the environment to be a supportive and loving one, and thus progress to stage 2 with a positive sense of self. If their needs are not satisfactorily met, they begin to perceive that the world is a hostile, unfriendly place and that they have to fight for their very existence. These experiences shape individual children's personalities. The more positively each stage can be resolved, the stronger the child's sense of self. This suggests a responsive, nurturing and caring role for the significant adults who interact with young children. Treat children thoughtfully, and do not ignore their needs or humiliate them when they make mistakes or do not meet your (adult) expectations.

We will explore the application of these theories in more detail in Chapter 10 and also investigate the place of attachment theory in shaping children's emotional wellbeing.

3.2.4 Cognitive theory: constructivism and sociocultural theory

Cognitive theory explains how people think and perceive the world; in other words, how they acquire, organise and use what they learn. There are a number of different cognitive theories, but we will explore just two of them – the cognitive constructivist theory of Piaget and the sociocultural theory of Vygotsky.

3.2.4.1 *Constructivism: Jean Piaget (1896–1980)*

Piaget believed that children's thinking is fundamentally different to that of adults. He outlined a number of stages to describe children's thinking at various ages (see Table 3.3). These stages are influenced by children's interactions with the environment, through which they build or construct their own understandings of the world. As they explore the environment, children continually reshape their ideas. They use their schemas (a mental framework for understanding incoming information) to enable them to think about the world. These schemas are shaped and reshaped as people gain increasing understanding of a concept.

Find out more

According to Piaget, the understanding of concepts happens through a process of assimilation and accommodation. Assimilation means that children take in new information and organise their understanding of this to fit what they already know. However, this way of categorising the new information or ideas does not always fit their current schemas. Often, as children learn new information about a specific idea or topic, they have to change their thought categories to gain improved understanding. Piaget called this accommodation. While children are trying to figure out a clearer understanding, they are said to be in a state of cognitive disequilibrium. When they achieve this understanding and a clear insight, they are said to gain a sense of equilibrium.

Very young children develop schemas through their senses – tasting, touching, smelling, seeing and hearing. Movement is essential to sensory development. Later this understanding is extended through language and pretend play (Gordon & Browne, 2017). For Piaget it is essential that children have opportunities to explore and discover for themselves rather than being told, explained or instructed by an adult.

Table 3.3 Piaget's stages of development

Age	Stage	Key ideas
Birth–2 years	**Sensorimotor stage** • Children gather information predominantly through the senses of touch and sight • Construction of knowledge is based on action – children learn through discovery; a trial-and-error approach	Object permanence (see Table 3.4 on visual and perceptual milestones). Children follow an object and demonstrate increasing understanding that things still exist even when they are out of sight (called object permanence). This is the beginning of memory and recall

➡

Age	Stage	Key ideas
2–6/7 years	**Preoperational stage** *Pre-conceptual stage 2–4 years* • Still gather information through sight and touch but language is becoming increasingly important • Children are egocentric; they see the world from their own viewpoint • Children believe everything has a consciousness, eg dolls have feelings • Beginning of symbolic play *Intuitive stage 5–7 years* • Hearing/listening becomes a more important way of gleaning information • Symbolic play becomes more complex • Abstract thought is still difficult	There is a transition from understanding based on action to understanding based on symbolic representation. Symbolic representation includes the ability to represent objects and events using mental symbols such as words or pictures, eg drawing a picture of their mother. It also includes using objects to represent something else, eg a wooden block to represent a car Symbolic play and language (see Table 3.4 Social development & play; speech, language & communication). They display increasing competence in language and socio-dramatic play
6/7–12 years	Concrete operational stage	Reasoning – the beginning of logical thought
12 years +	Formal operational stage	Abstract thinking

Find out more

Though we still support the idea that cognitive development occurs through assimilation and accommodation, age and stage theory is criticised. It has been shown that young children might acquire some cognitive skills at an earlier age than described by Piaget. Acquiring knowledge and skills is very dependent upon experiences, context and the refinement of other developmental skills such as motor coordination. The view that children are egocentric and only capable of seeing the world through their perspective has also been challenged. Young children can show concern and empathy for others.

It has also been argued that the language used and the types of questions asked play a role in children's understandings of a task. This means the teacher must use simple age-appropriate questions and language that the child can understand and follow. Think of what this means for children whose home language is not the one spoken in the ECCE centre.

- *Implications for care, teaching and learning*

Your role is to ensure the environment is safe, secure and stimulating so that young children can construct their own knowledge though a process of exploration and discovery (see guidelines for practice in Table 3.4). Children need sufficient time and concrete materials (see Chapter 6). Because they are learning predominantly through movement and their senses, stimulating play is an ideal way to support early learning as it provides opportunities to adapt and refine concepts (Neaum, 2016). At times, children require explicit encouragement to think and reason. Try to avoid telling children what to do or giving them the answer. Rather suggest or ask questions to prompt their thinking (see Chapter 8 for examples of questioning techniques).

We will explore the concept of language and how to support learning in more detail when we look at the next cognitive theorist, and in Chapter 12 when we explore language and literacy.

3.2.4.2 Sociocultural theory: Lev Vygotsky (1896–1934)

For Vygotsky, learning takes place through social interaction. He called it a sociocultural theory because he believed that learning is embedded in or linked to the child's family and cultural practices. The cultural influence can take many different forms such as a traditional Western perspective where the nuclear family is emphasised or, for example, a traditional African perspective where the extended family plays a more prominent role in childrearing practices.

Children learn best in a collaborative, interactive, language-rich environment. In such an environment the adult must have a good understanding of children's current level of understanding as well as their next steps in learning (Neaum, 2016). Vygotsky explained this process through what he called the zone of proximal development (ZPD). By this he meant that children's cognitive development is reliant on two levels. The first level is what the child can do by himself unaided, and the second (higher) level is what the child can do with the help of a more competent or knowledgeable other. Learning takes place in the ZPD, which is the space between the two levels. A more competent other could be a member of the family, a teacher or an older child.

Something to consider

Children's thinking is mediated by signs or cultural tools, the most important of which is language (Charlesworth, 2017). Today we talk about the concept of scaffolding to support children's learning. For example, a two-year-old is playing with blocks. She is trying to build a tower, but it keeps falling over. Her mother sits next to her and suggests that she starts with a big rectangular block followed by a slightly smaller block, and so on. With the support of the mother who guides the size and shape of blocks used, the child builds a tower of four cubes.

Another central concept in sociocultural theory is that of private speech. Vygotsky believed that the emergence of language is tied to what children are thinking. While young children are busy, they talk out aloud to themselves. After a while this self-talk becomes internalised and is no longer heard. Vygotsky believed that by talking to themselves, both out loud and internally, children self-direct – they think about and plan their behaviour. 'With age, private speech, which goes from talking out aloud to whispers, to silent lip movement is critical to children's self-regulation' (Gordon & Browne, 2017: 117).

Vygotsky (1978: 129) stressed that much of a child's learning takes place during play, describing this as 'in play it is though he were a head taller than himself'. This is because he takes on roles that are above his present level, such as playing mommies and daddies. Through play, a child learns self-regulation, language and a range of other cognitive and social skills. For Vygotsky, the teacher is more of a guide on the side than a transmitter of information (Neaum, 2016).

- *Implications for care, teaching and learning*

Each child's family and cultural context is acknowledged and accepted by adults caring for the child. Building positive teacher–child relationships is essential. Teachers teach intentionally based on what they know about the child to guide learning. Teachers support learning through the co-construction of knowledge (see Chapter 8) and promote sustained shared thinking. Teachers use empathy to guide social relationships and conflicts in a constructive way. As we have said, play is crucial for learning, and Vygotsky identified socio-dramatic play as being a lead activity for children between the ages of three and six (Karpov, 2005). The teacher should ensure, therefore, that there are many opportunities for this kind of play to occur. In short, socio-dramatic play not only helps children to regulate their behaviour, but also enables them to acquire the necessary behaviours to assist with the transition into primary school.

3.2.5 Early childhood and neuroscience

'Neuroscience specialises in studying how different parts of the nervous system function and the optimum conditions for development – and how these can go wrong' (Conbayir, 2017: 4). It makes use of imaging technology to take 'pictures' of the brain, which then have to be interpreted. Imaging technology has enabled us to more easily identify the effects that early childhood experiences have on the developing architecture of the brain – both positive and negative.

Neurons are the building blocks of the brain. The growth of new neurones – neurogenesis – begins after conception and continues throughout an individual's life. A neuron consists of three parts (see Figure 3.2) – a cell body and two different extensions called dendrites and axons. Dendrites carry information to the cell body and this is taken from the cell body by the axon. Information passes from the axon of one neurone to the dendrites of another.

The connection between axon and dendrite is called a synapse, across which the information is transmitted (conducted) with the help of chemical transmitters. The axon is covered in a white fatty substance called myelin, which helps with the transmission of the information.

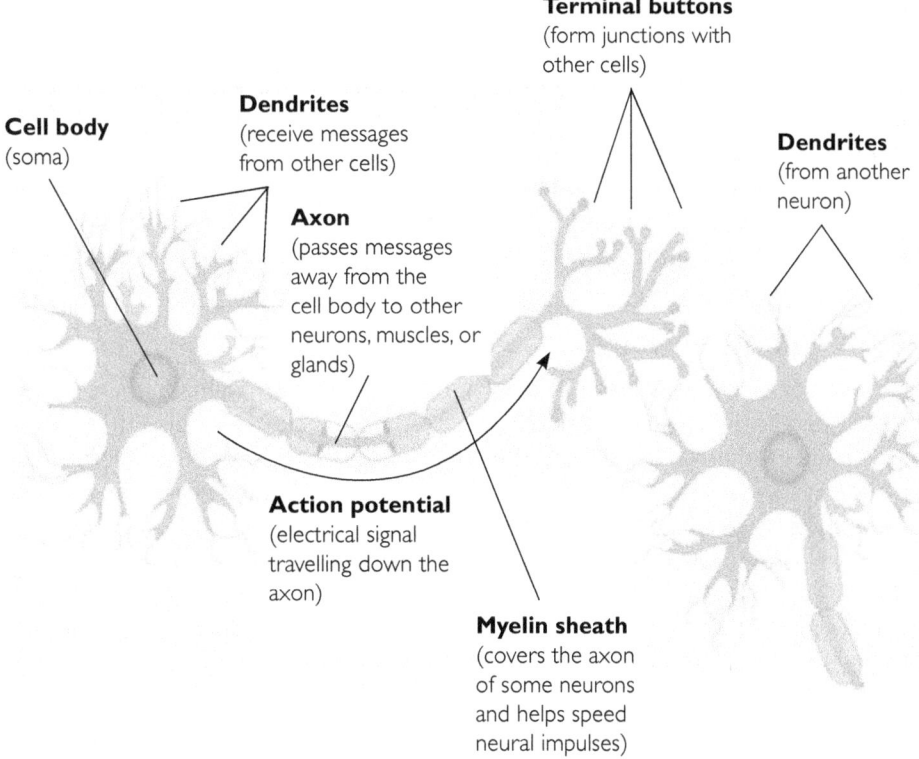

Figure 3.2 A diagrammatic representation of a neurone

At birth, the brain contains approximately 86 billion neurones, and this number continues to grow during our lifespan. Each neurone has about 2 500 synapses, and this number increases to about 15 000 by age three (Conbayir, 2017). This ability to increase the number of neurones and to change the structure and function of the brain is called neural plasticity. This is most rapid during early childhood, and is influenced by environmental experiences and interactions, both positive and negative. These experiences, good and bad, become the neuro-archaeology of the individual's brain (Perry, 2001). We know repetition of experiences not only strengthens the existing synaptic connections, but also leads to neurones creating pathways in different parts of the brain based on experiences.

3.2.5.1 Implications for care, teaching and learning

Favourable childhood experiences promote the growth and strengthening of neural connections, therefore opportunities to engage in quality play, including exploration and communication with others, and enjoying secure, responsive relationships with opportunities for repetition for the mastery of skills, are essential.

Neuroscience has also confirmed that there are sensitive periods or distinct phases in early childhood, specifically between birth to five years, when learning of specific skills appears to be more readily mastered. During this time, the brain is best able to receive and use information gained from experience in order to learn a specific skill. Early childhood is now known to be a crucial time for acquiring motor skills and language, and forming attachments (Conbayir, 2017).

> **Something to consider**
>
> We know young children learn through movement. This strengthens muscles and provides opportunities for sensory learning, which boosts brain development. Improved control of large muscles leads to better fine motor control, such as manipulating play materials and later writing. Thus make sufficient opportunities for large motor movements as these influence fine motor ability. One also has to consider the concept of sensitive periods when planning the learning day. This does not mean that young children have to receive direct instruction or be subjected to 'teaching'. Rather it means that the teacher plans the early learning environment carefully. It should be language-rich, support learning through movement and provide quality multisensory experience and sufficient opportunities for exploration in a safe and secure space (see chapters 6 and 7). In other words, it is important that children are given opportunities to regularly practise skills such as language, movement and exploration, reasoning and problem solving to build familiarity, competence and confidence.

3.3 DEVELOPMENTAL DOMAINS

Although developmental psychology has been widely critiqued, no study of early childhood is complete without considering the developmental domains that underpin holistic development or the development of the whole child. Drawing from the various theoretical perspectives, three broad areas of development are recognised. These are physical, cognitive, and affective (social and emotional). Other domains are embedded within these three (see Figure 3.3).

We now briefly describe the three domains:
1. **Physical:** this describes children's progress over the control of their bodies. Growth is biological and refers to an increase in size while development is characterised by an increase in skills and complexity of performance. The refinement of balance and posture go hand in

hand with increasing control of muscular movements which is called motor control. Control over the arms, legs, neck, shoulders and body (see posture and large movement in Table 3.4) is called gross motor development, while control over the smaller muscles is called fine motor development. Fine motor development refers to increasing dexterity (agility) in the use of muscles of the hands and fingers, feet and toes, eyes, mouth, lips, cheeks, etc. As we have said, physical development follows a specific sequence namely head to foot (cephalo–caudal) and from the middle of the body towards the outside (proximal–distal); for example, control of the shoulder precedes control of the arms and fingers. Aspects of perceptual motor development, especially spatial orientation and awareness behaviours and the eye muscle control of visual perception, also fall under the physical domain.

2. **Cognitive:** this refers to intellectual development and involves the development of thought processes. It is concerned with how we acquire, organise and use what we learn (Neaum, 2016). Language development – how we think and communicate – is an integral part of cognitive development. Certain aspects of perceptual motor development also fit under this domain, especially sensory perception, for example touch and visual discrimination. Cognitive development involves the development of conceptual thought, memory, problem solving and reasoning, imagination and creativity.

3. **Affective:** this refers to social and emotional development. Emotional development refers to the child's ability to feel and express an increasingly wide range of emotions. It also explores the development of self-image and self-concept, and is closely aligned with a feeling of wellbeing towards oneself and others. Social development describes the child's increasing ability to relate to others within a social context. The affective domain includes the development of independence and the ability to express empathy. The development of these skills is largely dependent on the opportunities children have to interact positively with others. The affective domain is largely responsible for the development of self-regulation and the ability of children to modify their behaviour.

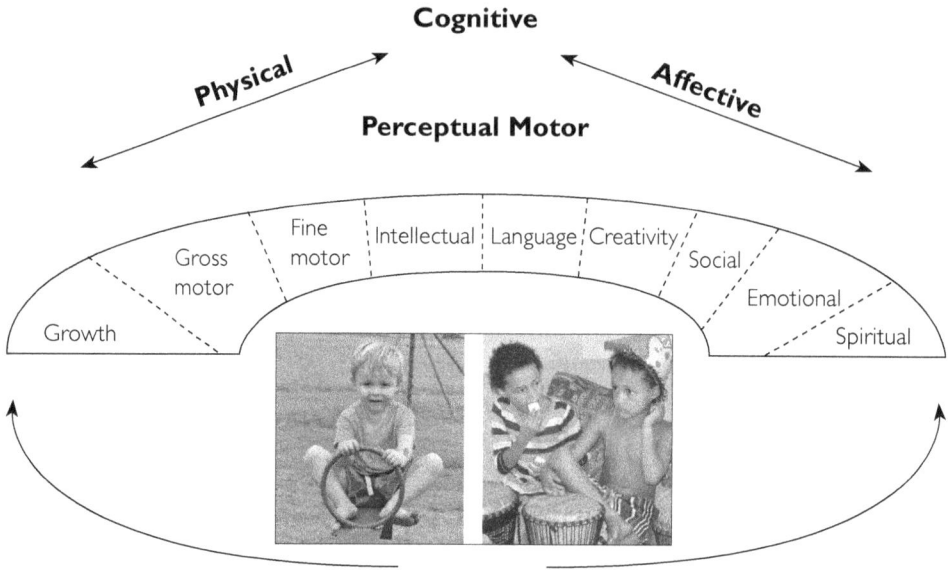

Figure 3.3 The holistic child – a concept of whole child development

Something to consider

For each area or domain, developmental milestones have been identified. It is important for all people who work and care for young children to be familiar with these milestones as they serve as a basis for observation and assessment of children. Through good observation and assessment, one can identify possible developmental difficulties or delays and seek, where required, specific professional help. Sometimes issues that might worry the teacher are of a contextual nature and through dialogue (conversations) with parents they can be addressed. Knowledge of developmental domains also serves as a guideline for practice. Activities and settings can and should be varied based on information obtained from observing children interacting with each other and their environment.

Table 3.4 on developmental milestones and implications for practice presents important milestones in a slightly different format. All the recognised developmental domains mentioned previously have been captured in different categories that enable the carer/adult to easily recognise the implications of each category for practice. The categories are posture and large motor development; visual perceptual and fine motor development; speech, language and communication; social behaviour and play; and self-care and independence (Sharma & Cockerill, 2014). The developmental domains have been clustered in a specific way to reflect new understandings of the processes underlying development and the shifts in emphasis on social communication, perception and attention control (Sharma and Cockerill, 2014). Contextual and cultural considerations are also reflected within these categories. The cognitive domain is not specifically represented in Table 3.4. As you read through the table you will see how cognitive development is closely related to visual and fine motor development, speech, language and communication. Social behaviour and play, as well as self-care and independence, are also closely aligned to the cognitive development of the child.

Table 3.4 Milestones of development and implications for practice

Development milestone	Description	Implications for practice
Newborn baby (neonate)		
Alertness and responsiveness	Long periods of sleep interspersed by short periods when baby is awake	Beginning of responsive relationship between carer and baby – start positively and continue throughout childhood in this vein
	Duration of wakefulness gradually increases; it includes fretfulness, crying and calmness	
Posture and large movement	Random movements of legs and arms	Handle baby carefully and gently when lifting, holding, feeding, etc. Support head and shoulders when lifting
	When pulled to a sitting position, marked head lag present	
	If lying prone (on stomach), head is turned sideways, and legs are tucked under tummy	
Primitive reflexes (automatic movement patterns – they slowly disappear between 3 and 6 months)	Moro reflex – occurs when support of head and shoulders is suddenly disrupted. The arms stretch open wide (abduction) and the hands also open. The arms then come together again	If each arm does not abduct (move outwards) in a similar way, refer for examination as there might be neurological problems

➡

Development milestone	Description	Implications for practice
Newborn baby (neonate)		
Primitive reflexes (automatic movement patterns – they slowly disappear between 3 and 6 months)	Rooting reflex – if the cheek is touched, the head turns in towards the touch. Sucking reflexes are for feeding and calming purposes. Later these become voluntary actions	When feeding, gently tickle the cheek closest to the mother's breast to encourage baby to latch onto it for feeding; dummy might soothe restless baby but do not place any sweet substance on it
	Palmar grasp – a finger placed in baby's hand causes its fingers to grip the finger tightly – disappears around 3–4 months	If this persists, refer baby for a developmental check
Hearing and vision	Sound is heard in the womb, and babies recognise their mother's voice and their native language soon after birth. Baby is sensitive to light and within a few days turns head in direction of light source	Talk, sing and read to baby while in the womb. Continue after birth on a daily basis. Look at baby, smile, soothe with gently touching movements. Hold and calm baby by gently rubbing different body surfaces
Touch, smell, taste	Babies are sensitive to touch especially on face, mouth, hands, soles and abdomen. Babies recognise mother by her smell	
Social interaction	Babies interact with carers through eye contact and facial gestures. Sound of mother's voice will relax baby. Beginning of emotional ties between baby and carers	Feed in tranquil environment; look at baby when feeding; talk to baby (do not play on cell phone and iPad). These are important moments to build attachments with baby

Age 1 month

Development milestone	Description	Implications for practice
Posture and large movements	Lies on back, keeps head to one side; random movement of arms and legs; hands mostly closed	Stimulate baby with mobile above cot
	If pulled to sit, baby lacks head control. Head falls back	Still support head when lifting, carrying baby
	Held in sitting position, back is completely curved	
	If held vertically on hard surface will make 'reflex' walking movements	Allow to sleep on firm surface, preferably on back
Visual perceptual and fine motor	Baby's pupils react to light, turns head towards light	Provide dangling toys for baby to look at
	Follows a pencil light briefly at a distance of 30cm	Look and talk to baby when feeding, dressing, changing, etc.
	Gaze is caught and held by dangling bright toy moved in line of vision; watches familiar face with increasing alertness when being fed or talked to	If eyes do not move together, refer for further investigation
	Defensive blink present from about 6–8 weeks	

➡

Development milestone	Description	Implications for practice
Hearing	Startled by sudden noise – stiffens, blinks, extends limbs, cries if hears sudden noise	If baby does not startle to sudden noise, refer for hearing test
	Starts to move head towards source of sound (small bell) but cannot locate source	Ideally hearing should be tested at birth
Speech, language and communication	When baby hears comforting human voice, stops crying and turns towards sound	When restless, talk gently to baby; attend to baby's needs immediately – do not leave baby to cry for too long; change when wet or soiled; feed when hungry
	Utters little guttural noises and vowel-like vocalisations when content	
	Responds favourably (moves arms and legs, and makes facial gestures) when known carers talk	
	Cries lustily when hungry or uncomfortable	
Social behaviour and play	Sleeps most of time when not being fed or handled	Place rattle in crib; hang mobile; talk and sing to baby; play gentle music
	Expressions vague but social smile and responsive vocalisations appear at 5–6 weeks	
	Stops crying when picked up and spoken to. Turns to look at speaker's face	
Self-care and independence	Sucks well	Feed on demand – usually 3–4 hourly; baby is totally dependent on loving adult so attend to baby's needs without too much delay – beginning to build a relationship of trust
	Needs head support when being carried, dressed or bathed	
	Passive acceptance of caring routines slowly gives way to greater awareness and more responsiveness	

Age 3 months

Development milestone	Description	Implications for practice
Posture and large movement	When lying on back, head in midline position; limbs more flexible, hands loosely open	Place rattle, squeaky toy or similar in cot or clip to edge of cot
	Brings hands together towards midline; kicks vigorously	Place something like scrunched paper under feet to encourage movement and provide stimulation
	When pulled to sit, little or no head lag; when held sitting, back mostly straight	
	Still needs support when being bathed and dressed	Change and dress/undress with care
	Lying on abdomen, lifts head and upper chest well above midline (waist)	Place on abdomen for short spells to strengthen tummy muscles
Visual perceptual and fine motor	Follows adults' movement within available visual field	Encourage baby to follow your hand and face with their eyes when tending to needs
	Follows dangling toy held at 15–25cm above the face and follows the toy from side to side	Place brightly coloured mobile above crib, encourage baby to follow a rattle, soft squeaky toy, etc, as you move them
	Watches movement of own hands when lying on back, engages in finger play	
	Eyes converge (come together) as dangling toy is brought towards face	Hold soft toys, rattle for baby to grasp
	Reaches to grasp toy with both hands from 16–18 weeks	
	Holds rattle for a few moments when placed in hand	

➡

Development milestone	Description	Implications for practice
Hearing	Turns eyes/head towards sound source; may move head from side to side as if searching for sound	Talk/sing to baby; make sure baby can hear you; watch carefully to see if baby follows direction of sound
	Quietens or smiles at sound of familiar voice unless baby is screaming	
Note: babies with a hearing impairment might be startled by carer's appearance beside cot		
Speech, language, communication	Cries when uncomfortable, annoyed or overtired	Pick baby up if crying, soothe, change, feed, etc
	Often sucks lips in response to sounds of his food being prepared	Talk/sing to baby – describe routines, etc (even though baby cannot talk, you are providing valuable language input)
	Shows excitement at sound of approaching voice, footsteps, running bathwater etc	
	Vocalises happily when pleased, also when alone	
Social behaviour and play	Anticipates feeding time eagerly; shows reactions to familiar situations by cooing and excited movements	Provide feeding cues, etc, for baby to anticipate what is going to happen
	Fixes eyes with purposeful gaze on parent's face when feeding	Make changing/feeding/dressing/bathtime fun. Take time to gently touch, even massage baby; continue talking/singing to baby
	Enjoys bathing and caring routines; responds well to being tickled and spoken to, and enjoys singing	

Age 6 months

Development milestone	Description	Implications for practice
Posture and large movement	Lies on back, raises head to be lifted	Encourage baby to lift head; allow baby to pull himself to sitting position by grasping your hands
	When hands grasped pulls self to sitting	
	Sits with support, with straight head and back, and turns head from side to side (sits independently without support at about 7 months)	Use cushions, pillows to support baby in sitting position – do not allow baby to sit unsupported. Surround baby with soft surface in case he falls over
	Can roll from front to back (5–6 months) and back to front (6–7 months)	Lie baby on tummy on floor to encourage rolling from front to back
		Do not leave baby alone on high surface as he might roll off
	Bears weight on feet and bounces up and down when held	Consideration of safe environment is essential
Visual perceptual and fine motor	Very curious, moves eyes in all directions; follows adult across a room with purposeful alertness; stares at small objects within 15–30cm	Provide bright, colourful environment; give soft toys with no sharp edges, rattles, fabric or plastic blocks of suitable size to bang together
	Stretches out both hands at same time to grasp. Reaches for and grasps small objects, usually with both hands but might use one hand only; uses palmar grasp; passes toy from one hand to the other; drops one object if another is offered	Offer baby toys to encourage him to reach out and grasp such as a soft cuddly toy
		Offer an activity centre
		Place under tree to watch leaves moving
	When toy falls from hand within visual field, watches it until it lands. When toy falls outside visual field, searches for it vaguely (early object permanence) or forgets about it	

Development milestone	Description	Implications for practice
Hearing behaviour	Turns immediately if he hears a familiar voice	Continue talking and singing to baby; observe his reactions
	Listens to voice even if adult is not in view	
Speech, language, communication	Vocalises tunefully to himself, uses sing-song vowels or single or double syllables (e.g. 'a-a', 'muh', 'goo,' 'der' (4–8 months)	Continue to provide enjoyable caring routines; smile often and encourage baby to laugh/smile back at you
	Laughs, chuckles and squeals aloud in play. Screams in annoyance	Recite nursery rhymes (eg 'This little piggy went to market'); sing songs and lullabies (eg Thula thula)
	Shows recognition of carer's facial expressions such as happy or sad. Responds selectively to emotional tones of voice	
Social behaviour and play	Shows delighted response to rough-and-tumble play; enjoys often repeated games; shows anticipation if carer pauses before key section in nursery rhymes or other action songs	Throw baby gently upwards and catch; tickle baby; sing action songs – start to increase the number of appropriate rhymes and songs to continue to stimulate baby
	When offered rattle, immediately reaches for it and shakes to make a sound. Manipulates objects, passing them from hand to hand. Puts everything in mouth	Provide a number of soft and other toys of suitable size. No small objects as baby could choke on them

➡

Development milestone	Description	Implications for practice
Self-care and independence	Still friendly with strangers but occasionally might show some shyness or anxiety in their presence	Even though baby might be holding a bottle do not prop feed, eg placing bottle on a pillow so that baby can suck unaided. Prop feeding could lead to baby choking or middle ear infection
	When feeding, places hand on breast or holds bottle. May attempt to grasp cup if used	
	Beginning to take semi-solids	Introduce pureed food, such as soft porridge, mashed butternut, etc – one new food at a time
		Do not sweeten food too much as this can be the beginning of poor nutritional habits

Age 9 months

Development milestone	Description	Implications for practice
Posture and large movement	Pulls himself to sitting position. Sits unsupported and can adjust body posture to lean forward to pick up and manipulate toys without losing balance	Ensure environment is safe – block off entrances, staircases, etc
		Furniture must be stable and secure if baby pulls self to standing position, etc
	Pulls himself from sitting to standing position (7–12months) but cannot lower self. Falls backward with a bump	Provide a variety of toys for baby to manipulate. Offer shape sorters and stacking toys. 'Posting' shapes through large slots is a fun activity
	Progresses on floor by rolling, wriggling or crawling from about 7 months	
	If held standing, steps purposefully on alternate feet	Occasionally place toys a little bit away from baby to encourage him to move forward

Development milestone	Description	Implications for practice
Visual perceptual and fine motor	Visually very attentive to people, objects and happenings in the environment	Place baby in a place where he can observe what is happening in the environment (eg under tree to watch leaves twirling)
	Baby starts to work out the position of objects – beginning of depth perception	Offer brightly coloured toys and equipment such as a spinning wheel; offer toys such as blocks of different shapes, largish balls he can roll, etc
	Immediately stretches out to grasp small toy if offered. Manipulates it and passes it from hand to hand	No small toys or toys with small breakable parts as most things go to mouth
	Pokes at small objects with index finger and begins to point at more distant objects with same finger	Under supervision allow baby to play with smallish objects, pegs, etc, to practise pincer grasp
	Picks up small objects between finger and thumb with 'inferior' pincer grasp	Play games like 'where is it?' – show baby an object and let it fall out of sight (beginning of object permanence – cognitive domain)
	Can release toy from grasp by dropping or pressing against a firm surface. Cannot yet release smoothly. Enjoys casting (throwing) objects over side of cot	Offer baby reasonably sized push and pull toys, eg a homemade wire car with wheels; a cart or a car on a string
	Looks in correct direction for fallen or falling objects (establishing object permanence)	Baby is starting to understand that he can affect the world around him. Offer toys that respond to baby's touch by making lots of noise and flashing brightly. This helps baby to work out that he can affect his world
	Beginning of early causal understanding, eg plays with cause-and-effect toys – pulls the string attached to a truck to bring the truck towards him	
	Watches activities of people and animals with sustained interest for several minutes	

Development milestone	Description	Implications for practice
Hearing	Eagerly attentive to everyday sounds	Continue talking/singing to baby; notice how responsive baby is to your presence when you enter the room
	Turns to search and localise faint sounds on either side of himself	
Speech, language, communication	Vocalises deliberately as a means of interpersonal communication; shouts to attract attention, listens then shouts again	Play 'talking' games with baby, eg pat-a-cake Use baby's name Be alert to vocalisations and double babbling. If baby stops, refer for immediate investigation for possible hearing problem
	Babbles loudly and tunefully in long repetitive strings of syllables, eg 'da-da', 'ab-ab-', 'mum-mum'. Babble is mainly for self-amusement but also to converse with parents	
	Responds to name when called (6–10 months)	
	Understands 'no' and 'bye-bye' (6–9 months)	
	Reacts to 'where's mommy/daddy?' by looking around	

Vocalisations of babies with severe hearing impediments rarely progress, ie they do not move onto tuneful double babbling such as 'ba-ba', 'ga-ga'. Vocalisation that lacks variation after 8–9 months could indicate a possible hearing problem

Development milestone	Description	Implications for practice
Social behaviour and play	Throws body back and stiffens in annoyance	Be present to reassure baby in the presence of strangers
	Clearly distinguishes strangers from familiar faces; clings to known person; needs reassurance if in presence of strangers (from 7 months)	Provide responsive, supportive, nurturing care
	Still puts everything to mouth	Play games such as peek-a-boo, pat-a-cake, etc
	Plays peek-a-boo and enjoys imitating hand clapping	Play hand-clapping games
	Watches toy being hidden under an object and finds it	Share simple picture books with baby
	Maintains interest for one minute when looking at pictures named by adult	Give cloth books six months
Self-care and independence	Holds, bites and chews small pieces of food	Offer food that is more lumpy; allow baby to feed himself if so wishes
	Tries to grasp spoon when feeding	Be prepared for a mess – do not shout at baby or prevent baby from trying new things (important for self-esteem)
		Place plastic mat on floor to enable easy cleaning up

Age 12 months

Development milestone	Description	Implications for practice
Posture and large movement	Crawls on hands and knees, bear walks or shuffles, pulls to standing and sits down again holding onto furniture; walks round holding onto furniture; may stand alone for a few moments (6–16 months); walks forwards and sideways with hand being held; may walk alone (9½–17½ months)	Provide safe environment where baby can explore Remove dangerous obstacles Furniture must be sturdy and secure Outdoor play area must be safe and secure as baby has no appreciation of possible dangers
Visual and perceptual motor	When outside watches people, animals for long periods of time; recognises familiar people approaching from a distance	Place in visually stimulating environment Offer appropriately sized toys – alter the variety and texture Encourage baby to build blocks – building tower of two blocks after demonstration is evidence of increasing understanding (cognitive skills)
	Has a mature grasp; picks up small objects with pincer grasp (thumb and index finger)	
	Uses both hands freely, but might show preference for one	
	Deliberately drops toys and watches them fall to ground	
	Points with index finger to objects of interest	
	Can release cube gently; by 13 months can build tower of two cubes after being shown how (can happen anytime between 11 and 18 months)	

➡

Development milestone	Description	Implications for practice
Hearing	Locates sound from any direction	When singing songs/reading story/saying rhymes, sometimes substitute child's name for the one in the rhyme; encourage child to join in; give appropriate praise
	Responds immediately to own name; shows recognition of familiar songs by trying to join in	
Speech, language, communication	Babbles loudly and incessantly	Continue talking to child

Avoid using 'baby' language like 'num-nums' for food

Do not mock or embarrass child by pointing out mistakes in speech or for not yet saying any words

Do not correct mispronunciations; rather repeat words correctly in a new sentence |
| | Shows by behaviour that some words are understood in context, eg 'Let's go in the **car**'; 'Would you like a **drink?**'. Understands simple instructions, eg 'Give it to daddy' (8–12 months) | |
| | Responds to familiar songs but pronunciation is inconsistent (12–15 months) | |

Development milestone	Description	Implications for practice
Social behaviour and play	Takes objects to mouth less frequently; little drooling unless feeding	Still needs a very safe and secure environment
	Will put objects in and out of box/cup when shown; quickly finds hidden object	Offer toys where child can place them in and out of containers, pack or unpack cupboards, etc Children like repetitive activities
	Plays pat-a-cake or similar game in home language, and waves goodbye both on request and spontaneously	Continue playing action games and songs with child, eg 'This little piggy went to market' Offer a variety of new toys – toys that make different sounds; toys that can be banged or knocked against something else, eg spinning top, drum
	Enjoys playing with adults – switches attention between adult and toy (joint attention)	Remember you do not have to buy expensive toys – boxes of different shapes and sizes, yogurt cups, milk cartons, empty tins (if edges are smooth) etc can be offered to children. These can be decorated by, eg painting them using colourful, non-lead-based paints
	Listens with pleasure to toys that make sounds; repeats activity that produces sound, eg repeatedly pressing a button	
	Gives toys to adults on request; demonstrates understanding by using objects appropriately, eg hairbrush, telephone	Children need the presence and reassurance of familiar adults
	Likes to be in sight and hearing of familiar people. Demonstrates affection to familiar people	

Development milestone	Description	Implications for practice
Self-care and independence	Drinks well from cup with a lid; holds spoon and will attempt to feed self but is very messy; munches pieces of food at side of mouth	Preferably offer cup; offer finger food, eg hardish biscuit, cucumber strip, carrot strips Encourage child to help with being dressed/undressed
	Sits and sometimes stands without support while being dressed by carer; helps with dressing by holding out arm for sleeve and foot for shoe, etc	

Age 15 months

Development milestone	Description	Implications for practice
Posture and large movement	May walk alone with uneven steps and legs fairly wide apart – feet wide apart, arms slightly bent and held above head for balance (9½–17½ months). Starts voluntarily but frequently falls or bumps into furniture	Make sure the area is safe and free from barriers and obstacles that might hurt toddler No slippery surfaces or accessible stairs Toddler requires constant supervision
	Sits by collapsing or falling forward onto hands	
	Crawls up stairs, and possibly down stairs backwards	A stair guard is useful as open stairways could be dangerous

Development milestone	Description	Implications for practice
Visual perceptual and fine motor	Enjoys coloured pictures in book, pats page; watches small toy pulled across floor; demands desired object by pointing index finger	Offer clear, simple illustrations and picture books Provide push–pull toys – pram, car, wire toy, etc
	Picks up string or small object with good pincer grasp using either hand	Provide such items Supervise closely
	Manipulates cubes and may build a tower of two cubes after being shown how (11–18 months). Can take objects out of container and put them back again, eg posting box containing different shapes	Provide wooden blocks of different sizes and shapes Provide a variety of toys in containers for toddler to empty and replace back through appropriate opening At home allow toddler to unpack the cupboard filled with plastic containers
	Grasps crayons with whole hand – palmar grasp; uses either hand to scribble from 14 months (11–18 months)	Provide large pieces of paper and short, stubby, non-toxic wax crayons

➡

Development milestone	Description	Implications for practice
Speech, language, communication	Uses jargon with intonation that sounds like speech, eg 'ga-ga', 'ba-ba', 'ma-ma'	Talk to toddler; describe what you/toddler are doing. Use grammatically correct language and pronounce words clearly Rhymes and song still important
	Says a few recognisable words (usually from 2–6) in correct context (12–18 months) e.g. 'mama', 'dada', 'gogo', 'no', 'baba'	Respond positively when toddler says a word
	Appears to understand some new words each week	
	Understands simple commands, eg 'Give me the bottle, ball', etc	Issue simple instructions, one at a time
	Communicates wishes by pointing, vocalising or screaming	Encourage child to keep on talking, respond positively. Model the correct word

➡

Development milestone	Description	Implications for practice
Social behaviour and play	Uses hands to push large wheeled toy on level ground	Provide large wheel toys, eg doll's pram, wheelbarrow, cart, small shopping trolley, etc
	Explores with lively interest properties and possibilities of toys, convenient household objects and sound-makers	Provide different toys and objects – make a shaker by adding beans to a small plastic bottle (seal well); offer an empty biscuit tin and plastic spoon for banging on it
	Engages in functional play, eg pushes car, pretends to drink from empty cup, bangs toy with hammer, etc	Provide a variety of different equipment (think of margarine and yogurt tubs, etc)
	Carries doll by limb, hair, clothing Repeatedly casts (throws) objects to floor, watches where things fall; finds hidden toy	Provide doll, teddy bear, etc. These can be bought or handmade (knitted, etc). Make a doll from waste – use a mielie cob wrapped in a piece of old material. Play peek-a-boo, hide and seek
	Enjoys 'give and take' games; very curious	Play 'exchange game' with toddler where you hand him something, he says 'ta' and then hands something back to you
	Emotionally unstable and closely dependent upon adults for reassurance. Looks to carer for support, especially in unfamiliar situations where toddler looks to the adult to affirm behaviour (social referencing)	Adult is responsive and uses verbal and non-verbal communication to continually reassure toddler that he is in a secure, nurturing environment, eg smiles, nods head or frowns to indicate that an action is inappropriate

Development milestone	Description	Implications for practice
Self-care and independence	Holds and drinks from cup; holds spoon, brings it to mouth and licks it; competent finger feeding. Chews well but still spills from mouth as not able to completely control lip movement	Provide cup and encourage self-feeding. Place food in curved bowl with a lip to make self-feeding easier. Provide eating utensils (spoon), allow to feed self
	Helps more constructively with dressing	Be patient, tell toddler what you want him to do, eg 'Give me your arm'
	Needs constant supervision for protection against dangers as he busily explores his environment	Safety is paramount; constant supervision is necessary. Place dangerous substances, eg bleach, out of reach. Be careful to safeguard all water points

Age 18 months

Development milestone	Description	Implications for practice
Posture and large movement	Walks well, feet only slightly apart; stops and starts safely; runs carefully, seldom falls but has difficulty negotiating obstacles, eg a chair in his pathway; walks upstairs with hand held (13–22 months); backs into small chair to seat self; crawls backwards downstairs	Ensure safety and constant supervision. Child-sized furniture is useful
	Pushes and pulls large toys and boxes	Provide variety of push-pull toys and boxes of different sizes
	May carry large bear or doll while walking	

Development milestone	Description	Implications for practice
Posture and large movement	Enjoys climbing	Provide suitably sized climbing frame; make sure that furniture child can climb onto is secure; make sure he cannot climb out of cot when you are not watching
Visual perceptual and fine motor	Picks up small objects immediately with delicate pincer grasp; enjoys putting small objects in containers and then taking them out – he is learning about the relative size of objects	Provide smallish objects such as Unifix cubes, buttons, small stones and bottle tops, corks and dry beans, eg broad beans. Supervise to prevent child placing small objects in his mouth and possibly choking, or pushing objects up his nose or into his ears Learning the relative size of objects is related to early mathematical knowledge
	Enjoys simple picture books, often recognising and placing finger on coloured pictures of familiar objects; turns several pages at a time	Provide different types of books – colourful cloth books; cardboard books enable easier turning of pages; draw and colour in pictures or take pictures from magazines to make books to share with child
	Holds pencil in middle or at top using whole hand; spontaneous to-and-fro scribbling using either hand or with crayon in both hands	Large pieces of paper, short sturdy crayons
	Builds tower of three cubes after being shown how	This activity stimulates memory acquisition
	Beginning to show hand preference	

Development milestone	Description	Implications for practice
Speech, language and communication	Chatters continually to self when playing – a mix of jargon and intelligible words	Continue speaking to toddler and name his actions Listen respectfully to what toddler has to say
	Listens and responds when spoken to; uses from 6–20 recognisable words; echoes last or prominent word in a sentence when being spoken to; growth spurt in spoken vocabulary (18–24 months)	Look at toddler when speaking to him; it is advisable to put yourself at his physical level when speaking to him Make sure he understands what you say Do not ridicule, shame or blame if he makes speech errors
	Demands objects by pointing and using loud vocalisations while looking to see if adult is responding to his demand	Provide responsive care; remain patient and caring at all times
	Enjoys nursery rhymes and singing	
	Obeys simple instructions, eg 'Fetch your shoes'; 'Shut the door' Points to own or carer's or doll's hair, nose, feet	Issue clear instructions, one at a time Give toddler time to respond Name and point out different body parts, eg during bath time

➥

Development milestone	Description	Implications for practice
Social behaviour and play	Explores environment energetically with increasing understanding; little awareness of possible dangers	Constant supervision Ensure a safe learning environment
	No longer takes toys to mouth, but still throws (casts) to floor when angry	
	Remembers where objects belong in familiar environment	Encourage him to tidy up
	Enjoys and imitates simple, everyday tasks such as feeding a doll, 'reading' a book, washing clothes (15–18 months)	Provide a variety of household experiences for toddler; use anti-waste to make a tea set or tools for home repair
	Pays good attention to tasks of own choosing; resists interference	Know when to intervene and when to remain silent
	Plays alone but still likes to be near familiar adult or older child Emotionally still very dependent on adult, alternates between clinging and resistance to being picked up	Make sure toddler can see or hear you if you are not in sight Tell toddler when you are going elsewhere Allow toddler to become increasingly independent Adult must be consistent, eg do not encourage child to feed himself one day and then refuse to allow him to the next day because you are in a hurry
	Exchanges toys with peers during play. Will snatch toy from another child if angry	
	Recognises himself in mirror	Provide a wall mirror and sit toddler in front of it. This enhances body awareness

Development milestone	Description	Implications for practice
Self-care and independence	Holds spoon and feeds self but might play with food; holds cup with two hands and drinks without spilling; lifts cup alone and hands back to adult	Encourage toddler to feed himself Do not chastise if he messes Feeding in highchair is ideal
	Assists with dressing and undressing, takes off shoes and socks but is seldom able to put them back on again	Tell toddler what you are doing, encourage him to help you dress/undress himself
	Beginning to be aware of toilet needs by becoming restless and through vocalisation. Might have bowel control (but very variable), might indicate wet or soiled pants	Ask if he wants to wee/poo Place on potty if toddler indicates he would like to do either. Do not scold if he does not produce a bowel movement or if he later soils his nappy

Age 2 years

Development milestone	Description	Implications for practice
Posture and large movement	Runs safely, stopping and starting easily, and avoids obstacles	Provide sufficient safe space for free movement Constant supervision
	Squats well to rest or play with objects and rises without using hands	
	Jumps on same spot after being shown how (17–30 months)	

Development milestone	Description	Implications for practice
Posture and large movement	Pushes and pulls large-wheel toys forwards and sometimes backwards; pulls small wheeled toy and shows awareness of direction	Provide different moveable toys, eg a large truck, a wheelbarrow, shopping trolley, wire toys; provide sufficient space, ideally with different surfaces
	Climbs on furniture to look out of window or to open doors; gets down easily	Check to ensure safety; consider where the child might land if he falls and if surface is appropriate for such a fall; be mindful of windows without burglar bars
	Shows increased understanding of size of self in relation to size and position of objects in the environment and to enclosed spaces such as a cupboard or cardboard box	Talk to toddler about his position in relation to other objects: 'You are in front of the table'; 'You are on top of the chair', etc
	Walks up and down stairs holding onto wall or rail, putting first one foot then two feet on the same step	
	Throws small ball overhand and forwards, without falling over	Provide different-sized balls – not too hard. Make balls from an old pair of pantyhose stuffed with newspaper or plastic bags
	Walks into a large ball when trying to kick it	
	Sits on small tricycle but cannot use pedals; propels it forward using feet	Buy strong sturdy tricycles that will last Plastic bikes are inexpensive and very durable

➡

Development milestone	Description	Implications for practice
Visual perceptual and fine motor	Good manipulative skills; increasingly adept in picking up small objects and putting them back in the same place, eg pegs	Provide colourful manipulative as well as construction toys Play dough and Duplo are useful
	Can match square, circular and triangular shapes in a simple jigsaw puzzle	Simple 2–4-piece puzzles
	Holds crayon towards the bottom nearer the point; uses thumb and first two fingers; mostly uses preferred hand	Still offer short stubby crayons Provide large pieces of paper
	Produces spontaneous circular as well as to-and-fro scribbles and dots; imitates a vertical line and sometimes a 'V' shape	Toddlers can also do these movements outside in sand; provide different kinds of materials such as crayons, paint, thick Kokis
	Builds tower of six or seven cubes	
	Enjoys picture books; recognises fine detail in favourite pictures; turns pages singly; can name and match pictures with toys or other pictures	Increase collection of picture books Make your own by drawing or cutting out pictures from a magazine to make a short book If possible, take child to the library for story time and to choose his own book
	Recognises self and familiar adults in photographs	Show child photographs of himself and family

➡

Development milestone	Description	Implications for practice
Speech, language and communication	Uses 50 or more recognisable words in context and understands many more; puts two words together to make simple sentences, eg 'More juice'; 'Want food' (18–30 months); starts saying 'no' and 'not'; constantly asks names of objects and people; may omit parts of words	Do not correct pronunciation or grammatical errors; model correct language Tell stories – you can make these up or draw on your own folklore (but remember to tell simple stories based on the child's world that have a happy ending) Provide a toy phone
	Begins to listen with more interest to general conversations; listens when spoken to but might need prompting to focus attention	Continue talking to child; describe actions and give words for what he is doing, eg 'You are enjoying your breakfast'; add some new words to increase vocabulary
	Refers to self by name or personal pronoun ('me'); talks to self in long monologue during play	Observe and record what child says This is a normal part of speech development theorised by Vygotsky
	Echolalia (repeating words) occurs frequently	You say goodbye and the toddler repeats 'bye, bye, bye'
	Can select a named object from a display of three or four	Supply a variety of objects such as a car, a rattle and a toy animal. Ask toddler to give you the car
	Enjoys and joins in nursery rhymes and action songs	Choose rhymes and songs that are culturally appropriate
	Can point to common body parts and items, eg hair, hand, feet, nose, eye, mouth, shoe, etc in pictures	Sing action song: 'Heads, shoulders, knees and toes'

Development milestone	Description	Implications for practice
Speech, language and communication	Carries out simple instructions, eg 'Go and see who is at the door'; follows a series of two commands, eg 'Fetch your doll and put her in the basket'	Marked increase in receptive language (the ability to understand information). This is part of cognitive development
Social behaviour and play	Follows adult around house, imitates domestic activities; will turn doorknob and run outside; very curious about environment; little understanding of dangers	Enjoys playing with household items Supervision essential
	Spontaneously engages in simple make-believe play; substitutes one item for another, eg a block becomes a car or a banana (beginning of symbolic play) (18–24 months)	Provide a simple home corner –this can be made from anti-waste materials; add dress-up clothing
	Understands that others might have wants that are different to his own	Encourage child to be tolerant and respectful of others
	Constantly demands adult's attention; clings tightly to show affection or, alternatively, if angry, fearful or tired; restless and rebellious if cannot get own way; resentful of attention given to other toddlers by familiar adults; tantrums when frustrated or trying to make himself understood; attention is usually easily distracted	Pay attention to child's needs and react accordingly. Do not shout at or fight with him If possible, prevent tantrums by diverting child's attention
	Defends own possessions with determination: 'It's mine'	Be tolerant. Focus on self and own possessions is a normal part of development at this age

➡

Development milestone	Description	Implications for practice
Social behaviour and play	Might take turns but has little idea of sharing either toys or attention of adults; unwilling to defer or modify immediate satisfaction of wishes	Not yet able to share so do not force child to do this
	Parallel play – plays contentedly near other children but not with them; beginning to cooperate with peers to achieve goals	
Self-care and independence	Feeds self competently with spoon but is easily distracted; lifts cup and drinks without spilling	Encourage self-feeding by making child sit down and eat Present food in manageable portions. Offer small portions
	Asks for food and drink	Child usually has three meals and two snacks per day Do not withhold food as punishment
	Usually attempts to verbalise toilet needs in reasonable time but is still unreliable	Encourage a potty routine but do not shame and blame if accidents occur

Age 2½ years

Development milestone	Description	Implications for practice
Posture and large movement	Runs and climbs well; negotiates stairs well, still places one foot then two feet on the same stair	Provide safe outdoor environment with appropriate climbing equipment Take to a park if no suitable outdoor play area at home
	Pushes and pulls large toys skilfully; might have difficulty steering them around obstacles	Continue to provide a variety of these toys

Development milestone	Description	Implications for practice
Posture and large movement	Can jump with two feet from a low step; stands on tiptoe if shown how to (16–30 months)	
	Throws ball from hand, somewhat awkwardly; kicks large ball gently and lopsidedly	Encourage children to throw and kick balls both to adults and to each other
Visual perceptual and fine motor	Recognises minute detail in picture books and self in photographs	Provide more detailed story books, read these to child and discuss pictures
	Begins to respond to social information on TV and other media as part of their world	Make sure children sit at least one metre away from TV; watch no more than one hour/day; adults to control what content is viewed
	Builds tower of seven+ cubes using preferred hand; inserts square, circular and triangular shapes into posting box; begins to correct the orientation of the shape from 33 months	Continue to encourage block play, discuss shapes; offer jigsaw puzzles with more pieces – anything from 6–20 pieces Make own posting boxes from ice cream containers or other containers that have plastic lids
	Holds crayon in preferred hand with improving pincer grasp	Offer large pieces of paper; variety of crayons Paint on easel
	Copies vertical and horizontal line and sometimes 'T' and 'V' shape	
	Matches 3–4 colours correctly (24–36 months)	Give child scraps of coloured paper and let him match the same colours

➡

Development milestone	Description	Implications for practice
Speech, language, communication	Uses 200 or more recognisable words (24–36 months) but speech structure and pronunciation show immaturities	Continue to speak to child using the correct grammatical structures Encourage child to speak; do not correct mistakes, but rather model correct form of language
	Speech is usually intelligible to familiar adults	
	Knows full name	Reinforce this information
	Still practising echolalia – imitating phrases	Play with language and encourage child to do same
	Can select pictures of actions, eg 'Who is eating?'; 'Who is sleeping?' (24–33 months)	Provide appropriate visual stimulation
	Recites a few nursery rhymes; enjoys simple familiar stories read from picture book	
	Provides a running commentary during play – to self and others	
	Requires physical or verbal prompts to shift attention to looking or listening to something in particular if engrossed in play	Speak respectfully to child as you request his attention

➡

Development milestone	Description	Implications for practice
Social behaviour and play	Very active and restless, and dislikes being constrained. Little understanding of dangers or need to defer immediate wishes	Sufficient place to play and move Safety is essential
	Throws tantrums when thwarted (frustrated) and not so easily distracted	Try to prevent tantrums from occurring by distracting him before he loses self-control
	Emotionally still very dependent upon adults; requires reassurance in unfamiliar situations	Continue providing responsive, nurturing care. Be patient, loving and respectful to child
	More sustained role play: putting dolls to bed, washing clothes, etc, but likes reassurance from familiar adult; acts out common activities using substituted material, eg has pretend tea parties with gravel on plate for cakes	Encourage playing in the home corner
	Plays meaningfully with miniature doll's-house-sized toys	Do not prevent boys from playing with traditional girls' toys, and vice versa
	Watches other children play with interest; joins in occasionally for a few minutes but has little notion of sharing either playthings or the attention of adults	Support children in their play; allow child to play for a considerable amount of waking time

➡

Development milestone	Description	Implications for practice
Self-care and independence	Eats skilfully with spoon, might use fork – consider culturally eating practices	Reinforce sitting down to eat and chewing with mouth closed (prevent choking)
	Pulls down pants when going to toilet but seldom able to pull them up again; may be dry through night – but very variable	Help with toilet routine Might still have accidents – do not shame and blame Encourage personal hygiene

Age 3 years

Development milestone	Description	Implications for practice
Posture and large movement	Walks alone upstairs using alternative feet; places one foot then two feet on same stair to come down; jumps from bottom step with two feet together	
	Agile climber	Provide low, sturdy apparatus for climbing
	Confidently negotiates way around obstacles with push-pull toys	Provide toys that child can push such as carts, wheelbarrows, prams and wire toys on wheels
	Increasing awareness of size and movements of own body in relation to external objects and position in space around them	Beginning to establish spatial awareness behaviours; encourage different types of movements, eg move in front of, behind
	Rides tricycle using pedals Riding a scooter helps establish balance	Provide sturdy tricycles. Tricycles also help to straighten knock knees and encourage hip and certain leg movements which plastic bikes do not

Development milestone	Description	Implications for practice
Posture and large movement	Can stand and walk on tiptoes; can momentarily stand on one foot (usually the preferred) when shown how	
	Can sit with feet crossed at ankles	
	Can throw ball overhand and catch large ball on or between extended arms, kicks ball forcefully	Provide largish balls for throwing, kicking, etc
Visual perceptual and fine motor	Builds tower of 9–10 cubes; by 3½ builds bridge of three blocks. Threads large wooden beads on shoelace (does not follow pattern)	Blocks remain valuable play materials; provide alternative materials to thread a string through – large buttons or raw macaroni
	Holds crayon near point between first two fingers and thumb using preferred hand. Copies 'V', 'H' and 'T'; imitates a cross. Draws person with head and might add one or two features	Provide short stubby crayons, and other drawing/painting media; large pieces of paper for drawing
	Can close fist and wiggle thumb	Make use of appropriate finger rhymes, eg 'Tommy Thumb'
	Matches two or three primary colours, usually red and yellow; might confuse blue and green. May know names of colours	Provide plenty of opportunities for children to match and sort using items such as different coloured pegs, wooden sticks or blocks
	Enjoys painting with large brush on easel, covers whole piece of paper; will name picture and talk about it if asked	Always have an easel outside with different coloured paint and different-sized brushes for children to do free painting

➡

Development milestone	Description	Implications for practice
Visual perceptual and fine motor	Cuts paper with scissors (neatly from 3½–4 years)	Have pairs of scissors readily available as well as paper to cut. Also provide left-handed scissors as well as the regular ones
Speech, language, communication	Able to modulate speech in terms of loudness and range of pitch; majority of vocabulary is intelligible to strangers; speech still contains immaturities of pronunciation and structure; uses personal pronouns (eg 'mine', 'yours') and plurals correctly, and most prepositions (eg 'in', 'between', 'on')	Encourage children to talk about themselves and others Model correct language usage rather than correct mistakes
	Gives full name, gender and sometimes age	Provide plenty of opportunities for children to learn these details in a fun way
	Still talks to self in monologue but also carries out simple conversations and is briefly able to explain past and present activities	
	Asks questions: 'Who?'; 'What?'; 'Where?'	Listen to children and handle all questions respectfully
	Identifies objects by function: 'Which one do we eat with?'; understands descriptive concepts such as 'big', 'wet', 'the same', 'different to', etc	Provide word games and make use of phrases that emphasise associations, eg a dog and bone; brush and comb; sock and shoe, etc
	Listens eagerly to stories, demands favourite ones over and over. Knows several nursery rhymes and enjoys singing	Continually introduce new rhymes and songs; tell a story every day; take time to read to children; let children tell their own stories

Development milestone	Description	Implications for practice
Speech, language, communication	Rote counts up to 10 but little concept of quantity beyond 2 or 3	Provide playful opportunities for counting during free-play activities; help children develop one-to-one correspondence through everyday activities such as setting a table for snack time or handing out mugs to each child: 'One for you, and one for you', etc. Encourage finger rhymes and songs
Social behaviour and play	Some ability to switch between listening and doing; needs to look at speaker when listening	Look at children and listen to what they say – be a good role model; encourage children to look at you when talking to you
	General behaviour more amenable. Can be affectionate; makes reference to emotions and can show empathy; shows affection for younger children	Encourage interactions between children of different ages
	Enjoys make-believe play inventing people and objects in addition to familiar activities; plays with other children, understands sharing but tends to follow own ideas	Have a well-resourced home corner. Change props from time to time to maintain children's interest; observe the symbolic play; provide dress-up clothes
	Enjoys playing on the floor with blocks, Duplo, trains, cars, boxes, dolls, etc, alone or in the company of peers. May build garage with blocks for cars, etc	Provide a range of educational toys; ensure thoughtful layout of play spaces and positioning of toys
	Shows some appreciation for the difference between past and present and of the need to defer satisfaction of wishes to the future	

Development milestone	Description	Implications for practice
Self-care and independence	Eats with fork and spoon	Encourage child to sit and eat; use the appropriate cultural utensils
	Washes hands but needs help with drying, can pull pants up and down but needs help with buttons and other fastenings	Supervise all toilet routines, providing assistance when necessary
	Likes to help adults with domestic activities including gardening, shopping, etc	Allow children to assist with household chores; in ECCE centre provide opportunities for washing dolls' clothes, dishes, etc
	Makes an effort to keep surroundings tidy – needs assistance	Encourage tidy-up routines; be consistent; suggest what each child can tidy up and support them as they carry out these responsibilities
	May be dry through night – very variable	Parents to ensure child goes to toilet before going to sleep; do not shame and blame if child has an accident

Age 4 years

Development milestone	Description	Implications for practice
Posture and large movement	Walks and runs up and down stairs in adult fashion; navigates obstacles skilfully; stands, walks and runs on tiptoe; climbs ladders and trees	Provide large blocks of time – at least one hour for outdoor play. Offer stimulating and challenging outdoor activities such as climbing frame, obstacle courses, etc. Use recyclable material such as old car tyres if commercial resources are not available

➡

Development milestone	Description	Implications for practice
Posture and large movement	Rides tricycle well, navigates corners, etc.	At the ECCE centre, have a cycle track with scooters, plastic bikes and tricycles for children to ride. Place handmade road signs on track
	Stands on preferred foot for 3–5 seconds and hops on preferred foot	Observe free play as it offers opportunities to assess a child and keep a record
	Sits with legs crossed	
Visual perceptual and fine motor	Builds a tower of 10 or more cubes. Builds three steps with six cubes (4–4½ years)	The problem solving involved in these activities is an example of early mathematics
	Holds crayon in tripod grasp; good control. Copies 'V', 'H', 'T' and 'O'	Continue to encourage free drawing and painting
	Draws a person with head, legs and trunk, and sometimes arms and fingers. Draws a recognisable house spontaneously or on request	
	Beginning to tell you what he plans to draw; attempts to build with a range of materials reflecting the ability to plan and execute ideas	Write a short description of children's drawings; provide different media for visual arts – collage materials, salt dough, boxes for box construction, etc
	Matches and names four colours correctly	Provide a variety of objects of different shapes but with colours that match

Development milestone	Description	Implications for practice
Speech, language, communication	Speech is grammatically correct and intelligible; utters few immature sounds – in particular the 'l-r-w-y' group, the 'p-th-f' group and 'k-t' sound group. Gives connected account of recent events; knows full name, home address and usually age	Continue to model correct language to children as opposed to explicitly correcting the child Provide rich language input by reading and telling stories
	Continually asks questions: 'Why?', 'When?' and 'How?', and the meaning of words	Answer questions respectfully; look directly at children when talking to them; introduce new words in context; repeat new words frequently in context
	Understands some abstract concepts such as 'before', 'after', 'if'	Use these words in relation to child's world, eg 'Before you go to bed I will read you a story'
	Listens to and tells long stories, sometimes confuses fact and fantasy	Be careful to ensure child is told that monsters, scary characters and superheroes who jump off buildings are not real
	Rote counts up to 20 or more – this does not necessarily mean that the child understands number concepts; beginning to count objects by words and touch in one-to-one correspondence up to 4 or 5 Before learning to count, a child needs to understand 'one-to-one correspondence'. This means being able to match ONE object to ONE other object or person	You can practice one-to-one correspondence in all sorts of different contexts. Laying the table in the fantasy corner, eg one cake to one soft toy, and another cake to a second soft toy. Continue to develop mathematical concepts through play-based activities – sandpit, water play, number songs, etc

Development milestone	Description	Implications for practice
Speech, language, communication	Enjoys jokes and made-up nonsense words; also enjoys phrases that are incongruent or out of place, eg 'the cow jumped over the moon'	Tell child humorous stories; encourage child to play with language and to find rhyming words even if they are not actually words, eg 'easy… peasy'
	Knows several nursery rhymes and can repeat or sing them correctly	Continue to extend child's knowledge of nursery rhymes and songs; consider all cultural groups. Rhyming is not a prominent feature in African languages
Social behaviour and play	More independent, strong-willed; adopts standards of behaviour of parents and other close adults	Continue to model desirable behaviours
	Can be cheeky to adults and quarrelsome with peers when crossed. May experiment with rude (swear) words	Pay little attention, if possible, to child swearing – no adult reaction tends to discourage use of undesirable language. It is not advisable to threaten the child with punishment or wash out the mouth with soap or other unpleasant-tasting substances
	Shows a sense of humour in play and social activities	Encourage children to explore different ideas and to enjoy activities
	Enjoys dressing up and make-believe play; engages in complicated floor games; tends not to be tidy	Provide a well-equipped home corner with variety: hairdressing salon, shop, office, fire station, etc. Have specific places for storing similar items. Encourage tidy-up time

➡

Development milestone	Description	Implications for practice
Social behaviour and play	Constructive outdoor building with any available materials	Provide blankets, sheets to cover climbing frame to make a tent; offer large cardboard boxes for outdoor construction
	Needs companionship of children with whom he is alternatively friendly and aggressive; understands need to argue with words and not blows; understands turn-taking and sharing	Beginning to play cooperatively, is sometimes able to share Encourage child to be assertive rather than to use physically aggressive behaviour: 'No, I do not like it when you do that', etc
	Shows concern for younger siblings and empathy for children in distress	Encourage child to play with toddlers and younger children
	Appreciates past, present and future	Tell stories related to different timeframes; children enjoy simple stories based on historical facts Children like to talk about events that have happened in their past, eg what they did over the weekend, etc
Self-care and independence	Eats well with spoon and fork, can spread a soft substance on bread with knife, eg jam	Encourage child to feed himself; make his own sandwich, etc
	Washes and dries hands; brushes teeth; can dress and undress self except for doing up laces and tying bows, etc (4–5 years)	Reinforce personal hygiene after toilet or before eating; allow child to choose what he wants to wear and to dress himself

Age 5 years

Development milestone	Description	Implications for practice
Posture and large movement	Walks easily on narrow line; runs lightly on toes; active and skilful in climbing, sliding, swinging, digging, and doing various stunts; skips on alternate feet; can touch toes without bending legs	Offer a wide variety of different physical activities every day so child can hone skills; encourage child to walk on a balancing beam; plan for movement rings with different activity stations Supervise risky and adventurous play
	Can stand on one foot for 8–10 seconds (both right and left); can stand on preferred foot with arms folded; can hop 2 or 3 metres forward on each foot separately	Include these activities in movement rings and obstacle courses, eg hop three times to the hoop
	Moves rhythmically to music	Play different types of music; offer creative dance and movement rings. Provide a range of different swings, eg tyre swing, a swing with a simple plank as the seat, etc
	Grips strongly with either hand	Continue to offer a variety of manipulative activities to strengthen hand and toe grip. Try to include monkey bars in outdoor equipment
	Throws and catches ball well, though catching with one hand only develops around ages 9–10; enjoys ball games and can follow rules	Provide different-sized balls for both free play and teacher-guided movement rings; provide bats for hitting balls and skittles and other objects, eg clown or similar figure with open mouth for children to use as bowling game. Old two-litre cooldrink bottles half filled with sand make good skittles

Development milestone	Description	Implications for practice
Visual perceptual and fine motor	Picks up and puts back objects	Provide different manipulative activities – pick-up-sticks, Lego, clothespegs, pair of tweezers to pick up small objects and place into another container, etc
	Holds cubes in dominant hand with ulnar (little) finger tucked in; builds elaborate models	Provide a large number of and different-shaped blocks
	Copies many letters – 'X', 'L', 'A', 'C', 'U' and 'Y' added to those already mastered; copies squares and triangles; good control of pencil; writes a few letters spontaneously	Continue offering a variety of creative visual arts activities; still offer large pieces of paper as well as smaller pieces, painting easel, etc. Encourage free drawing; encourage child to write name in top left-hand corner
	Draws recognisable man with head, trunk, legs, arms and features. Draws house with door, windows, roof and chimney; spontaneously draws other pictures containing several items; colours neatly and can stay within lines	Encourage free drawing where children can bring their own interpretation and creativity to their work. Ask child to draw a picture of himself at the beginning of each term. Keep each picture to track child's increasing understanding of his body image. Provide different types of drawing and painting resources (see Chapter 11)
	Cuts strips of paper neatly; cuts on zigzag line	Provide plenty of cutting experiences on straight, curved and zigzag lines
	Names four or more colours and can match 12 different colours	Encourage visual matching games, eg find the matching button; match different shades of green, etc

Development milestone	Description	Implications for practice
Speech, language and communication	Speech is fluent and grammatically and phonetically correct; might confuse 's-f-th' group	Have a selection of story and picture books for children to 'read'; tell and read stories to them on a daily basis; remember children like to have the same story repeated, especially when being read to at home. Encourage children to tell their own stories; you could, for instance, ask the group to tell a progressive story where one child starts the story and the next continues it, and so on. Provide opportunities for dramatic play. Make use of rhymes and songs; riddles, jokes and word plays, eg use Dr Seuss books
	Loves being read to or being told stories; will act them out later. Delights in reciting or singing rhymes and jingles; enjoys jokes and riddles	
	Gives full name, age and home address and usually birthday	Reinforce child's learning of personal details
	Can listen to instructions while engaged in activities	Encourage speech by listening to what children have to say; answer their questions and ask them open-ended questions. Ask them to tell you about their pictures and then you write on the picture itself a short sentence that captures what they have said
	Constantly asks meanings of abstract words and uses them appropriately	Continue to talk to children, introducing new words and ideas. Remember to make your input contextually relevant
	Understands time and sequence concepts and uses terms like 'first', 'then' and 'last'	Model mathematical language to child during free play, teacher-guided activities and routines, eg 'We will first pack up the toys, then wash our hands before eating'. If the children are playing with blocks, ask who has the most, the least, etc

Development milestone	Description	Implications for practice
Social behaviour and play	Developing self-regulation; general behaviour is more controlled and independent with wide variability in different situations; able to hide/regulate emotions and express socially appropriate responses to events	Encourage social interactions in group games. Allow sufficient time to engage meaningfully in games; ensure there are sufficient resources and space to play; ensure that props are culturally diverse and appropriate; encourage active participation and an interactive learning environment
	Follows tidy-up routines but needs reminding	
	Continues to enjoy dramatic play. enjoys stories about strong, powerful characters; plays creatively; symbolic play present	Encourage all types of activities, make-believe play, games with rules, educational toys, outdoor games, etc. Use this time to observe and document children's behaviour and progress – all aspects of physical, cognitive, social and emotional development
	Plans and builds constructively inside and outside	
	Chooses own friends; plays cooperatively with peers; understands need for rules and fair play	
	Increasing understanding of the wishes and feelings of friends; engages in bargaining, compromise and reconciliation. Tender and protective towards younger children and pets; comforts playmates	Allow children to make own rules and to sort out any conflicts – only interfere if the situation becomes out of hand
		Support learning through thoughtful intervention and co-construction of learning (see Chapter 6 on play)
	Definite sense of humour	
	Beginning to understand the meaning of time as it appears in the daily programme	Copy of the daily programme illustrated in pictures should be on the classroom wall at a level the children can see

Development milestone	Description	Implications for practice
Self-care and independence	Uses knife and fork competently	Competence with eating utensils will be influenced by cultural determinants
	Washes and dries face and hands, but needs supervision in relation to cleanliness for the rest of the body; can undress and dress himself	Give child independence in self-care tasks, but keep an eye on the progress; encourage children to tidy up after themselves, eg hang up clothes, place them in the laundry basket, etc

SOURCES: ADAPTED FROM SHERIDAN (1973); SHARMA & COCKERILL (2014)

Something to consider

As we have stressed, developmental tables are necessary but are only guidelines. They give an indication of what we can expect from individual children at different stages and ages of development. They can inform our practice so that we can ensure it is appropriate and suitably challenging for all children. We have given some ideas of how to do this in Table 3.4 in the column 'Implications for practice'. Knowledge of appropriate age-related milestones enables us to make tentative assessments of each child's developmental progress. This provides us with a base to investigate further if we think there is a possible problem related to the child's growth and development as early intervention is the best remediation of this.

3.4 FACTORS THAT INFLUENCE OVERALL WELLBEING OF YOUNG CHILDREN, IE GROWTH, DEVELOPMENT AND LEARNING

Today it is generally agreed that growth, development and learning is dependent upon a complex interaction of biological (nature) and environmental considerations. If these considerations are predominately favourable, children will fall within acceptable parameters (boundaries) of development. If not, they will show signs of atypical development (Neaum, 2016).

No study of children and childhood is complete without exploring some of the factors that impact on children's early growth, development and learning. Children do not live in isolation; they live within some type of family structure, therefore factors affecting families affect children.

We have drawn on Bronfenbrenner's ecological systems theory (Donald, Lazarus & Moola, 2014) to represent a biopsychosocial–environmental model (see Figure 3.4) that provides a comprehensive lens though which to explore the many factors that impact children's overall growth, development and wellbeing. In this model, recognition is given to the importance of the family, neighbourhood and broader community, as well as to environmental and biological factors. In addition, this model recognises the value of a multi-disciplinary approach in addressing challenges and constraints.

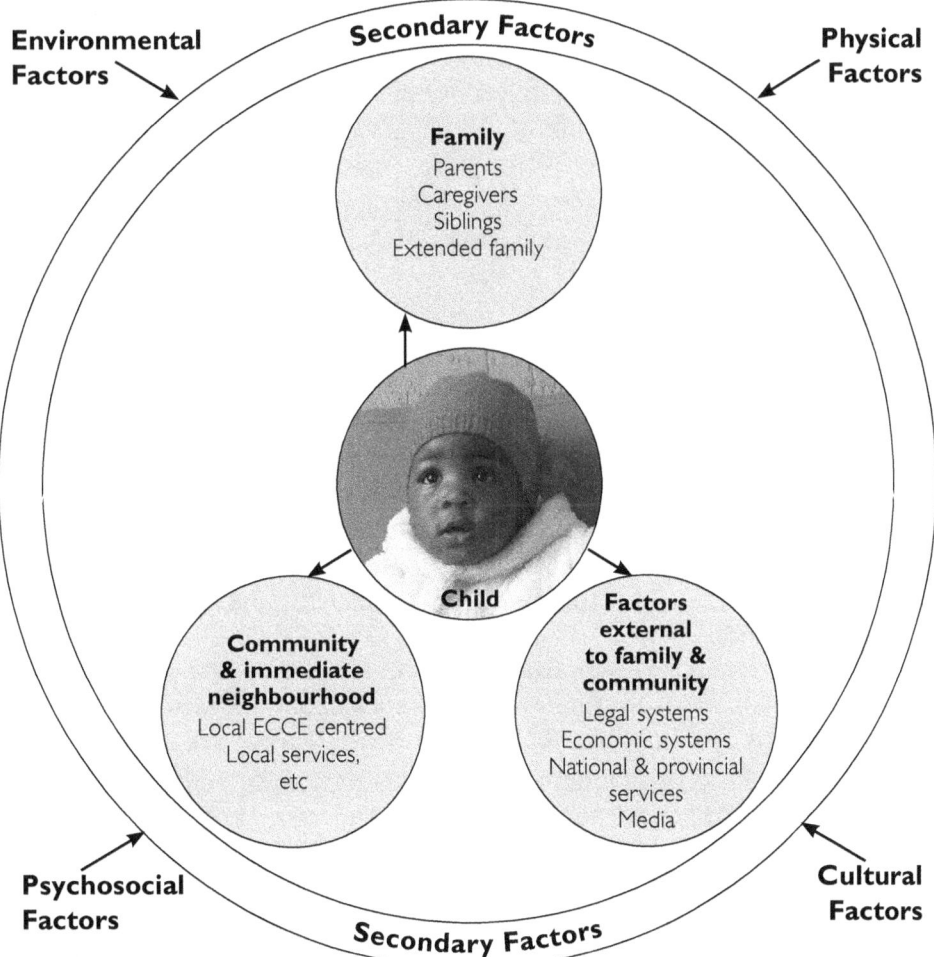

Figure 3.4 Factors influencing overall well-being (growth, development and learning) of young children

Figure 3.4 is a diagrammatic representation (adapted from Bronfenbrenner, as cited in Donald et al, 2014) showing factors influencing overall well-being of children. This diagram comprises four circles. The child is centrally placed in the inner circle and the primary factors influencing wellbeing are housed in the three outer circles. The family, comprising parents, caregivers, siblings and extended family members, are placed within the second circle. Within the third circle, we find the community and immediate neighbourhood. Different ECCE services and contexts fall within this realm. The fourth circle demarcates those factors external to the family and community. These external factors have been grouped into four categories Firstly, we mention the legal system including relevant laws and policies that influence children's wellbeing. Think, for example, of The National Integrated ECD Policy (DSD, 2015) – see Chapter 15; The National Curriculum Framework (DBE, 2015); The National Early Learning Standards (DBE, 2009); the Children's Act of 2005 including later amendments (RSA, 2007). These policies provide the framework for ECCE provisioning.

Secondly, we consider the availability of services such as health, welfare, education or judicial that are offered by local, provincial and national government as well as civil society. For example, some available health services for young children include offering expectant mothers adequate antenatal care to ensure a live, healthy newborn baby and providing immunisation services to babies and toddlers (Kibel, Westwood & Saloojee, 2013).

The third category is the media – think of the impact of television, radio programmes and social media and how these might influence child-rearing patterns, for example. Mothers make lifestyle changes based on the media and advertising. For example, despite knowing the advantages of breastfeeding, they decide to bottle feed because it is more 'fashionable'.

A fourth factor is an economic one. Economic factors refer to the distribution of income, wealth, and the family's ability to afford sound health and quality care, and education for young children. Currently, for example, in South Africa with the high rate of unemployment, economic hardship is weighing heavily on many communities and families. Strained socioeconomic factors are a prime cause of poverty and child neglect in South Africa (Kibel et al, 2013).

Superimposed on these four external factors and cutting across all the circles are a number of important secondary factors that can also have a positive or negative influence on the developing child. Some of these are environmental, cultural, physical and psychosocial (Kibel et al, 2013). All these factors are interdependent and influence all aspects of a child's growth, development and learning. To elaborate:

- **Environmental factors** that impact on optimal development include housing, the availability of safe water, sanitation and refuse removal. In addition, community resources such as antenatal services; the availability of local health services (eg immunisation and well-baby clinics); recreational facilities including parks, a library or toy library; etc, are also important.
- **Physical factors** include exercise, diet, smoking, age of mother and genetic inheritance. In addition, physical factors also consider the type of stimulation and care given to babies and young children. Choices made

by parents impact directly on the growth, development, learning and wellbeing of young children.
- **Cultural factors** refer to lifestyle choices such as personal hygiene, nutrition, perceptions of health and disease, and traditional practices, including child-rearing practices. All these factors are determined by the society in which one lives as well as class, gender, religion and socioeconomic factors.
- **Psychosocial factors** are numerous and are acknowledged as being a major determinant of optimal growth, development, learning and wellbeing in young children. Psychosocial behaviours include a number of negative behaviours such as violence, aggression, abuse, parental problems including drug abuse, alcoholism, dietary deprivation (malnutrition), stress and anxiety, among other things. Negative situations include all children in stressful or neglectful relationships, families living in poverty, as well as parents (both mothers and fathers) or teachers who are depressed and unable to form responsive relationships with their children. Children and their families require support if the children are to enjoy and benefit from their childhood interactions.

Something to consider

Within early childhood education there is a strong correlation between different theoretical perspectives, the factors affecting growth, development and learning, and developmental domains. We acknowledge that context, culture and developmental factors are equally responsible for ensuring the wellbeing of children.

3.5 SUMMARY

Based on all that has been presented in chapters 2 and 3, we draw out some key messages that influence the growth, development, learning and wellbeing of young children. These include the following:

1. Pre- and postnatal experiences are major determinants in the long-term health and development progress of children.
2. The first 60 months of a child's life are critical in determining their future development. The quality of care, affection and stimulation received by the child during the first five years of life have been shown to shape a child's life chances (Richter et al, 2012).
3. There appear to be developmental phases that all children go through, but their individual progress is shaped by their experience and culture.
4. From birth, children are competent and skilful learners with a wide range of skills that are further shaped by their family and community, and experiences.

5. Children are born curious, which drives them to experiment, explore, interact with and make sense of their world. They seek active experiences, often through play.
6. Young children learn with and through other people, especially their parents, carers, teachers and other children.
7. Social and emotional wellbeing are crucial to support positive development and self-regulatory behaviour (see Chapter 10).
8. Important characteristics or learning dispositions that support lifelong academic success are laid down in the early years; these include developing trust in other people, curiosity, a sense of responsibility, perseverance and self-esteem. There are many others.
9. Education for democracy through democracy begins in the early years. Children make choices and learn that these have consequences. As we discussed in Chapter 2, the child has voice and agency. The child should ideally be in a respectful environment where tolerance and equity are key.

REFERENCES

Bertram, T & Pascal, C. 2010. Introducing child development, in Bruce, T. *Early childhood: A guide for students*. London: SAGE.

Charlesworth, R. 2017. *Understanding child development*. Boston, MA: Cengage.

Conbayir, M. 2017. *Early childhood and neuroscience: Theory, research and implications for practice*. London: Bloomsbury.

Department of Basic Education (DBE). 2009. *National Early Learning Development Standards*. Pretoria.

Department of Basic Education (DBE). 2015. *The National Curriculum Framework from birth to four*. Pretoria.

Department of Social Development. 2015. *National Integrated Early Childhood Development Policy*. https://www.google.co.za/webhp?sourceid=chrome-instant&rlz=1C1CAFA_enZA657ZA657&ion=1&espv=2&ie=UTF-8#q=Guidelines+for+Early+Childhood+Development+Services.+2006.+Department+of+Social+Development:+Pretoria (Accessed 6 April 2017).

Donald, D, Lazarus, S & Moola, N. 2014. *Educational psychology in social context*. 5th ed. Cape Town: Oxford University Press.

Empson, J & Nabuzoka, D. 2004. *Atypical child development in context*. Basingstoke, UK: Macmillan.

Gordon, AM & Browne, KW. 2017. *Beginnings and beyond. foundations in early childhood education*. Boston, MA: Cengage Publishing.

Hardman, J. 2012. *Child and adolescent development in South Africa*. Cape Town: Oxford University Press.

Karpov, Y. 2005. *The neo Vygotskian approach to child development.* New York: Cambridge University Press.

Kibel, MA, Westwood, T & Saloojee, H. 2013. *Child health for all: A manual for Southern Africa.* 5th ed. Cape Town: Oxford University Press.

Neaum, S. 2016. *Child development for early years students and practitioners*, 3rd ed. Los Angeles: SAGE.

Perry, BD. 2001. The neurodevelopmental impact of violence in childhood, in Schetky, D & Benedek, EP (eds). *Textbook of child and adolescent forensic psychiatry.* Washington, DC: American Psychiatric Press Inc. 221–238.

Pritchard, A. 2005. *Ways of learning. Learning theories and learning styles in the classroom.* London: David Fulton.

Republic of South Africa 2007. Children's Amendment Act 41 of 2007. Pretoria: Government Printer.

Richter, L, Biersteker, L, Burns, J, Desmond, C, Feza, N, Harrison D, Martin, P, Saloojee, H & Slemming, W. 2012. *Diagnostic review of early childhood development.* Pretoria: Human Science Research Council (HSRC).

Sharma, A & Cockerill, H. 2014. *Mary Sheridan's 'From birth to five years': Children's developmental progress.* London: Routledge.

Sheridan, M. 1973. *From birth to five years: Children's developmental progress.* Slough, Berkshire: NFER Nelson Publishing Co Ltd.

Vygotsky, L. 1978. *Mind in society. The development of higher mental processes.* Cambridge, MA: Harvard University Press.

Walsh, D. 2005. Development theory and early childhood education: necessary but not sufficient, in Yelland, N (ed). *Critical issues in early childhood education.* Berkshire: Open University Press.

Chapter 4

Professional spaces: reimagining the role of the teacher

Vivien Linington, Nontokozo Mashiya and Lorayne Excell

In this chapter we consider:
- who today's early childhood teachers are
- the characteristics of an early childhood care and education (ECCE) professional educator
- a code of ethics for an ECCE professional educator
- creating an inclusive learning and teaching environment
- the role of reflection in becoming a professional.

4.1 INTRODUCTION

Quality care and education demand ethical professional practice. In this chapter we unpack what constitutes this form of practice and the characteristics of a teacher whose practices are steeped in professionalism. In South Africa today ethical professional practice must be inclusive of diversity in relation to race, class, gender, disability, language, ethnicity and religion as well as a range of other diverse factors including children with special education needs. Finally, we explore the role of critical reflection in professional development.

4.2 WHO ARE TODAY'S EARLY CHILDHOOD TEACHERS?

An ECCE teacher in South Africa in 2020 could be a graduate with a formal ECCE qualification, a certificate, a diploma or a degree. She could also be a teacher qualified in another phase who put her career on hold to have children of her own and then returned to work with younger children. She might have a qualification in nursing, a short course perhaps that enabled her to become a nursing aide. Or she could have a childcare qualification, gained after a short or long course at a recognised college or a non-governmental organisation (NGO) offering accredited childcare certificates. She could also be a township 'gogo' with 20 or more young children in her care during the day but no formal qualification. The thread that draws them together – the highly qualified, the semi-qualified and the unqualified – is, one would hope, an interest in, if not passion for, ECCE and, in some instances, a wealth of contextual and wide-ranging experience – experience steeped in adaptability. The different contexts these teachers have encountered requires them to draw on this adaptability to try to ensure that all children receive quality care and education.

Something to consider

Read the vignettes below and reflect on the variety of personnel who could be working in the ECCE field and thus impacting the future of our country. Consider, furthermore, the wide range of skills, knowledge, attitudes and values that these teachers bring to the education and care of the young child.

Educator one

Bronwyn qualified as an Intermediate Phase teacher and then chose to work in a disadvantaged school context, sharing a vision of hope with children whose parents/caregivers were mostly unemployed. When one of the children she had taught entered university – the first member of their family to do so – Bronwyn's joy was almost as great as the family's. Bronwyn then left to have children of her own and took great care to learn as much as she could informally about the development and stimulation of the young child. She has now returned to teaching, working in a crèche in an informal settlement that cares for children from three months to five years of age. She is also investigating how to gain further ECCE qualifications.

Educator two

Thandi chose a career in ECCE after gaining a university pass in her Senior Certificate at a former Model C school in a middle-class, semi-rural area. She qualified as a dietician and then took an early childhood development (ECD) postgraduate diploma course. Her interests in nutrition and young children led to her taking a post with the two- to three-year-old group in an independent early childhood centre.

Educator three

Mamkulu is nearly 60. She has spent her life in Soweto and watched it change from an unlit 'satellite' township to a vibrant area where tourists wander and wonder as tours take them to Vilakazi Street and other township landmarks. It is here where history presents itself, and the resilience and resistance that form an integral part of our history humble many a visitor. Mamkulu has touched hundreds if not thousands of lives since she started looking after babies in her informal crèche. Their mothers drop them at Mamkulu's as early as 6am as they scurry to catch minibus taxis and report for work. Mamkulu is delighted to hear that there is a possibility that she can now obtain an ECCE qualification.

➡

Educator four

Jabu always wanted to work with young children. He is the eldest in a family of seven children and, through circumstances not of his choosing, was very involved in the upbringing of his younger siblings. When he finished school, he worked at night and weekends as a waiter to fund his studies in childcare. He now heads a crèche in Evaton and is constantly faced with astonishment as people realise he has chosen this career. Jabu loves the spontaneity of young children. The teachers are all women and they have learnt to respect his commitment to ECCE. Jabu says that his vision for South Africa begins in the cot and that is why he loves focusing on the challenges and possibilities inherent in ECCE.

Reflection

- What do you think each of these educators can bring to the socialisation of the children in their care? Socialisation is a sociological term which refers to 'the transmission of conduct, roles, attitudes and values from one generation to another' (Chetwynd & Harnett, 1978, in De Witt, 2016: 238).
- What qualities and dispositions do you think each of these educators will encourage in the children?
- How do you think these qualities and dispositions will help the children in their life path?

Each teacher will bring the outcomes of their socialisation into their professional practice. This will result in different foci and approaches to their interaction with the children and to the delivery of the curriculum. It will also impact their professional identity. Certain characteristics, however, should be apparent in all professional ECCE educators.

4.2.1 Characteristics of an ECCE professional educator

The characteristics of a professional ECCE educator should ideally embrace a wide range of quality and competences. Jones and Pound (2008, in Bruce, 2010) view leadership and management as an integral part of being a professional ECCE teacher.

Leadership and management, according to Jones and Pound (2008, in Bruce, 2010), is 'a people-orientated, problem-solving, culturally influenced process of reflection'. It should also involve a consistent effort by individual teachers working together with parents and others to improve learning outcomes for children.'

These ideas spell out the qualities required to become a good ECCE professional teacher, and also point to the width and depth of the knowledge, skills and attitudes required.

If we begin to unpack these ideas, the required characteristics of an ECCE professional educator start to emerge. An ECCE educator is a leader not only in collaboration with the children in her class but also in her relationship with their parents and caregivers and other stakeholders in the ECCE field. This requires a number of interpersonal skills such as negotiation and flexibility.

Being a leader does not mean that all decisions are made top-down (ie the teacher pronounces what is right and the other stakeholders follow). Rather, in the context of ECCE it means a professional teacher who works collaboratively, modelling respectful and insightful teaching and learning. It will also involve guiding parents on how best they can participate in their child's growth, development and learning. The teacher, for example, might suggest that, time permitting, a child is told a story every night at bedtime. The story can be read or told. The importance of this 'together' time cannot be underestimated. Not only is language, vocabulary and language structure being enhanced, but the social emotional benefits of this close, fun experience form bonds that enhance a sense of belonging. Furthermore, cultural norms, values and beliefs are mediated through both the choice of the stories that are told and the way in which they are presented (see Chapter 12 for further details).

Reflection

As Jones and Pound (2008, in Bruce, 2010) claimed, leadership and management are important professional roles that should be part of an ECCE professional profile.

- What do you think it means for an ECCE teacher to be people orientated?
- What behaviours, attitudes and skills would such a teacher display?
- Who must they be orientated (or turn) towards?
- Why is this characteristic so important in the context of ECCE?

Did you, in your reflection, think about the partnerships based on trust, integrity and openness that a professional ECCE teacher needs to build with those people who have a direct influence on the life of the child in their care? These people may be parents, guardians, caregivers, other teachers or members of professional support services such as play therapists.

4.2.2 The role of emotional intelligence

In 1995, Daniel Goleman proposed a new kind of intelligence, one that clearly resonates with the kind of professional profile suited to an ECCE educator. Goleman called this new kind of intelligence emotional intelligence (EQ). He explained that EQ was 'a new kind of intelligence and a new way of thinking about the ingredients for a successful life' (Goleman, 1995, in Gordon & Browne, 2017: 493).

Goleman's idea of EQ was built on Gardner's theory of multiple intelligences. Goleman maintained that five basic emotional and social competencies define EQ (Goleman, 2012, in Gordon & Browne, 2017: 493):

1. **Self-awareness:** knowing what we are feeling in the moment and using those feelings to guide our decision making; having a realistic assessment of our abilities and a well-grounded sense of self-confidence
2. **Self-regulation:** handling our emotions so that they facilitate rather than interfere with the task at hand; being conscientious and delaying gratification to pursue goals; recovering well from emotional distress
3. **Motivation:** using our deepest feelings to move and guide us toward our goals, to help us take initiative and strive to improve, and to persevere in the face of setbacks and frustrations
4. **Empathy:** sensing what people are feeling, being able to take their perspective, and cultivating rapport and attunement with a broad diversity of people
5. **Social skills:** handling emotions in relationships well, and accurately reading social situations and networks; interacting smoothly; using social skills to persuade and lead, negotiate and settle disputes, thereby enhancing cooperation and teamwork (Goleman, 2012, in Gordon & Browne, 2017: 493–494).

A young child's ability to notice and label feelings corresponds, Gordon and Browne (2017: 494) suggest, to Goleman's 'self-awareness' dimension. A good ECCE educator will help children by assisting them to find a label for their feeling of anger or sadness so that they have words to describe particular feelings (Gordon & Browne, 2017) (see Chapter 10).

Find out more

Read the vignettes below which present situations that may occur in ECCE contexts. Then consider how you could use your EQ to bring the conflict to a successful resolution. Identify which particular social competence or combination of competencies of EQ we have just discussed could help you in the contexts that follow.

- Two mothers are arguing about which of the children first splashed water on the other's painting. The argument is going nowhere and the children are just looking on, scowling at each other.
- A four-year-old is in tears. He had a birthday ring and had brought hotdogs for all his friends. One, a Muslim child, refused to accept the hotdog and then told the other children they should hand theirs back.
- You have been working at a crèche for five years and are offered a promotion. It involves a great deal of administrative work, which you do not like so you turn down the offer. The owner of the crèche is disappointed and suggests that you are unlikely to be offered another promotion post.

4.2.3 Professional ethics

We now turn to another aspect of professionalism – ethics. Ethics are what guide the decisions we make, both in our professional and personal life. They are concerned with what is 'right' or 'wrong'. Would you, for instance, discriminate against a child whose father was a gangster? This knowledge has been shared with you, in confidence, by the child's mother. Would you now share this information with other parents? This is an ethical issue.

Something to consider

Gordon and Browne (2017: G-4) define ethics as follows:

> A theory or system of stated principles and standards; what is 'right and wrong'; one's values; the principles of conduct governing both an individual teacher and the teaching profession.

The notion of a profession and a professional is complex and not easy to define, but a good starting point is with the idea of 'agency'. It relates to our practice, ourselves, the decisions we make and how we act on those decision. Agency, another sociological concept, refers, as we have said, to the ability to act, to make choices and act on them. Educators use their agency as they demonstrate, day by day, 'principled practice' (Reed & Walker, 2015). According to Reed and Walker (2015: 256), 'principled practice' is value-based practice grounded in ethics from which principles are derived. These principles recognise the needs of the child and parents as central, with the 'professional' as a facilitating partner. Let us unpack that idea and illustrate what we mean with an example.

Principles are beliefs or attitudes that guide the decisions we make. For example, if we believe that it is important to listen to what children think as opposed to simply telling them what we think, we will build into our daily programme opportunities for hearing what our children have to say. They could be talking, for instance, about the actions of a character in a story we read to them or about what materials they want to use to depict 'an alien' in creative art. What we are doing is including the children's voices in decisions to be made. There will, of course, be some exceptions.

Reflection

Think about the scenario below and whose agency would take prominence.

A child says 'no' to taking medicine that is vital to his health. He is in fact exercising his agency or making a choice. Does that mean that we use our agency to go against parental instructions and follow the child's wishes? What do you think?

We would argue that in this case you need to use your knowledge as a professional to counter the resistance from the child and dispense the medicine.

Find out more

As we have already noted, Reed and Walker (2015) described principled practice as 'value-based practice grounded in ethics'. Values and ethics are both complex concepts. Values refer to one's judgement of what is important in life. They are important beliefs or ideals often shared by members of a culture about what is good or bad, and desirable or undesirable. Our values shape our attitudes and influence our behaviour. If, for instance, we value respect, this will guide our interactions with parents, colleagues and the children. We will know that culture and context play an important role in making people who they are and in shaping their identity. We will take this into account when coming face to face with views that may be different from our own.

The last part of Reed and Walker's (2015: 256) definition of 'principled practice' is the phrase 'grounded in ethics'. Ethics, as we have indicated, is concerned with what is good for individuals and society. Practice that is grounded in ethics would therefore demonstrate respect for key moral principles that include honesty, fairness, equality, dignity, diversity and individual rights.

Try this out

Fill in the table below and then discuss it with a partner to see if you have a similar understanding. We have started the table for you with an example of our own.

Concept	Definition (own words)	Think of an example that relates to your own practice
Inclusion	Accepting difference as normal and working with it – not against it.	Your principles relating to inclusion mean that you carefully observe your children while they are playing outside to make sure no one is left out
Fair play	Giving all participants an equal chance – applying fairness and justice in all situations	
Integrity	The quality of being honest and following moral principles	
Collegiality	The spirit of cooperation among colleagues	

Concept	Definition (own words)	Think of an example that relates to your own practice
Partnerships with parents/teachers	A partnership approach where teachers and parents work together and share information to improve learning outcomes, which often involves mutual decision making	
Child-centred pedagogy	The curriculum begins with and responds to the needs and interests of the child	
Equality	Providing equal opportunities for all involved	
Equity (impartiality)	The quality of being fair and impartial	
Trust	Being able to rely on someone and accept what they say is true	

Find out more

A code of ethics for an ECCE professional educator

NAEYC has drawn up a list of core values that inform ethical behaviour. These are:
- appreciating childhood as a unique and valuable stage of the human lifecycle
- basing our work with children on knowledge of child development
- appreciating and supporting the bond between the child and the family
- recognising that children are best understood and supported in the context of family, culture, community and society
- respecting the dignity, worth and uniqueness of each individual (child, family member and colleague)
- respecting diversity in children, families and colleagues
- recognising that children and adults achieve their full potential in the context of relationships that are based on trust and respect.

These values apply to a teacher's work with children, families, colleagues, the community and society. A code of ethics 'states the principles by which each individual can measure and govern professional behaviour' (Gordon & Browne, 2017: 161). These principles are based on 'collective wisdom', and assist us in making decisions that are ethically defensible.

In South Africa, teachers in the formal schooling sector must be registered with the South African Council of Educators (SACE). Currently this stipulation does not apply to ECCE teachers, but the new qualifications in ECCE will undoubtedly be linked to a set of ethical standards appropriate to ECCE and not dissimilar from those of the SACE.

> **Try this out**
>
> Based on all that you have read in this chapter so far, try to draw up your own code of ethics applicable to the context in which you work.

4.2.4 The core value of inclusion

Many of the NAEYC core values speak to the issue of inclusion. In South Africa, inclusion is also an important core value. The policy on inclusive education in South Africa was formulated and passed more than a decade ago. The White Paper 6 (DoE, 2001) was designed to transform the South African educational system by building an integrated system for all learners (Engelbrecht, 2006). Its ultimate purpose was to address problems related to children with disabilities and special learning needs. Inclusion is equally applicable to ECCE where many of the foundations of self-esteem and self-worth are laid.

4.2.4.1 Who is the inclusive ECCE teacher?

We have previously noted that professional teachers should be agents of change. However, teachers are not born with agency; they acquire it (Priestley et al, 2015). The most effective agents of change, according to Emirbayer and Mische (1998), have embraced three different dimensions of this concept. Firstly, they are rooted in past experience. Secondly, they have a wide repertoire of experience and, thirdly, they always act in the present shaped by their current reality. This current reality will include the existing resources and constraints, as well as the ability to imagine many ways forward.

According to the European Agency (2012), such teachers are sensitive to diversity and will display the following core values and areas of competence:
- Valuing diversity in children: diversity is seen as a resource that enriches the learning environment.

- The teacher's view of difference in children: teachers should acknowledge children's differences and support them accordingly. They should have high expectations of every child and provide pathways for them to realise their potential.
- Working with others: collaboration and teamwork are key at all times when working with parents and families as well as a range of other educational and health professionals.
- Personal professional development: teachers should be lifelong learners and reflective practitioners.

Something to consider

An inclusive teacher will deliberately choose teaching approaches that promote inclusive education for young children. All children thrive in the presence of their peers. Children with disabilities should therefore have opportunities to interact with those who do not have disabilities. From a centre management perspective, ECCE teachers should note that children with special educational needs in inclusive ECCE centres may display mild to moderate learning and/or behavioural challenges. Sometimes it will take a particularly high level of commitment by teachers to handle these challenges constructively.

Creating a learning environment for inclusive centres that is well managed with clear structures and routines is of the utmost importance for children's success (Wong & Wong, 2014). Polirstok (2015) outlines six management strategies teachers might use in an inclusive context:

1. Creating a supportive learning environment
2. Ignoring certain behaviours where appropriate
3. Focusing on structure and routine during the learning day
4. De-escalating (defusing) behavioural crises before they get out of hand
5. Promoting self-regulation by offering children opportunities to make behavioural choice by themselves
6. Limiting the use of punishment.

Further detail on how to implement these strategies can be found in chapters 6, 7 and 8.

Find out more

Specific activities can enhance learning in diverse contexts and implicitly foster quality education. When designing activities, the theory of multiple intelligences (MI) can be used as a guiding tool. In this theory, Davis, Christodoulou Seider and Gardner (2011) propose eight intelligences (abilities). The thinking behind this theory is that children possess different kinds of minds and therefore understand, learn, remember and perform in different ways (Gordon & Browne, 2017). MI theory acknowledges this pointing out that children use knowledge in different ways. MI is neither a curriculum nor a model of pedagogy, but it does allow teachers to appreciate the different abilities that children display. The eight MIs are as follows:

1. Musical-rhythmic
2. Visual-spatial
3. Verbal-linguistic
4. Logical-mathematical
5. Bodily-kinaesthetic
6. Interpersonal
7. Intrapersonal
8. Naturalistic.

Gardner (1998), from whom this theory originates, did not suggest that teachers must develop every activity to address all the intelligences. He maintained that this theory should empower children and not restrict them to one modality of learning. If each child exhibits a distinctive profile of different intelligences (abilities), then an environment rich in stimulating materials and activities can provide educational opportunities that enhance multiple intelligences and in so doing embrace inclusion (Gordon & Browne, 2017).

Try this out

Look at the children in your care and try to identify some of the intelligences that are already apparent, for example the child who shows strong interpersonal skills. The range of abilities already displayed by the children in your care can be seen as another form of diversity. Can you match particular children's abilities to specific intelligences identified by Gardner? Inclusive practice and special needs in relation to the young child are explored in further detail in Chapter 14.

A teacher who manages inclusion with insight, empathy and adaptability needs, as a professional, to constantly reflect on the suitability of his practice. Each of the areas of professionalism we have addressed in this chapter lends itself to reflection.

4.2.5 The role of reflection in becoming a professional

Becoming a truly professional ECCE educator is a lifelong process. Your qualification is the first step on a path that will include doubt, delight, trust and learning day by day as you engage with situations that will not quite fit the textbook scenarios you read as a student. You will make mistakes, and think, looking back, that perhaps you could have handled things differently. An essential part of your learning is your ability to critically reflect, and it is this that will enable you to move forward along that path of professional growth. Reflection deals with consciously looking at and thinking about our experiences, actions, feelings and responses so that we can interpret them and analyse them to help us learn (Schon, 1991; Brookfield, 2017).

When you reflect critically, this does not mean that you are being negative and destructive. It does, however, mean that you will not accept anything at 'face value'. You ask questions: What?, Who?, Where?, When?, How?, Why?, What if?, What next? and So what? Reflecting in this way will help you begin to connect with the big pictures of young children's lives in South Africa, for example the influence of class, social inequalities and socioeconomic conditions. It will help you look beyond the obvious – the 'face value' – to underlying factors, some of which you may need to address.

Critical reflection drives professional development. An ECCE educator who embraces professional development and utilises critical reflection will, be it unknowingly, support the belief put forward by Hanson and Appleby (2015: 25) that effective reflective teachers need to become 'agents of their own change'. They need, in other words, to consider a range of different perspectives on the nature of reflective practice and then develop, from an informed position, their own 'theory of action' (Argyris, 1995, in Hanson & Appleby, 2015). Both these concepts – agent of change and theory of action – point to your personal belief system about what constitutes quality ECCE practice in differing contexts.

As Nussbaum-Beach (2000) asserts, agents of change are those who intentionally or indirectly cause or accelerate social, cultural or behavioural change. They do this by reflecting on their own practice, identifying strengths, weaknesses and possibilities of change, and then drawing up a theory of action which they then implement and evaluate. It is a cyclical exercise where one observes, evaluates, plans and implements. It becomes one's own 'theory of action'.

Nussbaum-Beach's suggestions resonate with ideas put forward by Hanson and Appleby (2015), who suggest that the degree of autonomy and level of engagement generated through critical reflection will enable teachers to question and develop their role in enhancing the quality or provision of care and education for children and families (Hanson & Appleby, 2015). This should be their professional goal underpinning all that they do in ECCE.

Try this out

Think of a situation in your life where you still sometimes wonder if you handled it the right way and whether the outcome was, in fact, beneficial to all involved.

Now reflect critically on the whole situation, the people involved, the context, the outcome. Use the questions: What?, Who?, Where?, When?, How?, Why?, What if?, What next? and So what? to guide your reflection.

If you could, what would you change about your approach? Did you exercise your agency? Did you emerge with a plan of action? If not, try to draw one up now and, if appropriate, implement and evaluate it.

4.3 SUMMARY

In this chapter, we explored the role of professionalism in ECCE and noted that there are many different ways of acquiring ECCE qualifications. However, regardless of the type of qualification or the pathways followed to obtain a qualification, all ECCE teachers should strive to become professional teachers. Professional teachers exhibit specific characteristic such as integrity, respect and a deep desire to always act in the best interests of the child, which means that issues of inclusivity and diversity are always at the forefront. Being professional also means not only considering what constitutes an appropriate early learning curriculum and environment, but also having regard for parents, other family members, the community and other stakeholders. Finally, professionalism means continually thinking about one's practice and about ways of improving it. Becoming a self-reflective teacher is an ongoing journey that requires persistence and a commitment to keeping oneself up to date with research in the field.

REFERENCES

Brookfield, S. 2017. *Becoming a critically reflective teacher.* 2nd ed. San Francisco: Jossey-Bass.

Bruce, T. 2010. *Early childhood: A guide for students.* London: SAGE.

Child Professional Support Coordinator. 2012. *Plan effective transitions for children in education and care services.* Child Australia, Western Australia.

Cohen, G. 2011. Social psychology and social change. *Science,* 334(6053): 178–179.

Conn-Powers, MC, Ross-Allen, J & Holburn, S. 1990. Transition of young children into the elementary education mainstream. *Topics in Early Childhood Special Education,* 9(4): 91–105.

Davis, K, Christodoulou, J, Seider, S & Gardner, H. 2011. The theory of multiple intelligences, in Sternberg RJ & Kaufman SB (eds). *Cambridge handbook of intelligence* Cambridge, UK; New York: Cambridge University Press: 485–503.

Department of Education. 2001. *Education White Paper 6: Special Needs Education: Building an inclusive education and training system.* Pretoria: Government Printer.

De Witt, MW. 2016. *The young child in context. A psycho-social perspective.* 2nd ed. Pretoria: Van Schaik.

Donohue, D & Bornman, J. 2014. The challenges of realising inclusive education in South Africa. *South African Journal of Education*, 34(2): 1–14.

Dunlop, AW & Fabian, H. 2006. *Informing transitions in the early years.* England: McGraw-Hill International.

Emirbayer, M & Mische, A. 1998. What is agency? *American Journal of Sociology*, 103: 962–1023.

Edyburn, D. 2004. A synthesis of the special education technology literature. *Journal of Special Education Technology*, 19: 57–80.

Engelbrecht, P. 2006. The implementation of inclusive education in South Africa after ten years of democracy. *European Journal of Psychology of Education*, 21(3): 253–264.

European Agency for Development in Special Needs Education. 2012. *Young views on inclusive education.* Odense, Denmark: European Agency for Development in Special Needs Education.

Gardner, H. 1998. A reply to Perry D Klein's 'Multiplying the problems of intelligence by eight'. *Canadian Journal of Education,* 23(1): 96–102.

Gordon, AM & Browne, KW. 2017. *Beginnings and beyond. Foundations in early childhood education.* Boston, MA: Cengage Learning.

Giddens, A. 2006. *Sociology.* Cambridge: Polity Press.

Hanson, K & Appleby, K. 2015. The undergraduate journey, in Reed, M & Walker, R. *A critical companion to early childhood.* New York: SAGE.

Haymond, M, Kappelgaard, AM, Czernichow, P, Biller, BMK, Takano, K & Kiess, W. 2013. Early recognition of growth abnormalities permitting early intervention. *Acta Paediatr,* 102(8): 787–796.

Hodkinson, A. 2009. Pre-service teacher training and special educational needs in England 1970–2008: Is government learning the lessons of the past or is it experiencing a Groundhog Day? *European Journal of Special Needs Education*, 24(3): 277–290.

Knight, T. 1999. *Inclusive education and educational theory: Inclusive for what?* Paper presented at the British Educational Research Association Conference, University of Sussex, at Brighton, 2–5 September. http://www.leeds.ac.uk/educol/documents/000001106.htm (Accessed 8 August 2018).

Kovaˇcevic´, J, Rahimic´, Z & Šehic´, D. 2018. Policy makers' rhetoric of educational change: A critical analysis. *Journal of Educational Change,* 19(3): 375–417.

McWilliam, RA. 2010. *Routines-based early intervention.* Baltimore: Brookes Publishing Co.

Nussbaum, M. 2000. Women's capabilities and social justice. *Journal of Human Development,* 1(2): 219–247.

Polirstok, S. 2015. Classroom management strategies for inclusive classrooms. *Creative Education*, 6: 927–933.

Priestley, M, Biesta, GJJ, Philippou, S & Robinson, S. 2015. The teacher and the curriculum: exploring teacher agency, in Wyse, D, Hayward, L & Pandya, J (eds). *The SAGE handbook of curriculum, pedagogy and assessment.* London: SAGE.

Reed, M. & Walker, R. 2015. *A critical companion to early childhood.* New York: SAGE.

Schon, DA. 1991. *The reflective practitioner: How professionals think in action.* Aldershot: Ashgate Publishing Ltd.

Shirley, D. 2016. How to lead educational change. *Journal of Educational Change*, 17(3): 281–285.

Silman, F, Yaratan, H & Karanfiller, T. 2017. Use of assistive technology for teaching–learning and administrative processes for the visually impaired people. *EURASIA Journal of Mathematics, Science, and Technology Education*, 13(8): 4805–4813.

Waghid, Y. 2014. Pedagogy out of bounds: Untamed *variations of democratic education.* Rotterdam: Sense Publishers.

Wong, H & Wong, R. 2014. *The classroom management book.* Mountainside, CA: Wong Publishing.

Zirpoli, T. 2012. *Behavior management: Positive applications for teachers.* 6th ed. Upper Saddle River, NJ: Pearson.

Chapter 5

I am because we are: the role of community in the development and learning of the young child

Susan Greyling, Lorayne Excell and Vivien Linington

What the best and wisest parent wants for his own child; that must the community want for its children – **John Dewey (Brewer, 2014)**

In this chapter we consider:

- the role of parents and families in relation to three different understandings of the term 'community'
- how these three forms of community are built, maintained and deepened
- collaboration between colleagues, families and community systems to create, maintain and enhance environments that promote the holistic development and constructive learning of babies, toddlers and young children
- how to create and maintain communication channels that establish and support the meaningful involvement of and partnerships with all stakeholders
- the process of referral, if necessary, to support services
- who the key stakeholders are in the various environments in which babies, toddlers and young children develop and learn.

5.1 INTRODUCTION

This chapter addresses the meaningful involvement of parents, teachers, playroom assistants and community stakeholders whose role in ensuring quality learning experiences for children from birth to four years is paramount. Perhaps the most important condition influencing young children's personal and social development and wellbeing is the type of parent–child relationship during the childhood years. Parents are young children's first teachers as they perhaps explore nature, 'read together', cook together and count together. As the young child's first teachers, the parents' role is multifaceted. They support, guide and model appropriate interactions, as they provide learning opportunities that help the child discover his world. Parental involvement enhances learning success, and this involvement should not end when the child enters an early childhood care and education (ECCE) centre. As a teacher of young children, knowledge of the community in which you are working is important. It will provide insight into the particular context of the babies, toddlers and young children and their families with whom you interact. It will also enable you to provide these young children with learning experiences that are meaningful and relevant to their lives.

Effective engagement is based on building relationships, and relationships take time to develop. One should never underestimate the value of these relationships, as ECCE is strengthened through the cooperation and full support of the parents and the community. This chapter explores the importance of effective parent, teacher and community partnerships, and suggests strategies that can enable the initiation and maintenance of such partnerships.

In addition, this chapter outlines the different stakeholders that are involved in the life of babies/toddlers/young children. There is a specific emphasis on their role in relation to the referral of children for further support and enrichment.

5.2 PARENTS AND COMMUNITY INVOLVEMENT AND PARTNERSHIPS

Involvement is difficult to determine as the phrase is used to embrace a wide range of activities such as parents serving on school governing bodies (SGBs), school councils, parent– teacher associations (PTAs), parent committees, fundraising events or even parents' financial contribution. Involvement is often centre driven, and teachers determine the types and levels of parental involvement in activities (Barnyak & McNelly, 2009; Hedges & Lee, 2010). According to Van Wyk and Lemmer (2009: 14),

> … the one common theme running through various definitions is that all these activities seek to bring together in some way the separate domains of home and school in the interest of the child's learning and development. Parent involvement can be described as the willing and active participation of parents in a wide range of school and home-based activities.

Community can be broadly defined as

> … all individuals and institutions, both in and out of the school, that have a stake in the success of the children in school and in the well-being of children and families. The community does not only include the neighbourhood where learners' homes and schools are situated, but also any institution, organisation or structure that has an influence on children's learning and development (Van Wyk & Lemmer, 2009: 110).

The idea of parent and community involvement and partnerships can be seen as a continuum. The starting point is involvement, which rests on parental participation. There is no guarantee that this will happen (Barnyak & McNelly, 2009; Hedges & Lee, 2010). Often, parent involvement in education and early schooling happens when parents are active in the centre through volunteer activities in the playroom or in centre governance, attend centre-based events and take part in parent–teacher communication (Ashton & Cairney, 2001; Berthelsen & Walker, 2008; Fan & Chen, 2001).

As one moves along the continuum towards a partnership, four key elements are added: mutuality, reciprocity, shared decision making and joint responsibility.

1. **Mutuality** refers to a collaborative relationship where teacher and parents support one another. Sensitivity to individual family contexts and issues related to these is a vital ingredient.
2. **Reciprocity** in the context of a parent–centre partnership refers to a relationship of mutual dependence or action or influence. There is give and take from all involved.
3. **Shared decision making** gives parents voice and agency. It is dependent upon good communication skills, including active listening and a consideration of views other than our own as we negotiate towards a common goal. Negotiation entails communicating with others to reach an agreement or compromise.
4. **Joint responsibility** in the context of partnerships means that both parents and teachers are accountable or answerable. All partners should be trustworthy, dependable, reliable and credible.

Different stakeholders (eg health workers, community developers, NGOs, social workers, etc) are involved in the life of the young child, therefore ECCE cannot take place without the cooperation and full support of parents and the community (Van Wyk & Lemmer, 2009: 7, 110; Calitz et al, 2009: 9). These stakeholders are discussed later on in this chapter.

5.2.1 Parent involvement and partnerships

Parents, refers to the adults responsible for the young child's upbringing as well as physical and emotional care (Van Wyk & Lemmer, 2009: 7–8). As we mentioned in Chapter 1, 'parent' refers to the child's primary caregiver, for example a grandparent or another adult who plays a significant role in the child's life. According to Gordon and Browne (2017: 250) and Van Wyk and Lemmer, (2009: 8), research has found that children whose parents were involved in their early learning displayed high levels of social skills, were more cooperative and self-controlled, and engaged more actively in both the home and ECCE environments. These children also performed better academically than those whose parents were not as involved in their education.

Parent–centre interactions can in fact be seen on two levels. One involves working with the child on the home front, and the other involves working in partnership with the ECCE centre.

On the home front, parents should actively engage with their children – reading and talking to them and playing with them, for example at bath time when parents can count toes together and experiment with sinking and floating. Involved parents will also ensure that their children have a healthy diet, get enough rest and have all the necessary requirements, for example diapers if they are going to an ECCE centre for the day. Preparing in advance makes life less stressful for both parents and their children.

The second level of interaction is that of parent–centre partnerships. As we have already said, a partnership involves four elements. In the context of ECCE, an instance of joint decision making could focus on a feeding schedule or a potty-training routine. For older children, this could be a joint decision on an outing, such as going to the museum or a visit to the park. In this way, parents feel valued as their opinions form an integral part of any decision making (Brewer, 2014: 89; Van Wyk & Lemmer, 2009: 86).

The young child will benefit from a healthy parent–teacher relationship (Van Wyk & Lemmer, 2009: 57). When families are involved early in their young children's education and partner with the teacher, the children perform better and have a more positive attitude. Furthermore, healthy parental attitudes are important for personality development (Van Wyk & Lemmer, 2009: 56). In addition to help with and promoting learning at home, parent involvement includes communicating with the centre, volunteering in the playroom and participating in parent–teacher organisations (Van Wyk & Lemmer, 2009: 83).

Something to consider

When parents feel that their role as partners in their children's development is acknowledged and appreciated, they will take up the responsibility as educators at home (Brewer, 2014: 522; Gordon & Browne, 2017: 250). Brewer (2014) suggested that teachers focus on seven principles to encourage parents to get involved in the centre:

1. Babies', toddlers' and young children's successes and achievements. Share these with parents on a daily basis, if possible. Send personalised information to parents about their child.
2. How to include the extended family to support babies, toddlers and young children where possible.
3. Extending frequent invitations to parents. If possible, have an open-door policy so parents feel welcome and able to approach the teacher.

4. How to use playroom staff and parent volunteers in creative ways to organise and enrich programmes.
5. Encouraging joint decision making with administrators, parents and teachers in relation to planning.
6. Alternative ways to make parents feel welcome in the centre, especially the playroom. Consider, if possible, serving refreshments, providing nametags, reimbursing parents for transportation and babysitting costs, etc. Consider meeting venues that are accessible for parents, such as community centres. Planning events at different times and on different days might also increase accessibility for some parents.
7. Recognising and affirming parents and staff for their efforts (Brewer, 2014: 516–517).

Find out more

Special activities can be successful when applying the seven principles. These activities could be parent visitation/observation days, special events for families such as family fun events or bring-and-share occasions. Invite a parent to come by at a time that suits you both, and hold an informal discussion. Consider arranging parent information workshops where they can learn about technology, child development, discipline and health-related issues. Organise a special people's day where the children are joined in their daily programme by people who are important in their life (this would naturally include grandparents). Invite parents to contribute to the theme, where appropriate. Parents can become members of teams involved in making recommendations for babies, toddlers and young children with special needs (Brewer, 2014: 517).

Something to consider

Starting at an ECCE centre

The first time a child goes to an ECCE centre and says goodbye to the parent(s) can be a stressful occasion for both child and parent(s). The expression of this stress will differ greatly depending on the age of the child and the reaction of both the parent(s) and the teacher. From about the age of seven months when babies have the capacity to recognise and remember a parent, many children weep as though they have been eternally forsaken when mom or dad walks out the door. Toddlers cling to their mothers when they sense their imminent departure. Separation fears may be more intense in children who are temperamentally 'slow to warm up' and have difficulty making transitions or entering new situations (De Wit, 2016; Brewer, 2014). They can experience a variety of emotions such as anger, guilt, jealousy, confusion, hurt and fear. Older children may regress to outgrown behaviour like whining, crying and bed-wetting, or may become more aggressive and demanding. A favourite toy or blanket can help a child feel more confident and secure. Research shows that babies, toddlers and young children who are given 'transitional objects' cry less when they are separated from their parents. These children are also able to explore their environment more actively, and focus on and learn new tasks better than children not in possession of a favourite item (De Witt, 2016). What follows are some general guidelines on how both parents and teachers could handle the situation.

Points for parents

1. Be patient and thorough when explaining the reason for your departure to your child. This can help the young child feel confident that you will return, and that the child has not done anything 'bad' to make you leave. This misunderstanding could arise because young children lack a real understanding of cause and effect, and therefore may not be clear on points that the parents consider obvious.

2. If your young child does regress to outgrown behaviour, you may need to adjust your expectations and standards.

3. Strive to establish a consistent routine. Pay particular attention to basic needs such as sleep, meals and exercise. The child needs to feel that you are dependable and that he can count on you to do as you say you will. Use separations as opportunities to build the level of trust between yourself and your child. For example, tell the child when you will be coming to fetch him. Link it to a particular event, for example after story time as the child does not yet have a real understanding of time. Make sure you arrive to fetch your child when you said you would.

> 4. Celebrate your child's entry into the centre in some small way. For example, for older children make sure that you can go with them to the playroom at least twice before they start at the centre.
> 5. Do not make an issue if your child has had an 'accident', for example wets his pants.
> 6. Remember, if age appropriate, to ask your child about his day. Listen carefully to the responses.

> **Some suggestions for teachers**
> 1. As the teacher, make sure you extend a warm welcome to all young children on their first day.
> 2. Make sure you have some self-help activities (such as play-dough or free drawing) that allow other children to be actively engaged so that you can give the new child your undivided attention. It is also worthwhile to consider staggering the number of new entries per day so that as a teacher you have time for all of them.
> 3. On the child's first day encourage the parents, if they are able, to stay for a while.
> 4. Give parents a list of useful advice – for example, suggest they include a change of clothing – encourage them to approach you with any concerns, and give them an outline of the daily programme, including arrival and departure times, etc.

Archbishop Desmond Tutu (2015: 38) defines community in a particular sense. He says:

> None of us comes into the world fully formed. We would not know how to think, or walk, or speak, or behave as human beings unless we learned it from other human beings. We need other human beings in order to be human. I am because other people are. A person is entitled to a stable community life, and the first of these communities is the family

Another understanding of community is one that includes all people and institutions, which we will now explore.

5.2.2 Community involvement

A community can be seen as all people and institutions, inside and outside the care and education environment, that play a role in the successful development and learning of babies/toddlers/young children. A community should focus on the strengths of its members, which would include different people such as parents, teachers, business owners, entrepreneurs, and people involved in the service and construction industry. Various organisations and educational opportunities might exist within the community. Partnerships between ECCE centres and the community should feature cooperation, coordination and collaboration. Open communication channels are key to success. ECCE–community partnerships should collaboratively set goals and objectives, and identify key people to help drive the partnership (Van Wyk & Lemmer, 2009: 113). The notion of community resonates with the African proverb that says: 'It takes a whole village to raise a child'. In a South African context, this proverb is inextricably linked to the value or principle of 'Ubuntu'. As Tutu (2015: 38) said, Ubuntu is not 'I think therefore I am'. It says rather that 'I am a human because I belong, I participate'. In other words, we can only be human together, and nowhere is this interdependence more important than in education (Tyatya, 2018). Because young children come to the ECCE centre from many different backgrounds and with a wide range of experiences, it is often community members with similar experiences who can provide enriching support. This enrichment can help promote inclusivity and the recognition and celebration of diversity.

Something to consider

Community involvement can take different forms. It may include extended family members and friends as well as collaboration with businesses and organisations, including relevant government departments and non-profit organisations (NPOs). Ideally, community partnerships should place the child's wellbeing at the centre. The teachers' knowledge of the community and the resources available therein can provide valuable insight into the optimisation of each child's particular context and needs.

Reflection

Explain in detail how you would involve parents and the community as essential stakeholders in the young child's educational development.

5.3 CONTINUOUS COMMUNICATION AND MEANINGFUL INVOLVEMENT WITH RELEVANT STAKEHOLDERS

In South Africa's diverse communities, communication with parents is vital. To make it effective, teachers need to consider factors such as:
- the language with which they communicate
- the communication channel that is most suitable, for example verbal such as a telephone call or face-to-face interaction, or non-verbal such as an SMS, WhatsApp message, email, a written note, a newsletter or a poster, always considering the literacy level of parents so that miscommunication

does not occur (Gordon & Browne, 2017; Van Wyk & Lemmer, 2009). It is the teacher's responsibility to ensure that parents stay informed about two matters: firstly, what the programme/centre offers and, secondly, the wellbeing of their child. Some form of communication should be sent home regularly throughout the year (Van Wyk & Lemmer, 2009; Brewer, 2014).

There are at least four ways to keep parents informed of their child's progress.
1. Newsletters, for instance, can set out what is happening in the ECCE centre, for example informing parents about the possible themes to which they may be able to offer additional resources and any special events that will take place in that week.
2. Parent meetings can be held where parents can see and experience some of their child's work and activities first-hand. Parent–teacher meetings can also take place when teachers or parents identify a particular problem with a child. The teacher arranges a time to meet with the parents so that the problem can be discussed, and possible options or solutions decided upon (Van Wyk & Lemmer, 2009).
3. Parents can be invited to come and see what is happening in the ECCE centre and contribute perhaps towards some of the stimulatory or caring activities, for example reading a book to the group or telling a story that comes from an old tradition.
4. Spontaneous brief discussions when parents drop off or collect their children can also provide useful information about the child. For example, someone in the family may be sick or a father or mother may be absent for some reason and this could impact the child's sense of wellbeing.

As already mentioned, parental involvement positively affects a child's ECCE centre experience, including later academic achievement, behaviour such as social adjustment and attitudes towards the centre in general (Gordon & Browne, 2017; Van Wyk & Lemmer, 2009; Brewer, 2014).

Establishing and maintaining an open line of communication with the ECCE centre is a key component of parental involvement. In order to gain full support and understanding of what happens in the birth to four-year-old ECCE centre parents, family and community members need to be continuously informed about and involved in children's education through ongoing communication (Van Wyk & Lemmer, 2009; Brewer, 2014).

As they are the primary educators of their children, their involvement should ideally begin when the child starts at the centre.

Find out more

Parent evenings (or similar set times for parents to engage with you) are important because they give the parent an opportunity to discuss what the child is doing at the centre and find out how they are progressing. Parents also have an opportunity to cover any issues they may want to talk about with the teacher. By attending such evenings, parents can become better involved in their child's development and learning. Sometimes parents find it difficult to attend these evenings for a number of reasons, ranging from those that are work related, transport difficulties or other children who need to be attended to at that time. As a result, these parents may feel they do not have sufficient time to discuss their child with the teacher. Teachers must be aware of these factors and work together with parents to arrange alternative meeting times (Excell & Linington, 2015; Van Wyk & Lemmer, 2009; Brewer, 2014).

Something to consider

One way to communicate with parents is for a child to have a 'message book'. Information about the child's daily routines such as eating, sleeping and 'toileting' can be shared with parents on a daily basis. If this form of communication is chosen, make sure parents are able to access the written information. Be vigilant about the choice of language used in the messages and avoid terms that parents might not understand such as 'perceptual motor development'. Invite parents to read the information written in the book on a daily basis and use the book to communicate with you if they prefer this method. If the child has a problem or does not feel well, the parent could write a message in the book and place it on the teacher's table on arrival at the centre. Some problems, however, are nearly always better dealt with on a verbal basis. If, for instance, you suspect a hearing problem, make an arrangement to talk to the parents privately (Calitz et al, 2009; Excell & Linington, 2015; Van Wyk & Lemmer, 2009; Brewer, 2014). Remember good communication is the cornerstone of a healthy relationship between the parent, the community members and the centre.

Reflection

Why is it necessary to understand the necessity of continuous communication and meaningful involvement with the relevant stakeholders, such as parents, family members and the community? Give reasons for your answer.

There is a third understanding of community that is relevant to ECCE, and that is a community of children, which, ideally, should embrace the notion of Ubuntu. As Archbishop Tutu (2015) says, a person with Ubuntu has a proper self-assurance that comes from knowing that he or she belongs in a greater whole. For the ECCE child, that greater whole includes both the earlier understandings of community, the family and the community at large.

We have already spoken about these first two understandings. We will now consider the third understanding – a community of children and the environment in which this community can flourish.

5.4 HOW THE LEARNING ENVIRONMENT CAN BUILD A COMMUNITY OF CHILDREN

The learning environment creates space for building a community of children in the ECCE centre, where teachers establish common ground among all the children and encourage them to interact constructively. In building a community, a teacher bases her decisions on the knowledge that young children learn best in the context of social relationships and that they need to feel accepted, respected and confident that their individuality is encouraged despite the emphasis on group dynamics.

Find out more

The building of a sense of community should be apparent from the beginning as a new child is welcomed into the centre. The teacher should refer to each child and parent by name and, as part of the welcoming process, guide them towards the child's own space, a locker or cubbyhole, or a hook for their personal belongings. This space should be labelled with the child's name and symbol. Crates stacked and secured with ties provide a good alternative should funding not allow for lockers.

Another approach to building a community of children is to bring appropriately aged children together to share ideas and information through group discussions. These could be based on the theme of the week, for example the season. Another way to facilitate group discussion is to present stories that contain problems to be solved. Children can then be encouraged to offer solutions, make choices and give reasons for these choices (Calitz et al, 2009; Van Wyk & Lemmer, 2009).

An environment that encourages the construction of a community must be an inviting space where staff and children respect each other, and differences are accepted as a natural fact of life.

Something to consider

The ECCE teacher's role is to support babies, toddlers and young children emotionally, socially, physically and cognitively so as to optimise learning in an appropriate play-based learning environment. Such an environment would, of course, be not only safe but also hygienic (see Chapter 9). As you plan and reflect on the environment that you create, ask yourself whether you have made both guidance and care major priorities. As a teacher you are, to refer back to Vygotsky, a guide on the side. The type of care you provide will, of course, differ for young babies, boisterous toddlers and active young children.

Planning a suitable learning environment will include the place where learning happens (it can be the physical environment, including the indoor and outdoor environment, as well as the people and the learning programme (Excell & Linington, 2015; Brewer, 2014). The place you create must be inclusive and accommodate children with various special needs. For example, you may have a child in a wheelchair and therefore need to consider whether he can access all the areas.

The learning environment should be attractive, colourful and comfortable, and speak to all the senses of a young child. This takes, as we have already suggested, thought, planning and hard work.

An appropriate and therefore inherently inviting learning environment will include the following:

- A comfortable space for parents to meet, hold discussions and receive information about the progress of their children
- A space where members of the community can come and support the children, both individually and in groups, perhaps by telling stories or talking about the history of the community
- Suitable challenges for babies, toddlers and young children that invite them to explore and learn using relevant resource materials such as building blocks
- Sufficient space for children to move and experiment with the materials on a regular basis without bumping into one another (Brewer, 2014).

The social and emotional benefits of feeling part of a community cannot be underestimated. It fuels a sense of belonging. Creating a community of children in the ECCE centre has a significant impact on how children interact and play together. It also impacts how they adjust to the centre and view the relationships they build with each other.

Reflection

Think about how the creation of a community of children draws on the four partnership principles: mutuality, reciprocity, shared decision making and joint responsibility.

> **Find out more**
>
> The Reggio Emilia approach positions the environment as the 'third teacher'. They argue that many explorations, thoughts, philosophies, concepts and ideas can be inspired by the environment itself. It will be up to you as a teacher to utilise this environment, for example by gathering a big pile of dry leaves in autumn and letting children play among them, jump on them, roll in them and listen to them rustle, crunch and crackle, and sometimes break. Older children could sort and compare different leaves.
>
> A true Reggio approach deals with a relatively small number of children, but you are more likely to have a fairly large group of children and, ideally, centre assistants to help you. Some parents also might be available as volunteers to help with the daily programme.

5.5 PLAYROOM ASSISTANTS AND VOLUNTEERS IN THE BIRTH TO FOUR-YEAR-OLD CENTRE

In South Africa, teachers might be challenged by the size of the group in their care. Centre assistants and volunteers are, in this instance, a valuable and enriching resource, and can add considerably to the quality of teaching and learning in the centre. Assistants and volunteers could include parents, students from universities or technical and vocational education and training (TVET) colleges, senior citizens, family members, religious groups or other community members.

All playroom assistants and volunteers should be screened. They will need police clearance and some training before they join the staff (see Chapter 15 on ECCE policy in this regard). Their training should include a thorough knowledge on the goals and activities of the programme offered at the centre (Brewer, 2014). Teachers should communicate clearly with assistants and volunteers, taking the time to discuss the centre's philosophy, the programme, appropriate discipline and other pertinent information. Furthermore, they should have a clearly defined list of duties to prevent misunderstanding and possible conflict.

> **Something to consider**
>
> Assistants and volunteers can help the teacher by presenting specialised activities, for example a weather chart, music, story reading or telling individually or in groups, creative arts, etc. They could also help with some of the routines, for example toileting and snack time. Supervision of outdoor activities, such as taking a small group for a walk around the playground, is also appropriate. Be careful not to assign the menial chores to them. Include them in the professional development programmes that are offered at the centre, and invite them to participate in staff meetings. Most important is to remember to always thank them for their help and reflect with them on the day's activities (Brewer, 2014).

Reflection

How would you accommodate volunteers in the birth to four-year-old ECCE centre?

Another role that a teacher must fulfil is to identify possible problems with children that might need investigation and referral to support services.

5.6 REFERRALS TO SERVICES FOR SUPPORT AND ENRICHMENT

The four partnership principles are necessarily based on trust, which is extremely important when discussing a possible problem with a parent. Hopefully the teacher will be able to share any information relevant to the possible problem so that the way forward is informed by collaboration and joint decision making. A relationship of this kind will ensure that whatever action is taken is in the best interests of the child and reflects the shared goal (Van Wyk & Lemmer, 2009; Brewer, 2014). Communicating problem areas to parents should always be accompanied by guidance on how they can support their child at home in the best possible way.

Something to consider

One possible intervention that may be seen at some ECCE centres is occupational therapists working with slightly older children where it has been observed that they have, for instance, perceptual motor problems. Occupational therapists typically use techniques and routines that may seem like play, but are designed to target areas of delay and difficulty. Children who have sensory motor integration difficulties usually benefit from occupational therapy.

If intervention by a professional is required, then the professional, teacher and parents should work together as a team to assist the child in the best way possible. The child's progress should be assessed continuously and recorded on a regular basis.

Table 5.1 encapsulates the process and people involved in the event of a possible difficulty.

Table 5.1 The process and people involved in the event of a possible difficulty

ECCE teachers	ECCE teachers are usually the first to notice developmental or learning difficulties. They could discuss what they have observed with parents and, where appropriate, give advice on how to handle the situation. Other teachers could also be approached for input on how to manage the problem in the playroom. Teachers should also approach the principal or centre manager for a possible way forward
Principals or supervisors	Principals or centre managers support teachers in coping with difficulties. They should also be involved in making decisions about referrals. A task team can be set up to help the teacher keep records and collect information about a child's specific difficulties
Nursing support	A nurse, either on site or within the district, can help the teacher identify possible health problem and offer advice on issues such as colic, nappy rash or teething difficulties
Occupational therapists	Occupational therapy helps children achieve their developmental milestones, such as fine motor skills and hand–eye coordination. The acquisition of these skills is important for successful play and later academic activities
Speech and hearing therapists	Speech and hearing therapists support children with language development and auditory perception, and can help teachers to identify difficulties with hearing or speech
Physiotherapists	Physiotherapists work with children to improve balance and posture, low muscle tone and overall motor skills
Teachers who assist children with special needs	These teachers assist in understanding learning and other difficulties. They can also advise on teaching methods that make learning easier for children who are struggling. These teachers tend to work with slightly older children
Social workers	Social workers deal with family problems that impact the young child's development and wellbeing. At the time of going to print, in the South African context the Department of Social Development registers ECCE centres and can provide help on a wide range of social issues from child abuse to poverty. They can also advise parents on how to support their child at home. Teachers who suspect that a child is a victim of abuse are required by law to report these suspicions to the relevant authorities (RSA, 2005)

Educational psychologists	Educational psychologists deal with children who have emotionally based difficulties often linked to behavioural problems. They can advise on how to respond to the child, both at home and in the centre. They can do formal assessments to identify development and learning problems, usually with older children
Medical doctors	All children are issued with a Road to Health chart shortly after birth, and this should accompany all children entering the centre. Health difficulties that arise after admission may require medical intervention. Parents should be advised if a teacher feels this is necessary. Medical services are available through provincial hospitals, clinics or private health care. There is also a range of alternative and culturally based medical services. Teachers should consider parents' preference
Resource centres such as NGOs, Training and Resources in Early Education (TREE), Early Learning Resource Unit (ELRU), Cotlands (toy library), Ntataise, Ilifa Labantwana	These centres can provide a wealth of information and some resources, and a number of them also offer training for ECCE staff We suggest you Google these organisations to explore the different services that they offer

Although these people and organisations have been linked to specific difficulties, they are also a rich source of consultation on quality ECCE practice in general. Teachers could, for instance, ask a clinic nurse to come and talk to parents about common childhood illnesses and the importance of immunisation.

Reflection

Now that you understand the importance of good relationships with parents/caregivers, families and other stakeholders, reflect critically how you would establish good relationships with all stakeholders.

5.7 SUMMARY

This chapter has emphasised the importance of community in the development and learning of the young child. It has looked at the importance of ECCE partnerships and given ideas on how these can be built and deepened. It has presented three understandings of community – community as family, community in the broader sense in partnership with an ECCE centre, and a community of children. At the centre of all these understandings is the wellbeing of the young child and the values, care and guidance that each 'community' can bring to the child's optimal growth, development and learning.

We have looked at the elements, processes and strategies that are important in creating what is essentially a triad – a bringing together of the three senses of community. We have considered how difficulties can arise and how a teacher can begin to identify possible problems for referral.

The underpinning philosophy of this chapter is Ubuntu: 'I am because we are'. Ubuntu as a 'lived practice' will automatically embrace diversity, which is a major feature of South African society. With its emphasis on 'we', the concept of Ubuntu resonates with the team approach that is essential in care and guidance.

REFERENCES

Ashton, J & Cairney, T. 2001. Understanding the discourses of partnership: An examination of one school's attempts at parent involvement. *The Australian Journal of Language and Literacy.* http://ezproxy.uws.edu.au/login?url=http://search.informit.com.au/documentSummary;dn=110275;res=AEIPT

Barnyak, NC & McNelly, TA. 2009. An urban school district's parent involvement: A study of teachers' and administrators' beliefs and practices. *The School Community Journal*, 19(1): 33–58.

Berthelsen, D & Walker, S. 2008. Parents' involvement in their children's education. *Family Matters*, 79: 34–71.

Brewer, JA. 2014. *Early childhood education, preschool through primary grades.* Boston: Pearson.

Calitz, EM, Faber, RJ, Grobler, HM, Orr, JP & Van Staden, CJS. 2009. *The day care handbook.* Cape Town: Kagiso Education.

De Witt, MW. 2016. *The young child in context. A psycho-social perspective.* 2nd ed. Pretoria: Van Schaik.

Excell, L & Linington, V. 2015. *Teaching Grade R.* Cape Town: Juta.

Fan, X & Chen, M. 2001. Parental involvement and students' academic achievement: A meta-analysis. *Educational Psychology Review*, 13(1): 1–22.

Gordon, AM & Browne, KW. 2017. *Beginnings & beyond. Foundations in early childhood education.* 10th ed. Boston: Cengage Learning.

Hedges, H & Lee, D. 2010. 'I understood the complexity within diversity': Preparation for partnership with families in early childhood settings. *Asia-Pacific Journal of Teacher Education*, 38(4): 257–272.

Lemmer, EM. 2007. Parent involvement in teacher education in South Africa. *International Journal about Parents in Education*, 10: 218–229.

Republic of South Africa (RSA). 1996. South African Schools Act 1996 84 of 1996. *Government Gazette*, 377 (17579). Pretoria.

Republic of South Africa (RSA). 2005. The Children's Act 38 of 2005. Consolidated Regulations pertaining to the Children's Act, 2005. Government Notice No R261. Pretoria: *Government Gazette,* 1 April 2010. No 33076.

Tyatya, K. 2018. *It takes a village to raise a child*. News 24.com.https://www.google.com/search?q=news24.comkhaya+ Tyatya&rlz=1C1CAFA_enZA657ZA657&oq =news24.comkhaya+ Tyatya&aqs =chrome..69i57. 157 37j1j7 &sourceid=chrome&ie=UTF-8 (Accessed 7 January 2018).

Tutu, D. 2015. *10 Pieces of wisdom from Desmond Tutu on his birthday.* http://www.tutufoundationusa.org/2015/10/07/10-pieces-of-wisdom-from-desmond-tutu-on-his-birthday/ (Accessed 24 October 2019).

Van Wyk, N & Lemmer, E. 2009. *Organising parent involvement in SA schools*. Cape Town: Juta.

Chapter 6
Playful pedagogies: creating playful spaces and places

Lorayne Excell and Nontokozo Mashiya

In this chapter we consider:

- different understandings of play and some of the challenges to play-based learning
- the characteristics of play
- theoretical underpinnings of play, and the relationship between play, learning and teaching
- the complexities of play-based pedagogies
- different types of play
- how to implement play and playful learning throughout the day
- how to plan for, choose and design appropriate resources for different ages and stages of development, including indigenous and culturally specific games and toys
- the reflective role of the teacher in ensuring an integrated and responsive playful early learning environment for young children

6.1 INTRODUCTION

The right to play is enshrined in the United Nations Convention of the Rights of the Child, which South Africa ratified in 1995. This right is captured in the South African National Curriculum Framework (DBE, 2015) and the importance of learning and teaching through play endorsed in the new qualification framework for early childhood care and education (ECCE) (DHET, 2017). Planning playful learning experiences for children, however, is a complex matter requiring deep insight into children and their particular context, the learning environment as well as the curriculum. In fact, as emphasised by Scott (2010: xvii, cited in Moyles, 2015), 'teachers plan for play by creating high quality learning environments and ensuring uninterrupted blocks of time for children to develop their own purposes through their play'. In this chapter we will investigate some of the theoretical underpinnings of play, and explore how to create, implement and maintain playful learning spaces in a variety of ECCE settings. You will also be encouraged to reflect upon your role in ensuring an integrated, responsive, culturally appropriate and playful learning environment.

6.2 WHY PLAY?

When children are immersed in a rich play-based environment, they show essential characteristics (behaviours) necessary for success in the 21st century (Moyles, 2010). Read the following case study and identify some of these characteristics.

> **CASE STUDY**
>
> Lebogang (L), Jonathan (J) and Mavis (M) are playing 'shop shop' in the fantasy corner.
>
> L: I will be the shopkeeper and you two are my customers.
>
> J: All right, but next time I want to be the shopkeeper.
>
> L: Yeah, sure.
>
> J: Next time.
>
> J: Mavis, you can be the mother and I will be your husband.
>
> M walks around the shop looking at the items on display. J walks next to her. She picks up a shopping basket and begins choosing some groceries. She takes various items off the shelf, turns them around to examine them and keeps on saying, 'Um … I wonder.' She then turns to J and asks, 'Could you please take that tin of beans down for me?' J obliges and hands it to M who puts in in her basket. M continues shopping. She looks left and right.
>
> J: What are you looking for, Mavis?
>
> M: We need bread and milk. I can't see the milk, can you? Will you please ask the shopkeeper where he keeps it? I am going to get some rice and look for a bigger bag of mielie meal. This bag is really too small. We must also get rice to eat with our chicken stew tonight.
>
> Thuli (T) walks into the shop and asks, 'Can I also play?'
>
> M: Yes – you can be the child.
>
> Immediately M says to T, 'Where have you been? We were worried about you. You know you cannot just wander off by yourself. Your father is very annoyed with you.'
>
> The children continue playing in the fantasy corner until it is story time.

Try this out

How many and which behaviours or characteristics did you identify among the players? A list of important behaviours for children to acquire follows. Look for examples of each type of behaviour in this case study. Did you mention any of the following types of behaviour?

Children were:
- making choices
- generating decisions
- negotiating
- pursuing their own interests
- showing independence in thought and action
- using their own ideas
- exhibiting intrinsic motivation
- being physically, intellectually, socially and emotionally active in a sustained way
- operating from a basis of what makes sense to them
- setting their own goals and targets
- relating their play to what they have observed in their own lives
- using their imagination to create playful possibilities.

Other essential characteristics, attitudes and skills developed through individual and/or collaborative plays include:
- becoming confident and preparing for a challenge
- experimenting, exploring and investigating ideas and objects
- learning new behaviours
- making and following rules
- acquiring new skills and interests
- using a range of social and interpersonal skills such as putting someone else's wishes ahead of you own and turn taking
- using the language and skills of emergent literacy and numeracy in a playful context
- engaging in symbolic play where one item, for example a block, can represent an entirely different object (adapted from Moyles, 2010).

Something to consider

Golinkoff and Hirsh-Pasek (2016) suggest that playful experiences allow children to develop what they have termed the 6Cs. These include children being able to **communicate** ideas, **collaborate** with others, initiate **creative** solutions to problems, think **critically** and evaluate data, have the **confidence** to try new things and be willing to fail, and, importantly, have the **content knowledge** which is the foundation underpinning all other functions.

According to Liu et al (2017), there are five definitive characteristics that define playful learning experiences:

1. Play should be a joyful experience – this allows for the release of dopamine in the brain, which is linked to the improvement of cognitive functions such as memory, attention, mental shifting (changing how we think), creativity and motivation.

2. Play should be meaningful – the child should be able to make connections between familiar and unfamiliar stimuli. This enables easier learning through the enhancement of analogical thinking (a method for solving problems), and the improvement of memory skills and metacognition.

3. Play should involve active engagement, which promotes children's agency and decision-making abilities. Through active engagement, children's memory and retrieval processes are enhanced. Executive control (which is goal focused and centres on self-regulatory behaviours) is improved through children developing skills which enable them to become less distracted, and improve short-term memory and lifelong learning.

4. Play should be iterative or involves repetition. Children acquire important learning characteristics such as perseverance and ultimately greater flexibility in their thinking.

5. Play should encourage social interaction, which should include positive caregiving practices. Social interaction leads to the healthy development of social emotional regulation and the lessening of learning barriers such as stress. It also helps children cope with challenges later in life.

Find out more

Moyles (2010) notes that the human mind is a pattern collector and young children are natural seekers of pattern. Patterns help children to make sense of everyday experiences and to establish order in their world. Play-based learning provides children with the opportunity to both create and discover patterns. Athey (1990, in Halpenny & Pettersen, 2014) claims that as young children play, they show repeated patterns of behaviour. For example, they 'transport' (ie carry objects from one place to another) and also rotate – turning, twisting or rolling themselves or objects. Athey (1990, cited in Halpenny & Petterson, 2014) also noted other behavioural patterns including 'containing' – children putting themselves or objects and materials into different containers – and envelopment, which is covering themselves, objects or a space. These opportunities should relate directly to the children and involve first-hand experiences.

Try this out

Observe children between the ages of approximately two and four years playing. Can you identify those creating and using patterns in their forms of behaviour or as they play with objects either inside or outside? Record what types of patterns are used and how often they occur.

6.3 WHAT IS PLAY?

Whitebread et al (2012) describe play as being an action that children do naturally. De Witt (2009) and Niland (2009) both assert that play lays the foundation of almost everything the child learns during the preschool years. Play is any voluntary activity that children perform solely for the pleasure it gives them. Play takes many forms, but the heart of play is pleasure. Play is intrinsically motivated and relatively free of externally imposed rules, as it is the process not the outcome that is important (Feeny, 2007).

Play allows children to find out about themselves and explore the world or environment around them (Lucich, 2011). Berk (2007) states that play offers children an opportunity to be independent, to make decisions on their own and thus become self-reliant. In this way, children's self-confidence is promoted, which leads to a positive self-image (Mayesky, 2006). Ridgway & Quinones (2012) also highlights that play encourages language as well as personal development.

Lucich (2011) asserts that play fulfils an important role in contributing to children's total humanisation. These meaningful, interactive experiences form the basis of long-lasting learning. In brief, through play children develop a plethora (many) of skills (Department of Basic Education, 2008), learn new and reinforce existing concepts (ideas and facts), as well as lay down attitudes and values that will influence their future behaviour.

Reflection

As a teacher (or parent), think carefully about the types of playful experiences and equipment you plan for the children in your care. Do they allow for inclusive, participatory, experiential learning opportunities that are culturally responsive and developmentally appropriate?

To ensure that play is inclusive, participatory and culturally responsive, we need to carefully consider our understandings of play and playful learning and teaching.

Something to consider

Play is elusive (obscure). It defies narrow definition as it has many different meanings, which differ in different contexts. It is now widely accepted and advocated that play is an important vehicle to support early learning. In fact, it has been established that much of the successful learning that happens in formal schooling emanates from the playful experiences of young children. Therefore, as a teacher it is important to understand some of the theoretical claims that underpin the role of play in teaching and learning.

Different theorists view play through different lenses. However, most theories identify similar characteristics and underpinning principles of play. This commonality presents, therefore, agreement about the various facets and pivotal role of play in ECCE.

6.4 THEORETICAL UNDERPINNINGS OF PLAY

We first consider a number of theorists and educationists who have had a significant impact on early learning play theories in the past 100 years. There are, however, many other theorists whose views are also important. We will consider some of these other theorists when we present an overview of underpinning characteristics of play.

In previous chapters (see chapters 2 and 3), we discussed a number of theorists who have made a considerable contribution to our understandings of play.

6.4.1 Piaget

Piaget (1962) argues that there are two major principles that guide the intellectual growth and biological development in children and enable them to survive in a specific environment. These are adaptation and organisation. For Piaget, learning is a process of adjustment to environmental influences. As we discussed in Chapter 3, Piaget described two basic mental processes which drive this adjustment – assimilation and accommodation.

6.4.2 Vygotsky

Vygotsky's social constructivism gives high priority to language in the process of intellectual development. Dialogue becomes the context through which ideas are considered, shared and developed. He suggested that children use play as a means of social growth (Rollins & Riggins, 2013) and to interact with each other using language and role play. This was illustrated in the previously mentioned sociodramatic play case study.

6.4.3 Sigmund Freud

Freud felt that play was a means of expressing and releasing emotions and tensions (Monighan-Nourot, in Branscombe et al, 2003).

6.4.4 Erikson

Erikson built upon Freud's theory. His psychosocial theory specifically explores play from a socio-emotional perspective. He viewed play as a necessary factor for social development.

6.4.5 Other theorists

Other theorists whose perspectives on play add to our understanding of its importance include Pestalozzi, Froebel, Maria Montessori and Loris Malaguzzi who developed the Reggio Emilia programme.

6.4.5.1 Pestalozzi

Pestalozzi's (1746–1827) approach has significantly influenced modern early childhood pedagogy. He emphasised not only what is taught but also how it is taught (see playful pedagogies). He viewed play as essential to a child's development and advocated, among other things, that education should:

- be child-centred and thus informed by the interests and needs of the child
- promote active rather than passive participation in the learning experience
- promote the freedom of the child based on her natural development balanced with self-discipline so that she can function both as an individual and as part of society
- allow the child to have direct experience of the world and make use of natural objects in teaching
- encourage children to use their senses to heighten observation and inform their judgement
- encourage cooperation between the school and the home, and between parents and teachers
- be based on authority founded on love, not fear.

6.4.5.2 Froebel

Froebel (1782–1852), founder of the kindergarten (which today is often referred to as Grade R), was influenced by Pestalozzi. He suggested that play is the highest level of child development. It is a spontaneous expression of thought and feeling. It is never trivial. It is serious and deeply significant, not only for what children learn about the world, but also for its spiritual significance (Kerry & Tollitt, 1987). Froebel argued that children should play until age seven, as it is only then that they are ready for the demands of formal schooling.

6.4.5.3 Maria Montessori

Maria Montessori (1870 – 1952) was an Italian physician and educator. The Montessori Method is based on the idea that children learn best when the environment supports their natural desire to acquire skills and knowledge. It is an approach to learning which emphasises active participation, independence and cooperation in accordance with each child's unique pace of development. In addition, it emphasises individuality and independence in learning based on self-directed activity, hands-on learning. It does however also support collaborative play. For Montessori, play is the work of childhood; children work in groups and individually to discover and explore knowledge of the world and to develop their maximum potential.

6.4.5.4 The Reggio Emilia approach

The Reggio Emilia approach, which was founded by Loris Malaguzzi (1920 – 1994), is named after the town of Reggio Emilia in northern Italy where the approach originated following the devastation of World War II. It has become an influential early childhood programme and draws on the progressive ideas of early educationists such as Pestalozzi and Froebel, whom we have previously mentioned. The Reggio Emilia approach also promotes a child-centred pedagogy based on an emergent curriculum that acknowledges that children are capable of constructing their own learning as they are driven by their interests to understand and know more. Learning is a collaborative process, and children are constructed as capable and competent beings (see Chapter 2 on the constructions of children) who are encouraged to use language playfully to interact with others.

A well-planned environment is key as it is recognised for its potential to inspire children. The environment is in fact called the 'third teacher'. There is also a strong emphasis on documenting children's thoughts – documentation is an important assessment tool in the Reggio approach (see Chapter 14).

> **Find out more**
>
> Malaguzzi explicitly acknowledged that children show their understanding and express their thoughts and creativity in a variety of ways, which he referred to as the Hundred Languages of Children. These 'languages' include drawing and sculpting, dance and movement, painting, pretend play, modelling and music. By encouraging playful teaching strategies, the Reggio approach emphasises hands-on discovery learning that allows children to use all their senses and all their 'languages' to learn and express what they have learned. Consequently, each one of these Hundred Languages must be valued and nurtured. The Reggio approach has reinforced the value of playful teaching strategies in early learning. Observe a child at play and identify how the idea of a hundred languages of children is being used.

> **Reflection**
>
> Reread the different approaches we have discussed. Observe the children in your care while they are playing. Identify the similarities and differences between their approaches and the ones we have discussed.

6.4.6 Playful pedagogies

The concept of playful pedagogies provides an alternative lens through which to view play. Informed by sociocultural theory, the emphasis shifts not only to how children learn through play, but also to how teachers teach playfully (Wood, 2009). The playful pedagogies approach is gaining support because it places the child at the centre of the learning and teaching process and acknowledges the role of the teacher. Playful pedagogies reinforce the well-accepted benefits of playful learning (see section 6.2) and the underpinning principles and characteristics of what children learn and how they learn through play (see sections 6.5 and 6.6). In addition, playful pedagogies explore how to teach playfully, and outline an exciting role for teachers as co-constructors of knowledge and supporters of sustained, shared thinking (Siraj-Blatchford, 2009). Together, teachers and children explore concepts and in so doing co-construct knowledge. Learning is a reciprocal event.

Something to consider

Playful pedagogies focus on the social nature of play rather than on the individual development of the child. In so doing, the approach provides an alternative to the creeping formalisation of early education. In playful pedagogy, children have an opportunity to explore the notions of agency, power and control (in other words, who controls what happens during play? Is the adult all powerful or do children have some opportunities for making choices and decisions during their play?). This means that they explore their world on their own terms. They can negotiate rules and meanings, are free to use their imagination and engage in multi-layered types of play. For example, pretend play regains its place of importance as children are enabled to exercise agency and control.

According to Wood (2009) and Rogers (2011), playful pedagogies consider the ways teachers make provision for play and playful approaches to teaching and learning. The approach also focuses on the planning of the learning environment, the pedagogical decisions the teachers make (such as the strategies and methodological approaches) as well as the time allocated to play and the choice of resources. In playful pedagogies 'play is sustained through reciprocal and responsive relationships, and is situated in activities that are socially constructed and mediated. While children's interests remain central to curriculum planning the subject disciplines enrich and extend the children's learning' (Wood, 2009: 27).

Try this out

Read the above quote carefully. Choose three of the main points Wood is making and elaborate on their meaning. For example, what do you think is meant by a reciprocal and responsive relationship?

Something to consider

Did you perhaps mention that it is an open, collaborative relationship where control is shared so that activities can be initiated by either party? Spontaneity, respect and warmth are key features of the relationship Wood envisages.

Wood (2009) also points to the value of an emergent curriculum which is culturally driven and based on the child's interests. Wood (2010) uses the term 'emergent responsive approach' to capture a playful pedagogical perspective based on acknowledging the significance of the cultural context in which children grow and learn.

6.4.6.1 An emergent responsive approach

An emergent responsive approach:

- allows the teacher to respond to children's choices and interests, and to their emerging knowledge, skills and understandings
- encourages interactive, participatory learning where knowledge is co-constructed with others as children participate both individually and collectively in their social and cultural worlds
- recognises ways of knowing and participating in different sociocultural practices which embody the beliefs, rules, behavioural practices, language, 'norms' and expectations within communities
- enables learning to become culturally and contextually relevant (see chapters 2 and 3) (Wood, 2010).

In brief, this approach recognises the knowledge that children bring to the setting. Children's knowledge and abilities can be identified through observing their interests, motivation and choices, and through multimodal representations (in other words, the many different activities such as drawing, painting, constructing, role playing, etc) through which children express themselves. Children's engagement/participation will also increase as they become more confident, knowledgeable and skilful (Wood, 2010). For Wood (2010), an emergent responsive form of play is the opposite of many current approaches towards play-based learning and teaching, which she calls a cultural transmission/directive approach.

6.4.6.2 A cultural transmission/directive approach

According to Wood (2010), this approach carries the beliefs of those who have the most power in society, and play becomes 'educational practice'. For example, children manipulate materials to improve fine motor coordination to promote a good pencil grip. They also complete worksheets aimed at teaching a specific skill, such as visual matching. These worksheets are often used to replace creative (imaginative) art activities. The richness of story time is lost as it becomes a phonics lesson.

In other words, the essence of play is lost as children are 'trained' to acquire preparatory skills and basic knowledge deemed essential for formal schooling. The role of the teacher is to transmit knowledge, skills and understandings that are deemed suitable and valuable to children. The teacher or adult has all the power, and controls the type, amount, time and resources made available for play. Children have limited ownership and control over their own play experiences. Imagination and creativity are restricted. This approach tends to regulate children and make them all the same. It negates the uniqueness of childhood.

Reflection

To what extent does the cultural transmission/directive approach we have discussed reflect your current approach to play-based teaching? Do you consider difference and diversity when you plan? Do you consider children's interests and allow them to make their own play choices, or is your approach similar to 'educational practice'?

6.4.6.3 Moving from a cultural transmission to emergent responsive approaches

Podmore (2009) notes that teachers often need help to make the transition from a cultural transmission/directive approach, which has a specific focus on the becoming child, to an emergent responsive approach, which focuses on the being, belonging and becoming child. To adopt an emergent responsive approach, you will have to think differently about:

- children
- the type of programme offered to them
- who initiates activities
- working with families
- assessment.

There is still a place for a cultural transmission/directive model as it is important for children to learn about and value their cultural heritage. At home, for example, parents or caregivers will use the transmission model to impart important cultural information. However, always try and ensure that children do not view their own culture as superior or inferior to others, as this can lead to negative cultural attitudes towards other people.

6.4.6.4 Some concluding thoughts

Play, from a theoretically and methodologically perspective, is a contested terrain. As Wood (2010) asserts, studies are useful to identify the benefits of play, but making links between play and learning and play and pedagogy remains a subject for debate. However, we do know that many and varied opportunities to play from birth onwards is vital if children are going reach their optimal development and learning potential. We also know that the role of the teacher/adult is pivotal in promoting rich play-based experiences for children. It is important when considering play to think about power. Who is controlling what and for what reason? Who, for example, is included and who is excluded? Do some children have to learn to play? To provide a context for these questions we will now look at the underpinning principles and characteristics of play.

6.5 UNDERPINNING PRINCIPLES AND CHARACTERISTICS OF PLAY

Research on play displays a number of commonalities. These include the following:

- All children play; it is a universal activity. It is, however, culturally bounded. Children from different cultures might play differently.
- Play is voluntary. Children choose to play. Adults, however, might have made the decisions about what, where, when and with whom (Bruce, 2010).
- Play is spontaneous. Children shape it as they go, changing the characters, events, objects and locations. Play as an active, enjoyable and pleasurable activity is self-motivating and is in itself a reward for children.
- It is often a social activity, and children share information in a variety of verbal and non-verbal ways. At times it can be a solitary undertaking.
- Children often experience a feeling of personal satisfaction when playing, which promotes a sense of independence and boosts their self-esteem. Play is also therapeutic in that it helps children to express and work through emotions and experiences. Play can therefore be seen as a major role player in emotional and social development.
- Play is process oriented; it is a means unto itself and might not have an end or goal in sight (Bartlett, 2010). Play can be adventurous and risky, and helps children explore the unknown.

Something to consider

Play is deeply intellectual and meaningful for children. It is closely linked to self-regulated learning and metacognition. It is an important context for coming to know oneself and developing helpful learning behaviours such as perseverance, curiosity, responsibility and a positive self-concept (Carr, 2001). Resilience, playfulness and reciprocity are other learning dispositions acquired through play (Carr & Claxton, 2002). Positive learning dispositions are central to successful engagement in lifelong learning.

Play presents concrete learning experiences which provide the context for the emergence of symbolic thought. Symbolic thought allows the child to imagine objects or events that are not present, which is a forerunner to abstract thinking (Worthington, 2010). During play, children imagine and pretend. They try out ideas, feelings and roles. They re-enact the past and rehearse the future. Through these processes they are enhancing skills that form part of emergent literacy and numeracy, for example the concepts of 'more than' and 'less than'.

6.6 CLASSIFICATION OF PLAY

Parten's 1932 classification of play has withstood the test of time. She classified play according to children's ages and the extent to which they interacted with each other. Modern thinking around play, however, questions the age/stage relationship.

- **Solitary play:** children play alone, absorbed in their own play. They are unaware of what other children are doing. According to Parten, babies and toddlers engage in solitary play, but today we acknowledge that other older children might also play this way. Examples are:
    - children who are egocentric
    - children who are not able or ready to share and cooperate during play
    - child who are emotionally and socially immature
    - children who choose to play alone.
- **Spectator play:** the child watches others playing without joining in. This often occurs in younger children but can occur at any age, depending on circumstances.
- **Parallel play:** children play alongside other children, notice what they are doing but continue with their own activity. They do not really interact socially with other children. In addition to toddlers, children who play in this way include those who are perhaps shy, who would like to become more involved with other players but are not sure how to do this.
- **Associative play:** children begin to play together, developing interactions through imitating what the other children are doing or playing with similar equipment. Three- to four-year-olds often demonstrate this type of play.
- **Cooperative play:** children interact, take turns, share and decide how and what to play. They collaborate, develop and negotiate ideas for their play. They may, at first, only play cooperatively for a short while. Later they may want to join in a group game or do what the group is doing. They are prepared to put aside their own desires and interests in order to follow those of the group. Children usually play cooperatively from about five years of age, but, of course, this may begin at an earlier age.

Piaget also classified play according to ages and stages. Once again, the age/stage criterion has been challenged, but knowledge of this classification remains relevant today. His classifications are:

- **Sensory-motor/practice play:** this begins in infancy and today it is acknowledged that this form of play continues throughout life. Much of this play is just for the pleasure of exploring through one's senses. It can also involve a lot of repetition, for example a baby throwing down blocks, or a child swinging on a swing or throwing a ball.

- **Symbolic (make believe, fantasy or pretend) play:** this begins somewhere towards the end of a child's first year when children start to give a different meaning to an actual object. For example, a doll becomes a baby; the swing could now become a rocket ship travelling into space; a block could become a cell phone. Wadsworth (1989: 60) points out that in 1967 Piaget wrote that 'its [symbolic play's] function is to satisfy the self by transforming what is real into what is desired'. Today it is also acknowledged that this type of play can continue throughout childhood.
- **Games with rules:** children begin to make and agree to rules that will govern their play. They might invent their own games and make up the rules as they go along. This form of play is typical of children aged from five years onwards, but, like cooperative play, they may engage in games with rules from an earlier age. Think, for example, of playing a game of peek-a-boo with a baby, who can follow the 'rules' albeit for a short time.

Reflection

Can you recall a time when you observed children engaging in each category of play identified by Parten and Piaget? Give an example of the occurrence and name the play features which determined your classification.

The classifications could be seen as 'how' children are playing, for example alongside each other. The next section looks at play from the 'WH' perspective – what, why, when and where. We gather the four WHs under the heading 'types of play'. It is important to note there are many ways of describing the different types of play.

6.7 TYPES OF PLAY

Play can be described according to the location, for example indoor or outdoor. There have also been descriptions relating to various aspects of development such as physical play, creative play, etc. More recently, descriptions have been related to subject disciplines such as nature, science (discovery play) and even language play. Sometimes play is described as a particular type such as socio-dramatic (fantasy) play, and sand and water play. There is no one correct way of naming play. When planning children's play experiences, teachers need to make sure that children have access to all types of play and a variety of resources are available, even for similar types of play.

We are now going to apply our 'WH' framework as an organising principle for capturing the many aspects of play.

6.7.1 Functional play

This form of practical play starts in infancy and includes playing with toys or objects that have a particular function. Through functional play a child learns to control his actions and make things happen, such as shaking a rattle or casting (throwing) objects. These simple and repetitive actions that emphasise the physical actions of play are slowly replaced by more complex forms of play. However, functional play is enjoyed by children throughout their childhood as they practise and master new skills allowing them to experience a sense of achievement. Functional play:

- involves balance, posture and movement including large muscle development (crawling, running, hopping, etc)
- encourages small (fine) muscle development (grasping, sucking, cutting, blinking eyes, squeezing, etc)
- involves movement control (hand–eye, foot–eye coordination, etc)
- encourages physical movement which is an important steppingstone for the development of perceptual motor skills and early literacy and numeracy
- involves exploration of the environment (closely related to nature and scientific play)
- involves the use of the senses (remember children are sensory-motor learners)
- is often played for its own sake (Smilansky & Shefatya, 1990).

Supporting functional play

- Ensure sufficient time and space.
- Allow for indoor and outdoor functional play opportunities.
- Resources must be safe to use and differentiated where necessary to be suitable yet challenging for children of different ages and skills ability.

Examples include squeeze toys for babies, push–pull toys for toddlers, climbing equipment, wheel toys, balls and bats, swings, large open spaces to run around and explore etc; in other words, a considerable variety.

6.7.2 Construction play

Construction play:

- occurs when the child's physical movements become more controlled
- becomes more complex over time – compare a baby beginning to build with blocks to an older child building a tower of five blocks
- involves constructive, creative and imaginative use of play materials
- is play with a purpose, encouraging problem solving and reasoning abilities
- supports the development of emergent mathematics.

Supporting construction play

Provide sufficient items so that children can achieve a sense of satisfaction through building.

Items include blocks of different shapes, sizes and colours; Duplo (for younger children) and Lego (for older children); boxes of different shapes and sizes such as biscuit, match, cereal, toothpaste boxes, etc; and cartons such as margarine containers, yogurt tubs and milk cartons.

6.7.3 Manipulative play

Manipulative play refers to activities where children move, order, turn or screw items to make them fit. It allows children to take control of their world by mastering the objects they use.

- It involves mostly the small muscles of the hands and fingers but do not forget about the feet and toes, as well as the muscles of the face and eyes.
- It involves a range of different levels of difficulty.
- It requires children to manipulate (use, work with) objects such as rattles, activity boards, lacing cards or pegboards. Make sure to include a range of different puzzles as puzzle building is not only manipulative but also enhances spatial and visual perceptual motor behaviours. Start with two-piece puzzles and gradually increase the number of puzzle pieces.
- It also promotes the development of cognitive (intellectual) and imaginative skills.
- It includes sand and water play, as well as manipulating play dough or clay, etc.
- It is important for the development of finger strength and ultimately a strong pencil grip.

Supporting manipulative play

Encourage babies to grasp objects such as a rattle, transfer blocks from one hand to the other and play with an activity centre if available. Toddlers could pick up tiny objects such as small pebbles, grains of rice, dried beans, etc, between thumb and forefinger. Watch carefully to make sure children do not put inappropriate things in their mouth. Safety considerations are paramount. Also encourage sand and water play as well as drawing and painting activities. Older children can play finger games like clicking or flicking fingers; encourage children to pick up marbles or a piece of string with their toes; to wriggle their toes; provide lacing cards, puzzles, pegboards, sand and water play as well as many different creative art activities.

6.7.4 Socio-dramatic play (fantasy, pretend play, make-believe play)

For Vygotsky, socio-dramatic play is the lead activity for children between ages of three and six years. By this he meant that it is through socio-dramatic play that children acquire and refine many of their self-regulatory behaviours (Karpov, 2005).

Socio-dramatic play has the following advantages:
- It allows children to use and develop their imagination.
- It provides opportunities to create an inner world within which children can make things happen in whatever way they wish. This includes pretending with objects, actions and situations.
- It gives children opportunities to act out frightening situations, putting themselves in control.
- It allows children to practise language and literacy skills as well as develop emergent mathematical understanding. They also get the chance to play with different forms of information and communication technologies (ICT), such as discarded mobile phones, computers, keyboards, cameras and calculators. Sometimes the community may have supplied old ICT items for use in fantasy play; but children could also make use of other objects to symbolically represent ICT equipment.
- It enables children to act out real-life events in a home or fantasy corner. As children get older the play becomes more complex. They make up stories and scenarios, and take part in fantasy play about things that are not real, such as fairies or superheroes.
- It allows children to use concrete objects such as blocks, toy animals, cars or toy people as symbolic representations (making something stand for something else).

Supporting socio-dramatic play

Adults must let children know that they support this type of play. 'Read' the children. Know when to intervene and join the play, and when to stand back and allow the children to play in their own way and on their own terms. At times provide prompts/stimuli to promote fantasy play, for example a short discussion, a visit to, for instance, a fire station, reading a story, supplying a variety of props such as a stethoscope, rubber stamps, toy fruit, empty food boxes and dressing up clothes, etc. Parents and teachers can help with the gathering of these resources.

Open-ended props such as pieces of material, different clothing and shoes, boxes, pieces of paper and crayons, etc, often allow for more imaginative and creative play than setting up a specific fantasy corner such as the hospital or *spaza* shop. Vary the offerings and allow children to have different types of play experiences.

Allow children to decide on where, what and how they are going to interact with each other and the equipment.

6.7.5 Games with rules

Games with rules have the following advantages:

- They encourage children to play in groups
- They allow children to negotiate their own rules – at first these might be flexible, but later children might well insist that rules cannot be broken.
- They are best played when children are intellectually able to understand and follow the rules.
- They encourage children to share and take turns when they are mature enough socially to play cooperatively.
- They are more easily followed when children are able to cope with the physical skills involved in the games.
- They are especially enjoyed from about five to eight years of age and upwards. However, younger children can engage in simple games with rules, but usually do so with an adult. Think of playing the 'ta' game with babies and toddlers where an adult and child pass an item to each other after the word 'ta' is said.

> **Supporting games with rules**
>
> Provide cards, or homemade or bought games such as board games. Examples include Snap, Ludo, Dominoes, and Snakes and Ladders. Games with rules can also be played outdoors, for example catch, hopscotch and hide-and-seek. Include song games such as 'Ring-a-ring-a-rosies' or musical chairs, which can also be successfully played with two- and three-year-olds. Draw on games within the child's culture to add familiarity, to provide fun and affirm identity.

We will return to the various types of play in other chapters that are focused on, for instance, mathematics and understanding our world.

> **Reflection**
>
> Reread the section on types of play and reflect on how each type could fit into one or more of the 'WH' (what, where, when and why) categories outlined at the start of this section. Identify an appropriate example in each type of play for babies, toddlers and young children.

A key player in this whole context is the teacher. In the next section we look at the role of the teacher in the establishment of a constructive play environment.

6.7.6 Implications for care, teaching and learning and the role of the teacher

Smith and Pellegrini (2013) state that quality childhood settings and programmes are characterised by a healthy balance of providing structure, giving children choices and ensuring a variety of playful learning opportunities. The adult must be in a positive caring relationship with the child and responsive to the needs of the child. To plan environments and experiences which foster learning through play, teachers have to fully understand play, and especially understand how to set up the learning environment from the perspective of the child.

Teachers should know how to make time and space for play and be able to listen to children and respect and trust their judgement. In a constructive environment, children's needs, interests and wishes are always considered. In other words, children are encouraged to have agency; their voices are listened to and they are allowed to make their own choices about, for example, which material they want to use to make a nature collage. Furthermore, the adult's role is one of a guide on the side. When appropriate, teachers contribute to the play process by offering support (scaffolding), for example in the construction of a new puzzle.

An important role of an adult during play is to provide a structure or a series of steps for the child to explore a new experience successfully and add to their initial learning. According to Niland (2009), the adult should know how to provide steps that are small enough for the child to gain success, but challenging enough to motivate and take the child's learning forward because children do not only practise what they already know but they also learn new things. Siraj-Blatchford (2009) refers to this process as co-construction of knowledge through sustained shared thinking between adult and child.

Find out more

To better understand the role of the teacher, the idea of a play/teaching continuum which ranges from no or minimal intervention by the teacher to the teacher taking control of the group of children is useful. A play/teaching continuum would move from free play or child-initiated activities to Teacher-guided/directed ones:

- **Free play or child-initiated activities:** these are times when children make their own choices (with whom, what, where and how to play). Children take the initiative and follow their own interests. Teachers observe but do not interfere or become involved unless invited or a crisis is imminent, for example to prevent an accident such as when a child runs in front of a swing. The teacher respects the children's ideas and activities, and responds appropriately in a number of different ways – doing nothing, remaining silent, suggesting, facilitating and, if asked, participating.

- **Collaboration between teacher and child/ren:** at times, even within the free-play context, opportunities arise for the teacher to join in. The teacher decides if she should intervene and scaffold to enhance the children's learning. In these instances, teacher and child/ren engage in shared sustained thinking and co-construction of knowledge. An example of this could be when the child is building a tower and the teacher suggests, after the tower has collapsed several times, that the child should try using the bigger blocks as a base. Teachable moments can also arise spontaneously as, for example, when the girls will not allow the boys to join them in the home corner because they say that boys should have nothing to do with the preparation of food. In this context, the teacher could ask the question, 'Why do you think boys can't take part in the cooking?'
- **Teacher-guided/directed activities:** these are at the other end of the play/teaching continuum. They are the times when the teacher takes greater control of the group, and plans and organises the activity. An example of this would be a morning ring. Depending upon the strategies used, the teacher might engage the group in a playful pedagogical activity or take the lead and instruct the children providing perhaps a demonstration of a particular activity, for example when showing them how to follow a recipe in a baking activity.

Wherever the teacher's practice can be placed on the continuum, there should be one constant: all forms of pedagogy should be approached playfully. Playful teachers use materials and resources in an imaginative and flexible way. They are open to change. For example, if a helicopter hovers overhead and the children are so excited they first want to go outside to see it and then talk about it. Chapter 8 discusses a number of playful ways of interacting with children, as well as different pedagogical approaches.

Reflection

The implementation of effective play-based programmes requires self-reflective teachers who reflect on play, pedagogy and learning. They purposefully try and locate any biases they may be harbouring, and reflect on their own thinking and practices, and in so doing clarify their attitudes and beliefs and theories about play. Thoughtful teachers know when to seize the teachable moment. They also understand the child's capacity for self-regulation and are able, through play and playful teaching, to enrich children's learning and development. As children gain self-regulation, disputes between them are minimised. Self-regulation is a process, not an end product, and takes time.

Try this out

How do you think you could provide children with the support, props, time and space to develop their play? List five ideas linked to particular types of play. In addition, identify two types of self-regulating behaviour you could encourage children to develop during play.

6.8 PROBLEMATISING PLAY

We have already mentioned that play does not necessarily benefit all children all of the time. All children do not play in the same way, nor do they always learn positively through play. Some may be consistently left out, therefore any good overview of play-based learning and teaching must challenge the universal assumptions about the uncontested value and worthwhileness of play. Walkerdine (1984), for instance, identified the power relations involved in children's play and interactions with one another and with adults. In this sense, 'play' may involve conflict and concession, and power may be played out through means that relate to age and size, gender, language, socioeconomic status or any number of other factors that influence children's play. This means that there may be winners and losers, beneficiaries who are already positioned more favourably and those who are marginalised. Play and active learning in educational contexts can therefore be a source of inequality, sometimes called 'dark play' (Grishaber & McArdle, 2010).

As a teacher, think about and question the following:

- The way play is positioned in various policy documents such as the National Curriculum Framework (NCF) (as being good and right for all).
- Assumptions (that are often accepted on face value) about the possibilities and benefits for all children regarding free choice (are all children allowed to and able to choose?) Could this cause cultural confusion?
- The notion of child-centredness. Do you practise this in your ECCE centre? Do you, for example, follow an emergent curriculum based on the children's interests or are the topics to be covered in the curriculum determined at the beginning of the year and never altered?
- Why play is positioned as both universal and culturally bounded. In other words, given the right circumstances, all children play, but as we have said they do not always play in the same way, nor do they all feel free to help themselves to the play resources on offer. Do you make appropriate allowances for cultural and contextual differences?
- If the play experience is sufficiently challenging? If children are not adequately challenged. this might become boring and repetitive, and no worthwhile leaning will take place.

- If you allow children to take sufficient risks? Today, safety concerns often place restrictions on play. For example, children are not allowed to climb a big tree in the playground because of the risk of falling, or rough-and-tumble play is banned because a child might get hurt. How do you balance the tensions between the perceived safety risks of outdoor play and the learning potential of risk-taking play?
- How play and active learning in educational contexts can be a source of inequality, especially if some children are positioned more favourably and others are marginalised because of their cultural and contextual situations, aspects over which they have no control. As a teacher you should always be an agent for change and be alert to factors that might cause marginalisation.

Something to consider

Wood (2010) maintains that we need to adopt an integrated approach to play where adults are involved with children to plan for play and child-initiated activities based on the teacher's observations and interactions. We should avoid an approach where adult-directed activities take centre stage in planning and assessment, and child-initiated activities are side-lined We need to adopt an emergent responsive approach to play-based learning and teaching (see the section on playful pedagogies in this chapter.)

6.9 SUMMARY

In this chapter we explored play through a theoretical as well as practical lens. We made a strong argument for the introduction of playful pedagogies that consider children's contexts and cultural backgrounds. We also considered how playful pedagogy can embrace both learning and teaching. We examined how, through a playful pedagogical approach that encourages children's participation and allows for differentiation, all children are included in the daily programme.

In the following chapter, we show how the early years' curriculum is realised through a play-based approach by considering the in- and outdoor learning environments. In Chapter 8 we explore a number of different teaching strategies that support the adoption of a playful pedagogical approach to early learning.

REFERENCES

Barblett, L. 2010. Why play-based learning? *Early Childhood Australia*, 16(3).

Berk, LE. 2007. *Development through the lifespan.* 4th ed. Boston: Allyn & Bacon.

Branscombe, N, Castle, K, Dorsey, A, Surbeck, E & Taylor, J. 2003. *Early childhood curriculum: A constructivist perspective.* Abingdon, UK: Routledge.

Bruce, T. 2010. *Early childhood: A guide for students.* London: SAGE.

Carr, M. 2001. *Assessment in early childhood settings: Learning stories.* London: Paul Chapman.

Carr, M & Claxton, G. 2002. *Tracking the development of learning dispositions.* London: Taylor & Francis.

Cherry, K. 2012. *The concrete operational stage of cognitive development.* New York: Adams Media.

Department of Basic Education (DBE). 2008. *Grade R practical ideas.* Pretoria: Government Printer.

Department of Basic Education (DBE). 2015. *South African National Curriculum Framework from birth to four years.* Pretoria: Government Printer.

Department of Higher Education and Training (DHET). 2017. *Policy on minimum requirements for programmes leading to qualifications in higher education for early childhood development educators.* Pretoria.

De Witt, M. 2009. *The young child in context. A thematic approach.* Pretoria: Van Schaik.

Duffy, B. 2006. The curriculum from birth to six, in Pugh, G & Duffy, B (eds). *Contemporary issues in the curriculum.* London: SAGE.

Feeny, S. 2007. *Who am I in the lives of children? An introduction to teaching young children.* Minneapolis, MN: Burgess.

Golinkoff, M & Hirsh-Pasek, K. 2016. *Becoming brilliant: Reimagining education for our time.* https://www.brookings.edu/blog/education-plus-development/2016/05/20/becoming-brilliant-reimagining-education-for-our-time/ (Accessed 1 April 2019).

Grishaber, S & McArdle, F. 2010. *The trouble with play.* Oxford: Oxford University Press.

Halpenny, AM & Pettersen, J. 2014. *Introducing Piaget. A guide for practitioners and students in early years education.* London: Routledge.

Hännikäinen, M & Rasku-Puttonen, H. 2010. Promoting children's participation: The role of teachers in preschool and primary school learning sessions, *Early Years*, 30(2): 147–160.

Hoisington, C. 2008. *Let's play! Using play-based curriculum to support children's learning throughout the domains.* California: Excelligence Learning Corporation.

Ivon, H. 2013. Features of children's play and developmental possibilities of symbolic puppet play. *Croatian Journal of Education*, 16(special edition1/2014): 161–180.

Karpov, Y. 2005. *The neo Vygotskian approach to child development.* New York: Cambridge University Press.

Kernan, M. 2007. *Play as a context for early learning and development.* A research paper commissioned by the National Council for Curriculum and Assessment, NCCA.

Kerry, T & Tollit, J. 1987. *Critical perspectives on early childhood education*. Oxford: Prentice Hall.

Khuphe, C. 2014. *Indigenous knowledge and school science: Possibilities for integration*. Unpublished PhD thesis. University of Witwatersrand.

LeBlanc, M. nd. *Johann Heinrich Pestalozzi*. https://www.communityplaythings.co.uk/learning-library/articles/johann-heinrich-pestalozzi (Accessed 29 November 2018).

Lucich, M. 2011. *Childcare healthcare program*. California: California Training Institute.

Liu, C, Solis, SL, Jensen, H, Hopkins, EJ, Neale, D, Zosh, JM, Hirsh-Pasek, K & Whitebread, D. 2017. *Neuroscience and learning through play: A review of the evidence (research summary)*. The LEGO Foundation, DK.

Mayesky, M. 2006. *Creative activities for young children*. New York: Thomson, Delmar.

Mc Clary, A. 2004. *Good toys, bad toys: How safety, society, politics, fashion have reshaped children's playthings*. London: McFarland.

Moyles, J. 2010. *The excellence of play*. Berkshire: Open University Press.

Moyles, J. 2015. *The excellence of play*. Milton Keynes: Open University Press.

Niland, A. 2009. The power of musical play: The value of play-based, child-centred curriculum in early childhood music education. *General Music Today*, 23(1): 17–21.

Piaget, J. 1962. *Play, dreams, and imitation in childhood*. New York: WW Norton & Company, Inc.

Podmore, VN. 2009. Questioning evaluation quality in early childhood, in Anning, A, Cullen, J & Fleer, M (eds). *Early childhood education: Society and culture*. London: SAGE. 158–168.

Ridgway, S & Quinones, G. 2012. How do early childhood students conceptualize play-based curriculum? *Australian Journal of Teacher Education*, 3(12): 46–56.

Rogers, S. 2011. *Rethinking play and pedagogy in early childhood education*. Oxon: Routledge.

Rollins, L & Riggins, T. 2013. *Society for research in child development*. Washington State Convention Centre.

Romero-Little, ME. 2010. How should young indigenous children be prepared for learning? A vision of early childhood education for indigenous children. *Journal of American Indian Education*, 49(1&2).

Smilansky, S & Shefatya, L. 1990. *Facilitating play: A medium for promoting cognitive, socio-emotional and academic development in young children*. PS&E Publications.

Siraj-Blatchford, I. 2009. Conceptualising progression in the pedagogy of play and sustained shared thinking in early childhood education: A Vygotskian perspective. *Education and Child Psychology*, 26(2): 77–89.

Smith, PK & Pellegrini, A. 2013. Learning through play, in *Encyclopaedia on early childhood development*. Montreal: Centre of Excellence for Early Childhood Development.

Sylva, K, Melhuish, EC, Sammons, P, Siraj-Blatchford, I & Taggert, B. 2004. *The effective provisioning of pre-school education (EPPE) project: Technical paper 12 – the final report: Effective pre-school education*. London: DfES and Institute of Education, University of London.

Vygotsky, L. 1978. *Mind in society. The development of higher psychological processes*. Cambridge, MA: Harvard University Press.

Wadsworth, BJ. 1989. *Piaget's theory of cognitive and affective development*. Chicago: Longman.

Walkerdine, V. 1984. Someday my prince will come: Young girls and the preparation for adolescent sexuality, in McRobbie, A & Nava, M (eds). *Gender and generation*. London: Palgrave Macmillan. 162–184.

Watson, M. 2003. *Learning to trust*. San Francisco: Jossey-Bass.

Whitebread, D, Basilio, M, Kuvalja, M & Verma, M. 2012. *The importance of play: Report on the value of children's play with a series of policy recommendations*. Commissioned by the Toy Industries of Europe.

Wood, E. 2009. Developing a pedagogy of play, in Anning, A, Cullen, J & Fleer, M (eds). *Early childhood education: Society and culture* London: SAGE. 27–38.

Wood, E. 2010. Developing integrated pedagogical approaches to play and learning, in Broadhead, P, Howard, J & Wood, E (eds). *Play and learning in the early years*. London: SAGE.

Worthington, M. 2010. Play is a complex landscape: Imagination and symbolic meanings, in Broadhead, P, Wood, E & Howard, J (eds). *Play and learning in educational settings*. London: SAGE.

Chapter 7

A creative and responsive curriculum for early childhood care and education

Lorayne Excell, Vivien Linington and Nontokozo Mashiya

In this chapter we consider:

- what constitutes an early years curriculum: care, nurturing and early learning
- the South African National Framework from birth to four
- what constitutes an appropriate early learning environment
- how to create and maintain different playful spaces in a variety of early childhood care and education (ECCE) settings
- how to create the intellectual and social and emotional environment
- the temporal environment and how the daily programme is adapted for different age groups
- how to implement a responsive, differentiated and inclusive early years curriculum and to recognise and respond to barriers to learning.

7.1 INTRODUCTION

A curriculum is a plan for teaching and learning. Until recently there was no national curriculum in South Africa for ECCE. Teachers followed a number of different programmes with varying degrees of success. In some instances, they even followed the Curriculum and Assessment Policy Statement (CAPS) for Grade R for teaching younger children. This is not a good idea as the CAPS document has been drawn up for schooling in the Foundation Phase and is therefore not ideal for younger children. There is wide consensus that a curriculum for ECCE should be play-based (see Chapter 6) and be informed by the children's needs, interests, contextual situations and cultural backgrounds (see chapters 2 and 3). In this chapter we will explore what constitutes a quality play-based curriculum for the early years (from birth to five years).

7.2 WHAT IS A CURRICULUM?

A curriculum provides a framework for teaching and learning. It is informed by a philosophy of education which is based on a specific understanding of teaching and learning; children and childhood; and how children grow, develop and learn, and what they need to know. It is important to remember that the philosophies of education that underpin a curriculum are drawn essentially from two sources. Firstly, a National Department of Education will embed its philosophy of education in the curriculum. Secondly, an individual teacher will have her own philosophy of education which she will use to interpret and shape her understanding and implementation of the national curriculum.

A curriculum provides a timeframe for teaching, and reflects the yearly, weekly and daily teaching and learning plans. All planning, written and otherwise, should be based on this framework. It should consider the contexts of the different stakeholders (children, parents, teachers and the broader community), and outline the purpose, the learning content, the methodology and the teaching material, as well as evaluation and assessment strategies for both the children and the teaching and learning process.

Something to consider

Any curriculum is influenced by political, economic, historical, social and cultural factors (see chapters 1 and 15 of this book for examples of these factors). For example, the overall aims of the South African curriculum are to give expression to the values underpinned in the South African Constitution (RSA, 1996). The curriculum aims to include the knowledge, skills and attitudes and values we would like our children to acquire. It proposes that children acquire this learning in a way that is meaningful to their own lives. It is therefore important to include local knowledge and child-rearing practices into teaching plans while being sensitive to global imperatives. The curriculum also aims to equip all children, irrespective of their contexts or cultural backgrounds, to be able to participate meaningfully in a democratic society; in other words, to develop voice and agency.

Reflection

Does your practice comfortably align with the curriculum features we have raised? How do you think these features relate to the idea of the being, belonging and becoming child discussed in Chapter 2? Did you consider, for example, that the being child would be acknowledged for what he can do at this time rather than always looking forward to what he might become? A curriculum that makes sure that learning is meaningful to children's own lives is acknowledging both the being and belonging child. In contrast, a curriculum that always considers what a child has not yet achieved and rarely acknowledges what a child can currently bring to the learning environment is inclined towards the becoming perspective.

7.2.1 Why a specialised curriculum for young children?

Babies, toddlers and young children are extremely vulnerable. They are totally dependent on adults for their survival and care. Therefore, in the early childhood context a curriculum has to emphasise a care and nurturing component as well as appropriate stimulation and early learning. Both aspects are critical to promote optimal growth, development and learning in young children. Thus in recent years the international focus has been to explore ways in which we can combine care and nurturing with early learning and teaching (see Chapter 1). These four features are in fact inseparable and essential to ensure effective ECCE provisioning. With these thoughts in mind, we will now have a brief look at the National Curriculum Framework (NCF) which was published in 2015 by the Department of Basic Education (DBE, 2015). As you study the NCF, try to identify how provision has been made for care and nurturing as well as early learning. Also identify how the different constructions of childhood, namely the being, belonging and becoming child, have been included in the curriculum. The NCF can be accessed from the following website: http://www.education.gov.za/Curriculum/NationalCurriculumFrameworkforChildrenfromBirthtoFour

To complete the 'Reflections' sections in this chapter, you should download this document so that you have your own copy.

7.2.2 The South African National Curriculum Framework

South Africa, following international trends, introduced an early childhood curriculum, the NCF, which has been informed by the National Early Learning Standards (NELDS) (DBE, 2009). Both these documents acknowledge the uniqueness of all children as well the importance of holistic development, and that children are competent, participatory and active learners. The documents suggest a specific role for adults working with young children. This role envisages adults who are caring and nurturing, and responsive to the interests and needs of all children. They also envisage self-reflective adults who have thought deeply about their commitment to children and to playful teaching and learning (DBE, 2015).

The NCF has introduced some important shifts in how we think about children and their learning. The first shift has been on how we view children. The focus has moved from a predominantly developmental one (the becoming child) to one which views children as competent beings who should be recognised for who they are now and what they can achieve in their current situation. This does not mean that the developmental one has been ignored but it is considered in a much more integrated way in the context of a child's overall wellbeing.

The second shift has been the introduction of six learning areas that incorporate the developmental domains, such as physical and social, etc. In addition, the NCF has also included subject disciplines such as mathematics, literacy and understanding the world, which incorporate subjects such as history, science, etc).

A third shift has been the recognition of the importance of the family in ECCE and their pivotal role in early learning. The result of this has been a further shift in the focus of ECCE from being predominantly centre-based to include greater recognition of other forms of early childhood provisioning such as child-minding services, home-based care and mobile ECCE services (see Chapter 15).

Something to consider

The shifts we have discussed have necessarily led to a reconsideration of how we should implement the early learning curriculum. We have to find a way to merge these new trends (alternative views of children, learning areas, developmental domains and wellbeing). Now we cannot simply focus on learning areas that compartmentalises knowledge into separate subject disciplines. Instead, subject content is woven into the learning areas as a whole to provide integration. We know children need knowledge but in today's world it is not possible to give them all the knowledge they need as it is constantly changing. For children to cope and thrive in this ever-changing world, they will need flexible and agile minds. We cannot simply focus on developmental domains as we know that if we do this we will not cater for the needs and interests of all children in contextually and culturally appropriate ways. The traditional idea of the universal child is being challenged. We know from brain research that babies and young children need a safe, healthy, nutritious and stimulating environment; they need consistent positive interactions with responsive adults and opportunities for sensorimotor exploration and discovery in an 'atmosphere free from stress but with a degree of pleasurable intensity' (Duffy, 2006: 88–89). Thus we have to become sensitive, thoughtful teachers who adopt a broad and flexible curriculum approach.

7.2.3 The child and the NCF

The NCF is based on three themes written from the perspective of the child. This is to emphasise that we are working with and for children, and that their needs and interests are foregrounded. This is apparent in the NCF themes which are as follows:

1. I am a competent person.
2. My learning and development is important.
3. I need strong connections (with adults).

Each theme is informed by four principles that underpin important aspects of children's wellbeing and development (DBE, 2015). These themes and principles are presented, as we have said, from the child's perspective. They are as follows:

Theme 1: I am a competent person
Principles

1. I am a competent person who actively creates my own identity and my own understanding of the world.
2. I am unique and have a unique life story.
3. I flourish when attention is paid to equality of opportunities where I can participate to develop my own potential.
4. I am sensitive to individual and group differences, and must be educated in ways that help me to celebrate difference.

Theme 2: My learning and development is important
Principles

5. I am curious, energetic and active, and I learn by taking up opportunities to make meaning of the world around me.
6. Appropriate local and indigenous knowledge and skills are resources that can be used to promote socially, culturally and linguistically sensitive learning environments for me.
7. Play and hands-on (active) experiences enhance my learning and development.
8. A comprehensive early childhood development (ECD) learning programme for quality and equality of opportunities pays attention to:
   - ✓ my developmental domains (social, emotional, cognitive, physical – with a focus on health and nutrition)
   - ✓ the content areas (languages and mathematics) and my strong links with my family and, later, my links to schooling.

Theme 3: I need strong connections with adults
Principles

9. Parents and families in their different forms play a central role in my overall development.
10. I benefit from a close and loving relationship with an adult.
11. Adults have the responsibility for the protection and promotion of my rights regardless of my age, background, ethnicity, ability and gender.
12. I would like adults to promote my wellbeing, positive identity, inclusivity, child-focused activities and competence for living and coping with life (DBE, 2015: 7).

The NCF (DBE, 2015) also sets out six early learning development areas (ELDAs). These are:

1. **Wellbeing**, which includes the emotional, social as well as the physical aspects of children's development. Wellbeing is very important because when children are healthy, physically active and well nourished, they are motivated to learn.
2. **Identity and belonging**, which is closely linked to wellbeing. This is about personal development, social development, secure relationships and celebrating difference. The stronger the child's identity and sense of belonging, the more resilient the child will be.
3. **Communication**, which underpins all interactions. Most children are born with the ability to communicate. Verbal and non-verbal communication (and assisted communication for children with special communication needs) is extremely important. Children use many ways to communicate that go beyond words, phrases and sentences. Children are multimodal meaning makers; in other words they use many different ways to communicate– a gesture, a smile or an outburst.
4. **Exploring mathematics**, which is about children developing an understanding of how to solve problems, how to reason and how to use mathematical concepts in their environment. Mathematical concepts develop as children investigate and communicate their ideas about numbers, counting, shape, space and measurement.
5. **Creativity**, which refers to the exploration and production of new and useful ideas, and solutions to problems and challenges. To create is to invent and to find solutions by asking questions. The main purpose is to encourage children to be creative, imaginative individuals, with an appreciation of the arts and insight into the importance of critical thinking and problem-solving skills.
6. **Knowledge and understanding of the world**, which refers to children's immediate and surrounding environment. This includes their immediate physical surroundings (people, animals, vegetables and minerals of all kinds); the history of their own families and later on their neighbourhoods; the geography of their surroundings (eg hills, rivers, flat spaces, rocks, weather and climate) and the tools that they use such as pencils, scissors, cutlery, household equipment, as well as cameras, mobile phones and computers. Children are curious about the world. They grow in confidence when they are encouraged to show their knowledge and skills in practical ways.

To reiterate, the six ELDAs reflect a broadening of developmental domains as well as a shift in how these domains are viewed. The focus, as we have said, has shifted from an emphasis on each individual domain to learning areas where a number of domains might feature.

- Wellbeing, for example, does not only refer to the physical aspects of development, but includes social and emotional wellbeing as well as self-regulatory behaviours which are integral to the concept of holistic development.
- Creativity includes both cognitive as well as the physical domains of development.
- The inclusion of subject disciplines as early learning development areas such as Mathematics and Understanding the World (Science, History, Geography, etc) could draw, depending on how this is approached, on each of the domains.

Something to consider

To implement a quality early childhood curriculum, teachers still need a good understanding of the developmental domains (Chapter 3) in addition to good subject and pedagogical content knowledge (PCK) in order to be able to immerse children in a quality play-based curriculum. Water play, for example, draws on both mathematical and science concepts as well as social and emotional skills. The chapters in this book reflect these curriculum shifts and provide guidelines to help teachers implement excellent playful teaching and learning opportunities – in other words, playful pedagogy.

The table on developmental milestones (Table 3.4 in Chapter 3) reflects the shifts set out in the NCF. This table also provides guidelines on how to implement good contextually aware practice across different developmental domains. In so doing, it provides a way for teachers to bridge the gap between nurturing and care, and appropriate stimulation and learning in the early years; in other words, an integrated child-centred curriculum.

Try this out

Study the milestones of development in Chapter 3. Now look at the six ELDAs. Consider the relationship between the two. For example, ELDA 1 is wellbeing, both physical and social. Show how this ELDA could be addressed appropriately with, for example, a two-year-old child using the developmental milestones as a guide. Remember to look at the description given for each milestone as well as the implications for practice. Base your exemplar on the following example. We have based this example on a one-year-old. You need to expand on your example.

Posture and large movement	Meeting ELDA 1
Crawls on hands and knees, bear walks or shuffles, may walk alone (9½–17½ months)	Provide a safe environment where baby can explore
	Ensure there are no dangerous obstacles
Social behaviour and play	Place a toy that is visible to a child but outside their reach to encourage them to crawl or walk
Will put objects in and out of box/cup when shown; quickly finds hidden object	Child needs a very safe and secure environment
	Meeting ELDA 1
Plays pat-a-cake and waves goodbye, both on request and spontaneously	Offer toys where child can place them in and out of containers; pack or unpack cupboards, etc.
	Play repetitive games with child
Listens with pleasure to toys that make sounds; repeats activity that produces sound, for example repeatedly pressing a button	Children like repetitive activities
	Offer toys that make enjoyable sounds – squeaky toy, toys that can be banged or knocked against something else, for example a spinning top, drum

From an exploration of the NCF it will be clear that an ECCE curriculum is a dynamic guideline for teachers who are faced with decisions about how to plan and organise the learning day and how to interact with babies, toddlers and young children. A curriculum helps answer questions such as: 'How do I arrange the play space?'; 'What are appropriate resources for children?'; 'What is it that children need to know and be able to do?'; 'How do I manage children's behaviour?'; 'What do I need to know to facilitate quality care in education?'; 'How do I know that learning and development are happening?'; 'How do I find out what I don't know?'; 'How do I build a partnership with parents and other caregivers'? An appropriate curriculum should be flexible enough to accommodate differences in children's ability, and embrace cultural and contextual considerations, as well as incorporate any new ideas and happenings. It should also be flexible enough to respond to ongoing research in the field.

To summarise what we have addressed so far:

The implementation of an appropriate curriculum is an integral part of the teacher's overall programme quality and should address:

- the value of an integrated approach which emphasises whole-child development and learning
- the integration of different learning and development theories, including new perspectives such as the sociology of childhood
- the importance of a developmentally appropriate and culturally and contextually responsive approach
- the recognition of the importance of a play-based approach to learning and teaching

- the recognition that children are active, participatory learners who have voice and agency
- awareness of the essential nature of an inclusive approach that accommodates all children and their families
- observation and assessment of young children.

Something to consider

An ECCE curriculum includes everything that happens during the day (Gordon & Browne, 2008). It is the thread that links care and nurturing to teaching and learning, regardless of the ECCE setting. It informs decisions about content (chapters 11, 12, 13), how to organise the setting or learning environment (Chapter 7) and how to guide and respond to children's behaviours (Chapter 10) and the use of teaching strategies (Chapter 8), and the principles of assessment (Chapter 14). Also, it is important to bear in mind that all that is taught and learnt, regardless of whether it is intended or not, will impact children's understanding of the world in which they live. From a sociological perspective, this is called the hidden curriculum.

In brief, therefore, a curriculum is:

- what is planned and not planned
- what is visible and also what is not visible (eg the teacher's beliefs about how children learn)
- everything that happens during the learning day
- the understandings of the world that children gain even if the teacher did not make them explicit (eg that not everybody has the same amount of power).

It is the teachers' interpretation of the concept curriculum that will guide, sometimes almost unwittingly, their professional practice. In the next section we will explore the relationship between play, learning, teaching and the early childhood curriculum.

7.3 PLAY, LEARNING, TEACHING AND THE EARLY CHILDHOOD CURRICULUM

In chapters 2 and 3, we explored various theories in relation to learning and development. We have repeatedly emphasised that children learn through play and we have considered to some degree how that learning occurs; for example, Piaget says that children must act on things to discover their properties and possibilities. Children should, for instance, construct their own tower using big blocks and therefore discover for themselves what stands and what falls. That is one context for learning, but the actual concept 'learning' is much broader. We will now look at this in more detail, acknowledging how an effective ECCE curriculum provides excellent learning opportunities for young children.

7.3.1 Understanding learning

Learning refers to the gaining of knowledge or skills. According to the behaviourists, learning can be seen as a permanent observable change in behaviour brought about through the reinforcement of desirable actions. For example, a child who puts his toys away is rewarded with a sweet that he likes. He begins to associate tidying up with getting a reward, and the action becomes a habit. From a behaviourist perspective, learning occurs through instruction, memorisation and habit formation enhanced by conditioning. It occurs when the child interacts with the environment and is rewarded for appropriate behaviour (Mwamwenda, 2004)

From a cognitive developmental perspective, learning refers to discovering, constructing and developing deep insight into a specific concept. In other words, it refers to a shift or change in cognitive structures (in Piaget's terms 'schemata' and in Vygotskian terms 'working in the zone of proximal development (ZPD)'. If deep learning occurs, the person should be able to evaluate (examine something to determine its value), analyse (scrutinise), infer (conclude) and deduce (work out); in other words, develop and then apply higher cognitive skills or what Vygotsky (1978) called 'higher mental functions' to different situations.

Development and learning theories tell us that there are certain conditions that must be met if children are going to experience meaningful learning opportunities:

- Learning must be authentic (real). We therefore start with what we know about individual child and their interests. We begin with what they know and then build on that knowledge. For example, young children will learn what a dog is, but it is only when they go to school that they are taught that a dog is part of a larger group called mammals.
- Good learning builds on the children's everyday lives. We must connect what happens in the home to the ECCE centre. For example, the parents teach children about their culture, and the teacher should reinforce this learning by using relevant content and resources. For instance, the word the child uses for 'mother' in the home context should be used in the ECCE centre as well. Another example could be the eating utensils. Find out what the parents encourage the child to use and follow suit. Be sensitive to sharp contrasts between what happens at home and at the centre. Parent–teacher communication is critical to ensure that the norms at the centre do not make a child feel alienated.
- Learning must be rewarding or satisfying. Children become motivated when they succeed, and they succeed when they have sufficient time and appropriate resources to practise new skills and experiences. Being allowed to make mistakes is an important part of learning. Encourage children to persevere (try again). Encourage initiative and do not make a

child feel guilty for trying something new even if the end result is messy and essentially nondescript. Learning is a process – the end result is not important.

- Learning requires good basic health, both physical and psychosocial (see chapters 9 and 10).
- Learning makes use of all the child's senses.
- Learning requires children to move – they are sensory motor learners. Physical and motor development are closely aligned to other areas of development, both cognitive and social and emotional (see Chapter 3).
- Learning requires concrete apparatus and many opportunities for hands-on participation.
- Learning is best realised through an appropriate play-based curriculum.

These pointers should underpin any early learning curriculum.

7.3.2 Understanding teaching: a playful pedagogic perspective (see chapters 6 and 8)

The teacher is crucial in implementing an effective ECCE curriculum – a curriculum is only as good as the people implementing it. Teachers require content knowledge and the interpersonal skills to enhance adult–child interactions (connections).

7.3.2.1 Content knowledge

Teachers' content knowledge (see chapters 11–13) is a key element in determining learning outcomes for young children (Sylva et al, 2004). Subject knowledge, for example where the rain comes from, or whether the earth goes around the sun or vice versa, provides the 'stuff' or the content to explore, but detailed subject knowledge should not be the focus in ECCE. Appropriate content should be able to contextualise the skills, attitudes, concepts and language that we believe is important for young children to learn. For example, it is important that young children learn to brush their teeth, but understanding the underlying value of oral hygiene may well be too advanced for them when they are very young.

Something to consider

What knowledge do you think is important for teachers of young children to acquire?

Did you think of the following?

- Subject discipline knowledge such as local history, science, and knowledge of numbers and other basic mathematics concepts such as shape and measurement, etc
- Knowledge of how to manage an ECCE centre; for example how to establish a health-promotion centre and knowledge of the available referral services
- In-depth knowledge of child development and how children best learn, including how language develops and the basic structure of the language through which you are teaching as well as others you might use with the children.

Once you have studied this textbook you need to add other knowledges that you now consider, on reflection, important.

7.3.2.2 Good adult–child interactions (connections)

The interactions between children and adult are crucial in constructive development and learning. Warm, responsive, nurturing interactions are essential, and so too are interactions that promote sustained shared thinking (Sylva et al, 2004). Sustained shared thinking is when 'teachers and children work together in an intellectual way to solve a problem, clarify a concept, evaluate an activity or extend a narrative' (Duffy, 2006: 89).

Each ECCE setting is unique, and the curriculum must show this. Thus, teachers have to be reflective, understand theory and how it informs practice, and ensure that the unique needs and interests of each child are met through an inclusive, culturally responsive environment. So while there are many different approaches that can be adopted when implementing an early years curriculum, we need to focus on what is most important for young children and what they need to be doing at each particular stage of their development (see Chapter 3, Table 3.4). In this way, we will promote the optimal wellbeing, development and learning of all children in our care. According to Duffy (2006), through good teaching children acquire a number of important behaviours including the following:

- Being social, making attachments, being with others, sharing experiences, becoming flexible and independent, showing care for oneself and others and all living things, understanding that people have different needs, interests, views, beliefs, cultures and all should be treated with respect (see Chapter 10).

- Developing positive dispositions and attitudes, and a willingness to try new things and take reasonable risks, showing confidence and enjoyment, being able to be involved and to persevere, and to have a sense of pride in one's own achievements (see Chapter 10).
- Being able to communicate well though verbal and non-verbal means. Children should enjoy using words and speaking. They should be able to listen to others and respond appropriately in line with their age. They should be attentive and respond with enjoyment to stories, rhymes and song. They should be finding out about books and writing. Provide children with opportunities to respond to comments and questions (see Chapter 12).
- Being creative. Encourage children to be curious, and to investigate and explore their surroundings. They should have opportunities to question, experiment, note similarities and differences, see and construct patterns, and realise ideas through the use of a wide variety of materials (see chapters 11 and 13).
- Ensuring their own health and safety. Provide a healthy, safe and hygienic environment and encourage children to develop understandings of healthy practices with regard to eating, sleeping, exercise, dressing and undressing, hygiene (personal and environmental) (see Chapter 9). Provide opportunities for children to refine their movement skills. They increasingly move with greater agility and coordination, and handle tools and materials with increasing competence (see Chapter 11). If they feel safe and secure and are comfortable in their interactions with adults, they demonstrate a feeling of trust and belonging, develop a positive self-image and are able to stand up for their own rights. They feel comfortable within themselves (see Chapter 10).

Reflection

Do you have a warm and responsive relationship with the children in your care? Does your ECCE curriculum provide opportunities for them to develop the behaviours to which we have referred? Give three instances of routines or activities that have enhanced the acquisition of these behaviours and reflect on your relationship with the children during these times.

7.4 IMPLEMENTING A PLAY-BASED CURRICULUM

The curriculum is framed by guiding principles that have been informed by various theories of early learning and development. These guiding principles (which closely relate to the principles informing the NCF) are described in the sections below.

7.4.1 Holistic development and wellbeing

In this book, these domains have been categorised in a slightly different way to easily accommodate the nature of learning and development in babies, toddlers and young children (see Table 3.4). These categories are posture and large motor development; visual perceptual and fine motor development; speech, language and communication; social behaviour and play; and self-care and independence. This categorisation has emphasised important domains of development in young children, namely gross and fine motor development as well as language, social and emotional domains. The importance of the cognitive domain has not been forgotten; rather, the categorisation allows readers to understand how cognition is a thread that runs throughout these focus areas.

7.4.2 A culturally responsive, inclusive and integrated curriculum

Children do not come to school in a vacuum (Romero-Little, 2010). They have already had a wealth of experiences, many of them culturally based. The content of the curriculum should identify with their culture so that they remain motivated and keen to learn. Romero-Little (2010) argues that, when teaching diverse cultural groups, their community's indigenous knowledge should be central to the design of any educational programme. Though we acknowledge that all children play (play is a universal activity), many of the activities are culturally bounded, as we have already noted. It is important to accommodate both universal and indigenous play in the curriculum to enable learners to fit within the bigger community and also know their roots. Many indigenous games and activities also affirm the child's home language and culture, as well as possibly offering other children different experiences. All learning opportunities are thus informed by relevant cultural and contextual factors that help to bridge what is learnt in the home and the ECCE centre. In young children, learning is integrated. This means different aims and objectives could be met through any specific activity, be it child initiated or teacher guided.

Make sure all children feel welcome and are able to participate in the daily programme. Teachers should make sure that activities are differentiated and that there are suitable activities for all children. There is no such thing as a one-size-fits-all curriculum. Content and learning opportunities are tailored to suit the learning needs and interests of individual children.

7.4.3 Language as a tool for learning in a stimulating learning environment

The more interaction children have with language, the more they will use and understand it. We know children react to their mother's voice while in the womb. From birth onwards, children gradually master language by listening to speech, by reacting to sounds, through cooing, gurgling, babbling and then imitating sounds, and finally by speaking. Even though babies are not yet talking, it is crucial that they are spoken to. Language is critical for learning and for thought development, thus language acquisition in the early years is crucial for later literacy proficiency and academic success.

7.4.4 Responsive and caring adults who interact meaningfully with young children

Responsive teaching involves educators being deliberate, purposeful and thoughtful in their decisions and action. Intentional teaching is the opposite of teaching by rote or continuing with traditions simply because things have 'always' been done that way (DEEWR, 2009). Positive interactions between children and adults are crucial to promote intentional teaching.

7.4.5 Learning through play

Reflection

The fifth principle of learning through play takes us back to many of the features of play-based learning that we have already discussed. As you read, try to recall how this principle complements what has already been said.

Something to consider

Play is not a break from the curriculum – it is the curriculum. Neither play nor learning can be rushed; they are both processes that take time. A play-based curriculum is not a prescriptive one. It defies rigid learning outcomes because it is flexible, sometimes messy and creative, and under the control of the children (Lucich, 2011). Confident young players become lifelong learners who are capable of independent abstract thought, and who are able to take risks in order to solve problems and gain understanding (Elkind, 2007).

According to Moyles (2010), play in an educational setting should have learning consequences. Teachers need to know and make explicit what these consequences are and what children are learning in that particular educational setting. This is what separates play in an educational context from recreational play, which commonly happens at home. A quality ECCE setting will offer both these forms of play. Decisions around the percentage of time given to each one can be challenging and will depend to a considerable extent on the individual children's age and if they are in full day care. Very young children and those in full day care need space for both. Play can just be fun but it can also scaffold learning and remain fun.

7.5 REALISING THE CURRICULUM

Realising and implementing the curriculum includes knowing both the children's and the ECCE setting's context (eg socioeconomic, cultural, family makeup, etc); setting goals (aims and objectives – these are informed by the ELDAs and, of course, by the child); knowing what to teach (content – see chapters 11–13); planning pedagogies (methodologies) (see Chapter 8) including resources; and assessment (see Chapter 14). All these aspects require reflection by the teacher to ensure a relevant and effective curriculum. In addition, specific emphasis has to be given to the learning environment to ensure the promotion of optimal development and learning through the provision of quality play experiences. The environment can be intentionally planned in four main ways, which will now be discussed.

7.5.1 Creating playful learning spaces

The physical environment considers the use of space, the placement of furniture, and the provisioning of resources. Look at both the indoor and outdoor learning environment. The layout will differ for different age groups. Safety considerations, including supervision by responsible adults, are paramount for both in- and outdoor environments.

7.5.1.1 Indoor learning environment

Babies require cots and a nappy-changing area. Toddlers also require cots, possibly a nappy-changing area and also a facility for potty training. Both require a safe indoor play space. For older babies, mattresses, doughnuts or blankets on the floor might suffice. Toys are placed on the floor or hung above babies, and should be easily accessible. Toddlers will need more floor space as they will be moving – crawling, shuffling and some walking. Highchairs are helpful for feeding time. Hygiene is paramount throughout (see Chapter 9).

Older children will need appropriately sized tables and chairs, both when doing activities as well as for mealtimes. They also need sufficient floor space for other activities. Provide a carpeted area or carpet squares on which the children can sit for teacher-guided activities.

Provide sufficient storage space for toys and other learning resources. There should be a variety of equipment to keep all children occupied (see Chapter 6). Place the resources on low shelves so that they are easily accessible to the children. This also allows them to choose what they would like to play with. Provide a variety of different toys and equipment such as construction materials (posting boxes, blocks), manipulatives (rattles, threading games), puzzles, and games with rules such as dominoes and lotto (see Chapter 6).

Additional learning areas could include:
- a book area or corner for all age groups
- a creative art area
- a fantasy area for socio-dramatic play
- a music area for both listening to and making music
- a listening area (which would be a quiet area to encourage active listening)
- an interest table relating to the topic under discussion – this is an interactive table, meaning that children can touch and play with items on it and bring new ones during the week from home
- additional tables such as a nature table, a discovery or science table.

There should also be a storeroom so that additional resources can be safely packed away and rotated to provide variety for children.

Reflection

Consider how you will construct and present activities and materials so they are arranged in thought-provoking and inviting ways to encourage exploration, learning and inquiry.

7.5.1.2 Outdoor learning environment

There should also be a safe outdoor play area with a variety of toys and other equipment available. There should be separate outdoor play areas for babies, toddlers and young children. Ensuring a physically safe environment is essential. There should also be sufficient protection from the sun. The area should be securely enclosed, the entrance gates should all have safety catches, and all large equipment should be fixed to the ground. Equipment must be age appropriate and well maintained. This means it must be regularly checked to ensure it is child friendly.

Try this out

Make a list of the equipment you would include if you were planning an outdoor play area for babies, toddlers and young children. Include a rough layout of what you would place where in each of the areas.

Did you think of the following?
- Climbing frame with slide, monkey bars, etc
- Low swings –where children can be securely seated
- Old tyres securely dug into ground for children to crawl through or over
- Sandpit with tools such as buckets, spades, old plastic cups, containers, etc. Even tins can be used but make sure they have no sharp edges

Try this out

- Container for water play, such as a low water trough/large plastic bowl. Provide funnels, jugs and old plastic containers for children to pour water. Let them wear plastic aprons to help keep them dry. Make sure there is continuous adult supervision
- Wheel toys and other push and pull toys
- Sensory tray – add a variety of sensory equipment such as squeegee balls, cornflour (Maizena), bubble wrap, sawdust, miniature toy animals, etc
- Various bats, balls, hoops, skittles, ropes, etc, to add variety and enhance gross and fine motor development
- An easel for painting, which should be put out every day on the veranda with a variety of different coloured paints and brushes.

7.5.2 Creating the social and emotional environment

We have already pointed to the importance of secure, warm and trusting relationships so that children feel confidently supported in their explorations and risk taking. Assist children to make connections (interact) with others, develop friendships and regulate their behaviours. Together, children and adults set the emotional and social tone of the environment. Chapter 8 will explore various pedagogies that promote a responsive social and emotional environment. In Chapter 10, we will explore other approaches to support emotional and social development and wellbeing of children.

7.6 THE INTELLECTUAL ENVIRONMENT

At times children need to be left to play freely. There should also be times for intentional conversation, or a well-placed question or query that will extend the children's learning. The ability to create shared sustained conversations (Siraj-Blatchford, 2009) is the hallmark of effective early childhood teachers. There are also times when the teacher says nothing but merely observes while children make their own choices and explore independently.

The intellectual environment also talks to content. What is it that children need to know and do and value? The knowledge component will be the specific focus of chapters 11, 12, 13 and 14, and the skills component has been addressed in Chapter 3. Chapter 10 has a focus on social and emotional development, and addresses important values that should be acquired in early childhood.

7.7 THE TEMPORAL ENVIRONMENT: USE OF TIME IN THE ECCE SETTING

This explores how the teacher allocates the time available during the day to the different aspects of the daily programme. (See Appendix 7.1 for an example of daily programmes.) The programme will, of course, vary depending upon the age of the child. The teacher plans for three essential components which comprise the daily programme:

1. Routines
2. Teacher-guided activities or focused teacher time with babies, toddlers and young children
3. Child-initiated activities (free play).

The daily programme brings a balance and structure into the day. It ensures that children have their needs met as well as sufficient time for interaction, communication and stimulation. The time allocated to each component is flexible. Time allocations will also differ to meet the particular needs of each specific group of children.

7.7.1 Routines

Routines are the everyday activities that provide the framework in which all other activities are planned. They provide a basic structure to the day and therefore give children a sense of security – they know what is happening next. By following a specific daily sequence, children have a practical way of gauging time. Routines have other important functions related specifically to children's emotional and social development. Through routines related to such activities as nappy changing, toilet time, and feeding and snack time, children begin to develop some independence. They also begin to learn about self-regulatory behaviours – such as keeping the bathroom clean and tidy, washing their hands, and tidying up after themselves. Routines also provide opportunities for learning about hygiene and nutrition, and offer an initial introduction to important subjects such as sexuality. Boys, for example, will notice they are different from girls, and vice versa. They might want to know where they came from. Teachers should be prepared to answer these questions honestly (see Chapter 10).

Something to consider

Routines will be different for each age group. Think about nappy-changing, feeding and sleeping routines for babies (see Chapter 9). These will vary from the routines implemented for toddlers, which might include potty training, different eating times as well as specific nap times. Routines should be adjusted for older children to accommodate their increasing independence and competence in self-help and care behaviours. Routines must be flexible. Adapt them to suit individual children's needs and to meet other demands made upon the daily programme such as an unexpected visitor.

7.7.2 Teacher-guided activities

These are times when the teacher takes control of the group, often called rings or circle time. Teachers might work with large or small groups. For babies, this time could be used to interact one-on-one and provide stimulating activities, or the teacher might interact with a few children who are, for example, lying or sitting on a blanket.

The time allocated to rings also varies; the younger the children, the shorter the ring.

- Toddlers approximately 5–10 minutes
- Two- to three-year-olds approximately 10–12 minutes
- Three- to four-year-olds about 12–15 minutes
- Four- to five-year-olds about 15–20 minutes.

If children are attentive and obviously enjoying participating, the time can be extended. If a child does not want to be part of the ring, do not force him. If children have lost interest, end the ring. There is no point in forcing children to listen or to do something in which they have no interest. Developing their interests will enhance their learning. Trying to get them to focus on something in which they have no interest is, in fact, teaching them how not to learn. It is simply dampening their curiosity.

Ring times are planned interactions. The teacher usually has a particular aim or goal, and will decide on a specific methodological approach and resources to mediate the chosen content to the children. It is important to think ahead; teachers therefore should do specific written planning for their rings. See Appendix 7.2 for an example of a written plan. Some more ideas of written planning are given in chapters 11–13.

Rings have different foci that will differ according to the age of the children. Language (discussion), music and movement rings are examples of this. For older children there may be maths, perceptual and science rings. There is also a daily story ring where suitable stories are told to the children. Even older babies enjoy listening to a story and very young babies enjoy a song. Other enjoyable rings include show and tell, birthday rings and possibly a library ring where children are allowed to choose a library book to take home. Even toddlers can be encouraged to select an appropriate picture book to 'read'. The way teachers engage with children will differ according to their age. For instance, teachers will spend one-on-one time with babies, but will not do a ring for them in the formal sense of the word.

Something to consider

One way for a teacher to engage with a few babies at the same time is to place them in individual doughnuts (large round cushion with the middle indented where baby can be placed) or make use of a long 'snake-/caterpillar'-shaped cushion. This cushion could be curved with two to four children supported by the curves. The teacher could then interact with a few children at the same time.

During ring times, teachers facilitate learning. They do this by co-constructing knowledge with the children to develop their thinking, reasoning and questioning skills. This is therefore not a time when teachers simply instruct children. Through thoughtful suggestions and the asking of appropriate questions which generate sustained shared thinking, teachers encourage the active participation of children. Chapter 8 provides some ideas on how to support playful learning. The implementation of teacher-guided activities will be addressed in the relevant chapters, for example, 11, 12, and 13.

Try this out

Read the following case study. (See appendix 7.2 for more details)

You are teaching a group of younger children between the ages of three and four years, and exploring different modes of transport. This is a rural community where walking and riding in a donkey cart is still a popular means of transport. Your morning ring could explore transport, asking the children about ways in which they have travelled. Here is an outline of a possible discussion ring.

Settle the children with an appropriate song or rhyme such as 'The wheels of the bus' or **mbombela westimela** (about a steam train) or **ibhaysikili** (a bicycle).

Initiate discussion with the children, exploring the different modes of transport they have travelled on and others they may have heard of or seen.

Ask them how they came to the ECCE centre that day.

Listen carefully to what they say, encouraging them to elaborate if possible and perhaps ask other children if they have also travelled that way.

Then invite the children to look at the theme table, which ideally has some concrete representations of forms of transport such as a model car, bicycle, donkey cart and a pair of shoes. There should also be pictures of different types of transport taken, for example, from magazines or downloaded from the internet. These could include aeroplanes, trains and boats to extend the children's knowledge base.

Ask some children to briefly discuss the item they have selected, and invite others to add something if they wish, perhaps saying why or why not they like or don't like that form of transport. To include some active participation, allow the children to lie on their backs and move their legs as if they were riding a bicycle. Tell them the bicycle will now slow down and ask them to stop 'pedalling' and lie quietly on the floor to represent the end of the trip and a calming conclusion. Tell the children when you touch them (perhaps use a feather) they can get up and move to the next activity.

Keep the ring simple and short – the children are only three years old.

Reflection

What aspects of playful pedagogy can you identify in this ring? (eg sustained shared thinking and co-construction of knowledge.)

Would you present such a ring to babies or toddlers? Why or why not? How do you think you could adapt this ring, especially for toddlers? How would you best initiate teacher time with babies?

7.7.3 Child-initiated activities (free play)

Children need time to develop play themes and ideas, therefore allocate at least 45 minutes to an hour for a session of free play. When planning activities for children from birth to five years, it is important to consider their ages and stages of development as well as their observed capabilities. In other words, know the children (their needs and interests) in order to provide appropriate resources and materials that are both stimulating and challenging. In essence, this means providing a variety of different resources that offer different degrees of challenge in order to accommodate all the children. This is called differentiation and is an important aspect of an inclusive approach to teaching and learning.

As we have already said, all children, especially babies and toddlers, are sensory motor learners, therefore encourage movement. Sharman, Cross and Vennis (2000) assert that babies from birth to 24 months of age require the adults to be the instigators of movement since some children in this category are non-mobile and others are still learning to move or walk.

Try this out

Take babies and toddlers' hands in order to encourage them to play; move their legs; encourage them to crawl. Make sure the environment is safe.

The main resource that is needed for babies is sufficient space to encourage movement. Make use of rolling toys that will trigger movement in babies, and sturdy furniture that will allow them to practise pulling themselves up as they try standing on their own.

Toddlers are already mobile, so it is important to provide toys that will assist them to walk. For example, a large ball can motivate movement in a child, as can push-along toys. De Witt (2009) also suggests that teachers encourage the use of toys that have the potential to promote speech, as language acquisition is an important developmental domain. By the age of three to four years, children are gaining more control of both gross and fine motor skills, therefore a variety of manipulative objects (see Chapter 6) should be offered to them. In Chapter 6 we explored how to plan for, choose and design appropriate resources for different ages and stages of development. Remember to include indigenous and culturally specific games and toys.

It is important to consider cultural diversity. Different communities have different knowledge and ways of doing things (Khuphe, 2014). Children differ in terms of, for example, language, religion, culture and preferences. It is important to integrate indigenous knowledge into the curriculum of young children and to provide resources that are appropriate to each child's culture. This is called an additive approach; the child's home knowledge and context form the basis upon which new knowledge is built.

Reflection

Think about your particular cultural context. Write down some of the toys that you would provide for babies and toddlers in your setting. They should be both bought and handmade. How can you make sure that you provide culturally responsive activities for all children? What can you do to ensure that you have provided differentiated activities for the different age groups and competencies? Share your ideas with your colleagues.

Something to consider

The role of the teacher during child-initiated activities (free play)

Teachers should have good insight into the development and learning opportunities that play offers. As already mentioned (see Chapter 6), these opportunities include developing skills and abilities, providing occasions to cooperate, building self-esteem and self-confidence, learning to regulate behaviour, developing friendships, taking turns, resolving conflicts and solving problems, and developing knowledge and understanding of the world. During free play provide children with:

- a safe and stimulating supportive learning environment where there is continuous adult supervision
- adequate space and time to engage meaningfully in their play experiences
- sufficient and stimulating props and other resources and equipment to develop their play. Think of something different that you can introduce each day for the various groups of children, for example cardboard boxes on one day, funnels in water play on another, etc
- meaningful intervention where appropriate (remember the teachable moment, the co-construction of knowledge and the different elements in the play continuum).

In addition, the teacher should:

- take time to observe, document and assess learning (see Chapter 14)
- where relevant, consult with other teachers or parents to ensure that play opportunities are contextually and culturally responsive. Sometimes this means encouraging and giving children permission to play and make their own choices.

In other words, as the teacher you set the boundaries and create the context so that children are able to engage safely in quality free-play opportunities.

7.8 SUMMARY

In this chapter, we have considered the multifaceted nature of playful pedagogies and the role they play in a creative curriculum. We have discussed the daily programme and its components, and the need for teachers to be constantly reflective and alert in relation to contextual and cultural issues. One way to do this is to construct your own educational vision and use this as a guideline to inform your professional practice.

REFERENCES

DEEWR. 2009. *Being, Belonging and Becoming: The early years learning framework for Australia.* Barwon, ACT: Commonwealth of Australia. https://www.scirp.org/(S(351jmbntvnsjt1aadkposzje))/reference/ReferencesPapers.aspx?ReferenceID=1115526 (Accessed 3 April 2019).

Department of Basic Education (DBE). 2009. *National Early Learning Development Standards.* Pretoria.

Department of Basic Education (DBE). 2015. *The National Curriculum Framework from birth to four.* Pretoria.

De Witt, M. 2009. *The young child in context. A thematic approach.* Pretoria: Van Schaik.

Duffy, B. 2006. *Supporting creativity and imagination in the early years.* Maidenhead: Open University Press.

Elkind, D. 2007. *The power of play: How spontaneous imaginative activities lead to happier, healthier children.* Massachusetts: Da Capo Press.

Gordon, M & Browne, KW. 2008. *Beginnings and beyond: Foundations in early childhood education.* 8th ed. New York: Thomson Delmar.

Hoisington, C. 2008. *Let's play! Using play-based curriculum to support children's learning throughout the domains.* USA: Excelligence Learning Corporation.

Khuphe, C. 2014. *Indigenous knowledge and school science: Possibilities for integration.* Unpublished PhD thesis. Johannesburg: University of Witwatersrand.

Lucich, M. 2011. *Childcare healthcare program.* California: SAGE.

Mwamwenda, TS. 2004 *Educational psychology: An African perspective.* 3rd ed. Sandton: Heinemann.

Moyles, J. 2010. *The excellence of play.* Buckinghamshire: Open University Press.

Republic of South Africa (RSA). 1996. *The Constitution of the Republic of South Africa.* Pretoria: Government Printer.

Romero-Little, ME. 2010. How should young indigenous children be prepared for learning? A vision of early childhood education for indigenous children. *Journal of American Indian Education*, 49(1&2): 1–25.

Sharman, C, Cross, W & Vennis, D. 2000. *A practical guide. Observing children.* London: Continuum.

Siraj-Blatchford, I. 2009. Quality teaching in the early years, in Anning, A, Cullen, J & Fleer, M (eds). *Early childhood education: Society and culture.* London: SAGE.147–157.

Sylva, K, Melhuish, E, Sammons, P, Siraj-Blatchford, I & Taggart, B. 2004. *The Effective Provisioning of Pre-school Education (EPPE) project: Findings from pre-school to end of Key Stage 1.* Institute of Education: University of London. http://wwwdcsf.gov.uk/research/data/uploadfiles (Accessed 10 January 2009).

UNESCO. nd. *Local and indigenous knowledge systems.* New York.

Vygotsky, L. 1978. *Mind in society. The development of higher mental processes.* Cambridge, MA: Harvard University Press.

Appendix 7:1 Daily programme

We have presented a composite daily programme that provides a framework for babies, toddlers and young children. It can, of course, be adjusted to accommodate the different needs of the three age groups.

Times	Infants	Toddlers	Preschoolers
6.30 am – 8.00 am	Welcome: bottle if necessary	Welcome: free play in/outdoor	Welcome: free play in/outdoor
8.00 am – 8.30 am	Breakfast; diaper change	Breakfast and tidy up; diaper change/ potty offered	Toilet routine; breakfast and tidy up
8.30 am – 9.00 am	Nap time; manipulative toys – rattles, activity centre, etc	Morning ring (including morning greeting and songs, register, weather chart); potty offered	Morning ring (including morning greeting and songs, register, weather chart)
9.00 am – 10.00 am	Outdoor free play – swing seat; place babies in doughnuts etc; provide visual/auditory stimulation	Creative art Free play	Creative art Free play

Times	Infants	Toddlers	Preschoolers
10.00 am – 10.30 am	Baby games, rhymes and songs	Interactive songs and games	Outdoor free play
10.30 am – 11.00 am	Story time and language games	Snack Diaper change/potty offered	Toilet routine Snack time and tidy up
11.00 am – 11.30 am	Diaper change	Indoor/outdoor free play	Second ring (eg movement, music, perception, etc) Outdoor free play
11.30 am – 12.00 pm	Lunch/bottle	Story time and language games	Outdoor free play
12.00 pm – 2.00 pm	Naptime; gentle music	Lunch Diaper change/potty Nap time; gentle music	Story time Lunch Nap; gentle music
2.00 pm – 2.30 pm	Gentle wake-up time	Gentle wake up Potty/diaper change Books	Gentle wake up Toilet routine
2.30 pm – 3.00 pm	Bottle, snack if appropriate; diaper change and indoor play	Snack time and tidy up	Snack time and tidy up

➡

Times	Infants	Toddlers	Preschoolers
3.00 pm – 4.00 pm	Baby games, and songs and rhymes	Indoor free play (manipulatives, table/floor work)	Indoor/outdoor play Books, manipulatives, construction toys Art activity Organised outdoor games
4.00 pm – 5.00 pm	Outside play and swing seat	Outdoor play Diaper change/potty	Toilet routine Indoor/outdoor free play
5.00 pm – 6.00 pm	Indoor play; swing seat and baby doughnut	Indoor play	Indoor play

The programme is an all-day one to accommodate working parents. Children may start leaving from lunchtime.

Times are approximate; they will need to be adapted to suit the context and group. Remember to offer a block of time for free play – at least 45 minutes to an hour

Appendix 7.2 Example of an activity plan: language ring

Teacher-guided activity: morning (language) ring

Topic: Transport Age group: 3-4 years				
	Teacher	**Activity**	**Resources**	**Activity outcome**
Introduction	Ask children to sit in a ring Sing a song to settle children and gain their attention	Sing a song – *Mbombela westimela**		Children are encouraged to sit down and focus

➡

Topic: Transport		Age group: 3-4 years		
	Teacher	**Activity**	**Resources**	**Activity outcome**
Body	Ask: 'Can you tell me how you came to the centre today?' Ask: 'Who else has travelled this way?' Can you think of any other way you could have come to the centre? Ask: 'Who else has travelled this way?' Teacher: 'Do you know what sound a car (a truck, etc) makes?' Ask a few children to go to the theme table and select one mode of transport Make suggestions, if necessary, to support children Invite other children to also respond, eg 'Who else would like to say something?'	A few children have turns to answer the question. (They might say by car, taxi, with my daddy, etc.) Children offer their experiences of similar modes of travel Possible answers include walking, being pushed in a stroller, coming with a friend, etc Children all make the sound of a car – moving fast, slowly, a truck etc Children go up to the theme table and select an item. Each child comes back to his place and has a chance to talk about the item. While the child is speaking, the item can be passed around so that all the children can take a close look Once child has spoken, he returns the item to the table	Theme table: concrete items such as toy cars, motorbikes, trains, boats, etc Picture of different types of transport, eg children/ people walking, someone riding a horse, a donkey cart, etc	Children: • practise listening skills and answering simple questions • talk about their different experiences and also practise turn taking by waiting for their turn to respond • are given an opportunity identify to select and discuss different types of transport • have an opportunity • to make a choice and to give reasons for their choice • are given a chance to express themselves though using language

Topic: Transport Age group: 3-4 years				
	Teacher	**Activity**	**Resources**	**Activity outcome**
Conclusion	Say to the children: 'Lie on your back and move your legs as if you were riding a tricycle' (Remind children not to bump each other)	Children lie down, legs in the air and pedal. They move legs fast, then slow, fast, then slow, according to the teacher's suggestions		Children practise: • gross motor skills by moving their legs in a circular motion
	Say: 'You are very tired; you have had a long journey. You are now pedalling slowly, more slowly. You are coming to a stop' Using a feather, say: 'When I touch you, get up slowly and tiptoe outside' (calming conclusion)	Children pedal more and more slowly. When they stop pedalling, they place their legs on the floor and lie still, breathing deeply. When children feel the feather, they get up quietly and tiptoe to the next activity	Large feather	Children have an opportunity to lie back and relax

* **Words *for Mbombela westimela***

Mbombela, mbombela westimela × 2
Wenzani lo mama, encish abantwana ×2

Chapter 8

Supporting playful teaching and learning: a pedagogy of possibilities

Lorayne Excell and Vivien Linington

In this chapter we consider:

- different ways of communicating with babies, toddlers and children (verbal and non-verbal) to support playful learning and teaching along the teaching–play continuum
- pedagogical possibilities for babies, toddlers and young children
- the organisation of play spaces as a pedagogical strategy to support play-based learning
- the grouping of children as a pedagogical strategy
- self-reflection as a tool to enhance playful teaching approaches.

8.1 INTRODUCTION

New approaches to how we think about children and how we ensure contextually relevant learning environments means we have to re-examine how we think about teaching. This means we have to think more carefully about what we do and say and, of course, how we do and say it. Teaching approaches based on 'one size fits all' have been increasingly challenged as a result of shifts in how we think about children and the early childhood curriculum (MacNaughton, 2003). If we are to deliver quality early childhood care and education (ECCE) provisioning, it is crucial for teachers to reflect on their practice to try to ensure that they implement an inclusive, culturally responsive play-based early learning curriculum where both playful teaching and learning are foregrounded (Wood, 2013).

In chapters 6 and 7, we explored play-based pedagogies and how to set up a quality early learning curriculum including the learning environment. We now consider some of the ways of teaching, with the focus on playfulness.

8.2 PLAYFUL TEACHING APPROACHES

Playful teaching approaches are based on intentional teaching that contains an appealing, fun-based element. This includes setting up high-quality learning environments, encouraging child participation, and joining in, when appropriate, in the children's activities. Skilful teachers 'read' children and the learning context, and teach accordingly. Playful teaching approaches include all the general teaching strategies (MacNaughton & Williams, 2004) as well as some contemporary approaches. It is for teachers to decide which strategy or strategies are the most useful at any given time. The way and frequency with which these strategies are used determine how teachers position themselves on the teaching–play continuum (see Chapter 6). This also determines their attitude to participatory, interactive learning that will impact their approach to care, nurturing, teaching and learning in the ECCE setting.

Something to consider

General teaching strategies include and skilful teachers know:
- when to tell and instruct children
- when to demonstrate or model behaviour
- when to describe or discuss objects or events
- when to facilitate or suggest
- when or how to question so that they begin to understand their children's thinking.

In addition, skilful teachers know the following:
- When to help, encourage, praise and give feedback
- When to differentiate the level and type of task
- When to include movement, dance, song, rhyme, story and drama
- When to listen
- When to remain silent and allow children to play on their own
- When to group children, and when to allow individual activity
- How to position furniture and equipment to support teaching and learning.

Some contemporary approaches include:
- scaffolding and mediation
- documenting learning through recordings, photographs, videos, etc (MacNaughton & Williams, 2004).

All these strategies allow the teacher to interact in a responsive and positive way with young children. Notice how they reinforce the idea that all learning and teaching happens throughout the daily programme: routines, free play and teacher-guided activities (see Chapter 7).

Reflection

Study the general teaching strategies mentioned above. Write down the type and frequency of each teaching strategy that you have adopted throughout the day, and position each one on the teaching–play continuum. Continue to do this exercise for one week. Draw up a teaching–play continuum similar to the one referred to in Chapter 6, ranging from teacher-directed/-guided activities though varying degrees of collaboration to child-initiated activities or free play.

Analyse your findings. What type of teacher are you? Do you engage playfully with the children, or do you instruct too often and suggest too infrequently, for example. Would you describe your pedagogy as being a play-based one? Is it participatory, culturally relevant, inclusive and responsive? Could you articulate the why behind the choices you make? In other words, do you teach intentionally prioritising the children's care and wellbeing, or are you perhaps, without realising it, following a teacher transmission model?

Use your continuum as a reflective tool as we now explore a number of teaching strategies. As you study these different strategies, you will realise that they are closely connected. In fact, there should be a seamless flow from one strategy to another. Often, you will use more than one method at any given time to support the children's learning.

8.3 PROMOTING A PLAYFUL APPROACH IN THE IMPLEMENTATION OF GENERAL TEACHING STRATEGIES

General teaching strategies can be incorporated in playful and sometimes different ways for the various age groups. The context sometimes determines the strategy, sometimes it is the chosen activity and sometimes the specific content or skill to be developed or learnt. As a teacher, ask, 'Is the chosen strategy the best for this particular situation?' Consider also the time taken to use this strategy, the number of times it is used and the type of voice you adopt. The choice of words, the way you modulate your voice as well as your body language go a long way to determining if the chosen strategy is playful or not. These sorts of choices will be informed in part by your emotional quotient (EQ) which we considered in Chapter 4.

8.3.1 Demonstrating

To demonstrate is to show how something is done. Demonstrating becomes useful when, for example, the teacher shows children how to use a piece of equipment safely, such as a hammer, or how to play a musical instrument correctly, such as a tambourine or shaker. Appropriate tasks can be demonstrated to children of all ages along the play continuum.

Babies continually try to make sense of the world. They hit, bang, suck and grasp different items. They intentionally imitate others. The teacher can show babies how to do things to make different sounds or movements. For example, give baby a toy and show him how to press the button so that it squeaks. Sheila is a *toddler* who has just started at the centre. She is almost three and does not know how to cut with a pair of scissors. The teacher demonstrates how to hold them and how to cut a piece of paper. She also tells Sheila, 'We place the offcuts of paper in the wastepaper basket.' She then gets up and puts the paper scraps into the wastepaper basket. Thandi is *four*. She is playing in the fantasy corner. She wants to cover her head like her Islamic friend Moeniera. The teacher takes a scarf from the shelf and demonstrates to Thandi how to do this.

By intervening and showing children how to do certain tasks the teacher prevents them from becoming overly frustrated, saying 'I can't' and giving up. Purposeful, sensitive intervention encourages children to persevere, which is an important learning disposition.

When demonstrating a task,

- give clear, unambiguous verbal instructions
- break the task into small sequential (successive or progressive) steps – young children can only follow one or two simple instructions at a time
- plan in advance and make sure you know the task well yourself so that you do not confuse the children by showing them incorrect steps (eg if you cannot play the game yourself, you cannot show the children what to do)
- provide children with lots of opportunities to practise the new task or activity.

Make sure the children are focused on you before you demonstrate a skill or technique. When children are involved in creative activities or their own play that is giving them satisfaction, they will not give you their full attention.

8.3.2 Describing

This means using words to explain how something or someone looks, feels, moves, sounds, smells or tastes. A description is like a word picture. We use it as a teaching strategy to help children make increasingly finer and more complex distinctions between events, people and things in their daily world; to distinguish, for example, between sweet and sour. Good descriptions draw children's attention to the specific characteristics or features of an object or an event (MacNaughton & Williams, 2004). They also help build the children's vocabulary.

We often make use of description in an ECCE context. Children ask plenty of questions and our answers are descriptive. Know how to answer questions effectively. This means you must have some content knowledge about topics being explored. If, for example, children are interested in garden creatures, you need to do some research so that you can answer their questions accurately. Do not be reluctant to tell the children if you do not know the answer. Suggest that you both try to find out. Go to the local library, Google information, ask someone who has specialised knowledge, but find the appropriate information. Through description you can encourage sustained shared learning by asking good open-ended questions (another teaching strategy). Make sure descriptions are used as part of conversations to encourage children to respond and interact with adults and share what they already know about a subject or event. Descriptions are often used in teacher-guided activities, but can also be helpful in joint teacher–child playful interactions (connections) and managing routines. With older children it can also be a useful evaluative tool. For example, 'Sipho please bring me the red pencil'. You are assessing if he knows specific colours.

Something to consider

Remember, children are active learners and require concrete learning materials in order to learn effectively. Provide a suitable learning environment and relevant learning materials that encourage children to explore and then describe what they found. For example, you might say to a **baby** who has grasped a fluffy teddy bear, 'This is a soft cuddly teddy' (describing how the bear feels). A **toddler** might be playing in the sandpit. You say, 'Busi, you look very busy and determined to put sand in the bucket' (describing how the child looks and acts). Three-year-old Jan has taken a bite out of his sandwich. He says, 'Yum, I like this.' You reply by describing what he is talking about. 'I can see you do. You have eaten your sandwich so quickly. You must like peanut butter. What does it taste like?'

8.3.3. Encouraging, praising and giving feedback

When you encourage a child you are reassuring them and supporting their actions (responsive teaching). Encouragement is useful when the child is having difficulty with a task or experience. Through appropriate encouragement, children are helped to persevere, try again, and ultimately acquire new knowledge or skills. Encouragement might be verbal or non-verbal.

Verbal encouragement includes making helpful suggestions. For example, a child who is scared to jump down from a standing position on a solid branch can be encouraged to sit on the branch and then push himself off with you standing next to him. This means there is still a sense of achievement. Words must extend and not inhibit (prevent) learning. Encouragement should extend children's thinking. 'That is a splendid construction' praises the child's efforts but does not extend the child's thinking (MacNaughton & Williams, 2004). If you follow the comment with, for example, 'I wonder how else we could make this car', this encourages the child to think of other ways of completing activities. Encouragement happens while children are busy with a task.

Praise is usually given when children have completed the task or part thereof. Remember, praise must be deserved and meaningful. If children have not done anything praiseworthy, do not praise them. Praise is individually earned. Praise new achievements or consistent effort. Praising children for tasks that require little effort from them does not motivate them to try harder. There is no uniform standard that becomes praiseworthy. Individualising praise is useful. For example, Johnny, who is usually a very fussy eater, eats all his food at lunchtime. This is worthy of praise. Matsie, who always eats well, finishes all her food. Though this is commendable, it is not necessarily praiseworthy. But today if she has eaten a few carrots and has never done this before, this then becomes praiseworthy.

Use praise sparingly and try to praise all children, not only the 'good' children or those who do well. You might sometimes be reluctant to praise naughty or difficult children. They are often the children who are never praised; they only always seem to get into trouble. Make a special effort to praise these children. Through careful observation, you will always find something to praise in each child. For example, if a child rarely completes an activity, when the child does so, remember to praise his efforts. For example, Jabu hardly ever sits still and listens to the story. Today he has been engrossed and has not moved, listening carefully to all that has been said. This becomes praiseworthy. Ask him what he found so interesting about this story, which might help you to manage his behaviour more effectively in the future.

Non-verbal encouragement usually happens when some physical help is provided. It takes many forms and can take a moment or involve longer periods of time. For example:

- The teacher moves the toy a little way away from the baby lying on her stomach to encourage her to wiggle towards it.
- The teacher stands next to the slide and holds the toddler's hand to encourage him to slide to the bottom.
- The young child is concentrating hard to place the puzzle piece into the correct slot. The teacher looks at James and smiles to let him know he is progressing well.

Small amounts of encouragement can make the difference between children experiencing a happy and satisfying day or a frustrating and disappointing learning experience.

Feedback is giving the child information before, during and/or after an activity. It might be verbal or non-verbal (ie a word or a smile). Feedback supports children's learning when it provides them with clear, specific information that helps them think about what to do next. Feedback should be appropriate to the child's learning style and developmental abilities. Verbal feedback is most successful when you describe what the child is doing rather than placing a value judgement on it.

> **Find out more**
>
> Verbal feedback describes specific events, interactions and behaviours. For example, Nkosi is trying to make a sandcastle. He is patting down the sand in his bucket using the spade, but is not managing to get it to form a shape. You say that he is doing it the right way and he is almost there. By pressing down the sand more firmly, however, he may get the sandcastle to stand. Acknowledging what the child is achieving is a useful technique to positively reinforce desirable behaviour, and supports the development of positive self-esteem. It is similar to praise, but a little bit more detailed. Explicit feedback helps children understand how their learning is progressing and what else it is they can do to successfully extend their activities (MacNaughton & Williams, 2004).
>
> Think of the last time you gave feedback to a child? Into which of the categories we have discussed do you think it fitted?

8.3.4 Facilitating and suggesting

As a *facilitator* you guide, making access to learning clearer. To facilitate well means you have to observe carefully to ensure that learning opportunities are appropriate to the children's needs and interests. Good facilitation also requires teacher reflection. Ask yourself, 'How can I make the task more accessible for children without too much intervention?' and 'How can I adjust the learning environment to better support positive learning experiences?' Facilitation includes organising space such as moving furniture to enable sufficient play space, timing specific activities or providing appropriate resources. These are ways of supporting children's learning, and possibly redirecting their attention to alternative possibilities. MacNaughton and Williams (2004) note that facilitation is a particular approach to teaching and learning emanating from theories like Piaget's.

Babies and toddlers enjoy repetitive play. They also practise the many new motor skills they are acquiring through repetition. Teachers facilitate motor movements by providing sufficient space for gross motor movements and by offering a variety of different equipment that enables children to practise these skills. For example, two toddlers are trying to grab the same toy. The teacher says, 'Mary, why don't you bounce the bright green ball?' Mary looks at the ball the teacher is holding, and the teacher has averted a conflict situation by redirecting Mary's attention to another object.

Suggesting is to offer advice, give ideas or make a recommendation. A suggestion infers that there is a better or more effective way of doing or saying something. By suggesting, you are giving the child a choice of whether or not to follow the advice given. There are times, of course, when you need to tell rather than suggest such when a young child is toddling towards a hot stove. Many teaching techniques include suggestions. For example, if you suggest, 'Have you thought about moving the plank to one side because …?', that is both a suggestion and a question. If you want the children to move the plank to the side you would tell them, 'Please move the plank to the side so that the other children do not hurt themselves.'

Many suggestions start with phrases such as the following:
- You could try it this way …
- If you do this … then … would happen.
- This might help ….
- What about …?
- Have you thought about …?

Make positive suggestions. Children are much more likely to follow them. Suggestions help children achieve their goal without becoming too frustrated and the teacher becoming too controlling. It is a way of encouraging perseverance. They also help to redirect children's attention. Suggestions also help to enrich children's play. For example, in the fantasy corner a suggestion by the teacher might lead to more enriching play experiences. They could also counter bias; for example, if two girls are playing 'house house' and resist a boy joining them because of his gender, you could suggest that a different role for him, such as setting the table.

Suggestions also help children relax and regain control of their emotions. For example, suggesting children breathe in deeply and breathe out helps to refocus them. You could also suggest that they march like soldiers or plod like elephants as this often helps to calm them and redirect their energy. Remember self-regulation – gaining increasing control over your emotions – is a process that continues throughout childhood, and in fact life.

Try this out

When a two-year-old in your care is throwing a tantrum, have you considered how would you handle it? How do you think suggestion would help resolve the situation?

Have you considered that instead of simply ignoring her, you try to redirect her attention by suggesting she chooses an activity of which she is particularly fond? Later when she has calmed down, you can talk to her about getting angry and try to give her some words to use to express how she is feeling rather than simply screaming. Try a phrase like, 'I feel angry because …'; 'It hurts me when …'; '… makes me cross' to redirect her attention (see Chapter 10).

8.3.5 Telling and instructing

Telling is to order, to let know or command. Instructing is a definite statement telling someone to do something. Telling is a way of providing children with information. It has its place in pedagogy and should not automatically been seen in a negative context. It is a conventional teaching technique when someone with knowledge passes this on to someone else. It is often associated with direct instruction and often referred to as 'chalk and talk'. You can tell children about ideas, concepts and reasons for doing things. You can also tell children to do (or not to do) things. When you tell children something, use clear, easy to understand language. Avoid words that might be unfamiliar to them. Make sure they understand what you have said. When telling, children might listen more carefully if the message is supported with non-verbal gestures.

Telling allows little opportunity for participation. However, it does sometimes have a place in teaching. For example, when the children are playing in the sand pit and begin to throw sand at each other, you tell them to stop it immediately. Later you can talk about why they should not throw sand, but do not use telling too often as this might result in passive learners with inhibited voice and agency. We tell when it becomes important to give children information.

Opportunities to tell include, for example, the following:

- Safety issues, for example 'Do not touch the hot stove – you will burn your hand.'
- To inform children about something that they would have difficulty in finding out for themselves, for example, social conventions, reading from left to right or not to masturbate in public (MacNaughton & Williams, 2004). Young children often tend to play with their private areas out of curiosity and because it gives them a sense of pleasure (see Chapter 10).
- To instruct children how to use a new tool or piece of apparatus. You tell (and show) a toddler, 'This is the way you hold a pair of scissors' or tell a young child to 'place the Prestik on the back of the piece of paper so that you can stick it firmly onto the table'.
- Telling a baby what you are doing. 'I am going to change your nappy, wash my hands and then give you your bottle.'
- Supporting children to deal with a disability. For example, you have an Albino child, Thabo, in the group who is visually impaired and cannot go in the sun. After checking with parents, the teacher can explain the situation to the other children and tell them how to interact with the child to accommodate his specific needs.
- Story telling – which is an extremely effective form of telling and should happen daily in the ECCE centre. Stories can be told or read to children from babyhood. Reading to children as a teaching technique is used to help them make meaning of their world and the surrounding world. Through story, many a sensitive issue such as losing a parent can begin to be addressed.

> **Something to consider**
>
> Never tell if there is an opportunity for children to discover something for themselves. Telling, like demonstrating and modelling, is positioned at the teacher-directed point on the teaching–learning continuum. Do not develop an over-reliance on these approaches.

8.3.6 Listening

Listening means paying attention and concentrating on what you hear. If you are listening well, you should also think about what it is you have heard. Hearing is simply the act of perceiving sound by the ear. Listening, however, is something you consciously choose to do. Listening requires concentration so that your brain processes meaning from words and sentences.

As a teaching strategy, you listen with the intention of understanding what children say and what they mean. Listening encourages children to have a voice and supports interactive pedagogies.

> **Find out more**
>
> Listening to children is important for the following reasons:
> - It is a way of making them feel valued and included.
> - It allows the teacher to decide if and when to intervene in children's play; if you listen carefully you will have a better idea of when children would benefit from adult guidance, support or control.
> - Good listening allows you to develop an emergent curriculum based on children's interests and needs. By listening carefully, you will be in a good position to respond to and extend their interests.
> - By listening carefully to children, you encourage them to develop their thoughts and explain their ideas to others. It helps build their vocabulary and contributes to language development.
> - Good listening also allows children an opportunity to express their questions, worries and anxieties after suffering a traumatic event. In South Africa, many children are subjected to, for example, various forms of violence and need to be encouraged to express their understandings of what it is they have seen, heard or experienced.

We all need to improve our listening skills. Some ways of doing this include the following:
- Making time to listen. It is estimated that children in an ECCE centre spend between 25 and 50 per cent of their time listening to staff (MacNaughton & Williams, 2004). If teachers are so busy talking, what opportunities do children have to make their own choices and to be

heard? This is especially important if you believe children's needs and interests should underpin the curriculum.
- Waiting after you have asked a question or given an instruction so that children have time to process what has been said and think of an appropriate response. Ask yourself, 'How often do I answer my own questions?'.
- Thinking about what it is that children have said and then responding to their ideas thoughtfully.
- Getting down to their physical level. When you can easily look children in the eye, it is much easier to listen to them and to respond appropriately.
- Writing down what children have said, when appropriate. This is a wonderful way of documenting children's thoughts. It is particularly helpful when children are describing their drawings and other works of art. It can guide your planning of the emergent curriculum.
- Not looking at or using your cell phone when listening to children.
- Modelling active listening skills to children. When children (or adults) are talking to you, do not become distracted, preoccupied or forgetful. One way is by looking at children when they talk to you. Stop what you are doing, and look and listen to them. Children do realise when you are not listening to them.

Reflection

Read the following true incident and then think about whether you see yourself in this scenario.

Andrew's mother was a busy working mother. Often when Andrew talked to her, she was busy doing something else. One day, in distress, he said, 'Mommy, look at me'. When she turned around and bent down to comfort him, he grasped her face in his two hands, stared into her eyes and started talking to her.

As we have already said, children do not always listen well. This can be because of a variety of reasons such as high ambient (surrounding) noise levels, too much visual stimulation, too many distractions, etc. It is therefore important to 'teach' children to listen carefully and to model listening behaviour to young children.

Try this out

There are a number of activities that promote listening. In the 'do this, do this, do that' game children are required to copy the actions that accompany 'do this', and ignore the ones that go with 'do that'. Children can also close their eyes and listen to and then talk about and name the noises they hear outside their playroom. Ask them if they think the noise is coming from near or far. When you are talking to children, sometimes whisper and then ask them what you have said.

8.3.7   Modelling

Modelling is a process through which children copy or imitate the behaviours of others. Many social behaviours as well as self-discipline are acquired through observing others, often adults, model appropriate behaviours and values (see Chapter 3). Modelling is useful to help build socially inclusive playrooms, to encourage children to play cooperatively, as well as to solve problems.

> **Important point for teachers and parents**
>
> Modelling can also increase children's interest and desire to read and write, so it is important for parents and teachers to model reading behaviours for children. There is evidence that children coming from print-rich homes are more likely to develop successful reading skills (Hill, 2006).

Teachers and parents should draw children's attention to the behaviour being modelled. This increases the likelihood of them adopting the modelled behaviour. In other words, teach by example. If you want children to share, create opportunities where you can model sharing to the children (MacNaughton & Williams, 2004). Decide on the values and behaviours you want children to acquire. During a staff meeting, teachers can collectively decide on the behaviours they want to model for children, for example conflict resolution, sharing and respect for others. Then, as a team, the teachers plan specific times and/or activities when this behaviour can be modelled to children.

Something to consider

- Remember to be alert to unplanned and incidental teaching moments when the desired behaviour can be modelled. Remember also that young children are not natural sharers. Sharing is a learnt social norm.
- Stories are a good way of making certain desirable behaviours explicit. Choose appropriate stories that depict the behaviour you want the children to acquire. Reinforce the message in the story by modelling that particular desirable behaviour at appropriate moments.
- Be prepared to model behaviour over time. Children need to have lots of good role modelling if they are to acquire the desired behaviour(s).
- Children are more likely to model the behaviour of people whom they like and respect.
- The desirable behaviour is more likely to be adopted through the use of positive reinforcement (praise or some other form of recognition etc)

8.3.8 Positioning of people and equipment

This teaching strategy considers how you position yourself near to other individuals, groups or objects, and how you position equipment and resources to support the children's learning. It includes all play spaces, indoors as well as outdoors (see Chapter 7 on creating the learning environment). The overall aim is to create a safe, secure, pleasant and productive learning environment where responsive intentional teaching happens.

> **Find out more**
>
> When placing objects and equipment consider the following:
> - **The social organisation of the learning environment.** Does it encourage children to interact and collaborate with each other?
> - **The physical space.** Is there sufficient space for meaningful engagement with various activities? Are there sufficient play spaces or is the activity set out in such a way that it causes overcrowding and results in frustration in children? Is the equipment placed within easy reach of children? If children are in groups, can each member access the materials? Is there sufficient space to encourage individual learning, opportunities to stand, sit, kneel; for floorwork and tablework, etc? Consider the indoor–outdoor flow – is best use made of both these learning spaces?
> - **The time constraints.** Consider the planning of the daily programme. Is it planned to be flexible, to offer children a balance and variety of activities? For example, how much time is allocated to teacher-guided and free-play activities; is the teacher–play continuum taken into account?; is there a large block of time for child-initiated activities, etc?

Positioning people

Where do you position yourself? As a teacher, you need to consciously plan how you will position yourself so that children's learning experiences are enhanced. Thoughtful positioning enables good listening, communicating, suggesting, questioning and holding enriched conversations with children. All these strategies enhance meaning-making opportunities. When you are near to children, you can easily make use of teachable moments – you can be responsive to individual children's interests and engage in cooperative interactive learning moments and sustained shared thinking.

> **Something to consider**
>
> Do not underestimate the other aspect of positioning, which is linked to power. Where and at what height you position yourself in relation to the children sends out implicit messages about who is more powerful (MacNaughton & Williams, 2004). Position and power are interlinked.

Reflection

Have you thought about the relationship between positioning and power? Do you, for instance, sit at the same level as the children when you tell a story? Do you sit near to a particular child or group of children? Think about why you choose this particular position. You may, of course, be placing a child who is disruptive near to you as a management technique. When do you invite a child to come and sit near/next to you? Simply by repositioning some children, you often change the group dynamic and change behaviour patterns. Potential conflict can be averted, for example, by standing in between children who are about to irritate each other. Children pay better attention and become more compliant. Where do you position visitors? Does the choice of position influence children's interactions with you and/or each other? If so, how? Do you unwittingly enforce gender power by always grouping the boys together and letting them leave the playroom first or by referring to sports as 'boys' sports' and 'girls' sports'?

8.3.9 Grouping

As a teaching strategy, grouping involves taking decisions about when to bring children together to enrich their learning. There are different ways of grouping children, which include the following:

- Formal groups, which are often teacher-guided activities and planned to meet a specific learning outcome. Formal groups include:
    - large groups, which usually occur when the whole group comes together, for example during a planned ring such as morning discussion, story, music and/or movement ring.
    - small groups, which occur when four or five children come together for a specific activity. Science and perceptual-motor activities are sometimes offered as small-group activities. The teacher works with a small group of children exploring a specific skill, for example visual matching, auditory recall or exploring different tastes. The other children are able to play independently, doing, for example, free drawing, puzzles or construction. Remember, however, while your main focus will be on the one group, you must still keep an eye on what is happening elsewhere. Visual art activities, for example making a collage, though not usually a formal teacher-guided group activity, can also be offered as a small-group activity.

    Small groups can be randomly chosen or set up according to age and/or stage of development. Multi-age groups allow both younger and older children to come together. Though this type of grouping is not common in South African ECCE centres, think about using it occasionally. Multi-age grouping offers a different dynamic, encourages flexibility and is responsive to children's individual needs. It can also encourage peer-to-peer learning (see Chapter 3), as well as enhancing social skills. Research has shown that multi-aged groupings in a fantasy corner allow for peer scaffolding and promote social learning. They also decrease discipline problems and increase cooperative problem solving among children (MacNaughton & Williams, 2004).

- Mixed culture and gender grouping, and inclusive playrooms, support the development of multicultural learning as well as positive interaction between peers with and without disabilities. Staff should explicitly model prosocial behaviour for the children as well as provide opportunities for them to spontaneously explore cultural diversity.
- Informal groups, which arise spontaneously during the day. Members of the group are flexible and usually determined by the children. Examples include being involved in fantasy play, or the teacher reading a book to an informal group of children who have gathered in the book corner.

8.3.10 Supervision

In any ECCE setting, adults act *in loco parentis*. This means that they have to ensure the care and safety of all children in the same way that a reasonable parent would be expected to do, thus supervision is continuous and ongoing. The principal plans the daily programme with supervision of all areas in mind. Place teachers so that all areas and children can be seen at all times. Do not sit with your back to the majority of the children.

Find out more

Where there are high-risk activities, for example water play, make sure an adult is always nearby as babies and toddlers can drown in a very small amount of water if they land face down in something even as small as a basin.

Can you think of other potentially dangerous situations where supervision is essential? Did you think of some of the following?

- Allowing children to use sharp instruments such as gardening tools or knives
- Animals in the vicinity that might bite, sting or scratch children
- Using heat sources in, for example, a science activity on liquids and solids
- Avoiding activities with babies and toddlers that make use of small items such as beads that they could put in their mouths and choke.

Remaining near to children gives them an extra sense of security. You can promote feelings of wellbeing in children by interacting with them on a frequent and regular basis, smiling in approval, and frowning or shaking your head if they are doing something inappropriate.

8.3.11 Questioning

When we ask questions, we are trying to find out about something or encourage a specific type of behaviour. Questioning means we word a sentence in such a way as to enable us to gather information from the listener (MacNaughton & Williams, 2004). As teachers, we might be seeking a specific answer or prompting children to think about something, to reason or to solve a problem. We might be able to prompt them to reflect briefly on something they have just done to another child, such as snatching his toy. It takes time to learn how to ask children good questions that support learning.

There are two types of questions – closed and open-ended. Each of these should be phrased in such a way that it places demands upon the children's cognitive skills, their language skills and the need to go beyond what they already know. The ability to question both ourselves and the actions of others is an integral part of active citizenship, the seeds of which are planted in ECCE.

- Closed questions, often called yes/no questions, tend to seek a specific response based on what children know or want. They ask children to remember or recall what they have been told or experienced. Examples include, 'Can you tell me how many legs an insect has?'; 'Do you remember who came to visit us yesterday?' Closed questions definitely have a place in learning and in assessment. Asking children a closed question about a story they have been told can indicate if they have understood it. However, if the teacher asks too many closed questions about things that the children know nothing about, this could shut down learning because they cannot answer any of the questions and may well feel inadequate. Closed questions are often those that require only a one-word answer, or a yes/no answer. They do not necessarily encourage children to think deeply about an issue, encourage them to speak or explore their understanding of the why behind issues or events.

- Open-ended questions are more probing and assume there is no right or wrong answer. They allow for alternative answers and encourage children to think and offer their own opinion. Open-ended questions often stimulate the imagination and are useful, and can provide insight into the sense children are making of their social and natural worlds. They encourage language because a one-word answer will not suffice. They encourage children to be interested in an event or person or object, and promote reasoning and problem-solving skills.

    Examples of open-ended questions are the following:
    - How do you think…?
    - Why do you think this happened?
    - What else could we do?
    - How did you feel when Sean took your toy?

- Where else could we look for ...?
- If you were X what would you have done?
- Would you have liked this story to end in a different way? Why?

Find out more

When asking questions, use short sentences and make them simple. Use words the children can understand. Ask one question at a time and give them a few moments to think of a response. If a child gives an incorrect answer, do not shut him down by saying an outright 'no', or immediately ask another child to answer. Rather, gently let him know that the answer is not correct. Perhaps you could say, 'Umm ... not really', or make use of prompts to help the child reach the correct answer. Questions such as 'Have you thought about?' or 'Remember yesterday Charlie said ...?' etc, lead the child to offer an alternative answer. Or you can say, 'I think there might be another reason – who has a suggestion?'

If you ask the group a question, do not let everyone shout out the answer as this can become chaotic. By reminding children not to shout out, they begin to realise they have to take turns and that they cannot all talk at once. One way to prevent all children from answering at the same time is to start with a name, 'Jabu, do you ... ?'

Avoid:
- answering your own questions
- repeating the same question until children answer it
- encouraging children to chorus answers
- asking questions that require a yes/no response – this does not encourage language development
- asking too many questions. Research has shown that sometimes making a positive comment is more likely to elicit a response from children than always asking a question. Instead of asking, 'Tell me about your painting'. say, 'I like the bright blue sky'. Children often then tell you why they made it bright blue (MacNaughton & Williams, 2004).

Try this out

Choose a short story that is suitable for young children. Draw up at least four open-ended questions that would give you insight into how a young child has made meaning of the text. You can also make up your own story that relates to the reality of the children in your care.

Something to consider

Children, of course, also ask their own questions, which provides valuable insight into how they are thinking. Respond to children's questions with warmth and enthusiasm. This makes children feel that their question has been valued and was worth asking.

8.3.12 Singing and rhyme (see chapters 11 and 12)

These refer to making musical sounds or using words rhythmically. Singing is a particularly powerful tool in early learning, and is valuable for a number of reasons including:

- the development of listening skills
- promoting language acquisition
- the development of early mathematical concepts
- providing immense joy and a sense of pleasure.

Singing should happen throughout the day (during teacher-guided activities, routines and free play). It is also emphasised during certain teacher-guided activities such as music or music and movement rings. Singing helps with transitions (moving from one activity to another), and songs help children learn the daily routines. Use song to indicate a routine such as wee-and-wash or tidy-up time. Teachers can make up their own songs and chants using familiar tunes. For example, a well-known tune in the ECCE context is 'I hear thunder' which is sung to the tune of *Frère Jacques* ('Brother John'). You can change the words to suit any situation or context. For example, when it is tidy-up time you could keep the tune and change the words to:

Time to tidy × 2

Tidy now × 2

All of us together × 2

Pick up this, pick up that

Try this out

Take a tune that you are familiar with and adapt the words to fit one of the routines in your daily programme.

8.4 SOME ADDITIONAL STRATEGIES

Apart from general teaching techniques, there are also some identified additional strategies that work particularly well with young children (MacNaughton & Williams, 2004). These are gaining in popularity and have been fuelled by alternative constructions of children (see Chapter 2). They enable us to view children as competent, capable beings who have a voice in their learning context and provide a respectful space for adults to listen to what they have to say.

8.4.1 Scaffolding

A scaffold is a temporary structure used as a support during construction. Similarly, during a child's construction of knowledge, scaffolding can be used to enable the child to move through the ZPD to a higher level of functioning (see Chapter 3). The term 'scaffolding' was introduced to education by Jerome Bruner, who had been influenced by the work of Vygotsky. It explains how a more knowledgeable other can support a less competent person, usually a child, to become more knowledgeable. The social environment and mediation provide the scaffolding. Language, verbal or non-verbal (body language), is a major mediatory tool or what Vygotsky called a psychological tool. The many teaching strategies already mentioned can all be part of a scaffolding process, for example encouraging, suggesting, describing and reminding. The success in scaffolding lies in social relations and the use of mediational means such as language to suggest possibilities that fuel cognitive development (Pritchard, 2005).

Try this out

Read the following case study.

It is free play, and Yael is struggling to build a tower of blocks. You can see that she is becoming frustrated. You come and sit next to her and show her how to place the bigger block first and then place a smaller block on top of the first block. You ask her to try for herself and see what happens. Her construction stays put and you ask her, 'Why do you think that the tower has not fallen over?' Yael says, 'Because of the big block on the bottom.' You then say, 'Yes, your tower will always be more secure if you place the larger block at the bottom.' Yael then continues to build the tower by herself. In scaffolding, as children become more competent and achieve their goal, the scaffolding is gradually withdrawn until they are able to perform the task themselves.

Observe the children and note a similar situation where scaffolding would enable the child to move to the next level of competency or understanding.

Scaffolding in practice can play a role in the co-construction of knowledge.

8.4.2 Co-construction of knowledge

This methodology draws on constructivism and social constructivism. Children explore, discover and build or construct their own knowledge, and thereby make their own meaning (see Chapter 2). Piaget believed that young children are primarily sensory motor learners who learn through active engagement with their physical environment. They are hands-on learners and need concrete objects to facilitate their learning. Vygotsky (1978) also believed that children are active learners who construct their own knowledge, but an essential element is the social context in which the learning occurs. Language is the mediational means through which this learning happens. Children become knowledgeable and are able to give meaning to their world by negotiating meaning with others. Co-construction therefore depends on children being active, participatory learners, but it is the collaborative nature of learning that underpins the idea of co-construction of knowledge as being an effective teaching strategy (MacNaughton & Williams, 2004; Sylva et al, 2004).

Find out more

Through co-construction, children learn how to pose problems and solve them with others. It helps to extend children's current level of understanding and the articulation of this in any area of development. Co-construction affords the teacher an opportunity to provide children with an appropriate explanation for why things happen, and include the children's ideas in the process. Research has shown that knowing why something happens is what makes learning powerful. It is the 'why' behind the 'what' that is pivotal. This, of course, means that the adult has to have accurate content knowledge and know how to use mediational means to scaffold this information to further the children's learning. To construct knowledge means that children require a wide range of media and materials through which to express their understanding of the world and through which to share their understandings with others. Teachers also need to listen to and watch, and interact with children as they attempt to represent their meaning to others.

Babies are not yet talking or actively moving from place to place, but they do explore the world using their senses. Offer babies an environment where they can touch, move, listen, feel, taste and smell to afford them opportunities to explore their environment, construct understanding and provide teachers with opportunities to listen and interact with them to help further their understandings of the world. Babies may not yet have expressive language, but they can demonstrate their responses in a variety of other ways.

Toddlers are beginning to move and actively enjoy exploring their world using their senses as they move from place to place. Provide a range of appropriate toys, suggestions, questioning as well as positive non-verbal interactions to support toddlers and extend their thinking. For example, give toddlers a variety of objects such as blocks and balls. Make a slope using a plank which is leaning against a box and encourage them to experiment and find out which objects slide and which roll. This is encouraging early mathematical thinking.

Young children can be encouraged to explore ideas, a specific topic or a theme that interests them and to share their interpretations and understandings with others though visual art, movement, dance and music. For example, if children are exploring trees by discussing what a tree looks like and sharing specific aspects, they can draw/paint the tree. or they can be encouraged to express through movement how trees move in the wind or in a big storm, etc. Through playing musical instruments, they can express their understandings of the different sounds trees can make depending upon the weather. Teachers listen, suggest, encourage and support children to explore and express their understandings of the concepts being investigated (MacNaughton & Williams, 2004).

8.4.3 Documenting

Documenting is a process of gathering, putting together and organising information about an event or issue. As a teaching strategy, documentation provides a written or pictorial representation of children's learning. It often focuses on a specific process or event. As part of overall planning, documentation has long been a way of recording information about children and of programme outcomes. We make use of written observations, activity plans and daily programmes to record what happens during the learning day. Documentation as part of the Reggio Emilia approach has led to considerable research. The Reggio approach has shaped current understandings of documentation in the early learning context. Documentation is based on teachers observing children's learning, recording or documenting this learning, and then acting upon the findings (see Chapter 14).

Something to consider

It is best to document children's learning when they are absorbed in interesting projects worthy of documenting. Increasingly, there is a recognition of including children's ideas in the decision-making process of what to document. In other words, teachers are being encouraged to recognise the children's competence, agency and ability to make good choices and participate in decision making. There are different ways of documenting children's learning such as the following:

- Taking photographs of children's drawings, models, paintings, constructions or playing in a fantasy area or on outdoor equipment (today, documentation is easy because we can make use of smartphones and tablets, as well as digital cameras)
- Making written observations of children's work including the language they use (this is more like traditional observation)
- Audio-recording children's comments and conversations
- Making overhead transparencies of children's representations
- Video-recording the process and products of children's learning
- Collecting a portfolio of children's work.

Some examples of documentation are as follows:
- **Babies** could be videoed when gazing at and following the mobile hanging above their crib.
- **Toddlers** are playing in the sandpit. They have been given yoghurt tubs of different sizes, a few large plastic spoons and a sieve. The teacher takes photographs of the different constructions they make.

- **Young children** are drawing. The teacher asks them about the drawing and then writes what they say at the bottom of the page. James, aged three, made a lot of vertical round squiggles on his paper. When asked about the drawing, he said, 'This is Dorothy being blown by the whirlwind.' The teacher later discovered from James's mother that he had been to see *The Wizard of Oz*.

Documentation can help teachers and parents reflect on the teaching and learning in the ECCE centre. This allows for a useful visual trail and enables teachers to note children's progress. If the centre has the resources, photographs can be placed on a 'wall' and a visual picture of all learning during the year can be created. If teachers are able and choose to do this in their playroom, they must ensure that all children are represented equally. Photographs can also be sent to parents using a smartphone.

Remember, that any sharing of information must be ethically acceptable, and that pictures or recordings of what children say or do cannot be shared without the parents' or guardians' permission.

8.4.4 Empowering

Good pedagogy that encourages voice and agency can be seen as enabling or empowering the young child. In general terms, 'empowering' means giving or delegating the power of authority to someone else. The person with power does something to enable those who do not have any power to become more powerful (MacNaughton & Williams, 2004). It usually refers to the transfer of political, cultural, economic and social power to people who, because of injustice and/or inequality in a particular society, have had little or no opportunities to take control of their own lives and to participate more equally in society. The overall aim of empowerment is to promote greater social justice. MacNaughton & Williams (2004: 274) state that 'put simply people are empowered when they have the resources and the independence to direct their own lives in ways that are free from discrimination and oppression'. In an ECCE context, empowerment can be seen as helping someone to become stronger and more confident.

As a teaching strategy, empowerment involves giving children the power or ability to make some of their own choices; for example, do they want a polony or peanut butter sandwich?; are children able to decide in which learning experiences they would like to participate? This can be easily achieved during visual art activities. When the teacher sets out sufficient play spaces and briefly discusses the options with the children, they can make their own choice of where they would like to be. They also have the freedom to move between activities. Obviously ensuring children's safety must always be an important consideration.

Something to consider

By allowing children to make choices the teacher provides children with opportunities to:
- take increasing responsibility for their own care and learning
- continue learning with an enhanced sense of self-worth, identity, confidence and enjoyment
- learn through their own strengths and interests
- discover useful and appropriate ways of finding out what they want to know
- understand their own individual ways of learning and to be creative
- self-regulate their own behaviour.

Find out more

Empowerment as a way to combat social inequality and injustice stems from the work of Paulo Freire, a Brazilian educator who argued that education always has political and social implications and consequences (Freire, 2003). He believed that all educators have a moral, social and political responsibility to become involved in education for social transformation in order to create a more just and equal social order. Teachers therefore need to understand that knowledge is socially constructed and how some knowledge-based practices could be seen as unjust and oppressive for some children and their family, for example blatant gender discrimination; only boys allowed to play with a soccer ball.

What is your understanding of fair in your context? Would you consider it fair, for example, for all children to have exactly the same number of blocks to play with at any specific time?

Is there, in this situation another way that you could promote fairness?

To empower children, MacNaughton and Williams (2004) suggest that teachers:
- decide what skills or attitudes children need to acquire to experience greater control and participation in their own learning. According to Derman-Sparks (1985, cited in MacNaughton & Williams, 2004), these skills include:
  - helping children feel good about themselves
  - encouraging children to participate as much as possible in all aspects of the programme
  - helping children to interact positively with each other
  - teaching children to think about fairness and to solve issues relating to it
  - helping children to stand up for themselves
  - building children's capacity to think about issues and solve problems.

- choose teaching and learning strategies that enable children to achieve greater control over their own learning
- choose content that is compatible with greater equity (fairness) and social justice issues. For example, reflect continuously on your language policy and your attitude and activism in relation to religious and cultural practices, gender stereotyping and children with disabilities.

Reflection

As a teacher, critically reflect on your curriculum content. Is it just and empowering? For example, does the curriculum promote tolerance and acceptance of difference and diversity such as different family structures and lifestyles? Are you actually an agent of change when faced with social injustice which manifests as discrimination, bias and prejudice? Does your content and practice promote acceptance of racial diversity and seek to break gender stereotyping? Do you teach about fairness and the normality of difference? Do stories, rhymes and songs promote positive attitudes towards diversity? If they do not, either discard them from the repertoire or adapt them. Do you help children to stand up for themselves when injustices occur?

For examples of additional critical questions that can be used to reflect on your practice, go to the following website: http://www.education.sa.gov.au and type in the name 'Glenda MacNaughton'.

Remember many parents also require support to become more empowered so that they can better interact with the ECCE setting and support their children's learning. As a teacher you should be a promoter not an inhibitor of self-esteem in all your ECCE centre relationships.

8.5 SUMMARY

The focus in this chapter has been on how the teacher can use pedagogical strategies to optimise the caring, nurturing, and teaching and learning experiences of young children. We have stressed the importance of varying your approach, documenting what has happened and empowering the child and others in the ECCE setting. We have also highlighted the importance of reflection and the necessity for an awareness that the messages you send, often unwittingly, can be 'read' in a very different way from the way they were intended. For example, the exclusion of a child from an activity on safety grounds may come across as bias or prejudice if not properly addressed. Often it is a small gesture like a smile or a nod of the head that becomes the appropriate strategy for managing behaviour or affirming a decision taken. The role of language as a mediational means is pivotal. Think carefully about the words you use and your communication style.

REFERENCES

Freire, P. 2003. From pedagogy of the oppressed, in Darder, A, Bolyondano, M & Torres, RD (eds). *The critical pedagogy reader.* New York: Routledge Falmer. 57–68.

Hill, S. 2006. *Developing early literacy: Assessment and teaching.* Victoria: Eleanor Curtain Publishing.

MacNaughton, G. 2003. *Shaping early childhood.* Berkshire: Open University Press.

MacNaughton, G & Williams, G. 2004. *Teaching young children: Choices in theory and practice.* Berkshire: Open University Pres.

Pritchard, A. 2005. *Ways of learning. Learning theories and learning styles in the classroom.* London: David Fulton.

Sylva, K, Melhuish, E, Sammons, P, Siraj-Blatchford, I & Taggart, B. 2004. *The Effective Provisioning of Pre-school Education (EPPE) project: Findings from Pre-school to end of Key Stage 1.* Institute of Education: University of London. http://wwwdcsf.gov.uk/research/data/uploadfiles (Accessed 10 January 2009).

Vygotsky, L. 1978. *Mind in society. The development of higher mental processes.* Cambridge, MA: Harvard University Press.

Wood, E. 2013. The play pedagogy interface in contemporary debates, in Brooker, E, Edwards, S & Blaise, M (eds). *The SAGE handbook on play and learning.* London: SAGE.

Chapter 9

Nurturing care: a pathway to health

Joan Orr, Lorayne Excell and Vivien Linington

In this chapter we consider:

- various health policies that should be in place in an ECCE setting
- the promotion of good health practices relevant to the young child
- designing and implementing a health programme in an ECCE centre/setting
- the relationship between health and holistic development of the young child.

9.1 INTRODUCTION

The first few years of life provide the foundation for the healthy growth and development of the young child. Research over the past 20 years has emphasised the importance of brain growth and development as a crucial determinant for physical, emotional and social health (Aboud & Yousafzai, 2016: 242). We are reminded that early deficits in prenatal care, as well as problems with nutrition, illness, abuse or lack of psychosocial stimulation, may have long-lasting effects on children who might subsequently never reach their full adult potential. As adults working with this age group, it is our responsibility is to ensure that babies and young children have the best possible start in life.

The focus of this chapter will be on the various policies and procedures which should be in place to ensure the health, safety and nutritional wellbeing of young children in early childhood programmes. It is beyond the scope of this chapter to deal with maternal health and pregnancy issues, although it is acknowledged that these too have an important impact on the health of the young child.

9.2 KEY LEGISLATION IN SOUTH AFRICA FOR THE PROVISION OF SAFE AND HEALTHY CHILDCARE

This section will briefly mention some of the key legislation relating to standards required for the safe and hygienic care of children in ECCE settings. Legislation is continually being amended and this information should be regularly checked for accuracy.

1. The Children's Act 38 of 2005 and Children's Amendment Act 41 of 2007 legally regulate the establishment of ECCE centres – called 'partial care facilities' in this Act (DSD, 2006; RSA, 2008). These Acts protect the rights and best interests of children and promote their wellbeing. They provide for the registration of ECCE programmes and centres, and delegates this function to local authorities for implementation. They also, through regulations, (Regulations, Annexure B, Part I and II), prescribe norms and standards for programmes and centres as well as procedures for the reporting of suspected child abuse.

> A useful reference to the Children's Act is: Berry, L, Jamieson L & James M. 2011. *Children's Act guide for early childhood development practitioners*. Children's Institute, UCT and LETCEE. Cape Town: University of Cape Town.

2. The National Environmental Health Norms and Standards for Premises and Acceptable Monitoring Standards for Environmental Health Practitioners. Notice 1229 of 2015. National Health Act 61 of 2003. Annexure A, section 2 sets out the standards for childcare centres. The standards are required for the issuing of a health certificate for the operation of an ECCE centre. It specifies requirements such as indoor and outdoor space, hygiene and safety, toileting facilities, water supply, storage, medical care and sick-bay facilities. Each registered childcare centre should have a health certificate prominently displayed – this is issued by an environmental health officer and is valid for one year, after which it must be renewed.
3. The Occupational Health and Safety Act 85 of 1993 requires employers to provide a safe and healthy work environment for employees.
4. The Foodstuffs, Cosmetics and Disinfectants Act 54 of 1972 has regulations governing the general hygiene requirements for food premises and the transport of food. The issuing of a certificate of acceptability for food premises should be prominently displayed if food is prepared, stored or served at an ECCE centre.

Another important document which is not an Act but is a useful guide for parents and health caregivers on how to raise a happy, healthy child is the Road to Health booklet issued by the Department of Health. It is given free of charge to all new parents and can be accessed at: file:///C:/Users/00100574/Downloads/road%20to%20health%20booklet%20(2).pdfroad

This booklet gives advice on how to raise happy, healthy children. It gives a record of a child's expected growth and development, and other issues such as good nutrition, protection from disease and injury, and what constitutes appropriate early stimulation and nurturing of children as they grow and develop. It is used by health workers to ensure that all children get the care that they require at the correct time. It also provides for health workers to note down a child's growth and development pathway; the immunisations given to the child; and a range of other advice for parents on how to support the ongoing healthy development of their child.

When a child is admitted to an ECCE centre, you should ask to see their individual Road to Health record and note if there are any omissions such as incomplete immunisation. The Road to Health chart should inform the development of the centre's health and safety policies and the implementation thereof.

9.3 THE RATIONALE FOR A HEALTH AND SAFETY POLICY FRAMEWORK FOR CHILDCARE

Babies and toddlers being cared for in groups are at a greater risk for infections than older children because their immune systems are not yet fully developed, and they still explore objects with their mouths. They also have minimal control over elimination while still in nappies, have poor personal hygiene habits and may have incomplete immunisation status. In addition, where large numbers of children are grouped together, germ contamination of the environment is facilitated.

It is important for childcare staff to understand the common modes of transmission of harmful organisms (germs such as viruses, bacteria, etc) so that they can clearly understand the need for specific policies and procedures in childcare settings to prevent, where possible, this transmission.

There are four main methods of germ transmission in childcare settings:

1. **Transmission through the air** where respiratory droplets are spread through coughing and sneezing. This transmission can be minimised through regular handwashing, proper tissue disposal, good ventilation inside the building, the prevention of overcrowding, and the exclusion of children and staff from childcare if they have communicable illnesses. It is also important to keep immunisations up to date and ensure the thorough cleaning of surfaces and objects which are touched with hands or 'mouthed'.

2. **Blood transmission** where there is contact with blood or blood-contaminated body fluids. This can be minimised by using careful universal precautions when dealing with injuries and blood spills, which includes the use of disposable gloves for hand protection, proper disinfection of blood-contaminated body fluids on communal surfaces, and careful disposal of blood-contaminated waste. All cuts or injuries on adults and children should be covered with a waterproof dressing.

3. **Oral–faecal transmission** which occurs through contact with faeces. Transmission can be minimised through impeccable toileting and nappy-changing procedures and regular handwashing after toileting or nappy changing and before any food preparation.

4. **Direct contact** with infected skin or objects. Transmission can be prevented by daily cleaning of all surfaces that are frequently touched by hands, preventing the sharing of personal items like facecloths, towels and bedlinen, the covering of any open injuries or infections, and the proper disposal of contaminated items.

A coordinated approach is necessary to ensure that childcare occurs within a safe and hygienic environment. Policies and procedures exist to reduce the spread of disease-causing germs within the ECCE environment.

9.4   HEALTH AND SAFETY POLICIES IN ECCE CENTRES

Any health or safety policy should be contextualised within the national legislative and local sociocultural requirements and should be checked annually by a knowledgeable person with both early childhood and health expertise. The policy framework used in this chapter is adapted from the Model Child Care Health policies developed by the American Academy of Pediatrics (AAP, 2014).

Individual policies should be developed for each of the sections below, which clearly stipulate the reason for the specific policy as well as the action required (the what, how, where, when and by whom).

9.4.1. Environmental hygiene issues

9.4.1.1 Environmental design

There are some important design criteria that help reduce illness in childcare settings. These include providing sufficient space to prevent overcrowding; surfaces, equipment and toys which can be easily cleaned; sufficient ventilation; separation of food preparation areas from nappy-changing and toilet areas; and well-designed toilet and nappy-changing areas where there are facilities for handwashing and the cleaning of potties.

9.4.1.2 Cleaning and disinfecting

Regular cleaning and disinfecting of surfaces and objects is required to keep high-risk areas safe so that germ transmission is minimised. This applies particularly to food preparation areas, toileting and nappy-changing areas, play areas for babies and toddlers, and play objects used by babies.

If a systematic cleaning policy is followed, this will control most potential outbreaks of gastrointestinal and other communicable diseases (eg listeriosis – a food-borne bacterial illness which specifically affects pregnant women and people with impaired immune systems).

> Cleaning is needed to remove dirt and grease from surfaces before the surface can be sanitised or disinfected with a chemical solution to remove germs.

Something to consider

Cleaning and disinfecting usually requires a two- or three-step process – firstly, wash the surface with soap or a safe commercial cleaning product; next, rinse with clear water; and lastly, disinfect with a suitable disinfectant. It is important to check the specific instructions of the product used and to use one that leaves no toxic residue on surfaces.

An effective and economical disinfectant solution to use is a fresh daily mixture of a 1:100 dilution of hypochlorite (household bleach) and water – 5 ml bleach in 500 ml water (one teaspoon of bleach to two cups of water). Bleach is effective against most common organisms and, if used in the proper dilution, should not cause any damage to clothing.

No ammonia-based general cleaning products should ever be mixed with bleach as this will release toxic fumes. Environmentally friendly cleaning solutions are commercially available which only require a one-step process, but these are costly.

If mops are used for floor cleaning, then separate labelled mops are required for the baby room, toilets, kitchen and the rest of the centre. These should be clearly labelled, and disinfected in a bleach solution daily.

Table 9.1 shows the recommendations for a general cleaning routine.

Table 9.1 General routine cleaning guide

Area/Item	Clean	Rinse	Disinfect	How Often
Nappy-changing surface, potties and toilet seats	Soapy water spray 5 ml in 500 ml water	Clear water	Bleach spray 1:50 dilution	After each use or toilet routine
Floors	General cleaning product	Clear water	Bleach in water 1:100	Clean 1–3 times a day (depending on area)
Dustbins	General cleaning product	Clear water	Bleach spray 1:50	Daily

Area/Item	Clean	Rinse	Disinfect	How Often
General cleaning of surfaces (door handles, gates, taps, basins, sinks, cots)	General cleaning product	Clear water	Disinfect hand contact surfaces with bleach spray 1:50	Daily (more often during an outbreak or if dirty)
Children's tables, chairs	General cleaning product (full strength for marks, if necessary)	Clear water	Food tables sprayed with 1:50 bleach solution	Before meals and after art or messy activities
Baby toys	Soapy water	Clear water	Spray with 1:50 bleach solution	After use (daily)
Kitchen counters and cutting boards	Wipe counters with soapy water. Wash cutting boards	Clear water	Bleach spray 1:50 solution	Before and after every use
Fridges	General cleaning product	Clear water	Bleach spray 1:50	Monthly or more often if ice build-up
Microwaves	General cleaning product	Clear water	–	After each use
Crockery and cutlery	Dishwashing liquid		Rinsing water with 1:100 bleach dilution	After each use
Lockers	General cleaning product	Clear water	Bleach spray 1:50 solution	Weekly or more often when soiled
Walls	General cleaning product	Clear water	–	As needed

Area/Item	Clean	Rinse	Disinfect	How Often
Windows	Window cleaner	–	–	Monthly or as needed
Cot and bed linen, fantasy clothes and soft toys	Washing machine	–	–	Weekly or more often if soiled
Cushion covers	Washing machine	–	–	As needed – monthly
Dishcloths, kitchen	Washing machine or by hand with laundry detergent	Water	1:100 bleach sanitising solution	After each use – at least daily
High cleaning (windowsills, fans, heaters, etc)	General cleaning product	Clear water	–	Weekly or more often if needed

9.4.1.3 Dustbins, refuse removal and pest control

Dustbins containing waste food or contaminated body fluids and nappies are a potential source of bad odour and pest infestation.

- All dustbins (indoor and outdoor) containing contaminated waste should have close-fitting lids.
- Dustbins should be emptied often and disinfected daily.
- Nappy-disposal bins should preferably be pedal-operated so that hands do not touch their lids when opened.
- All dustbins should have plastic bin liners so that staff's hands do not touch the contents when emptying them.
- Small plastic bags should be available in staff toilets for sanitary towels or tampons before they are placed in the toilet dustbin.
- Pest infestation (cockroaches, flies, ants) can be minimised by proper disposal of food items in waterproof, covered containers.
- Pest-control should be done over weekend or holiday periods when children are not present at the centre.

9.4.2 Personal hygiene

9.4.2.1 *Hand hygiene*

Effective handwashing is one of the most successful methods of preventing the spread of disease (Azor-Martinez et al, 2018). Stringent handwashing has been shown to reduce diarrhoeal diseases by 50 per cent and reduce parental work absences and absenteeism of both staff and children (Kotch et al, 2007). Each centre should have a clear policy which specifies when hands are washed, how they are washed and who needs to wash hands.

It is important that water is not reused between children when hands are washed. Where no running water is available, the use of an alternative system such as a plastic drum or container with a tap, or a 'tippy tap' (plastic bottle on a rope that sprinkles water out of holes in the lid when tipped over) is recommended (RSA, National Environmental Norms and Standards 2015: 35).

Centres should also prevent the recontamination of hands during drying by using disposable paper towels or non-shared towels for both staff and children.

If alcohol hand sanitisers or wet wipes are used, a similar drying procedure must be followed. Washing with soap and water, however, is still the preferred method except in emergency situations where water is not available.

Who must wash hands?

All adults and children in the centre should wash their hands regularly.

The following guidelines apply specifically to adults and should be adapted to include children when appropriate.

When?

On arrival at work in the morning

Before handling food, feeding bottles or feeding a child

After wiping noses, faces or buttocks, or touching body fluids

After doing any cleaning or touching pets

After visiting the toilet, changing a nappy or helping a child with toileting

Before and after attending to an injury or removing gloves

Before and after giving medicines

➤

Who must wash hands?

How?

Wet hands with clean water and apply soap (liquid soap preferred)

Wash all parts of hands for 15 seconds (top and palms, between fingers, fingertips and wrists)

Rinse hands well with clean water

Dry hands on a clean towel or disposable towel (no sharing of towels)

Avoid touching the tap by turning it off using the same paper towel

Apply hand cream if required

When to use waterproof gloves

To protect an adult who has an injury or eczema on hands or who is pregnant (this is because pregnant women might be more susceptible to contracting certain communicable disease from young children)

When a child has diarrhoea or an oozing nappy rash

When dealing with any injury

When cleaning up blood-contaminated body fluids

9.4.2.2 Nappy changing and toileting areas

Oral–faecal contamination of nappy-changing surfaces and toilets is a common source of diarrhoea in childcare settings. To prevent this, it is important that:

- surfaces used for nappy changing should be waterproof, and be cleaned and disinfected between each nappy change
- nappy-changing areas should be separated from any food-preparation areas
- a procedure should be in place to prevent cross-contamination of clean nappy-changing supplies such as jars of cream and wet-wipe containers
- soiled nappies should be disposed of hygienically
- adult and child hands should be washed after the procedure
- staff who change nappies should have some means of clothing protection (eg disposable plastic aprons) if they also handle food
- potties must be cleaned hygienically after each use to prevent contamination of toilet areas and basins
- items like mops or other cleaning materials used in the toilets may not be used for cleaning in food-preparation areas.

> **Reflection**
>
> Think about the nappy-changing practices in your ECCE centre and whether they comply with the criteria we have just discussed. Where, for example, do you store each individual baby's clean nappies? Does each baby have its own labelled jars of nappy cream and similar items?

9.4.2.3 Non-sharing of personal care items

Items such as facecloths, towels, hairbrushes, toothbrushes and bedding should be for personal use only and not shared among staff or children.

Wherever possible, disposable items like paper towels or wet-wipes should be used to reduce cross-contamination in group settings.

Re-usable items should be regularly laundered or washed and be clearly labelled with the child's name.

9.4.2.4 Shoe-protection policy for baby play areas

During their first year of life, babies play primarily on the floor and frequently place their hands and other objects into their mouths. Because of this, the floor should be as clean as possible to protect them from dirt and contaminants often found on shoe soles. This can be done by:

- regular washing and disinfecting of floors where babies play (two to three times a day)
- covering adult shoes with disposable or washable shoe covers when walking on baby play surfaces (a cheap option is to use disposable hair covers over shoes, similar to those worn by people working with fresh food in supermarkets)
- removing outdoor shoes while inside the baby room and/or wearing indoor shoes or socks to protect the floor.

9.4.3 Nutrition, food and feeding practices

9.4.3.1 Water supply

If there is no reliable municipal water supply, then 10–25 litres of clean water per child per day are required for drinking and food preparation on the premises.

Clean water should be available for drinking purposes and be regularly offered to children, particularly during hot weather. In areas where there is no safe drinkable water, the available water can be boiled and then cooled for children to drink. A hypochlorite solution may also be used:

Add two drops of bleach (Jik) per litre of water. Stir it well. Let the mixture stand for half an hour before drinking.

9.4.3.2 Food hygiene requirements for ECCE centres

If food is prepared and served, then the centre should obtain a certificate of acceptability, which must be displayed on the premises (see section 9.2). The requirements below have been adapted to meet food safety legislation as well as recent hygiene requirements for listeriosis prevention.

Food hygiene requirements for ECCE centres

Provide in kitchen areas

Handwashing facilities with liquid soap and disposable paper towels

Liquid-proof dustbins with close-fitting lids, which are regularly emptied and disinfected daily

Clean cutlery, crockery, basins, and utensils that are not cracked or chipped

Working surfaces that are cleaned and sanitised before preparing and dishing up food (use the bleach spray).

Food storage

Fridges must be kept at temperature of 4 °C, which is recorded daily on a form (date and temperature)

Yoghurt, dairy products and perishable foods must be stored in the fridge

Fruit which is served unpeeled (eg apples, watermelon, etc) must be washed off with a 1:200 bleach solution before cutting (5 ml bleach in 1 litre water)

Food cooked early must be stored in the fridge until reheated (unless it is kept hot at a constant temperature of at least 65 °C).

All food must be in covered containers and dated when stored in the fridge.

Expiry dates on food items must be checked so that older items are used first (eg porridge).

Dry food items should be stored off the floor in rodent- and insect-proof containers with close-fitting lids.

Something to consider

The kitchen environment is, of course, very important, but consideration must also be given to hygiene in relation to the food servers and the serving of food.

Food servers

Food servers:
- should wear hair coverings, plastic aprons and plastic gloves (a clean pair for every mealtime)
- should cover any sore, cut or abrasion totally with a waterproof dressing
- should have clean fingernails, hands and clothes.

Must wash hands:
- when coming on duty or after a break
- after every toilet visit
- after blowing nose or after contact with a handkerchief or tissue
- after touching hair, nose or mouth
- after contact with money or a dustbin
- after handling raw vegetables, fruit, meat or chicken
- before handling ready-to-use food
- after hands have been contaminated for any other reason
- before and after putting on or removing gloves.

May not:
- touch food with bare hands (use clean gloves and a serving spoon or tongs)
- serve or handle food if they have a contagious condition or diarrhoea
- spit or smoke in an area where food is handled
- handle food so that it is contact with any exposed body part
- cough or sneeze over food
- lick fingers when handling food
- use a handwashing basin for cleaning purposes or for any purpose except handwashing.

Reflection

Which of the above procedures are used in your centre? If some of them are not used, do you think they should be introduced? If so, why?

Reheated food, some of which might have been prepared, may, of course, also be served. If you are serving reheated food think about the following:

- Food must be reheated up to a minimum of 70 °C in a microwave or oven before serving. Use a food thermometer to check this and record daily.
- When using a microwave for reheating, a glass bowl or microwaveable container should be used and not cheap plastic buckets or containers.
- Keep a small amount (about 50–100 ml) of the meat/chicken/fish every day in a labelled and dated container in the fridge. This can be discarded after 48 hours. If any case of suspected food poisoning occurs, then this specimen must be given to the health department for testing.

> NB. Food poisoning is a notifiable disease

(SOURCE: THIS INFORMATION ON FOOD MANAGEMENT IN THE CENTRE HAS BEEN ADAPTED FROM FOODSTUFFS, COSMETICS AND DISINFECTANTS ACT 54 OF 1972, NO R. 962, 23 NOVEMBER 2012; NATIONAL ENVIRONMENTAL HEALTH NORMS AND STANDARDS FOR PREMISES. NOTICE 1229 OF 2015; NATIONAL HEALTH ACT, 2003; NATIONAL INSTITUTE OF COMMUNICABLE DISEASES, RSA, 4 MAY 2018.)

9.4.3.3 Breast milk and breastfeeding

Staff should encourage breastfeeding and make it easy for mothers to either breastfeed in the centre or to use expressed breast milk to feed their baby. If the centre is located in, for example, a mother's place of work and she wishes to come to the centre and breastfeed her child, a suitable comfortable place must be made available for her.

Fresh expressed breast milk must be clearly labelled with the date and the child's name, and stored in the refrigerator until needed. It should not be stored for more than a maximum of 48 hours. If frozen expressed breast milk is sent to the centre, it can be stored for a maximum of two to three months. To defrost frozen breast milk, place the container into warm water. Defrosted breast milk should not be refrozen.

Never microwave breast milk as this destroys the antibodies and may also overheat the milk, causing burns.

Make sure that breast milk is given to the correct child (Marotz, 2011).

9.4.3.4 Bottle feeding

The centre needs an effective method to handle baby feeds to prevent milk contamination or the incorrect mixing of formula, and to limit the need for refrigeration. The following is thus recommended:

> Parents clean and sterilise baby bottles at home and fill the bottle with the correct amount of preboiled water.
>
> The teat of the bottle must be covered with a teat cover.
>
> The premeasured milk powder is decanted by parents into suitable containers – the correct amount of powder should be measured into individual containers for the amount of water supplied.
>
> Both feeding bottles containing preboiled water and premeasured milk-powder containers are sent to the childcare centre every day. It is recommended that parents provide one extra amount more than the baby is expected to need, just in case they are late in fetching the baby.
>
> All items must be labelled with the child's name.
>
> The bottles are stored in a container on a suitable clean surface (the bottles do not need refrigeration if the formula has not been added to the water). An added advantage is that this water does not require heating as it is already at room temperature.
>
> When the baby requires a feed, the staff member washes her hands and then removes the lid of the feeding bottle with the teat cover in place.
>
> Without touching the inside of the bottle, she tips the premeasured milk powder into the water.
>
> Next the teat and lid are replaced on the bottle, and then the bottle is shaken to mix the contents.
>
> Reconstituted formula must be discarded after two hours if it is not stored in the fridge. When the baby has finished drinking, discard unfinished milk – do not keep this to send home as it is possible that babies can be given old milk in error.
>
> Record the amount of milk the baby drinks.
>
> No medication or foodstuffs should be added to a bottle of milk unless this is on the written instructions of the child's health advisor.
>
> A baby who is not yet able to hold its own bottle should be held by an adult so that eye contact is made. Babies should be held at approximately a 45° upright angle when drinking to prevent choking.
>
> No prop feeding is allowed. Prop feeding is when the baby is fed from a bottle propped up with a cloth or other support and not held by an adult for feeding. Prop feeding can lead to choking and other health difficulties.

9.4.3.5 Introducing solids to babies

It is generally recommended that babies start with pureed or mashed foods from about five to six months of age. Staff should follow parental instructions about the type of food and the age to introduce solids (provided this does not seem unrealistic).

When feeding babies, make sure they are sitting upright and that they are given small amounts at a time to prevent gagging or choking. If a child is seated in an infant chair (highchair or feeding chair), he should be strapped in securely with a safety seatbelt. Protect his clothing with a bib.

Never force a baby to eat. When a baby shows signs of turning his head away from the spoon, stop offering food.

Always decant food into a bowl before feeding to prevent contamination of the food in the original container.

All bottles or containers of commercially or home-cooked baby foods must be labelled with the child's name and the date it is opened. Opened food must be used within 48 hours.

Be particularly vigilant once a child starts finger-feeding and make sure that foods offered are not choking hazards. At first offer the baby soft finger foods such as soft fruit or a soft biscuit (boudoir biscuit) for baby to suck. When the baby begins to cut teeth, offer different foods such as a piece of banana or avocado pear, or a piece of bread.

> **Common choking hazards**
> Foods that are round, hard, sticky, spongy or small are potential choking hazards for children under the age of four. Examples are rounds of Vienna sausages; hard sweets; nuts; whole grapes or whole baby tomatoes; large chunks of raw apple or carrot; popcorn; scoops of peanut butter; marshmallows; and large chunks of meat. If these foods are served, they should be chopped finely or cut into thin strips.

9.4.3.6 Feeding the toddler and young child

Children should be seated when eating. A proper mealtime routine should be introduced where children wash their hands and help, when able, with setting the table and serving the food.

From around nine months of age, children often show an inclination to feed themselves, either with their fingers or spoons. This should be encouraged as self-feeding promotes fine motor skills and independence. Toddlers should wear bibs to protect their clothing from food spills.

Encourage children to taste all food served, but do not bribe them to finish food. Dish up only small amounts of a disliked food.

Be aware of any food allergies or cultural or religious food prohibitions for children in the centre.

From about one year, encourage children to drink small amounts of water from plastic cups (without non-spill lids) as these cups cause less tooth decay than sippy cups (these are 'trainer' cups that prevent spilling because they have a tight-fitting lid with a spout or straw from which to drink).

It is generally recommended by speech therapists that by 14 months of age toddlers should stop using dummies, and by 18 months of age they should stop drinking out of bottles as these habits may reinforce an immature suck-swallow pattern which may delay proper speech development and cause orthodontic problems.

9.4.3.7 Food for birthday celebrations

Each ECCE setting should decide what will be allowed for birthday celebrations in the centre. It is best to limit treats sent to the centre and to also remember those children with specific dietary needs (eg allergies) during special celebrations. Also bear in mind that in some cultures, birthdays might not be celebrated.

9.4.3.8 Some important nutritional issues

Space limitations do not allow us to go in depth into, for example, nutrition policies, nutritional guidelines and menu planning for ECCE centres, and to consider common nutritional concerns such as feeding problems in babies, infants and young children, and certain nutritional disorders.

There is a lot of information available on these topics. We recommend that you consult the following resources for further details into these important and central areas that are an integral part of health growth, development and learning.

> **Nutrition guidelines for ECD centres**
>
> The following website gives a good overview of nutritional guidelines for ECE centres:
>
> http://ilifalabantwana.co.za/wp-content/uploads/2016/12/Nutrition-guidelines-for-ECD-centres_Draft-2_30-September-2016.pdf
>
> **Nutrition policy**
>
> The National Development Agency gives an excellent overview of nutritional policies:
>
> https://www.nda.org.za/publication/health-and-nutrition-in-ecd.
>
> For information regarding feeding problems in infants consult:
>
> https://www.google.com/search?q=feeding+problems+in+infants&rlz=1C1CAFA_enZA657ZA657&oq=feeding+problems&aqs=chrome.2.69i57j0l5.134772j0 j7&sourceid=chrome&ie=UTF-8
>
> and for obtaining information on feeding problems in toddlers the following website is useful:
>
> https://www.google.com/search?q=feeding+problems+in+toddlers&rlz=1C1CAFA_enZA657ZA657&oq=feeding+problems+&aqs=chrome.2.69i59j69i 57j0l4.8027j0j7&sourceid=chrome&ie=UTF-8

> **Nutrition policy**
>
> In addition, the following website will give some information on feeding problems in the young child:
>
> > https://www.google.com/search?q=eating+problems+young+child&rlz=1C1CAFA_enZA657ZA657&oq=feeding+problems+in+young+children+&aqs=chrome .2.69i57j0l2.11289j0j7&sourceid=chrome&ie=UTF-8
>
> We also suggest that you refer to the Road to Health booklet, where a brief overview on certain of these issues is given. The web address is given at the beginning of this chapter.
>
> > Also consult the National Integrated Early Childhood Development Policy 2015 (see Chapter 15 on policy). Chapters 2, 3 and 5 provide some information on nutritional issues. It can be sourced from the following website:
> >
> > https://www.unicef.org/southafrica/SAF_resources_integratedecdpolicy.pdf

Satisfactory increase in weight and height are the best indicators of healthy growth and development in babies and toddlers. All children should be weighed regularly and their weight recorded on their Road to Health chart. It is not the function of ECCE teachers to diagnose or treat a nutritional disorder. However, if you suspect a baby, toddler or young child of having a possible nutritional disorder, speak to the parents and refer the child for a medical assessment as good nutrition is fundamental to optimal growth, development and learning in young children.

9.5 REST AND SLEEP

Babies and young toddlers under the age of 18 months require two sleep periods during the day (morning and afternoon) while older toddlers and pre-schoolers will require one rest period after lunch.

Staff should introduce a proper rest routine where a tranquil atmosphere is created, which could include darkening the room, playing soothing music and reducing the noise level.

Cots and floor sleeping mattresses should be spaced a minimum of 750 mm apart. Racks to store mattresses are a good idea so there is no contact between the surfaces. Each child should have their own bedding and sheets that are labelled with their symbol.

Children should always be supervised during rest time.

If some older children do not sleep, they should be allowed to play quietly without disturbing those children who are sleeping.

Something to consider

The centre should draw up its own safe sleep policy for babies younger than 12 months of age. This is to reduce the possibility of sudden infant death syndrome (SIDS) (cot or crib death in babies under one year) due to asphyxia (suffocation) or entrapment. If parents do not agree with aspects of this policy, then they should provide a signed waiver or indemnity form to cover the centre. The website of the American Academy of Pediatrics at http://www.aap.org provides details of safe sleep policy criteria.

Safe sleep policy for babies

Babies should be placed on their backs to sleep on a firm surface. Once babies can roll back and forth from their tummies to their backs, they should be allowed to settle into a preferred sleep position. Placing babies to sleep on their sides is not safe, nor is the use of sleep-positioning devices such as wedges.

The cot mattress should be protected with a plastic mattress cover to prevent contamination of the mattress and to make cleaning possible. The SIDS policy recommends using a fitted sheet. No soft toys, pillows, bumper pads, duvets or sheepskins should be placed in the cot as these are suffocation risks. No cords from apnoea (cessation of breathing) monitors (which allow caregivers to monitor babies sleeping from a distance), blinds or curtains should be accessible inside the cot as these are a strangulation risk.

The baby's head should not be covered with a blanket or cloth nappy, and bibs, hooded clothing and items such as teething necklaces and dummy chains should be removed to prevent choking and suffocation.

A dummy is allowed during sleep time but should not be reinserted into the baby's mouth if it falls out while the child is asleep.

Babies should not be swaddled (wrapped tightly) for sleep as this is linked to abnormal hip development as well as suffocation risk if they roll onto their tummies and cannot roll back again.

For sleep, babies should be dressed appropriately for the room temperature so that they do not overheat.

Babies are not allowed to sleep in car seats, baby chairs, doughnut cushions, pillows or swings. If they fall asleep elsewhere, they should be removed and placed in their own cots.

Babies are not allowed to share cots.

When babies are awake, they should have supervised 'tummy time' to improve motor milestones, develop the shoulder girdle and reduce plagiocephaly (a flat head).

SOURCE: ADAPTED FROM THE AAP (2016)

Feeding, rest and sleep involve a number of safety issues, as we have discussed. We will now consider other safety issues that are particularly relevant in an ECCE context.

9.6 SAFETY

Adults are required to protect children from harm and this is done by adhering to legislative standards that relate either to staff or the physical environment. ECCE centres would be well advised to ensure they have insurance to cover any possible claims for staff or child injury. Accidents or what are now termed 'unintentional injuries' are one of the leading causes of death, permanent disability and non-fatal injury in young children. According to Marotz (2012), in an ECCE centre there are four steps that staff should take to prevent unintentional injury. These are outlined in Table 9.2.

Table 9.2 Steps to prevent unintentional injury in an ECCE centre

Identified steps	Description	Criteria to consider
Advanced planning	Planning of playroom layout Planning of selection of resources and other learning materials Thoughtful consideration of choice of activities Reflection on planning	Age and stage of development Are resources sufficiently challenging to promote acquisition of new skills? Do resources promote a sense of independence?
Establishing safety policy guidelines	These are statements about what is considered to be acceptable behaviour by children to ensure the safety of the individual child, the group and property These guidelines (rules) apply to both the indoor and outdoor environment Safety checklists should be drawn up for all areas and staff should be responsible for checking that all safety requirements are adhered to	Guidelines should be simple and easy for all to understand Give a brief explanation of why the guidelines are needed Guidelines should be applied consistently Guidelines should be stated (written) in a positive way, for example: 'Slide down the slide on your bottom with your feet first so that you can see where you are going' Avoid 'do not' and 'don't' Guidelines should be drawn up for both the children and adults

Identified steps	Description	Criteria to consider
Quality supervision	Young children are impulsive and do not as yet have an understanding of the many potential dangers that they might face. They cannot be expected to be responsible for their own safety	**Never** leave children unattended Supervision occurs whether children are awake or asleep If necessary, have more than one responsible adult overseeing children Have a roster for playground supervision that specifies the area and responsibility for each staff member Quality supervision is affected by the type of activities that influence the number of children a teacher can safely manage
Safety education	Children start to learn about safe behaviour as soon as they start understanding words Knowing about safety practices enables children to deal with possible emergencies Being aware of personal safety and self-protection practices can help children to avoid potentially harmful situations	Adults should model safe behaviour as children learn through imitation Safety practices are learnt incidentally as well as being explicitly taught and reinforced at suitable moments

SOURCE: ADAPTED FROM MAROTZ (2011)

Something to consider

Specific staff concerns

All adults working with children are required by the Children's Act (RSA, 2005) to have a police clearance certificate to verify that their name does not appear in the National Child Protection Register or the National Register for Sex Offenders.

Staff should receive training about the specific risks that are applicable to children of different ages in the ECCE setting. It is only with a good understanding of the developmental characteristics (see Chapter 3) of different age groups that hazards for a specific age group can be eliminated.

These hazards should be minimised as much as possible by ensuring that excellent safety precautions are in place. In addition, all staff should have basic first aid knowledge and undergo regular first aid training for the handling of common injuries. The centre should have emergency contact numbers at hand should a serious injury occur requiring medical attention. Table 9.3 gives an overview of risks, common causes and prevention of unintentional injury, which can occur both indoors and outdoors.

Table 9.3 An overview of risks, causes and possible prevention of unintentional injury

Type of risk	Possible causes	Possible prevention/ management
Transport-related risks, eg motor vehicle Walking – a pedestrian Wheeled toys, scooters and tricycles	Inadequate restraint Poor supervision on pavement/road unable to control scooter or tricycle, etc	Proper use of car seats Supervise near traffic; teach the rules of road where appropriate Check for suitability of wheeled toys; supervise consistently
Drowning	Swimming pool, fishpond, basin of water, bathtub, pond, toilet, bucket	All water sources such as swimming pools or fishponds should be made inaccessible; supervise all water play; buckets/basins of water must not be left on the ground

➡

Type of risk	Possible causes	Possible prevention/ management
Burns	Fireplace, brazier, heater, candle, stove/two-plate cooker, electrical outlet, corrosive substances such as ammonia causing chemical burns; fireworks	Fireguards; use wall mounted heaters, if possible; cover electrical sockets with safety plugs; store all chemicals out of children's reach
Suffocation	From plastic bags, bedding, clothing (neckties), pillows; entrapment in chest or appliance such as a fridge; aspiration (inhalation) of small objects	No soft pillows for baby; remove neckties before sleep; keep unused appliances (fridge, etc) locked; remove plastic bags; take care if balloons are being used for an activity
Falls	Stairs, furniture (cot, bed, nappy-changing table, chair, etc), play equipment, window	Use stair guards; never leave babies unsupervised on high surfaces; windows should have burglar bars, etc; ensure equipment is suitable for the age and size of child; always monitor play
Poisoning	Medication, cleaning products, insecticides, cosmetics, plants (eg oleander, syringa berries, certain mushrooms, etc)	All medication, cleaning products and insecticides should be kept out of reach of children; never decant paraffin (or other corrosive substances) into a clear cooldrink bottle; check the garden regularly for possible poisonous plants. Contact the poison control unit if necessary
Wandering unsupervised	Lifting a gate latch, climbing over a fence or through broken fencing	Childproof entrances/exits to possible danger points; check perimeter fencing

Something to consider

Adults working with babies should be trained in managing risks particular to this age group – choking, SIDS, shaken-baby syndrome (brain injury caused by forcefully and violently shaking a baby), etc. Consult https://www.healthline.com/health/shaken-baby-syndrome for symptoms, causes and treatment of this syndrome.

Toddler teachers should have specific training to deal with issues related to potty training (view the following website: https://pediatrics.aappublications.org/content/103/Supplement_3/1367/); biting (see Chapter 10); common accidents, both indoors and outdoors, such as falls; and risks related to water, hot substances, electricity and sharp objects.

Knowledge about how to protect children from possible sun damage is also essential as South Africa has the second highest rate of skin cancer in the world, and 80 per cent of skin damage occurs during the childhood years (CANSA, 2010). Eyes may also sustain sun damage, causing cataracts and other visual problems in later life.

Each ECCE setting should develop a sun-protection policy to ensure that all children and employees are protected from skin and eye damage caused by the harmful effects of the ultraviolet (UV) rays from the sun. The policy should include the following components:

Recommended components of a sun-safe policy

Sun-protection practices will be followed throughout the year and will apply to all skin types.

Sun protection will be included in the planning of excursions (hats and sunscreen).

Staff should act as role models for children, and demonstrate sun-safety practices (wearing appropriate hats, sunglasses and sunscreen).

Children should play in shaded areas between 10:00 and 15:00. Outdoor activities should be rescheduled to early morning or late afternoon when the temperature is lower.

Wherever possible, sandpits and metal equipment should be provided with shade cover. Artificial grass should be regularly sprayed with water to cool it down.

Parents should be requested to provide wide-brimmed hats or legionnaire-style hats (with a flap over the neck) for their child. Peak caps and sport caps are *not allowed* as they do not protect the ears, cheeks and neck from sun damage.

Parents should be encouraged to dress their children in loose-fitting clothing that covers as much skin as possible.

Parents should be required to provide water-resistant sunscreen with a sun-protection factor (SPF) of above 30 for their child.

➡

Written parental permission should be obtained to apply sunscreen to all children aged six months and older at least 20 minutes before the child goes outdoors, and should be re-applied every two hours.

Babies under six months of age should be kept out of direct sunlight since it is not recommended that they use sunscreen. Written instructions from a healthcare provider are required if parents request sunscreen to be applied to their baby who is under six months of age.

Sunscreen should be stored in a cool place out of reach of children.

Staff should monitor the expiry date of sunscreen and discard the product when out of date.

Water should be provided and offered frequently for children during outdoor activities.

Staff and children should be watched carefully for heat-related illness such as heat exhaustion and heat stroke. Symptoms of heat exhaustion include sweating, rapid pulse, dizziness, muscle cramps, nausea and vomiting, and headache. If not treated, this can lead to heat stroke, which can be fatal. Early symptoms of heat exhaustion in babies include irritability, refusal of bottles, fewer wet nappies, floppy posture and a sunken fontanelle (the space between the bones of the skill in an infant, often called the soft spot on the skull).

Find out more

A safety checklist for both indoor and outdoor areas should be drawn up by the staff together with parents. It should be applicable to all ages under review, but with specific focus on the individual age groups. Safety rules that cover outdoor and indoor environment must be clearly displayed (pictorially as well as written), and an emergency evacuation plan must be in place and practised at least once a term.

Try this out

Look at the following example of a safety check. Based on this example, draw up an outdoor and indoor safety checklist for your environment.

Safety checklist

Item	Watch points
Outdoor Environment	
Perimeter fence	This must be intact, approximately 2 m high, with no breaks, etc. All gates must close securely
Protective surfaces under equipment	Avoid compacted soil, uneven surfaces, concrete and tar. Surfaces should be loosely covered with materials such as wood chips, mulch, shredded rubber or soft mats or, in certain instances, appropriate AstroTurf
Playground	Ensure that the surface is safe (eg no protruding tree roots; large stones; litter; dangerous materials, such as broken glass; cans; twisted metal; cracked, loose, slippery paving stones; sharp objects; uneven paving where babies and toddlers could fall) Barriers must be put in place to prevent babies and toddlers from wandering off, etc
Climbing equipment	Correct height and size for specific age groups; no rough surfaces, splinters, rust, sharp points (eg nails, bolts, etc), missing rungs, broken steps, etc
Swings	Correct make and size for specific age groups. Watch for worn bearings that need to be oiled, damaged seats, frayed rope, etc
Flowers and plants	Certain plants are poisonous (eg oleander), as are many types of mushrooms, etc
Indoor Environment	
Playroom layout and maintenance	Playroom arrangement must be such that the teacher can see all children at all times; it must be litter free, the equipment must be stored properly, and the tables cleaned after activities; stair guards must be used to ensure that babies and toddlers are secure, etc
Floor surfaces	These should be clean and non-slip; carpets must be cleaned daily; spills must be wiped up immediately; there should be no uneven tiles; extra care must be taken in areas where babies and toddlers play, etc

Item	Watch points
Indoor Environment	
Adequate ventilation	Windows must be intact and able to open, burglar bars must be installed to prevent falls, air vents must be open, etc
Heating	There must be suitable fireguards; heaters should preferably be wall mounted, etc
Storage of equipment	There must be sufficient shelves that are easy for children to reach; all areas must be labelled properly; poisonous items/hazardous substances must be kept out of reach, and stored and labelled properly; free-standing shelves and cupboards must be secure, etc
Electrical appliances	Lights and other appliances must be in good working order, and cables must be clear of walkways; all plugs that are accessible to young children should have plug protectors, etc
Bathrooms	Toilets must be cleaned daily, and also after use; hand-washing facilities must be available with soap for washing hands; the hand basins must be clean with no dripping taps; clean towels must be provided to dry hands, etc
Add to this general list yourself	
Infant equipment safety list	
Cots and cradles	Slats must be no more than 6 cm apart; the mattress must be firm and fit snugly against the sides of the cot; surfaces must be smooth with no protruding bits that could cause injury; drop-side latches must not be able to be released by a baby, etc
Cot toys	Toys must have no strings longer than 178 cm to prevent entanglement; crib gyms or other toys must be securely fastened to prevent them from being pulled into the crib and injuring the baby; components of toys must be large enough not to be a choking hazard
Add to this list	

Keep the checklist in your classroom where you file other documents and policies, and use it once a week to monitor ongoing safety practices and ensure a safe learning environment.

Taking responsibility: Making the checklist work

In addition, there should be a roster of responsibility so that each week it is a staff member's duty to check and report on any issues that arise. These issues must be acted on as soon as possible before injuries occur. If they cannot be attended to immediately, affected areas must be out of bounds for children. One way to deal with problems identified is suggested below. Note the problem and action required, and when the problem was resolved.

Date	Item	Action required	Action completed (date)	Action taken by whom
Outdoor Environment				
20 June 2019	Fence	Repair hole in fence next to swings	Repaired 21 June 2019	Mrs Nkosi
Add ...				
Indoor Environment				
20 June 2019	Door guard leading to front outdoor play area broken	Latch door securely to prevent toddlers from exiting playroom until guard is repaired. Handyman contacted	20 Sep 2019	Mrs Tshepo
Add ...				

9.7 PREVENTATIVE HEALTH CARE

Many routine healthcare practices reduce illness and help keep children healthy. Good health is a prerequisite for learning, and staff at childcare centres should collaborate with local or community child-health clinics for accessing available services relating to dental health, vision and hearing screening, speech and language assessment, developmental assessment, immunisation administration and deworming.

Something to consider

No health assessment or treatment may be done on any child without the written consent of the parent or legal guardian. In addition, staff should be reminded that all personal and health information of parents, children or other staff members is confidential and may not be shared without the permission of the person concerned or the child's legal guardian.

ECCE centres and preschools are required, in terms of the Health Act 61 of 2003, to keep records of children's immunisations. ECCE staff should remind parents to consult their healthcare providers about any additional immunisations (eg influenza) which could provide extra protection in group childcare.

Download from the Department of Health

The mother, child health and nutrition booklet: http://www.health.gov.za/index.php/component/phocadownload/category/332

For the recommended immunisation schedule, Google the vaccination schedule in South Africa:

> https://www.parent24.com/Baby/Babycare/the-vaccination-schedules-in-south-africa-20171122

9.7.1 Children who become sick during the day

All ECCE settings should develop a policy in relation to the management of sick children. This should include information about which conditions require them to remain at home and when they may remain at the centre (see the box which follows shortly after this section) and what to do if they become sick during the day.

Families should be advised to have a backup plan for childcare for those times when their child cannot attend the centre or has to be sent home due to illness.

Staff should observe children for any serious signs of illness on arrival at the centre (morning health check) and should record these signs.

If a child becomes ill during the day, a staff member (usually the teacher or the principal) must immediately inform the parent/guardian and recommend that the sick child is taken to a health professional for further advice. The child should rest in a quiet place under the supervision of a familiar adult until the parent arrives.

Childcare settings are required by legislation to provide a separate area with hand-washing facilities for the care of ill children (RSA Environmental Norms and Standards, 2015).

When there are doubts about the condition of the child, a note from a health care provider may be requested to verify that it is safe for a child to return to the centre, e.g. when they are no longer infectious.

9.7.2 Conditions that do not normally require exclusion

Excluding children with mild illness is unlikely to reduce its spread as most of the germ transmission occurs before the symptoms of the illness become apparent. However, any child who is obviously ill should be kept at home until well.

> It is unnecessary to exclude a child with the following symptoms (AAP, 2014: 80–81; Aronson & Shope, 2013: 52–53):
> - Common colds and runny noses (regardless of the colour of the nasal discharge) unless the child is obviously unwell
> - A cough with no other symptoms, such as fever or breathing difficulties
> - A watery eye discharge without redness of the conjunctiva (the lining of the eye) and without eye pain or fever
> - Fever up to 38 °C without any other signs or symptoms of illness and where the child is acting normally (this, however, should be monitored over a few hours for any change in condition)
> - Rash without fever or any changes in behaviour
> - Oral thrush (white spots or patches inside the mouth)
> - Unusual chronic illnesses such as chronic hepatitis B infection, cytomegalovirus (CMV) infection or HIV infection where the child appears well.

9.7.3 Conditions where children should be excluded from group childcare

To maintain the health of children and adults in childcare centres, those with treatable communicable (infectious) diseases that pose a risk to other persons should remain at home to reduce the possibility of the spread of infection.

> **When to exclude a child from the ECCE setting**
> - Any illness which prevents the child from taking part in the normal activities
> - Any illness which requires more care than staff can provide without neglecting the wellbeing of the other children in the group
> - A sudden change in behaviour such as lethargy, lack of responsiveness, persistent crying, or signs of a stiff neck or any convulsions.

- A child with severe coughing or wheezing or who is making high-pitched whooping sounds, having difficulty breathing, becoming blue in the face or vomiting after coughing. A baby with a breathing rate of 50 or above, in the absence of crying, needs assessment by a health professional.
- A child with a fever of 38.3 °C or higher, accompanied by behavioural changes and other signs or symptoms of illness such as a sore throat, abdominal pain, rash, breathing problems, vomiting, diarrhoea or a stiff neck. Any baby under six months of age with an unexplained fever of 38 °C or higher should be evaluated by a health professional.
- A child with mouth sores who is drooling
- A child with watery diarrhoea or with three or more stools above what is normal for that child or with any blood in the stools (faeces)
- A child who vomits more than twice in a 24-hour period unless the vomiting is found to be caused by a non-infectious condition and the child remains well hydrated
- All children with conjunctivitis (pink eye), impetigo (infectious skin disease), ringworm (fungal infection), scabies (an infectious skin disease caused by a mite (insect) and head lice (small insects which infect the human head) until they have had 24 hours of appropriate treatment for that specific condition.

Children on antibiotics or any other newly prescribed treatment need only be excluded for the first two days of treatment unless they still meet some of the other exclusion criteria previously mentioned (Aronson & Shope, 2013)

The exclusion periods for the following common childhood infectious diseases are given in Table 9.4.

Table 9.4 Exclusion period for common childhood communicable diseases

Chickenpox (varicella)	Until all the blisters have dried
Shingles (herpes zoster)	
Hand, foot & mouth disease (HFMD) (Coxsackie virus A16 and Enterovirus 71) – usually causes fever, malaise, skin rash, sore throat, and small blisters that ulcerate	
Rubeola (measles)	Until four days after the onset of the rash, provided the child is feeling well
Rubella (German measles)	Until six days after the rash appeared provided the child is well

Roseola (baby measles)	Until the child has had no fever for 24 hours.
Respiratory syncytial virus (RSV) is a common and very contagious virus that usually infects children before their second birthday. In most instances it presents as nothing more than a cold, but it can cause more serious respiratory tract problems and should therefore be closely monitored. See the following website for more information: https://www.webmd.com/lung/rsv-in-babies#1	Until the child has no fever and is well enough to participate in activities at the centre
Mumps	Until five to nine days after the onset of swelling of the parotid (salivary) glands and the child feels well (whichever is sooner)
Pertussis (whooping cough)	Until five days after appropriate antibiotic treatment has started and the child is well
Tuberculosis	Until a health professional has determined that the child may return to childcare

For further information on common communicable diseases in childhood consult the following website:

http://www.porcupinehu.on.ca/en/audiences/educators/cdim/cccd/

9.7.4 Prevention of communicable diseases in the ECCE centre

The implementation of health practices to try to ensure, as far as is feasibly possible, the prevention of ill health and the promotion of good health is, as we have already said, an essential component of quality health practices in the ECCE centre.

To ensure the ongoing health of all children, staff and other stakeholders, the teacher needs to consider a wide range of different health practices that prevent the spread of communicable diseases and lead to the promotion of good health as well as positive attitudes towards health.

These health practices include the following:
- Ensuring good environmental health and hygiene – see section 9.4.1
- Implementing good personnel hygiene – see section 9.4.2

- Ensuring children have received the necessary immunisations and that their immunisation schedule is up to date. Space does not permit us to explore this schedule, but readers can consult the following website for details of the immunisation schedule recommended by the Department of Health:

    https://www.parent24.com/Baby/Babycare/the-vaccination-schedules-in-south-africa-20171122/. This website gives a good overview of the national routine immunisation schedule recommended in South Africa.
- Ensuring that children are adequately nourished – see section 9.4.3
- Provide ongoing health education for children and families to ensure the implementation of sound health practices – see section 9.8.

9.7.5 Medication administration in ECCE settings

Childcare staff should limit parental requests for the administration of medication to children because of safety risks and staff time constraints. However, in situations where the medication is essential for a chronic or acute condition and cannot be given outside of childcare hours, the following should apply:

Specifications for the administration of medicine
- The medication must be given directly to the teacher by the parent or legal guardian.
- The medication should have been prescribed by a health professional. Over-the-counter (OTC) medicines, tonics and vitamin syrups do not normally classify as sufficiently important for administration in an ECCE setting.
- The medication must be in the original container dispensed by the pharmacy with the name of the child clearly displayed and instructions for administration , which include the dose, the route (how it should be given, for example orally), the time of day it must be given, the prescribing person's name, the expiry date, for how long the medication must be given and any special administration or storage instructions.
- If medicine needs to be stored in a refrigerator, then the container should first be put into a Ziplock bag and closed so that there is no accidental contamination of food by the medication.
- Parents must give written consent for the administration of any medication in a childcare setting. An individual medication sheet is preferred for this purpose as the previously used medication books compromise confidentiality.
- Staff must complete the medication form and sign it once they have given the prescribed medication.
- The centre should add into their policy who will be responsible for medication administration in a specific group (eg the group teacher or one person for the whole centre.)

9.8 HEALTH EDUCATION

Health education is a key aspect of any ECCE ongoing health-promotion programme. It is an important responsibility of all adults working with young children, either at home or in an ECCE centre.

The health education programmes should focus on children, but teachers should consider all stakeholders, as their health attitudes and practices will directly influence the health of children. Health education should not only focus on the prevention of communicable disease, but should be broad enough to include overall health promotion.

Stakeholders include children, staff (both teaching and auxiliary), parents and families, the broader community, various organisations (such as non-governmental and non-profit organisations, various associations as well as officials from a number of government departments – national, provincial and local government). These people can assist teachers with the implementation of the health programme and at times also provide health services, for example health screening that covers weight and height, and visual and auditory screening.

The teacher and ECCE centre staff should make use of all incidental teaching moments when healthy attitudes and health knowledge can be taught and reinforced. Examples include reminding a toddler to sit down and eat his piece of apple to prevent choking, reinforcing the correct handwashing technique in young children, reminding kitchen staff to store all cleaning fluids on a high shelf out of the reach of children, and ensuring constant supervision of children by teaching staff. There should also be planned health education activities such as a theme on safety or telling a story about a child who has a chronic illness. Other examples include actively teaching toddlers how to wash their hands properly or practising an emergency evacuation drill with staff and children. Setting up a hospital fantasy corner is an example of a planned health education intervention where children actively participate in the activity or stage a role play on visiting the clinic.

To implement an effective health education programme, teachers require adequate content knowledge about a broad range of health issues. They should also be aware of the many health policies that inform their ECCE practice (see sections 9.2 and 9.3 as well as Chapter 15). Good health education draws on a variety of pedagogies (see Chapter 8) and should, like all other aspects of early education, be informed by a playful pedagogical approach to teaching and learning (see Chapter 6). Finally, teachers must remember that they are role models. Children (and others) learn through imitating good health practices, such as covering their mouth when sneezing.

> **Find out more**
>
> Think about your centre and the children in your group. Think of some additional health education topics that you could introduce to the children and to their parents. Choose one topic appropriate for parents. Write a letter to them in which you explain the importance of the chosen health issue for the wellbeing of their children and how this could be addressed in their daily home routine.

9.9 SUMMARY

In this chapter we have explored a wide range of issues relating to the healthcare of the child and the responsibilities of stakeholders. As we stressed at the outset, if children are not healthy, they will not be able to learn and benefit optimally from their early childhood experiences.

As this chapter has outlined, good health practices underpin every aspect relating to early care and education. They are fundamental to the good administration and management of the centre and are an integral part of quality at every level of operation. It is essential to communicate health matters to parents and staff as well as other stakeholders through a variety of media, for example posters and WhatsApp, newsletters, etc. In short, an adherence to health and safety practices is essential to ensure a quality learning environment. They should also be important components that inform pedagogical content and implementation.

REFERENCES

AAP Task Force on sudden infant death syndrome. SIDS and other sleep-related infant deaths. Updated 2016 recommendations for a safe infant sleeping environment. *Pediatrics,* 138(5): e20162938.

Aboud, FE & Yousafzai, AK. 2016. Very early childhood development, in Black, RE, Laxminarayan, R, Temmerman M & Walker, N. 2016. *Disease control priorities. Reproductive, maternal, newborn and child health.* 3rd ed (vol 2). World Bank. https://doi.org/10.1596/978-1-4648-0348-2

American Academy of Pediatrics (AAP) (Pennsylvania Chapter). 2014. *Model childcare health policies.* Aronson, SS (ed). 5th ed. Elk Grove Village, Il: American Academy of Pediatrics.

Aronson, SS & Shope, TR. 2013. *Managing infectious diseases in childcare and schools.* 3rd ed. Elk Grove Village, Il: American Academy of Pediatrics.

Azor-Martinez, E, Yui-Hifume, R, Munoz-Vico, FJ, Jiminez-Noguera Strizzi, JM, Martinez-Martinez, I, Garcia-Fernandez, L, Seijas-Vazquez, ML, Torres-Alegre, P, Fernandez-Compos, MA & Gimenez-Sanchez, F. 2018. Effectiveness of a hand hygiene program at childcare centers: A cluster randomized trial. *Pediatrics*. 142(5): e20181245. http://pediatrics.aappublications.org/content/early/2018/10/04/peds.2018-1245 (Accessed 13 October 2018).

Be SunSmart: A Guide for Schools. October 2013. Cancer Association of South Africa CANSA).

Be SunSmart, Play SunSmart. 2017. National Schools and Early Childhood Working Group. Cancer Council Victoria, Australia.

Berry, L, Jamieson, L & James, M. 2011. *Children's Act guide for early childhood development practitioners*. Children's Institute, UCT and LETCEE. Cape Town: University of Cape Town.

CANSA. 2010. *Fact Sheet – skin cancer*. Cancer Association of South Africa. http://www.cansa.org.za>files>2012/05>SKIN_CANCER_Leaflet_2010 (Accessed 29 October 2019).

Department of Social Development. 2006. *Guidelines for early childhood development services*. Pretoria: UNICEF.

Kotch, JB, Isbell, P, Weber DJ, Nguyen, V, Savage, N, Gunn, E, Skinner, M, Fowlkes, S, Virk, J & Allen, J. 2007. Handwashing and diapering equipment reduce disease among children in out-of-home care centers. *Pediatrics,* 120(1). e29-e36. doi:10:1542/peds.2005-0760

Marotz, LR. 2011. *Health, safety and nutrition for the young child*. 8th ed. Belmont, CA: Wadsworth.

National Institute of Communicable Diseases, RSA. *FAQ. Listeriosis.* Kitchen/shops disinfection_20180302. http://www.nicd.ac.za/index.php/faq-how-to-eradicate-listeria-from-your-kitchen-or-small-shop/

RSA. Children's Act 38 of 2005. Consolidated Regulations pertaining to the Children's Act, 2005. Government Notice No R261. *Government Gazette*, 1 April 2010. No 33076.

RSA. Children's Amendment Act 41 of 2007. *Government Gazette,* 18 March 2008. No 30884.

RSA. Foodstuffs, Cosmetics and Disinfectants Act 54 of 1972. No R. 962. 23 November 2012.

RSA. National Environmental Health Norms and Standards for Premises. Notice 1229 of 2015. National Health Act, 2003.

SunSmart Childcare. 2015. *A guide for service providers.* Cancer Council of Western Australia. https://www.cancerwa.asn.au.

Chapter 10
Building social and emotional wellbeing

Lorayne Excell

In this chapter we consider:

- understandings of emotional, personal and social development
- the role of theory in understanding emotional, personal and social wellbeing
- the importance of self-reflection in the understanding of self and in establishing warm, responsive adult–child relationships
- how to facilitate the development of the young child's identity and sense of belonging through responsive, participatory and play-based ECCE practices
- understanding social behaviours and developing self-discipline and conflict resolution skills in young children.

10.1 INTRODUCTION

Emotional, personal and social (affective) development involves helping children to develop a positive sense of themselves and others, to have confidence in their own abilities, and learn how to manage their feelings. Appropriate affective development supports the development of positive relationships and respect for others. Children develop social skills and begin to understand what constitutes appropriate behaviour. They acquire the skills to resolve conflicts in an acceptable way.

The strong attachment or bond which forms between babies and their primary caregiver is the foundation for healthy emotional, personal and social development. Infants develop a sense of trust in caregivers who respond thoughtfully to their requests for love and attention (see Erikson, Chapter 2). Research indicates that the first three months are critical for the development of attachment relationships. It is important for infants to be immersed in warm, nurturing, consistent, caregiver relationships, both with their parents and, if in care, their caregivers (Charlesworth, 2017). Social and emotional wellbeing is thought to be so important that in many early learning curricula, including the NCF, it is a separate learning area (DBE, 2015).

10.2 UNPACKING TERMS

10.2.1 Emotional development

Emotional development is concerned with how children come to recognise their feelings and how they begin to regulate or control and express them in socially acceptable ways. Children experience the same emotions as adults, such as happiness, sadness, fear, anger, contentment, jealousy, frustration, etc. Young children do not have the words to label these emotions and do not always know how to express themselves in an appropriate manner. Caregivers have to support children in understanding each emotion and provide them with the appropriate ways of expressing these emotions. Ultimately, children will also need the vocabulary to express how they are feeling, and caregivers play a pivotal role in their acquisition of these words.

10.2.2 Personal development

Personal development explores children's growing self-awareness and knowledge about themselves. It involves the development of their self-esteem and identity, and includes the following:

- Establishing dispositions and attitudes towards learning. Positive learning dispositions to be acquired by children include trust, curiosity, perseverance, tolerance, respect, responsibility and self-esteem. These dispositions encourage children to become interested in their environment and continuously explore its possibilities.
- Developing self-esteem and self-confidence. Self-esteem refers to children's growing sense of their own value and worth. Self-confidence relates to their feeling of trust in their abilities, qualities and judgement. It also relates to their perception of how they are viewed by others, as well as their sensitivity towards others (Bruce, 2018).
- Developing increasing self-care, independence and the competence to manage their own activities. An important focus is on how children gain a sense of self-respect and become aware of their own personal health and how to promote it.

10.2.3 Social development

Social development is the understanding of other people and how to build relationships with them. It is shaped by social cognition – the ability to think about social relationships, to understand how the social world functions and how one is expected to behave. Important informing aspects are:

- forming relationships with others and working amicably alongside them

- managing and controlling one's own behaviour – children begin to distinguish between right and wrong, and understand how their behaviour might impact others
- developing a sense of community as children begin to understand and respect their own needs, views, beliefs and culture as well as those of others (Meggitt, Bruce & Manning-Morton, 2016).

Something to consider

Emotional, personal and social development are closely interrelated, and it is not possible to completely separate them. However, when they are studied as one, specific aspects of each area can be overlooked. When observing and assessing children, care must be taken that all three areas are adequately considered.

Social, personal and emotional development are closely related to and influence cognitive development as well as children's understandings of social relationships and situations. We also know that children's emotional wellbeing determines how successfully they learn (or not). The concept of wellbeing maybe most closely related to positive social, personal and emotional development, but it also includes physical and spiritual development, as well as health and nutrition. In other words, the concept of holistic development underpins wellbeing.

10.3 DEVELOPING EMOTIONAL UNDERSTANDING: EXPLORING CHILDREN'S FEELINGS

Learning about emotions and how to regulate them is a long journey only fully completed in adulthood, and even that is questionable at times. Babies need care in order to survive, and to try to ensure they get this care they express their emotions intensely and immediately usually through crying or screaming. In very young babies, the expression of emotions is an unconscious act. They react to stimuli without conscious thought. Sometimes, however, it is hard to know what baby wants: food, changing the nappy, another blanket, etc. Adults caring for infants therefore have to know them well and be finely attuned to their needs. We also know that a caring, nurturing adult who responds speedily to a baby's signals for care is an essential role player in the support of positive emotional development. Leaving babies to cry is not good practice as it does not help the infant to develop a sense of trust in adults or in their environment. Older babies begin to show positive emotions and can be very affectionate when pleased or satisfied. They coo and smile in response to a familiar adult or if they hear preparations for their feed.

According to Meggitt et al (2016), by around the age of six months, infants begin to consciously relate to their emotions. They express anger, for example, if a familiar adult leaves them alone in a room, and from about nine months they might cry if held by a stranger. They might begin to show fear if left alone in an unfamiliar environment.

Toddlers have strong feelings. They can sob if sad, and may show jealousy and hit out if they think someone else has 'their property' (a toy) or if their primary caregiver shows another child attention. They cannot yet easily express themselves and may become very frustrated, especially if thwarted (not getting their own way). Tantrums (physical expressions of anger and rage including sobbing and screaming) are not uncommon. As they become more verbal (around age two), they are better able to express their needs and so tantrums tend to decrease. It is important to talk to children about their emotions so that they acquire the words to express themselves better.

Older children from about three to six years of age are better able to express their emotions. They scream less, and physical expressions of anger such as hitting, kicking or biting tend to become less frequent as they get older. Children might cover their eyes if they want to avoid something or use words such as 'go away' 'me no like', 'it's hard', etc, to express themselves. By the age of four they should have good language skills and will be using full sentences to express themselves, for example, 'This is mine; I was playing with it first', etc.

10.3.1 Emotions frequently expressed by young children

Fear is a very real emotion in young children. Fears become abnormal if they persist or if they interfere in the child's life. All children might be scared of loud noises such as thunder or the slamming of a door. Babies might also get scared if they have a sensation of falling or their body not being supported.

Toddlers may have many different fears such as separation (from parents or caregivers – including being left alone in a strange place), noises, falling (when climbing down a jungle gym), animals and insects, using the potty, bathing and bedtime, including being scared of the dark. Preschool children may have similar fears. In addition, they may be fearful of getting lost, separation from parents because of divorce or death, going to sleep in the dark and encountering monsters or ghosts, which are often related to bedtime.

Do not ridicule, tease or make fun of any child who is scared. Though you might not understand the reasons for their fear, it is very real to them and you must address it thoughtfully and sensitively (see section 10.3.2).

Stress or anxiety may occur when children are unsettled. They react in different ways, which will depend upon their personalities as well as what they have witnessed in their homes. Behaviours might include:

- aggressiveness
- withdrawal, tension, watchfulness
- reluctance to interact with other children

- refusal to eat, or overeating
- if potty trained, regression – beginning to wet their beds or soil themselves
- a return to more babyish ways (regression) and may want to reclaim a comfort object such as a bottle or their blanket/teddy, etc, and may also suddenly want help again with dressing, feeding, etc
- sleep problems such as refusing to go to bed or having nightmares.

Something to consider

Changes in their routines (eg going on holiday, returning to the centre after a long weekend), an absent parent (father/mother away on a business trip), a sick parent/grandparent, the birth of a new sibling, and poverty-related issues are recognised causes of stress in young children. We, as the caregivers, have to support children and help them to manage their anxieties. We cannot relieve children of all their anxious feelings. In fact, we know that small amounts of anxiety act as a stimulus, which often has a positive behavioural outcome. However, if there is no known cause for the stress and/or children are excessively anxious for a few weeks, it is advisable to talk to parents and possibly involve other professionals so that the situation can be effectively managed.

10.3.2 Strategies to deal with children's anxieties and fears

One strategy to deal with children's anxieties and fears is awareness of how children express their emotions, which includes recognising that they may not yet have the language to express how they are feeling.

Something to consider

Young children express their emotions predominantly through physical actions. It is only when they are older that they verbalise their feelings more readily. Be observant so that you can 'read' what it is the child is indicating. If scared or angry, they may run away, kick, hit, stamp their feet, scream and cry, or throw an object on the floor. When excited or happy, they may scream, shout or jump for joy. When sad, lonely or in need of attention they may want a cuddle or a hug or to sit on their caregiver's lap. A shy child might hover near to where other children are playing in the hope of being invited to join in. An impatient toddler might snatch the toy away from another child.

Some strategies to deal with children's anxieties and fears include the following:
- Develop a trusting relationship with children. Within ECCE centres, children must know who their particular caregiver/teacher is. Allowing children to build a close, trusting relationship with a specific teacher is key to ensuring healthy emotional development.

> **Reflection**
>
> Do the children in your ECCE centre all know who their primary caregiver is? Are they confident enough to turn towards this caregiver when they are distressed? If children do not have a primary caregiver in the centre, how can the care routines be altered to ensure all children have a specific caregiver to whom they can turn in times of discomfort?

- Create a calm, comfortable space where children feel safe and secure (see Chapter 7).
- Help children to talk about their feelings and fears. Put it into words for them. 'That loud noise gave you a fright; don't worry, it was only a truck backfiring'. Do not mock or tease any child for being fearful.
- Offer sensiopathic activities such as sand and water play, play dough and finger painting to help children express their feelings non-verbally. Fantasy or socio-dramatic play in the home corner is also a good way for children to express their anxieties. Younger children can be encouraged to take their fears out on a soft toy. Older children might be given a punching bag. (You can easily make one out of an orange bag stuffed with newspaper and tied to the branch of a tree.)
- Tell children stories about specific situations that relate to their cause of anxiety. Through the story, they hear how others overcame some of their negative feelings; in other words, you introduce the child to alternative coping strategies.
- Where appropriate, role model desirable behaviour to the child while being sensitive to her feelings. For example, if the child is scared of thunder you can reassure her while at the same time not showing any overt fear of the noise being made by the thunder.

10.4 PERSONAL DEVELOPMENT

Babies enter the world with unique characteristics and abilities. We have predetermined genetic features and characteristics that will shape the way we react to our environment and other people (see chapters 2 and 3). The development of self begins at birth and continues into adulthood. It is influenced by our genetic predispositions as well our environment, which includes physical challenges, our life experiences, cultural contexts and the people we meet.

Personal development begins with bodily awareness. Newborn babies make random involuntary movements, blink and briefly follow objects. They quieten when being held, and enjoy being fed and cuddled. They respond positively to a nurturing environment. As they grow and interact with their environment, they receive feedback about themselves and what it is that they can do with their bodies. They come to know their hands and fingers, their feet and toes;

they place objects in their mouths and start exploring the world through movement and sensory input. They realise that their actions (smiling, cooing, crying, etc) elicit a response from other people. If these responses are positive and satisfying for the baby, they begin to develop a positive sense of self (see Erikson, Chapter 2). As they grow, they explore what it is their bodies can do and slowly increase their capabilities.

Something to consider

Babies increasingly show that they have a mind of their own. They like to do things for themselves, which is called autonomy (see Erikson, Chapter 2), but they also seek adult approval before doing something. This approval is demonstrated through the adult's response to the child's action, which is then, seemingly, noted by the baby before they go ahead. This is called social referencing (Meggitt et al, 2016).

Toddlers like their efforts to be appreciated. They respond with pride and pleasure. A simple remark such as, 'Wow, you're building a beautiful sandcastle' helps children to feel emotionally safe and secure. However, they are also self-conscious. They quickly become embarrassed and show emotions of guilt or shame. Be careful of making negative remarks such as 'be careful, don't drop that' or 'no, the shoes don't go there'. Such remarks can result in toddlers feeling anxious or incompetent (Meggitt et al, 2016).

Reflection

Do you carefully consider how you talk and interact with young children to help them develop a positive self-image?

By the age of three, they have usually learnt that they are either a boy or a girl and increasingly understand that their gender identity remains stable. This contributes to developing a stable self-concept, which is deepened by being able to relate by the age of five years their age, full name and possibly their address. They increasingly want to be with others and feel accepted by others, but also want to be individuals in their own right. They identify certain emotions such as 'shy' and 'cross', and know certain social roles such as 'big brother' or 'baby sister' (Meggitt et al, 2016).

As part of their self-concept, children, also from about the age of two, begin to develop a social identity and increasingly the ability to identify with a social group. Gender, race/ethnicity and disability are determinants of identity, and from a young age, children are exploring how they are the same and how they are different. Much of a child's identity is socially constructed, as are the different expectations of how girls and boys should behave, and what they should wear and do. Culture, ethnicity and religious beliefs all influence a child's identity formation, self-esteem and self-concept (Raburu, 2015; Manning-Morton, 2014).

Find out more

To support identity development, you have to know each child really well. When planning staffing ratios, it is best to allocate the same staff members to care for the same children every day. In other words, the children have the opportunity to get to know who their specific caregiver is so that they can form a bond with them. It is also important to know the parents and their specific child-rearing practices. If these practices can be carried over to the centre, children will feel much more secure and at ease there. Observation is also essential so that the caregiver can 'read' and respond appropriately and positively to the cues given by the children. By 'reading' children accurately, appropriate, individualised play opportunities are provided for each child. This also ensures that each child's specific context is taken into consideration.

Reflection

It is important to value the child's home language and cultural practices, and to encourage other children to value each other's background. Ask yourself how you can give deliberate thought to the child's culture, home language and specific learning needs, especially if a child has a disability, and how to support individual children's learning. By considering and responding constructively to these questions, all children have the opportunity to build a positive self-identity and a positive self-concept.

10.5 DEVELOPING SOCIAL RELATIONSHIPS

Humans are social beings. We live in communities. We thus need to acquire sufficient skills to interact successfully with other people. We appear to be born with some innate (inborn) skills that enable us to relate to others, and how we do this is shaped by our sociocultural environment. However, not all social skills come naturally to all people and so children need to be supported to behave in socially acceptable ways. One of the most important roles of the caregiver is to model such ways and not only with older children (see Bandura, Chapter 3).

From birth, babies will look intently into the face of a person holding them; they turn their head in response to a voice and soon begin to smile in response to human contact. When upset, they are soothed by a familiar adult. As they get older, they may vocalise and smile when in the presence of other babies. (See Table 3.4 on developmental milestones for a detailed overview of social and emotional development.)

Try this out

Play a game such as peek-a-boo and pat-a-cake with babies who are about nine months old. Did they enjoy these games? Did they gurgle and babble in response to adult stimulation?

Reflection

Ask parents and other stakeholders in your centre about games they play, or could play, with their babies. Find out about some indigenous games that you could include in your resource file.

Something to consider

Older babies and toddlers begin to engage in social referencing – if they want to do something, they may first look at the adult to gauge the adult's response. If this appears to be one of approval, the toddler will carry on with the planned activity; if the response is more negative, the toddler may refrain from continuing with the activity.

Find out more

Toddlers also imitate behaviour; for example, they will copy an adult humming or clapping hands, etc. They generally cooperate during caring activities such as bathing or dressing. By the age of two, they copy other children. If one child drops a cup, the other one will follow. They make eye contact and laugh together. They might socialise for a small part of the day but will generally engage in parallel play (see Chapter 6). Even very young children can show empathy (compassion). They often become distressed when they see another person upset and may even offer them their comfort 'blanket'.

By the age of three, children can engage in associative play and by age four may at times play cooperatively. They enjoy making friends, but friendships are still somewhat unstable. They are starting to enjoy having some control over others and are beginning to develop a sense of what is right and wrong. They are able to argue with adults and are adamant that they are right. They are very reluctant to shift their position. By the age of four they are beginning to understand the meaning of sharing and can take turns. However, they do not like to wait for too long a period. Conflicts over property and territory are frequent, but children are beginning to understand what it means to compromise and are able, with assistance, to negotiate simple solutions. By the age of five they may indicate a preference for playing with their own gender. They are playing cooperatively and are beginning to enjoy games with rules, but do not like losing. Competitive games are for primary school and not for ECCE settings.

10.6 THEORETICAL PERSPECTIVES

There are many theories that explore different aspects of emotional and social development. We have already explored two theories that explain aspects of psychosocial development (see Chapter 2). Another theory which has relevance, especially when thinking about the very young child, is John Bowlby's (1907–1990) attachment theory. He claimed that babies have an innate, biological need to have a close, loving relationship with their primary caregiver, usually the mother. This type of relationship provides the infant with a sense of safety and security, which is the foundation of good emotional development. If, for some reason, this bond does not form or if it is negatively impacted, children's emotional and personal development can be disrupted and they may have difficulty in forming stable social relationships in later life.

Something to consider

Responsive, nurturing, caring behaviours from the caregiver that focus on a stable, consistent relationship provide the child with a secure base from which to venture out into the world. Gradually the child develops a sense of inner trust and gains in confidence and independence. If immersed in a stable secure relationship, the child develops a secure attachment to the caregiver. If the relationship with the caregiver is inconsistent or if the adult is unavailable, then the child develops insecure attachments. These can manifest in extreme dependency and very clingy children, or unhealthily independent children. These children are often identified as being troublesome in later life; they might seek attention in socially unacceptable ways or present with behaviour problems (Meggitt et al, 2016). The basis of the problem is emotional insecurity and having difficulty in forming strong emotional ties to others.

Find out more

Infants after about the age of six months and young children who are separated from their primary caregiver might exhibit separation anxiety. This causes them extreme distress because they are unable to resolve their anxiety by getting close to the caregiver. If separation anxiety is prolonged (over a couple or more days) (eg the caregiver is hospitalised or goes away on a holiday) this can result in prolonged emotional insecurity. Children can lapse into a state of despair and depression.

According to Erikson (see Chapter 3), anxiety of this nature can be addressed at a later stage in a child's life using specific intervention strategies.

10.7 SUPPORTING CHILDREN'S EMOTIONAL, SOCIAL AND PERSONAL DEVELOPMENT

As we have already mentioned, young children respond best to having one or two stable, consistent caregivers. Obviously in the home situation this is usually one or both parents. In ECCE centres, children should be cared for by familiar people with whom they have built a trusting relationship, and whom they know will see to their individual needs and care.

Reflection

In an ECCE setting, how do you as the primary caregiver respond sensitively to children's feelings, ideas and behaviours, and relate and interact with parents? Is there anything you would like to change about the way you interact with them?

Something to consider

Despite all the above aspects being in place, difficulties can still arise. As we have already said, some children find it hard to share their caregiver with other children, and become angry or jealous. The child may cry and show signs of anxiety separation when that caregiver is not there, for example she may be ill, on holiday or has gone for lunch. This is one reason why it is advisable to have two or three caregivers jointly look after a few children and ensure that supportive alternative arrangements are always in place so that children feel secure when change happens. Sometimes the parents become jealous and might feel that they are being displaced by the caregiver. Caregivers must always behave in a professional manner and never try to replace the parents.

Some ways of ensuring positive affective development

- Consistent routines (with some flexibility to adapt to specific needs) help provide a sense of safety and security to young children.
- Treat children and their families respectfully. Never insult children or speak down to them. Use appropriate language – not baby talk, but words and positive gestures that children will understand. Do not ridicule children, or shame and blame them.
- Provide clear, consistent boundaries to give children a sense of security. Where boundaries are not clear, children's behaviour might become more disruptive. Remember, when appropriate you can say 'no' to a child.

> **Some ways of ensuring positive affective development**
> - Provide an inclusive environment where all children and their families feel welcome. Make sure the posters and other environmental print in the centre are relevant to all families; ask yourself if issues related to cultural diversity, the home language of children, possible disability, different family structures, etc have been considered.
> - Allow children to make appropriate choices, and to make mistakes. This is how they learn.

10.7.1 Helping children settle into the ECCE centre

Settling children into a centre can be traumatic for both the child and the parent. This process takes time and requires sensitive, thoughtful management, which begins the first time parents visit the centre to explore ECCE options. When parents apply to admit their child to the centre, prepare them for what to expect. Show them around the centre and answer their questions honestly and truthfully. Explain the daily programme so that they have some idea of the routine. Find out about the child's specific needs, interests, likes and dislikes. Advise parents on how to help their child settle into the centre. The settling approach taken will differ according to the type of centre and the age of the child. Inform parents about the best way to contact you if they are concerned about anything.

Find out more

As the teacher, ensure the centre is organised and the atmosphere is inviting. If the newcomer is a baby, make sure the cot/play area is ready for the child. Let the child bring a special object from home – a blanket, a pillow used at sleep time, a special toy or a teddy that allows the child to maintain a connection with home while at the centre. For older children, have some enjoyable activities set out so that there is something to grab their attention. Welcome the child and the parent warmly. When children arrive, kneel down to greet them – it is always more reassuring for children if you interact with them on their level. Show them their symbol and locker/cubby. Allow the parents to spend some time in the playroom to settle the child. Suggest that the parents set a limit on how long they will stay. They could say to their child, 'I will do a puzzle with you and then I must go to work. I will fetch you after naptime'.

Find out more

Encourage parents to be consistent. When they say goodbye, they must mean it and leave. When they are ready to depart, go to the child and let the child know you are there for him. Hold him and make sure the parents say goodbye to him. He might cry but he knows his parents are leaving and he is not being abandoned. Tell the child when they will be back. Give a concrete example, such as after story time, or after the afternoon snack, etc. All children are different. Some will take a few days to settle, some may take a couple of weeks. Initially, some children appear to settle in very well and then shed some tears after a week or so. Tears are always more frequent after a weekend or when returning from a holiday, but if the familiar caregiver is present, they soon dry up. It is often, at the beginning of the year, a good idea to stagger the intake of newcomers to the centre so that special attention can be given to the child joining the group.

What are your admission practices? What strategies do you use to settle the newcomer?

Something to consider

Ideally, the child should spend some time in the centre with the parent before he actually attends on a daily basis. That way he has time to get to know the staff and possibly become familiar with the routine.

Try this out

Based on what has been written, write a short guideline for parents on what type of behaviour parents might expect from their child at home after they have joined an ECCE centre. Also provide some guidelines on how these behaviours might be managed. A written guideline helps to alleviate unnecessary distress on the part of the parents.

10.8 UNDERSTANDING AND MANAGING THE SOCIAL WORLD

Just as children have to learn about the physical world, they also have to learn about their social world, which is called social cognition (Meggitt et al, 2016). Children have to learn about relationships and also come to realise that these are not always predictable. People's intentions are also not always obvious, and children therefore have to learn to 'read' people and to know that through our behaviour we communicate our feelings and thoughts to others.

Find out more

Behaviour refers to everything we do – to our actions and how we respond to stimuli. As we have just said, through our behaviour we communicate our feelings and thoughts to others. Observation is therefore the adults' most powerful tool for understanding a child in their care. By simply observing children, we can 'read' so much about their behaviour. Children's behaviour is closely aligned to their developmental abilities. These include the ability to sit still, to wait their turn and to apologise with understanding (see Chapter 3).

10.8.1 Learning about social behaviour

As we have already said, for young children social relationships are the foundation of attachment behaviours. It is through strong attachments with adults that children develop an understanding of what constitutes acceptable moral behaviour. In other words, a sense of what is right and wrong. However, if children have experienced insecure attachments in their early years, they may be unable to make sound age-appropriate moral judgements, and this can impact their social behaviour and disrupt relationships with other children.

Learning the rules of social interaction takes time, and during early childhood acceptable behaviours should be made explicit for young children. They can be respectfully told, politely reminded, and adults, of course, can consistently model socially acceptable behaviours (Meggitt et al, 2016) (see Chapter 8 on pedagogical strategies).

Important social rules include:
- how to talk to different people in different situations
- how to be polite
- who is allowed to talk and when
- which behaviours are allowed in some situations and not in other contexts
- the different behaviours that are acceptable for some people and not others, which can be culturally related.

As we have said, these rules are dependent upon different contexts and reflect a particular sociocultural perspective. The question of power can be an influential factor, influencing who speaks first, who is deemed to require more respect, etc (see Chapter 2).

> **Reflection**
>
> In your ECCE setting, are both adults and children respectfully treated? Are the adults, because of their more mature age, given more respect than the children? How do you accommodate different cultural practices? Remember, social rules might change for different cultural groups. These rules may also differ according to the particular time of the interaction and the particular context.

> **Find out more**
>
> Learning social rules is a complex journey for young children. It begins with social referencing (referring to adults' expressions and tone of voice that children interpret to make sense of a situation and guide their response). Children are continually faced with a dilemma. On the one hand, they want to satisfy their own needs and interests, and on the other they are faced with the restrictions placed upon them by their parents and society. Initially, children experience a range of 'dos' and 'don'ts'. They acquire many basic socially acceptable behaviours through being immersed in a safe and secure environment, having their boundaries consistently reinforced and repeatedly being told certain things such as, 'Say please', etc. Gradually they come to understand more abstract rules, such as not to hurt others or take another's possessions. They become adept at controlling and regulating their own behaviour and by middle childhood begin to appreciate and conform to many of society's rules.
>
> Remember, young children lack good impulse control, so sometimes, even when they know something is wrong, they will do it because of immature emotional regulation. As caregivers, handle these situations sensitively. Reinforce the boundaries but do not ridicule or break their self-esteem. In other words, use discipline in a positive way.

Meggitt et al (2016) stress that as caregivers we should not focus excessively on turn taking and sharing as socially acceptable behaviours. We should rather highlight consideration, kindness, thoughtfulness and empathy, as these are important social behaviours. This is also a way to inform children about democracy and democratic forms of behaviour. For example, Thandi, two-and-a-half, happens to be watching as Rosemary trips and falls in the playground and grazes her knee. Thandi rushes up to Rosemary, helps her stand up and says what she heard teacher Busi say, 'Come let's go together and make your sore better.'

10.8.2 Conflict management

Conflicts are a normal part of life. Squabbles and disagreements are part of growing up, and managing children's conflicts sensitively is an important aspect in shaping social behaviours. Learning to resolve conflict should not be damaging to children's self-esteem; neither should it be destructive to the other person involved.

Conflicts arise over disputes regarding territory (space), property (toy) or people (caregiver/parent and friends) (Dinwiddie, 1994). Children find it hard to share any of these. The younger the child the more difficult it appears to be.

Something to consider

Toddlers are still developing a sense of self. Possession is thus important and whatever the object of interest, it becomes 'mine'. They are not yet ready to share. It is unrealistic to ask a toddler to share her favourite doll with another child. Likewise, it is not realistic to expect toddlers to sit still for any length of time. If another child takes the object (even if the toddler is no longer playing with it), conflict can result.

Similarly, older children compete with each other for friendships. They may not like it if a child whom they regard as their special friend plays with someone else. In fact, they may exhibit aggressive behaviour which may result in a physical outburst such as smacking another child or throwing down a toy in rage.

Managing conflict

- Model appropriate behaviours, especially for younger children. Play with them and demonstrate ways of communicating, cooperating and negotiating. For instance, say, 'I see you are finished playing with the car. Could I please play with it?'
- Support children to settle or resolve a conflict. Asking a child to say sorry is not a very effective strategy. Often the child is not sorry, so the apology is meaningless.
- Adapt the programme and the learning environment to suit the developmental stages of the child. This will help to prevent or minimise a number of undesirable social behaviours (see Chapter 7 on the learning environment). For instance, two children, Robert and Vusi, are sitting on the carpet playing with toy cars. Sam and Jabu are sitting next to them building with blocks. Robert drives his car into the block construction, and it falls over. Conflict arises. The teacher realises that this happened because the children do not have enough play space for activities of this kind. She suggests to Sam and Jabu that they move their blocks to the other side of the carpet to prevent any more accidents.

Reflection

Think about a recent conflict situation based on a space issue that occurred in your playroom. How could you have minimised the conflict by adapting the learning environment?

Try this out

Next time young children are involved in a conflict situation, try to involve them in the resolution process. Ask the culprit (offender), 'What can we do to make Sipho [who was victim] feel better?'

Something to consider

Sometimes it is hard to know who started the altercation (quarrel). We sometimes blame the child whom we saw hitting out at another child, yet if we knew the entire story we may find that the child being hit had snatched the other child's toy. Usually both children are in tears. Before you, as the adult, react, find out the full story. Calm both children. Let the child who is the calmer of the two tell his version, then ask the other child for his. By age three or four, most children can come up with a possible resolution. By asking children how they think the quarrel can be ended, you are giving them some agency and voice, as well as teaching them some positive negotiation skills.

Try to avoid possible conflict through the provision of sufficient resources. It is always easier to prevent conflicts than to sort them out. Try to ensure you have not only a sufficient but also a variety of resources that will allow for group play and individual play, as well as materials that offer children an opportunity to express their emotions. Suitable sensiopathic materials include water and sand play, finger painting and play dough. If you do not have sufficient resources, suggest that children choose what they want to play with and then, if necessary, rearrange the groups, for example: 'Sipho, do you think you could go to the play dough first and then I will make sure you can go to the cars.' Remember that anti-waste material can provide additional resources.

When dealing with conflict:
- always talk in a calm voice; there is never a need to shout at or threaten children
- ensure you are at the child's level; make eye contact and make sure the child can hear you; do not stand over children in a threatening manner
- gently touch children to divert their attention; we do not hit or use other physical force
- acknowledge the child's feelings: 'I see you are angry because you can't have all the toy animals'
- reinforce the rules or what needs to happen in a positive way: 'The blocks stay in the block corner. There is a handy shelf where we can pack them away.'
- threats and bribery are not appropriate. It you mention a consequence, enforce it, for example: 'the fantasy corner is now out of bounds. When you pack away the clothes you threw on the floor, I can think about allowing you to play in this corner again'.

> **Something to consider**
>
> Threats like sending children to the clinic for an injection, spending time in the first aid room or not giving them their snack are not helpful. You teach children to be fearful of medical contexts or you can cause them to have medical problems such as a low blood sugar by withholding food.

10.8.3 Childhood friendships

Children refine social skills through friendships. Through play with peers, children realise the importance of adapting their behaviour to remain part of a group. Friendships in young children are often changeable. They may spend brief moments together or might establish long-lasting friendships.

> **Find out more**
>
> Children often stay on the side lines watching other children play and working out what is happening. They may begin to imitate what the other children are doing. For example, an onlooker may take a few blocks and start building a construction, or begin to dig in the sandpit, possibly laughing with the other children. This is called using a side-by-side strategy (Meggitt et al, 2016). The child (the previous onlooker) may then do something different to gain the other children's attention. If successful, they all start playing together.
>
> Some children, however, find it difficult to join in when others are playing and require the positive support of the teacher. The teacher could verbalise the child's desire, 'Would you like to join in? Let's go and see what they are doing? Maybe you could do the same thing and begin to join in'. As Meggitt et al (2016) suggest, it is important to tell the child not to ask to join in because such a request is usually met with a firm no. If the child starts doing a similar thing to the other children, he is usually accepted into the group.

> **Something to consider**
>
> The above is also a useful strategy, if, as the teacher, you want to join the group. You can also model phrases such as: 'Could I have a turn next?' or 'Please can I have that when you're finished?' In this way, through modelling, you also provide children who are struggling to be part of the group with strategies that may help them to join in.

Some children are naturally socially competent. They have good strategies for joining in and mixing with other children.

10.8.4 Dealing with grief

Young children have not yet established a clear understanding of what death and its permanent nature means. Adults often describe the loss of a loved one using terms that children find confusing. For example, they have 'gone to sleep' or 'gone to heaven'. These types of descriptions can lead to children becoming frightened and not wanting to go to bed or having nightmares. They may imagine that they will also be taken to this place called 'heaven'. Give children honest, yet simple answers. Make it clear that the person will not be coming back. Often, our natural desire is to shield children from sadness and loss, but children are perceptive – they know something has or is happening. Obviously spare them any gruesome or horrific details, but give them a short, simple explanation. Acknowledge your sadness and sense of loss. By doing this, you also allow them to grieve and this helps them come to terms with their own loss in a more positive way.

Within the ECCE centre, have some books that tell stories about losing a loved one. Encourage children to play in the home corner to make sense of the loss. Having animals in the centre is a good way of allowing children to witness the cycle of life. Hamsters, for instance, who have a fairly short lifespan, can provide children with some realistic life experiences.

Something to consider

Helping children handle grief

Different cultures and religious groups handle death and the grieving process differently. Be sensitive to each family's cultural and religious traditions, but as far possible encourage parents to help children grieve by doing the following:

- Explain things to them – the death of a loved one, a terminal illness of a parent, a divorce or separation of parents, even going to prison. Make sure they feel in no way responsible for what has happened.
- Include them in the family process of grieving. Let them share the sadness and know it is normal to feel unhappy. Allow them to go to the funeral or to visit the grave. Experts suggest that this is advisable, but it is, of course, a personal choice. Grieving is a process that eases over time, and by allowing the child to grieve, you begin the healing process.
- Be there for them. Give them extra attention, reassuring them that the other parent/caregiver will not be going away. Be patient with them; be warm and responsive.
- Discuss the deceased person with them. Show them photographs or share a special object that belonged to the deceased with them. If, for example, a parent knows he has a life-threatening illness, that parent can put together a 'memory box' that can be shared with the child after the parent has died. Included in this box could be some photographs, special objects/toys, etc, that the parent wanted the child to have.

10.8.5 Disruptive behaviours

Meggitt et al (2016) ask an interesting question: 'What makes behaviour problematic?' Is it, one wonders, an adult perception of how children should be behaving even if they have not yet developed the ability and understanding of adult behaviour standards? Is it because the child's behaviour is perceived as antisocial and shows a lack of concern for others, or is it because the behaviour is disturbing and raises concerns about the child's wellbeing, for example excessive tantrums?

Find out more

Challenging behaviour has many causes. Feelings of insecurity are a common cause of difficult behaviours in children and stem from many reasons, both physical and emotional. Anything that causes physical discomfort can lead to challenging behaviour. This includes being hungry, tired, cold, feeling sick or even a minor injury. Different emotions might spark disturbing or disruptive behaviours. Emotions may be:

- anxiety (a parent has gone away, or the child is starting at an ECCE centre or even returning to the centre after a weekend)
- anger (perhaps at being left at a centre or not getting enough attention)
- fear (of monsters, specific animals, being left alone, etc).

Children may react differently, but common behavioural outcomes related to these emotions include crying, screaming, kicking, running around wildly, hitting out, biting, spitting, swearing, disrupting other children's activities, refusing to cooperate and/or wanting their primary caregiver. Other children may become sad and withdrawn.

Something to consider

Physical outbursts are a good way of attracting the adult's attention. This type of behaviour often results in the child being labelled naughty and soon the child lives up to this label (a self-fulfilling prophesy). When a child is labelled naughty, ECCE staff may begin to treat him as such. It is important to prevent this type of labelling from starting and if it does, break the cycle as soon as possible. There is always an underlying cause and it is therefore essential to identify it so that you can hopefully begin to change the child's behaviour patterns. This is not necessarily easy, nor does it happen quickly. It takes understanding, time and patience to effect a change in a child's behaviour.

Some strategies to help children modify their behaviours include the following:
- Becoming a self-reflective teacher. Identify your own feelings and emotions. Know when you are angry, frustrated or overly tired. Try to be honest about your biases – we all have them. Try to determine what causes you to become impatient and irritable with the children.

- Practising voice modulation. Talk to children in a calm, gentle manner.
- Asking yourself how you respond to children. Do you set the boundaries firmly and consistently? How do you reinforce them?
- Not threatening children. Always make sure that you can enforce what you have said, and, of course, NEVER use corporal punishment or leave children to cry helplessly for long periods of time.
- Trying to imagine what it feels like to be a child in the ECCE setting. Would you feel overwhelmed if you were just one of many children demanding the teacher's time and attention? Can you, the teacher, begin to imagine how a small child might feel in this situation?
- Making time to give each child some individual attention. Bend down when talking to young children – be at their eye level and listen to them. Mention a child by name. Know each child's favourite toy, security blanket, etc.

Something to consider

Consider the following:
- Does the child have a good relationship with a particular teacher? If yes, support this relationship.
- Are there sufficient activities on offer which this child will find enjoyable? Are there sufficient sensiopathic activities that will encourage the child to express her emotions?
- Are the learning environment and the daily programme appropriate for this child's age and stage of development? This includes routines as well as teacher-guided activities. For example, the child might still need help with toileting.
- Is the child hungry, thirsty or tired? Manage accordingly.
- Take appropriate action when disruptive behaviour happens. Reinforce the guidelines and explain that you cannot allow certain types of behaviour. Ensure that the consequences for disruptive behaviour are reinforced, but that these are not punitive but rather disciplinary in nature. The following case study is an example of how to deal appropriately with disruptive behaviour.

CASE STUDY

Read the following case study.

Eugene and Thabo were playing outside with the wheel toys. Eugene bumped Thabo, who tried unsuccessfully to smack Eugene, saying, 'Don't bump me, I don't want to play anymore.' Eugene jumped off his tricycle, picked up a stone and threw it at Thabo. It hit him on the arm and he started screaming. The teacher, who had seen what had happened, came over to the boys. She asked, 'What is happening here?' Thabo said, 'My arm hurts. Eugene threw a stone at me.' 'I didn't,' protested Eugene. 'Thabo tried to smack me.' The teacher comforted Thabo and said, 'Let's go and wash your arm to help you feel better.' When Thabo had calmed down, the teacher asked Eugene to show her where the stone that hurt Thabo had fallen. Eugene pointed to the stone. The teacher then said, 'Is this the stone you threw, Eugene?' He looked downcast, nodded his head and said, 'Yes'. The teacher reminded him about the rule of not throwing stones and not hurting other children. She did not shame or blame him, but she did introduce a consequence for his action. She told Eugene to play indoors for the rest of playtime. She also asked him why he thought the stone had made Thabo cry and if he wanted to say anything to Thabo before he (Eugene) went inside to play. Eugene mumbled, 'I didn't mean to hurt you, Thabo.'

Reflection

Read the case study carefully. Write down how the teacher followed the advice we have given about how to handle disruptive behaviour where children hurt each other.

Something else to consider

Always let the child know that it is the behaviour and NOT the child that is unacceptable.

Where feasible, ignore disruptive behaviour and when appropriate opportunities arise, praise the child's good or acceptable behaviour. Where possible, prevent situations that provoke disruptive behaviour. This in part means, as we have mentioned before, that the learning environment and use of space and resources are well planned. If you know what triggers certain behaviour in certain children, try to distract them by suggesting they play elsewhere or allowing them to rest, etc.

Find out if anything happened at the home (in the family life) to possibly trigger a behavioural change. You hopefully have a good relationship with parents. If the behaviour continues, speak to them to find out if the child has similar difficulties at home. Develop a strategy together for managing disruptive behaviours at home and at the ECCE centre.

It becomes important to work together with parents. Establish a partnership where teachers and parents collaborate and negotiate the way forward, and make joint decisions on how to manage the child's behaviour. Good communication is key.

10.8.6 Some specific behavioural problems

10.8.6.1 Temper tantrums

These occur more frequently in younger children usually between the ages of 15 months to about three years. This child is not yet able to easily express her needs and wants. Tantrums usually result from the child feeling confused, overwhelmed and frustrated. Children may lie on the floor and scream and kick, often in a public space. Children can also hold their breath and might go limp and turn blue. (The child will not suffocate; the body's own defence mechanisms will ensure that the child will automatically start breathing after a short while.)

- The adult needs to remain calm and stay near to the child, but ignore the tantrum.
- Other children should be encouraged to move away (another teacher can manage these children).
- Reassurances such as, 'I can see you are very upset' are helpful, but otherwise silence is best.
- When the child has calmed down, help her to regain self-control and to rejoin the group.
- Do not ridicule the child (there is no place for shaming and blaming) or allow other children to make fun of her.

We are aiming to help children manage their own behaviours and to encourage other children to treat all peers respectfully.

Reflection

If tantrums do occur in the centre, ask yourself the following questions:
- Are the routines sufficiently flexible? Are children given warnings about changes in activities and are they offered a choice so that they might return to the activity at a later time?
- Is the environment over-stimulating and perhaps too noisy? Is there a place for quiet and solitude?
- Are teachers readily available to intervene and prevent possible outbursts?
- Do adults engage in prosocial behaviours? Are they responsive and caring towards children so that the children's levels of frustration are minimised?

10.8.6.2 Bullying

Bullying is a form of antisocial behaviour. It occurs when a child who cannot easily defend himself is intentionally and repeatedly exposed to negative actions by one or more children (Olweus, 2013). These actions may be physical, such as hitting and pulling ugly faces; verbal, such as calling the child ugly names; or exclusion from the group. Bullying involves an imbalance of power and the victims are perceived as weak, vulnerable or different (Wolke & Lereya, 2015).

Find out more

Young children can display a host of undesirable behaviours such as snatching another's toy, pushing a child out of the way, pulling someone's hair and calling them names such as 'ugly' or 'stupid'. However, it is unwise to label young children as a 'bully' because once a child is labelled it becomes difficult to lose the label. Remember, young children are still developing behaviour controls and the adult's role is to help them behave in an acceptable manner. Remarks like, 'We ask if we can play with the toy' or 'No one is stupid' help to refocus the child's behaviour.

Help children, especially those who are more reserved, to ask politely for something: 'May I have a turn when you are finished'? Encourage children to become assertive. Teach them to say, 'NO, I don't like it when you push/snatch …' etc or, 'Stop that, it's hurting me'. As children get older, teach them conflict-resolution skills so that they can begin to negotiate their own solutions.

Try this out

Read the following example.

You say, 'It is Sipho's turn to ride on the tricycle. Why did you just snatch it from him? You are now going to have to wait until everyone has had a turn before you get your chance to ride' (the consequence).

Identify a moment when one child is displaying undesirable behaviour in your centre. Identify the unacceptable behaviour for the child and state the consequence of this behaviour. Write down the child's response, bearing in mind that this may not reveal exactly what the child is feeling.

Something to consider

By identifying the undesirable behaviour and verbalising a consequence, you help the child to recognise what behaviours are not acceptable. It is more beneficial than just saying, 'You have been naughty. Now you can't have a ride on the tricycle.' When it is the aggressive child's turn to ride, take him back to the tricycles and say, 'Now you can have a turn, but remember you cannot push other children or snatch the tricycle from them.' As the teacher, you stay in this area and ensure that all the children play together.

10.8.6.3 Biting

Biting might occur because the baby or toddler is teething, and biting into something or someone helps relieve the discomfort. There is no aggression. However, biting because of aggression is a problem that needs swift action. Aggressive biting is a form of attention-seeking behaviour, and because it results in a strong reaction, the biter continues even though the attention is negative.

The child who is bitten is distressed and the parents are often angry and upset. They might blame the staff for not properly supervising the children. The parents of the biter are often embarrassed and might feel helpless. Do not become angry with the child who bites. You cannot threaten the child or use corporal punishment. You definitely do not bite the child yourself or tell the victim to do so. Reinforce the rules and make sure your reaction to the incident is clear, assertive and consistent (Gordon & Browne, 2017). For example, first comfort the child who has been bitten. Then look at the biter, speak to him at eye level. Tell him that this is not acceptable behaviour and that it hurts to be bitten. Ask him how he thinks the bitten child feels. Do not ridicule or use physical punishment. Suggest an alternative form of behaviour, such as 'If you feel like biting something, tell me and you can go inside and I will give you something hard to bite into (eg a hard rubber duck or a biting ring).' There should be a consequence, such as the removal of the biter from a game.

Look for patterns – when, where and with whom does it occur? This requires careful and continuous observation. If you can establish a pattern, you can take preventative action. Explain to parents that biting is something that happens among children. You will not always be able to prevent it, but you will be vigilant and keep them informed.

10.8.6.4 Swearing

Young children quickly learn that swearing causes parents, teachers and other adults considerable distress. As with biting, the stronger the adult's response, the more likely the swearing will continue. Use your judgement so that you can respond appropriately. Remember, too, that children have heard the language somewhere, and are often imitating how their parents or other close adults react when angry or frustrated.

If it occurs in the centre, do not give it undue attention, especially if the child is frustrated or distressed. Be consistent, and do not get cross or threaten the child. Remind the child, 'I know you are upset but we do not use that type of language here.' Suggest another form of more acceptable language and a different way of expressing frustration, such as punching the punching bag to get rid of angry feelings or using a new phrase such as, 'I am so mad/angry with Sally'. Building the children's vocabulary will provide them with alternative words to express themselves in a more acceptable way.

Communicate with the parents. Encourage them to be careful about what they say around the house or what TV shows they watch in the presence of their children.

10.8.7 Managing discriminatory behaviours and language

Children often call each other names but in today's climate name calling can frequently become a form of 'othering' (MacNaughton & Williams, 2004). It reflects what is occurring in the broader society, and children repeat what they have heard adults say (see Chapter 2 on social learning theory). In South Africa we have many recorded incidents of racism, xenophobia and discrimination against gay, lesbian, transgender and bisexual individuals, as well as other forms of discriminatory and biased behaviours. Gender discrimination may also occur where girls, for example, are not allowed to climb a jungle gym or boys are not allowed to play in the home corner.

We need to support children from an early age to respect all living things, to be tolerant and to treat others with dignity and respect. The ECCE centre is an inclusive, caring, democratic environment and these values, inherent in our Constitution (RSA, 1996), should be adopted by all staff members.

Reflection

How do you construct a learning environment that supports an inclusive, caring and democratic approach towards all people?

Did you think of the following?

- Self-reflection. Consider your own attitudes and acceptance of diversity – are you proactive, tolerant and empathic, and do you treat everyone with dignity and respect? Make it clear that the staff will not support discriminatory behaviour, but will foreground anti-bias.
- Children learn through role modelling and imitation. Do you act as a constructive role model? Do you discourage judgemental behaviour, and model tolerance and social justice? Do you help children accept difference and diversity as a natural part of life? Do you encourage them to talk about difference as a naturally occurring phenomenon?
- Listen to what children say and be confident enough to join a discussion, thereby creating opportunities for shared thinking and the co-construction of knowledge. In a discussion of this kind you will be able to challenge negativity and redirect the conversation to promote an attitude of acceptance, for example, 'Yes, we all seem to have different people who care for us. Jeni has two mommies', 'Yasmien lives with her mommy and daddy, as well as her granny and grandpa, and you live with your mommy and daddy'. Families come in many different types and forms.

➡

- Discuss any incident with the parents. Parents should be informed if a child has been discriminated against and also told how the incident was handled. You will also have to meet with the parents of children who are using discriminatory language or exhibiting discriminatory behaviour.
- Ensure that the curriculum and learning environment support difference and promote positive attitudes to diversity.
- Have a clear ECCE centre policy. This will give staff guidelines on how to manage such situations. Remember, we aim to educate children, and promote tolerance and respect in the early years. We lead by example. We do not shame and blame, and we do not model disrespectful behaviour to the child who is exhibiting discriminatory practices.

10.8.8 Managing sexual behaviour

Children explore their bodies. They look at their fingers, toes, eyes and ears. In the same way, they explore their genital area and their feelings of sexuality. This is perfectly normal, and these children are not abnormal or perverts. Children might show an interest in anatomical differences between boys and girls during, for example, nappy changing or toilet routine.

Find out more

Respond in a matter-of-fact way. Name the body parts and explain differences in anatomical areas in a straightforward way. 'Yes, Peter stands when he has a wee and Lerato sits down. That's because boys and girls are made differently, aren't they?' Try to make use of the correct anatomical names. Boys have a 'penis' and girls a 'vagina'.

By allowing young children to share a bathroom, they can notice anatomical differences in a non-threatening and non-embarrassing way, but if a child expresses a desire for privacy, this should be accommodated. As children grow older (three to four years of age), they may play 'doctor, doctor' (explore each other's bodies) and may also masturbate. This is more noticeable during, for example, story time or naptime. Children do not place the same sexual meanings on this behaviour as adults. There is usually very little that is explicitly sexual about their behaviour; they are merely exploring and finding out about their bodies (Honig, 1998).

Something to consider

If children exhibit sexual knowledge or behaviour that is not age/stage related, then suspect that something is untoward. Observe and monitor that child carefully. According to the Children's Act (RSA, 2005) as a teacher you are obligated to report any suspected cases of child abuse.

Reflection

Before you can manage children's behaviour or questions in relation to sexual matters, you need to be comfortable with your own sexuality. Are you aware of your own prejudices and attitudes towards sex? Once you are comfortable with your own feelings, you can manage children's behaviour and parental anxieties about this subject much more realistically.

Find out more

Some ideas to manage children in relation to sexuality include the following:

- Reflect on your own feelings and attitudes. Do not become embarrassed or angry when you see children behaving in ways that might make you feel uncomfortable. Remain calm and rational. Do not shout at children or ridicule them if you see them exploring their bodies. Simply distract them. 'Perhaps say John is a boy and he has a penis and you, Jane, are a girl and you have a vagina. Now it is time to come and join the rest of the group'. The question of time and place is extremely relevant in relation to young children and sexuality. If a child, for instance, continually plays with himself during ring time, you might suggest to him privately that this is not really the time or the appropriate place for such behaviour.
- Always answer children's questions truthfully. Make the answer short – one sentence. If a child asks, 'Where do I come from?' Answer truthfully, 'A seed/egg.' Children will ask further questions when they feel the need to find out more.

Something to consider

Many teachers give the excuse that they cannot talk to children about sexuality (and some other issues) because of parental resistance. A well-written policy that is shared with the parents when their children commence at the centre will enable teachers to adopt a more proactive approach and enable them to manage all sensitive issues truthfully and professionally. Such a policy provides a guideline for staff, and ensures that behavioural issues are managed in an appropriate way to meet individual children's and family's needs.

This is important in the South African context where many sensitive issues are not discussed as adults could be embarrassed and therefore might hide behind the excuse that it is not part of 'their culture'. In a country that has a high teenage pregnancy rate, a considerable degree of child abuse and where the youth have one of the highest HIV/AIDS rates in the world, such excuses do not address the need for child education and protection.

10.9 SELF-REGULATORY BEHAVIOURS

An important aim of early childhood care and education is to help children develop self-discipline or what is also termed 'effortful control' (Meggitt et al, 2016). This means the ability to regulate their own responses, actions and behaviours in keeping with societal expectations. Self-regulation develops over time and is an interrelated function of brain development, and cognitive, emotional and social development, including positive social relationships (Meggitt et al, 2016). Exactly what has to be regulated will, in a number of instances, be culturally based.

Even adults can find self-regulation difficult. Saying no to something you desire can be difficult. Think of trying to follow a study programme or an exercise schedule, or how you have possibly reacted in anger to a minor offence such as someone pushing you out of the way in a queue. Road rage and domestic violence happen on a regular basis and can be closely related to lack of self-regulatory behaviour in adults.

As adults we help children move from having their behaviour regulated by an adult to encouraging them to take control of their own behaviour. All cultures and societies have specific child-rearing practices and as ECCE teachers we need to take cognisance of the practices found within individual families. This is all part of socialisation, and teachers and parents have to have a common meeting ground. As the adult and teacher, you remain responsible for upholding an acceptable behaviour code in your centre. Playful pedagogies facilitate self-regulatory behaviour as it allows children to take decisions, make choices and be aware of the outcome.

10.10 SUMMARY

In this chapter we have considered the emotional and social behaviour of the young child, and foregrounded the many issues that are related to this. We have discussed strategies for moving children towards self-regulation by focusing on possible reasons for disruptive behaviour and how to deal with it. We have highlighted the responsive, nurturing role of the adult as well as the importance of attachment theory in the foundation of social relationships.

REFERENCES

Bruce, T. 2018. *Early childhood education*. London: Hodder Education.

Dinwiddie, SA. 1994. The saga of Sally, Sammy and the red pen. Facilitating children's social problem solving. *Young Children*. Washington: The National Association for the Education of Young Children.

Honig, AS. 1998. *Psychosexual development in infants and young children: Implications for caregivers.* Paper presented at the Annual Meeting of the National Association for the Education of Young Children, Toronto, November. https://files.eric.ed.gov/fulltext/ED425848.pdf (Accessed 2 July 2019).

Charlesworth, R. 2017. *Understanding child development.* Boston, MA: Cengage.

Department of Basic Education (DBE). 2015. *The National Curriculum Framework from birth to four.* Pretoria.

Gordon, AM & Browne, KW. 2017. *Beginnings and beyond. Foundations in early childhood education.* Boston, MA: Cengage Publishing.

MacNaughton, G & Williams, G. 2004. *Teaching young children: Choices in theory and practice.* Berkshire: Open University Press.

Manning-Morton, J. 2014. *Exploring well-being in the early years.* Berkshire: McGraw Hill.

Meggitt, C, Bruce, T & Manning-Morton, J. 2016. *Childcare and education.* London: Hodder Education.

Olweus, D. 2013. School bullying: Development and some important challenges. *Annu Rev Clin Psychol*, (9): 751–780. https://www.researchgate.net/profile/Dan_Olweus/publication/234087483_School_Bullying_Development_and_Some_Important_Challenges/links/56b89a3b08ae44bb330d3426/School-Bullying-Development-and-Some-Important-Challenges.pdf (Accessed 24 June 2019).

Raburu, PA. 2015. The self – who am I?: Children's identity and development through early childhood education. *Journal of Educational and Social Research*, 5(1): 95–102.

Republic of South Africa. 1996. Constitution of the Republic of South Africa. Pretoria: Government Printer.

Republic of South Africa. 2005. The Children's Act 38 of 2005. Consolidated Regulations pertaining to the Children's Act, 2005. Government Notice No R261. *Government Gazette*, 1 April 2010. No 33076.

Wolke, D & Lereya, ST. 2015. Long-term effects of bullying. *Archives of Disease in Childhood*, 100(9): 879–885. https://www.ncbi.nlm.nih.gov/pmc/articles/PMC4552909/ (Accessed 1 November 2019).

Chapter 11

Creativity in early childhood

Myrtle Erasmus, Hantie Theron and Geo Westraadt

Creativity is a vital dimension of human intelligence **(Prentice, 2000: 145).**

Creativity stands at the centre of educating children who will be the scientists, inventors, artists, musicians, dramatists, innovators, and problem solvers of the future **(Kemple & Nissenberg, 2000: 67).**

In this chapter, we consider creativity in early childhood in relation to:

- its importance in early development and learning
- its impact on the holistic development and learning of the child
- arts activities and creative development in early childhood
- the role of music and dance in the holistic development and learning of the young child
- drama and imaginative play
- the role of visual arts in the development and learning of the young child
- the role of the teacher in the enhancement of creativity in the young child.

11.1 INTRODUCTION

Every child is born with infinite creative abilities. From the prenatal stage onwards, the human brain has the capacity to learn and to think in a way that is unique and individual. Infants develop gradually and pass through a series of well-identified milestones based on various movements, sounds, human contact and interactions. These milestones include being able to sit, crawl and walk; to gurgle, laugh; to imitate sounds and to speak and sing; and to play and learn. In this same progressive manner and with similar support, the baby will begin to observe, notice, absorb and start to imagine.

Imagining is thinking. It is to see something in the mind's eye. To imagine requires higher-order cognitive processes that develop as the young child becomes increasingly aware of his world. Creative development and imagination originate in the brain from the same centre as speech. Young children are naturally creative; it seems to be inborn. Children learn and solve problems through imaginative play, the visual arts (drawing, painting, modelling, making pictures), music (singing, making music with instruments and making rhymes), dance and movement. As they do this, they are investigating and discovering their world and questioning what they experience (DBE, 2015). These wide-ranging thought processes can be likened to creativity.

Creativity, according to the multiple intelligences theory of Howard Gardner (2006), is an aspect of intelligence and cognitive functioning. Thus, every child is born with creative potential; it is not a gift given to only a few, nor should it be interpreted as a child being talented or exceptional (Edwards, 2010).

11.2 EXPLORING THE MEANING OF CREATIVITY

Creativity is not easy to define. A simple definition would state that it involves the use of imagination, original ideas and thinking of something in a fresh and novel way that reveals inventiveness. If we observe young children's creativity, it is clear that each child is doing things in their own unique way and that as their experiences are enriched, they produce novel solutions to problems they encounter. The ideas that they produce are mostly exceptional and fresh, devoid of outside influences that restrict their unique way of thinking. The vast number of questions children ask from ages three to four indicate their curiosity. Their speech and expression of ideas often astonishes adults because of its originality and ingenuity.

Creativity is not limited to the arts and will be visible in every area of the young child's life. Encouraging children to think creatively, to imagine and be innovative develops critical thinking and problem-solving skills (DBE, 2015).

Teachers should realise that if creativity is nurtured, it will grow. Unfortunately, creativity can also be suppressed to such an extent (eg through the use of worksheets) that the child might cease to demonstrate any creative thinking. By providing plenty of opportunities to discover, explore and make, the innate creative potential of every child will develop.

11.2.1 Teachers of young children should nurture their creativity

Caring for and educating young children is an extremely responsible task. It requires an appreciation of holistic development as well as what constitutes contextual and cultural relevance for each child. Plan activities that provide opportunities for young children to play and explore in a safe but natural setting with sufficient stimulation to encourage the development of their inborn creativity. Depending on the age and readiness of the young child, activities can range from talking to them in suitable language; pointing at objects and naming them; using rhymes and songs, gestures and movements; listening to music; looking at pictures and real things, and recognising colours and shapes. The more the child sees, observes, hears and experiences, the more their creativity and imagination will develop. Stimulation should always be age appropriate, and balanced with periods of stillness and rest.

11.2.2 The importance of creative learning

Teachers and parents need appropriate information about the role of imagination and creative learning to enable them to structure an environment that supports playful learning and nurtures creativity. Opportunities for creative learning should be provided as part of a quality daily programme.

According to Krofliˇc (2012), arts experiences promote the development of engaged, sensitive, creative and prosocial attitudes in young children. Aesthetic experiences add to the emotional, spiritual and moral development of young children, bringing happiness and joy into their day. For these reasons, in the Reggio Emilia preschools, beauty and learning through the aesthetics are regarded as natural rights. The Reggio approach cultivates ways of thinking that lead to empathy, attention, sensitivity, surprise, humour and an appreciation of beauty in the natural world.

Creative experiences in the arts support collaborative learning. Through the arts, children are encouraged to respect each other, listen to each other and share ideas. The study conducted by Krofliˇc and Smrtnik-Vitulic (2012) showed that after well-planned and guided creative arts activities such as drawing, painting, symbolic play, making music and singing together, young children were more tolerant and peaceful in their interaction with their peers. They also noted that music rings and drama activities often resulted in the inclusion of formerly shy and reserved children into the group.

Koopman (2005) noted that the children's day became more satisfactory due to rich, pleasant and inspiring aesthetic experiences. Young children's involvement with the creative arts also refines their observation – a skill that enhances all learning. The sense of accomplishment arising from active learning and discovery can lead to fulfilled children confident in their self-worth.

11.3 THE ROLE OF THE CREATIVE IN LEARNING AND DEVELOPMENT

The first seven years of a child's life should provide many opportunities for optimal development and learning to take place. According to Piaget (1964) and neo-Piagetian learning theories (Case, 1992), children develop cognitively in hierarchical stages with each new stage building on the prior one (Casper & Theilheimer, 2010). Young children assimilate and accommodate (see

Chapter 3) the experiences gained in their daily lives. In this process there is an intricate interchange between thinking, imagining and creating. Knowledge is constructed through understanding and making meaning across a variety of contexts, codes and symbol systems (Deans & Wright, 2018). The environment and context in which the development takes place is important because children learn through active experience.

Vygotsky stressed the importance of the social context in the 'scaffolding' of cognitive development (Vygotsky, 1978) (see chapters 3 and 8). Teachers and parents should provide rich opportunities for children to engage in appropriate creative arts activities that provide a context for the co-construction of knowledge (Casper & Theilheimer, 2010).

An important aspect of creativity is that it draws on and can enhance all the developmental domains (areas) (see Chapter 3). As we have previously mentioned, for study purposes developmental domains are explored in isolation, but in reality they are interconnected and interdependent. We have already explored some specific developmental domains in Chapter 3. Revisit these domains in the relevant sections in this chapter.

11.3.1 Physical development

There is no doubt that healthy physical development will enable children to engage in creative play, movement games, dance and role play, all of which are essential for their creative development. Movement is an integral part of physical development that leads to the refinement of motor movements. In addition, movement stimulates the neurochemical synapsis of the brain (De Jager, 2011: 20). Dance and drama as forms of movement are excellent ways of developing gross motor skills in young children.

Movement also enhances fine motor skills including hand-eye coordination (Beaver et al, 2010) Fine motor behaviours include self-help skills related to dressing up, playing instruments, and handling art media and equipment. Children become increasingly skilled through maturation and practice. These skills include the ability to pick up a crayon or a brush to hold it and move it over a surface. Fine motor skills are also necessary to string beads, stack building blocks, cut with scissors and paste, as well as model clay and other media in the toddler stage. They can hold shakers or other instruments and move to the beat of music. Children will naturally build these skills through experiential play.

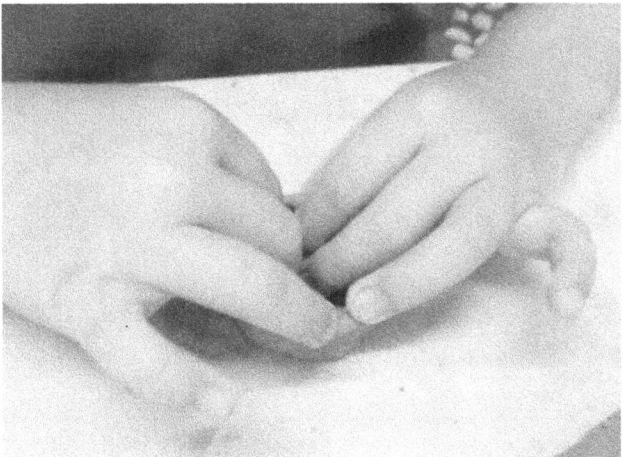

Figure 11.1   Photo of fingers making pinch pot

11.3.2 Coordinating gross and fine motor skills

Even though larger muscles usually develop before smaller ones, more advanced motor abilities require children to coordinate large motor skills with fine motor skills. Outdoor physical play such as climbing up playground equipment requires them to use the large muscles of the arms and legs to propel them upward and forward. At the same time, however, children must use fine motor skills to coordinate eye and hand movements, and to adjust their grip on the playground equipment. Children who are climbing must also coordinate the action of many muscle groups to maintain balance.

Likewise, dance and other movement activities to the beat of music, drama as well as the visual arts promote coordination of the small and large muscles and, of course, contribute to the refinement of the different perceptual motor behaviours.

What we have not considered in detail is perceptual motor development (defined in section 11.3.3). Though there is a much greater focus on perceptual motor development in the Grade R year, it is in the very young child and through creative arts and other forms of activities that the seeds of competence in the perceptual motor development area are laid.

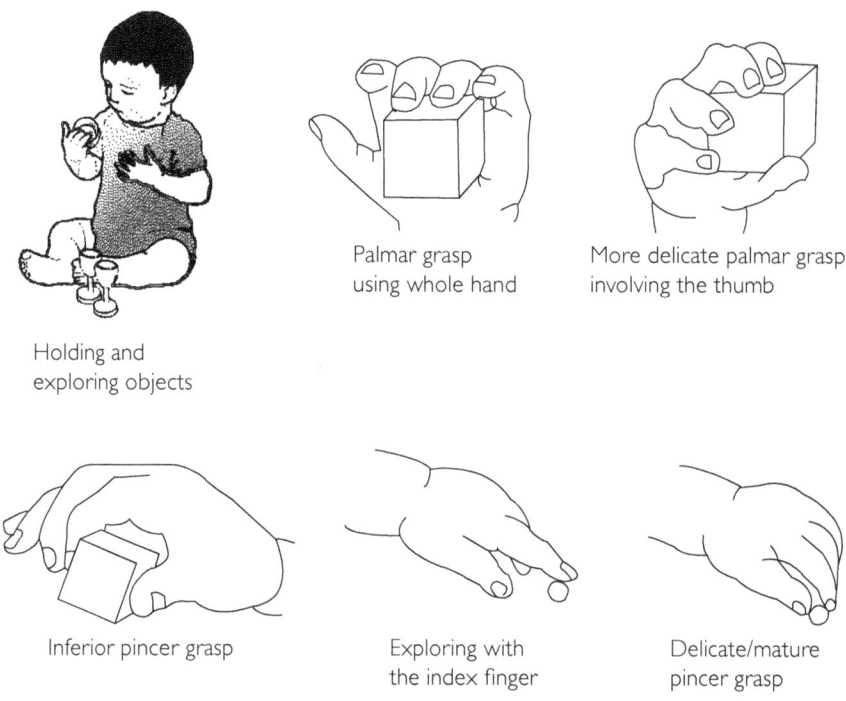

Figure 11.2 Fine motor skills development (Beaver, et. al, 2010).

11.3.3 Perceptual motor development

Babies are biologically driven to make sense of their world and it is the five senses that provide the input for meaning making. As young children see movements and shapes, hear sounds, smell odours, experience different tastes and touch objects in their gradually expanding world, they try to make sense of this input (sensory stimuli). Perception is the awareness, recognition and interpretation of this sensory stimuli. Motor skills refer to changes in children's ability to control their body movements.

Perceptual motor development is therefore a combination of sensory and motor skills. It enables a person to receive sensory stimuli, interpret it and then respond through the coordination of body movements. For example, a baby hears a voice and turns his head towards the sound and smiles; a newborn baby's sense of smell will be activated by close contact with the mother, and the baby will want to suckle. A toddler when riding a plastic scooter bike sees a barrier, interprets this information in the brain and slows down to move around the obstacle. In other words, the senses enable us to draw in information from a variety of sources, to interpret this information (or sensations) in the brain and then respond appropriately.

Perceptual-motor development is a process that starts at birth (if not before) and increases in complexity during the formative years. By the age of six or seven, the perceptual motor behaviours are generally refined (Gallahue & Donnelly, 2003). Ample opportunities, specifically in movement and the creative arts, should be provided for the development of these perceptual motor behaviours.

There are three broad categories of perceptual motor behaviours:
- Spatial awareness and orientation behaviours
- Temporal awareness
- Sensory motor development.

We will briefly outline these three types of perceptual motor behaviours.

11.3.3.1 Spatial awareness and orientation behaviours

Spatial orientation refers to how the body or body part is placed in the space it is in. A baby's spatial awareness behaviours develop slowly. As the baby reaches for a toy, he is beginning to explore the position of a particular body part in space. Later, as he learns more about his body image and specific body parts, he will come to know how he can move and manipulate these body parts in a given space. As he grows, he should ideally have many opportunities to deepen his spatial awareness by crossing the midline and becoming aware of the left and right side of his body and direction in general.

These spatial awareness and orientation behaviours, which are crucial for the acquisition of early numeracy and literacy, will be refined in later years. As children paint and draw, filling a large sheet of paper and moving across it, they are developing aspects of these behaviours.

11.3.3.2 Temporal awareness behaviours

Temporal awareness refers to children's ability to develop an inner and outer sense of time. This includes coordination and rhythmic movements. Moving to music with its inherent rhythm and beat is an excellent way of developing these behaviours.

11.3.3.3 Sensory motor behaviours

Sensory motor behaviours include the following:
- Visual perception
- Auditory perception
- Tactile perception
- Olfactory
- Gustatory perception.

Visual perception

Visual percpetion refers to the brain's ability to make sense of what the eye sees (Loubser, 2015). Visual perceptual skills fall into a number of different categories, which children will develop as they grow. These categories are outlined in Figure 11.3.

The Fourth Industrial Revolution (which explores the shifts in thought and action that we have to make in a technological world) requires a child to be able to quickly discriminate between a wealth of visual stimuli and choose that which is appropriate for her needs. These choices are stored in her visual memory. Although most children develop the ability to discriminate visual images as they grow, some will take longer to develop this and other visual skills, and may require some assistance.

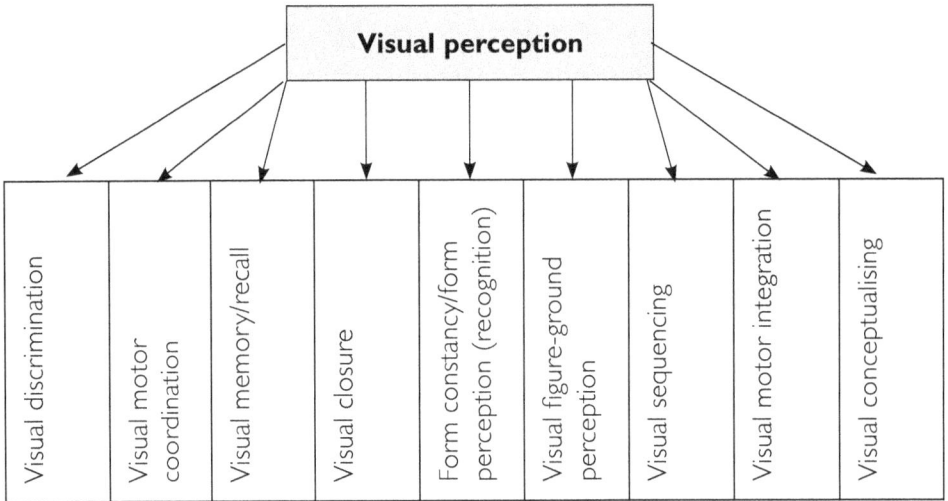

Figure 11.3 Visual perception

SOURCE: LOUBSER (2015: 67)

See Appendix 1 at the end of this chapter for a brief explanation of these terms.

Try this out

A large amount of learning occurs through observation. To provide opportunities for observation, parents and teachers should point at objects while discussing their properties. Choose a real object such as a chair and ask young children to talk about what they see. You could also use pictures and photographs to develop observation skills and enhance visual perception.

Something to consider

Visual acuity (being able to see) is essential if children are going to develop good observation skills. These skills include identifying shapes, colours, textures and lines which are some of the elements of visual art and might be used by the children in their visual art activities.

Auditory perception

Auditory perception refers to the ability to listen and interpret what is heard in a meaningful way (Loubser, 2015: 7).

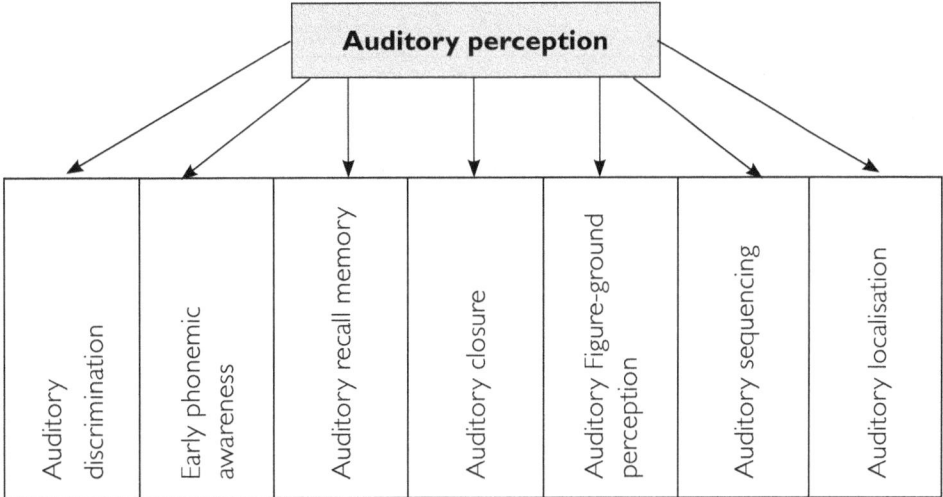

Figure 11.4 Auditory perception
SOURCE: LOUBSER (2015: 71)

See Appendix 1 at the end of this chapter for a brief explanation of these terms.

Auditory perceptual skills fall into a number of different categories, which children will develop as they grow. These categories are outlined in Figure 11.4. Children need to be able to distinguish between different sounds. Young babies will respond to their parents' voices at a very young age. Good auditory skills enable children to distinguish between different pitches (high and low sounds), volumes, and sources of sounds and words, which is essential preparation for learning to speak and emergent literacy. The ability to identify individual sounds in a word is an important part of early literacy. It is called phonemic awareness and four-year-olds, for example, can identify the sound or phoneme at the beginning of their name. This skill is part of auditory perception that is enriched through participation in the creative arts, in particular music and drama. Active listening allows a child to identify and respond to:

- soft and loud sounds in, for example, music
- beat and rhythm
- chants and songs
- stories and rhymes, etc.

Children's awareness of beat, rhythm and pitch prepares them for music making, while language is acquired for speech and communication. This will be discussed in more detail in the section on music.

Something to consider

It is important for adults to sing to babies as it allows them to develop their own singing voice.

Try this out

Children between birth and the age of four years explore and learn through their senses. It is important therefore to provide contexts for sensory stimulation from an early age. Table 11.1 sets out some practical ideas in relation to auditory discrimination that you could use with your children.

Table 11.1 Some practical ideas to promote auditory discrimination

Skills development	Benefits	Activity
Listening actively while walking	Builds awareness of everyday sounds	• Take a stroll to a park or through your neighbourhood • Draw your child's attention to the natural and human-made sounds in the environment around him • Hone in on any unusual sounds and ask him to predict what might be making that sound, for example a bird like a plover that makes its nest on the ground and shrieks in protest if someone goes near it
Auditory discrimination (making children aware of different sounds)	Experiment with sounds: present a playful introduction to music and singing	• Use shakers, rattles and drums • Encourage toddlers to sing along with you

Skills development	Benefits	Activity
Auditory discrimination (making children aware of different sounds)	Experiment with sounds: present a playful introduction to music and singing	Put dry beans, dry rice or dry noodles into a cleaned and dry water bottle. Use glue to ensure the cap is tightly fitted. Let the children hear each sound individually first and then name what is in that bottle. Then place each bottle in a clean sock and allow them to listen carefully and identify what is making the different sounds Older children can fill and decorate their own containers as part of a visual arts activity
		• Make two of each kind and see if your child can find the matching sound • Have your child shake the bottle first while it is not in the sock and then while it is in the sock, and talk about the differences they hear (Anthony, 2019)

Try this out

Allow babies to play with water and hear the sound it makes as they splash about. You could also make coloured ice balls by adding a dash of food colouring to the water in the ice tray. The children can listen to the sounds these balls make as they roll around a metal tray. You could also make patterns by encouraging children to roll the melting balls on a white tray.

Another possible way of developing aspects of sensory perception is to collect different kinds of wrapping paper and use it to promote auditory and visual perception. You could, for instance, ask them to pick out two pieces of paper or two drawings on the paper that match (visual matching). Place transparent wrapping paper (cellophane) under the feet and legs of babies. They will enjoy kicking it and listening to the rustling sounds they make when they move their feet over the paper. Think about how else you can stimulate perceptual skills using different types of wrapping paper. The paper could also be used for different visual arts activities.

Tactile perception (touch)

The tactile sense, also known as the sense of touch, is the largest sensory system. It plays an active role in both physical and mental behaviour as it receives sensations from different kinds of receptors, like touch, pressure, texture, pain, heat or cold (Ayres & Robbins, 2010: 40). It delivers information about shape, size, texture, pressure and temperature (De Jager, 2011: 34). In the uterus (womb), the tactile system is the first sensory system to develop, and is already functioning while the visual and auditory systems are in the beginning stage of development (Ayres & Robbins, 2010: 40). This emphasises why skin-to-skin contact is important for newborn babies. When enveloped in arms or in a blanket, babies become calm. When touched, they respond with reflexes such as grasping at fingers or movements such as turning their heads towards the object touching them. Caressing, comforting skin-to-skin contact makes them feel connected and safe. Daily massages with lotions and oils at bath time, during dressing or changing of nappies offer opportunities for sensory input. Toys, blankets and towels offer a range of different textures, all of which can contribute to sensory stimulation. During art activities, such as making hand- and footprints on different surfaces, young children will also experience different textures.

Olfactory and gustatory perception (smell and taste)

Olfactory perception is the ability to identify and interpret information sent to the brain through the sense of smell, and gustatory perception is the skill to distinguish and interpret information through the sense of taste (Loubser, 2015: 73).

According to Flemming (2014), babies are born with preferences for the smells and tastes they experienced from the foods their mothers ate during pregnancy. In the case of breast feeding, this continues because what the mother eats flavours her milk.

Find out more

Try out some of the following activities to enhance olfactory and gustatory perception, and record how the child responds:
- Add, for example, lemon essence to play dough or paint during creative art activities and ask children to describe what they smell.
- Try these baking and making activities:
    - Make different flavours of milkshakes
    - Bake chocolate and vanilla biscuits.

➥

Pinterest offers a wealth of recipes and other ideas suitable for young children
- Blindfold the child (this can work with certain children but be careful that the young child is not frightened by this activity):
  - Let him smell and identify different fruits/flowers/fragrances.
  - Let him taste and identify different fruits/vegetables/sweets, etc.
  - Let him experience the difference between salty, sour, sweet and bitter (these are the four basic tastes).
- Messy play: use instant pudding as finger paint – children can:
  - experience the texture of the pudding
  - smell and taste the flavour
  - see the colour.

Using food is not usually appropriate. But if there is some instant pudding left over from the children's lunch, it could be used for this activity.. Remember, children should wash their hands before beginning any food-related activity.

Something to consider

Understanding the role of the senses

As we have already said, one of the first ways children learn is through their senses – that is, as they hear, see, smell, taste and feel. Information gathered through the senses, namely sensations, elicits an electrochemical response. According to Ayres (2005), the sensations we experience provide three different sets of information:

1. The first set tells us where our body is in space and how it is moving. This information is provided in two ways. Firstly, by proprioceptors, which process the input about body parts and the body's position in space. This information is received through the muscles, ligaments and joints. For example, we see a step and know we have to move our lower body appropriately. Secondly, by the vestibular receptors, which also process input about movement, plus gravity and balance, and receives this input through the inner ear (Kranowitz, 1998).

2. The second set of information comes from the exteroceptors, which are linked to the five senses and enable us to respond to sensations or input coming in from outside the body. For example, we see a dog snarling and back away, or we hear a baby cry and run to comfort the child.

➡

Understanding the role of the senses

3. The third set of information comes through the interoceptors, which alert us to sensations coming from the visceral (internal) organs in the body. According to Price and Hooven, 2018), the interoception sense is about the physiological condition of knowing what is going on inside our bodies and assisting with emotional regulation. Interoceptive awareness is a means of integrating bodily sensations, for example hunger, tiredness, cognitive processes and emotional feelings such as stress and happiness.

When sensations from these three information sets are successfully integrated, the brain can use them to perceive and provide an appropriate motor response or action. In other words, the senses enable us to draw in information from a variety of sources, to interpret this information (or sensations) in the brain and then respond appropriately. For example, when a child is riding a tricycle and sees a road sign, he interprets it as a warning to slow down and applies the brake.

Try this out

The following activities promote the development of vestibular and proprioception. Try them out and record the child's responses and how they may differ from each other according to the position they are placed in.

- Carry baby around in different positions such as:
    - on your back
    - in front of you with his back towards your body
    - facing you
    - in carrycot, cradle or car chair.
- The interaction this provides is pleasurable for the baby while at the same time promoting a sense of trust between baby and carer.
- Play face-to-face with the baby.
- Move the baby's hands and feet together, as well as across the midline during bath or dressing time.
- During messy art, let the baby lie on his tummy and reach for finger paint.

Find out more

Just as the creative arts enhance vestibular and proprioception, they can also develop the sense of interoception. One of the reasons for discussing interoception in this chapter is that the creative arts can enhance this sense in a variety of ways. Children can experience an immense amount of satisfaction through participating in activities that form part of creative arts. These satisfying activities are called sensiopathic as they generate a sense of calm and wellbeing in the child. Music can be soothing and relaxing; and drama and socio-dramatic play allow children to express their fears and feelings without any constraints. The visual arts offer a way of expressing one's feelings through a tactile medium such as finger paint or modelling play dough.

11.3.4 Sensory motor integration

The sensory and motor functions are basic to all behaviours. As these functions mature, they react selectively to various stimuli to produce an integrated and coordinated response.

Sensory motor integration refers to the increasingly refined and complex relationship between the sensory system (nerves) and the motor system (muscles). Also, it refers to the process by which these two systems (sensory and motor) communicate and coordinate with each other. This is essential in the holistic development of infants and children. Difficulties in and with sensory motor integration is one of the most common reasons why children have difficulties in early academic learning. During early childhood, they need plenty of opportunities to practise and refine their sensory integration skills. Creative arts provide an ideal context for sensory motor integration as babies and young children use all their senses often simultaneously to receive and respond to information from their environment.

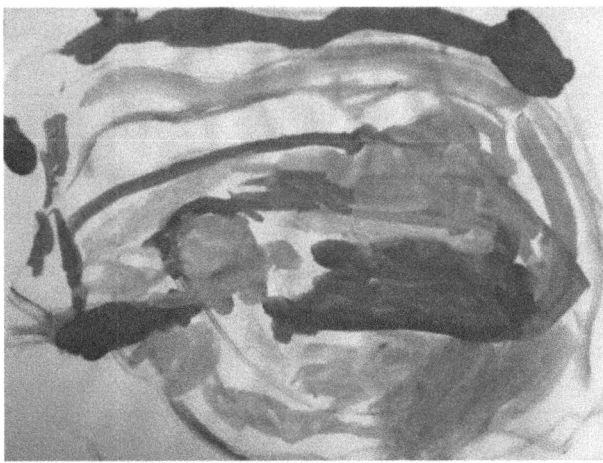

Figure 11.5 An example of finger painting

Find out more

We have discussed perceptual motor development and sensory motor integration, and the inextricable role the creative arts play in the refinement of these behaviours. Remember, however, that perceptual motor development cannot be viewed in isolation. It is closely linked to both physical and cognitive development (see Chapter 3). Revisit the milestones of development (see Table 3.4). Which ones do you think have specific bearing on creativity and creative development? Can you also identify the close correlation between the various domains and creative development? Hand–eye coordination, for example, plays a central role in finger painting see Figure 11.5.

11.4 ARTS ACTIVITIES AND CREATIVE DEVELOPMENT IN EARLY CHILDHOOD

The National Early Learning and Development Standards (NELDS) (DBE, 2009) flag creative activities as an important context for holistic development. The National Curriculum Framework (NCF) (DBE, 2015) positions creativity as one of the six early learning and development areas (ELDAs) (see Chapter 7). In the following section, we draw on the three developmental stages outlined in NELDS (DBE, 2009) to explore how to offer creative activities that are developmentally appropriate as well as contextually and culturally relevant for each age category. According to the NELDS (DBE, 2009: 9), developmental stages are divided into three broad categories:

1. Infant: birth to 18 months,
2. Toddler: 18–36 months
3. Young child: 3–4 years.

In the following section of this chapter, the development of creativity in early childhood in and through the art forms will be explored.

Something to consider

Arts activities is a collective term which encompasses several domains such as dance, drama, music and visual art in a wide variety of genres. Dance, drama and music form part of the performing arts, and in early childhood are presented in an integrated manner. Visual art is a collective description for two-dimensional (pictures on a flat surface) and three-dimensional creations (eg freestanding models, sculptures, and vessels or containers) and visual literacy (looking at photographs of artworks and other visual art forms followed by the children discussing what they observed).

According to Pramling et al (2009), the arts, in their own right, provide an essential foundation for early childhood development and learning. They should not be seen as mere teaching strategies for other subjects. The development of children's artistic capacity fuels aesthetic perception, which in turn leads to creativity and invention. For example, the knowledge a young child gains during the process of creating a unique and original picture or making a model in clay that depicts an individual interpretation that can often cannot be measured, but the lasting effect enriches and broadens several knowledge fields (Eisner, 2004).

11.5 MUSIC

Music plays a very important part in the everyday lives of children and can be introduced into a variety of social and educational contexts. According to Beaver et al (2010: 186), songs, rhymes and music include listening to music, moving to music (dance) and making music. The aim of these early musical experiences is to develop the innate interest of children in music and to heighten their awareness of music as a means of communication and self-expression.

11.5.1 The role of music in the holistic development of the young child

According to the NCF Birth to Four, music allows children the opportunity to creatively communicate, sing, make music (see figure 11.6), dance and explore movement (DBE, 2015: 57). Children have an innate and spontaneous affinity to music. Music can be played to calm and initiate the sensation of happiness and cheerfulness in young children. It can be seen, in fact, as a joyful and exciting tool to enhance the all-inclusive development of young children. According to Arya et al (2012), exposure to music is even beneficial to neonates (newborns). From birth onwards, humming and singing is associated with nurturing and care. Downs (2015) claims baroque and classical music (forms of Western music composed during the 17th–19th century) calms babies. Lullabies, for instance, maybe sung to infants when putting them down to sleep.

Figure 11.6 Making music

Steinhoff (2016) agrees and says that exposure to music from an early age helps young children to speak more clearly and develop a larger vocabulary, and enhances their social and emotional skills. Norton et al (2005) found correlations between musical perceptual skills and non-verbal reasoning (abstract thinking). Involvement in music making and listening improves memory as well as aural awareness for sounds and speech. In short, therefore, as Reimer (2004) states, musical experiences affect the brain, the body and emotions. Making music is therefore an essential element to incorporate into the early childhood curriculum.

Table 11.2 draws together the points we have made.

Table 11.2 The benefits of music making

Concept/skill	Benefits of music making	Activity
Literacy	Songs help children to learn new sounds and the meanings of words as they are presented in context Neural pathways are strengthened through musical activities	Action songs: • Head and shoulders • The wheels on the bus • Siyanqusha ('We are stamping mielies') Action rhymes Listening to music Playing instruments such as shakers, rhythm sticks, etc

Concept/skill	Benefits of music making	Activity
Coordination	Motor skills are developed through movement, dancing and percussion as children move their bodies to the beat of the music	Simon says game Percussion band Dance/move to rhythm, eg march, sway, clap Action songs, eg Hokey pokey; Shosholoza
Social	Children benefit from interacting with the other children in the playroom, sharing and learning to work in a group	Dramatise a song: • Five little ducks went swimming one day • Here we go loo-be-loo • Ring-a-ring-a-rosies Dance together with a friend/peer (cultural dances)
Creativity	Music is a creative outlet for babies, toddlers and young children, as well as for adults. It brings fun and joy to young and old	Shake rattle to the beat of a song Clap hands to the beat of a song/rhythm of music Use percussion instruments: shakers/drums/rhythm sticks/bells and even kitchen utensils or waste items such as an empty biscuit tin used as a drum Do different animal movements using appropriate music: • Slow and heavy = elephant • Fast and light = birds • Very slow = tortoise
Expression (emotional)	Music allows children to be expressive; they move to the rhythm and beat, and sometimes sing along as they try to mimic what they hear	Specific types of music can trigger certain moods Use musical instruments to express different emotions Wave scarves and flags to the beat of the music

➡

Concept/skill	Benefits of music making	Activity
Attention and concentration	The rhythmic beat of music helps children remember. Through repetition, babies and young children can recognise, remember and later recite familiar songs even if they cannot always understand the words	Finger songs: • Tommy Thumb, Tommy Thumb, where are you? • Incy wincy spider Action songs: • Head and shoulders • The wheels on the bus • This is the way I wash my face (to the tune of Here we go round the mulberry bush) Dance with a friend
Numeracy	Songs and/or the beat of the music helps children to explore early number concept	Action songs that involve number concepts: • One, two, buckle my shoe • One two, three, four five, once I caught a fish alive • Ten green bottles Action rhymes Listening to music Playing instruments such as shakers, rhythm sticks, etc
Spatial awareness and orientation behaviours; temporal awareness behaviours; sensory awareness behaviours	Music always involves movement and it is through movement that children develop these behaviours	All of the activities we have mentioned contribute towards the development of these behaviours. For example, Head, shoulders, knees and toes builds an understanding of high and low, while the Hokey pokey ('Put your left leg in, put your left leg out, etc') builds understanding of position in space, directionality and laterality
Aesthetic perception and creativity	Musical exposure enhances an appreciation for music as well as imagination and creative thinking	All enjoyable and fun music activities – such as those mentioned above

It is helpful to have some idea of the meaning of the musical terms to which we have referred. Some knowledge of these allows a teacher to be better informed about the why behind her introduction to music for young children. According to Isbell and Raines (2013), there are universal elements of music that feature in all genres and styles. For young children, important elements of music that ECCE teachers should understand to enable them to offer meaningful music experiences to young children include the following:

- **Beat** is the term used to describe the underlying constant pulse of the music that forms the basis of timing (repeating patterns of strong and weaker beats, eg in triple time (waltz time), beats will be presented as a continuously repeated pattern of three beats – **1**,2,3; **1**,2,3 where 1 = always the strong beat).
- **Pitch** refers to how high or low the sound is – going higher/ascending, going lower/descending, etc.
- **Rhythm** is a term that refers to the timing of music – a combination of short and long sounds (notes) and silences (rests), which is usually controlled by a regular pattern of beats (Le Roux, 2017:62) and organised together in groups that make musical sense (see Figure 11.7).

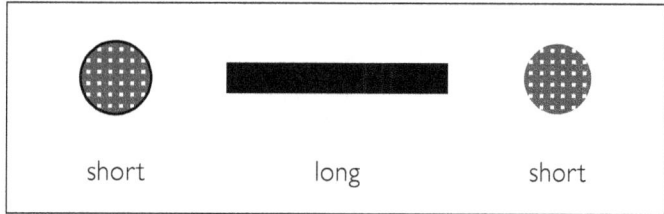

Figure 11.7 The timing of music

Try this out

- Tap *Mary had a little lamb* while saying the words.
- Beat a drum or any object to produce sound and keep the rhythm.
- Teach children the chant: **the beat, the beat, the beat is in my feet**, and let them move to this chant in various ways, eg stamping or on tiptoes, etc (Van As & Excell, 2018).
- Pick up the rhythm through clapping/hands/stamping feet/touching body parts.
- March to music like soldiers (left/right).
- Waltz to music representing ballroom dancing – **1**,2,3.
- Use rhythm sticks to tap rhythm.
- Move to the tune and words of *Shosholoza*.

- **Melody** is the tune of music. It is a musical sequence of high and low notes/pitches that moves by steps or skips. These symbols can also be represented by tapping different body parts on each step (Le Roux, 2017: 75).

Try this out
- Move your arms up and down to the melody of *Twinkle twinkle little star*.
- Likewise, wave your hands to the tune of *Nkosi sikelel' iAfrika*.
- Sing the universal nursery chant (*do-me-re-do*). This is usually the first tune that young children get to know.
- Young children can move their arms up and down to indicate high and low.
- Many teachers use the Solfa system (do, re, me, fa, so, la, te, do).

- **Texture** indicates light, heavy, thick or thin music. When playing a song to young children, they may be able to distinguish between male and female, high and low voices.

Try this out
- When using musical instruments, a triangle can be used to indicate the high tone and a drum for the lower tone.
- Imitate different animals according to musical instruments; for example, drums can be elephants, triangle can be birds or butterflies.

- **Tempo** indicates the speed of the music (Le Roux, 2017: 85). Fast movements can be associated with running like a dog, trying to catch a cat, etc.

Try this out
- Sing the song *Zig-zag dolly* and clap on the steady beat.
- Move according to the tempo of the music: run fast like a dog, slow as a tortoise or a snail
- Use the same song and repeat it in different tempos (*Mary had a little lamb*).

- **Dynamics** are sounds that increase and decrease in volume (Isbell & Raines, 2013: 186). The toddler can experience dynamics by listening to music that gradually grows softer or louder. The difference between loud and soft can be associated with sounds in nature.

> **Try this out**
> - Start a song softly, gradually grow louder and end softly again.
> - Loud can be as thunder, and soft as raindrops.
> - Children can illustrate it by stamping their feet (loud) like an elephant and tiptoe (soft) like a kitten.
> - Indicate 'loud' by stretching and opening arms, 'soft' by curling up.

11.5.2 Music implementation

Children love music and usually join in eagerly when music activities are presented. The main purpose of music with young children should be enjoyment and building a foundation for musical appreciation. Music thus needs to be part of the ECCE day. Music can be used to calm or soothe babies, to attract children's attention, or to move older children from one activity to another. A music ring is a useful way to involve older children in musical exploration, such as introducing a new song, playing instruments, etc. Culturally diverse music should be included, ranging from classical to contemporary and including the many different kinds of music popular in both African and Western culture. Your repertoire should naturally include many traditional and adapted nursery rhymes, children's songs and action songs. Pieces should not be too long and should be repeated so that children can memorise the tune and the words. Where feasible and age appropriate, make children aware of the elements of the music, like beat, rhythm and pitch, and guide them to listen and identify the repetition of phrases.

11.5.2.1 *Listening to music*

Listening is an essential skill for understanding, appreciating and using music. Children will not be able to recognise environmental sounds, learn new songs or move to the rhythm of music if they have not listened closely to a lot of music. The environment is rich in sounds, and these should be brought to the children's attention. While playing outside, the teacher can, for example, ask them to close their eyes and try to identify different sounds they can hear and which ones appear to be the closest.

Isbell and Raines (2013) state that from the first months of life an infant is receptive to music. Babies respond to environmental sounds by moving their arms and legs, or turning their head towards the source of a sound. Infant sounds, such as cooing and babbling, have musical qualities such as rhythm and pitch. If the mother/teacher repeats these sounds, interaction between adult and baby occurs. The baby realises these repetitive interactions bring attention and that sound is therefore important. By about six months of age, babies like to shake objects like rattles which make a pleasing sound. Babies will also reach out for a cot toy or moving mobile that makes sounds.

Toddlers enjoy echoing words and phrases that their parents or teachers use, and they are fascinated by the words and phrases that are frequently repeated in songs and finger rhymes. They can sometimes be heard humming unique sound patterns and words while they are playing and when trying to communicate with their teachers or parents (Isbell & Raines, 2013).

At age three to four, children's language becomes more refined and they enjoy singing songs with other children. The benefits that music brings to the young child should be acknowledged by using songs and music to complement the children's activities throughout the day. Children will enjoy experimenting and making up their own nursery chants (see Figure 11.8). The tune of the widely known nursery chant is the tune to which *Ring-a-ring-a-rosies* is sung. These words can be adapted and used with this universal chant. Children can also make up their own songs based on this tune and other familiar tunes.

Figure 11.8 A nursery chant

In the ECCE setting you could provide a listening centre with equipment such as CDs and earphones for older children to listen attentively to a variety of musical sounds. Attentive listening is crucial and can be enhanced if stories and poems set to music are included with the wide range of different music types (genres). To enrich the children's musical experiences, invite, if possible, musicians to sing or play instrumental works so that children can participate in live musical performances.

11.5.2.2 Moving to music (dance)

Dancing is a unique form of communication involving coordinated and rhythmic movements. Movement is a semiotic (meaning-making) tool like spoken language and can be understood in terms of artistic expression, with the body acting as an expressive instrument that enables a temporally and spatially oriented process similar to a dance dialogue (Deans & Wright, 2018). Music and movement often occur simultaneously. An example of this would be an infant lying on his back and reacting to fast music by moving his legs quickly (Isbell & Raines, 2013: 187).

Try this out

Music can create different moods. Play pensive (meditative), cheerful, lively and peaceful music, and get the children to respond through appropriate movement. Examples can be found under the heading 'Setting up music and dance activities' (section 11.6). Guide them to imagine a specific scene, for example a garden full of flowers with butterflies, a thunderstorm, a party or a river. Some music pieces like **Peter and the wolf** by Prokofiev can be used to create a music story that the children can dramatise. Other well-known examples that can be used to generate active listening and rhythmic movement are the **Dance of the sugarplum fairy** (from **The Nutcracker** ballet by Tchaikovsky), **The Marriage at Troldhaugen** by Grieg, **The flight of the bumblebee** by Rimsky-Korsakov and **Carnival of the animals** by Saint-Saens. The sound and the images in these examples can be related to the world of the young child. Also consider other cultural songs like **Ayo Ayo!**; **Thula thula baba**; **Qongqothwane** ('The click song' or 'Knock knock beetle'); and **Imvula** ('It's raining').

When responding to music, children need time and space to develop confidence in moving/dancing. Make sure to involve all children, but be patient and sensitive to the less confident ones (Beaver et al. 2010: 337). For young children, dance and moving to the rhythm of the music must be simple, joyful and relaxing. Children move to the beat of the music in an improvised manner. Scarves can be given to the children and they can be encouraged to move both the scarves and themselves in their own way to the rhythm of the music.

In a multicultural ECCE context, children use many different ways to express meaning through movement and dance. This provides an ideal opportunity to introduce different cultures and their types of music, dances and traditions. Ensure representation of all cultural groups by sourcing music from YouTube and other resources.

Find out more

Children learn songs and rhymes more easily when actions are added. Choose songs from all over the world that are, for example, funny, traditional, rhyming or silly. Once children have grasped the rhythm of songs, they can do simple accompaniment by clapping and body percussion. Always add new songs to their existing repertoire and allow children to request their favourite songs (Swim, 2014: 238).

Children enjoy action songs and rhymes like *Incy wincy spider, Head and shoulders, Hokey pokey, Ten little soldiers* (or *Ten little Zulu boys*), *The wheels on the bus, Here we go round the mulberry bush* and *Ring-a-ring-a-rosies* (Matterson, 1991).

Source some of these songs and rhymes, and try them out with your children. Note how they move and respond to the activities offered. Do you notice differences according to ages and stages of development?

11.5.2.3 Singing

Long before children sing, they listen to singing. According to the NELDS document (DBE, 2009), adults must speak, sing and read to children from an early age to support the development of their communication skills. Isbell and Raines (2013) comment that when listening to songs and music, babies, toddlers and young children are storing the melody, pattern and rhythm of the songs, and this provides the basis for singing and other forms of musical activities.

When young children are exposed to singing on a regular basis, they will begin to pick up familiar tunes. They will start to spontaneously repeat the phrase 'round and round' when hearing the song, *The wheels on the bus*. Young children often have favourite songs that they like to sing on a regular basis. The early childhood programme should encourage spontaneous singing and teach a repertoire of new songs.

Find out more

Le Roux (2017) emphasises that when choosing songs for young children, the following aspects should be considered:

- The song must be short.
- Choose a comfortable voice range (between C^1 and D^{11}) – which is just over an octave. This is very important because if the range is too great, small children will produce an undesirable chest or throat sound or they will just sing or shout out of tune.
- The melody must be easy.
- The words must be easy to understand and related to their world.
- There should be repetition of phrases and words. Allow the children to add their own nonsense words if they choose.

Identify at least five appropriate songs that meet the above-mentioned criteria for the different age groups.

Something to consider

Singing is the most important and accessible form of music making for children (Kodàly, in Houlahan & Tacka, 2008). Sadly, however, many adults have negative perceptions about their own singing voices and find singing embarrassing – usually because somewhere in their childhood they were told that they cannot sing (Van As & Excell, 2018). Remember, teachers and parents do not have to be musical experts to introduce the joy of music to young children. They do not need to be good singers. By introducing music to young children and singing to and with them, children begin to discover their singing voice and this will probably trigger a lifelong enjoyment of music.

11.5.2.4 Making music

From the earliest pot-banging days, young children enjoy opportunities to make music. They often use their body parts to keep rhythm. Body percussion refers to sounds which are produced by the use of the body parts, for example clapping hands on thighs. It includes clapping with the hands, clicking the fingers, tapping the shoulders and stamping the feet. In fact, any part of the body that can make a sound can be used. Young children find music making satisfying and even thrilling. At a very young age, children can shake rattles according to the rhythm or beat of music. Shaking percussion instruments or tapping out a rhythm can help children to feel in control.

Something to consider

Instruments need to be introduced one at a time, and the teacher must demonstrate during group activities how they should be used. Children should be given the opportunity to experiment with them.

Instruments such as drums, rhythm sticks, wooden blocks, tambourines, triangles, bells, castanets, maracas and cymbals are the most common musical instruments that young children can use (Tassoni, Bulman & Beith, 2009: 316; Isbell & Raines, 2013: 203). See Figure 11.9 for examples of frequently used percussion instruments.

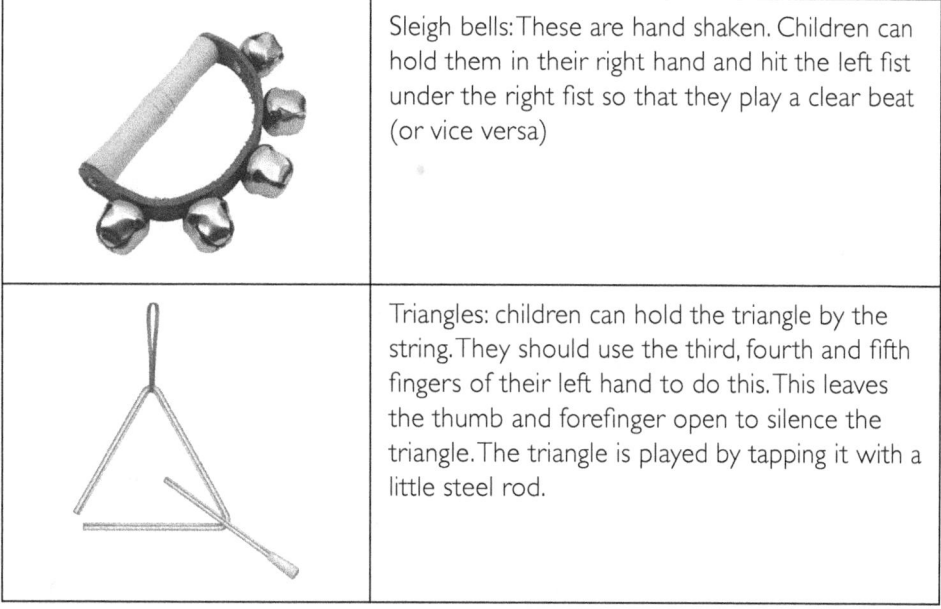

	Sleigh bells: These are hand shaken. Children can hold them in their right hand and hit the left fist under the right fist so that they play a clear beat (or vice versa)
	Triangles: children can hold the triangle by the string. They should use the third, fourth and fifth fingers of their left hand to do this. This leaves the thumb and forefinger open to silence the triangle. The triangle is played by tapping it with a little steel rod.

	Tambourines: these are beaten by hand. For an 'ordinary' beat, a wrist movement can be used and for a strong beat, a forearm movement.
	Rhythm sticks: these are knocked against each other to produce a clear 'click' sound. This can be done loudly or sofly, quickly or slowly.
	Maracas or rattles are shaken, holding one in each hand.
	Drums: these can be played by hitting them with the hands or using drumsticks or wooden spoons.

Figure 11.9 Examples of frequently used percussion instruments

Remember: the correct holding and playing of the instruments will depend on the child's age and hand–eye coordination skills.

Try this out

Making percussion instruments from recycled materials is an enjoyable and exciting activity for young children, and they can use a range of materials to make a variety of rhythm instruments. Empty coffee or biscuit tins can be transformed into drums, and empty pill containers or plastic cooldrink bottles can be filled with dry pebbles or sand to make shakers.

11.6 SETTING UP MUSIC AND DANCE ACTIVITIES TO PROMOTE CREATIVE LEARNING OPPORTUNITIES IN EARLY CHILDHOOD

The role of the teacher or parent is to create an environment with situations and activities that give children opportunities to experience music. McPherson (2015) argues that children from a young age are quite accurate at identifying the emotion expressed through music. Pramling et al (2009) emphasise the importance of having a clear purpose for the activity and to engage with the children in a conversation, pointing out variations in the music. This promotes auditory discrimination. The aim should be to enable children to express themselves in an appealing and creative manner. Music and dance are a powerful ways of getting in contact with one's emotions.

Try this out

Activities that can be presented by the teacher or parent to enhance musical appreciation

Infant: birth to 18 months

Sometimes the child will join in and other times you will need to model an appropriate response for the child.

- Hum and sing lullabies and appropriate songs accompanied by gentle movements.
- Listen together with the baby to a variety of music while tapping or clapping along. Sing along where applicable.
- Play music and move the body to the same tempo.
- Shake a sound making object like a rattle or play with a cot toy or mobile that plays music.
- Make babies aware of sounds in the environment made by birds, frogs and crickets.

Toddler: 18–36 months

- Sing together, in combination with movements and gestures.
- Body percussion, clapping hands, tapping the shoulders and stamping the feet to the beat of songs. Some older children may start clicking their fingers.
- Use shakers and play rhythm sticks.
- Listen to music from a variety of genres (types); use instruments to try to reproduce the beat, rhythm and tempo of the music.

Activities that can be presented by the teacher or parent to enhance musical appreciation

Toddler: 18–36 months

Sometimes the child will join in and other times you will need to model an appropriate response for the child.

- Play songs with a variety of tempos while children dance along. This encourages them to speed up if the music is fast, and slow down when the beat slows down.
- Young children can move their arms up and down to indicate high and low pitch.
- Children can begin to identify loud and soft tones by stamping their feet (loud) and tiptoeing (soft).
- Use a selection of pitch ranges and ask the children to stand on tiptoe when the pitch is high and bend down close to the floor when it is low.

Young child: 3–4 years

- Use percussion instruments and try to play to the beat of different songs.
- Include dancing with quick and slower movements, symmetrical and asymmetrical movements – encourage collaboration. Symmetrical movements are when both hands and/or feet are performing the same motion, for example clapping and jumping. Asymmetrical movements involve using one side of the body only at a time, for example moving either the left or right hand/arm/leg/foot.
- Play music and allow children to enact what they hear, for example walking like an elephant, flying like a butterfly, etc.
- Learn songs from other cultures and in different languages, and combine with dances where applicable.
- Introduce cultural dances from different ethnic backgrounds, making sure to include non-Western music in the programme. Have a look at the following links for culturally diverse music and dance resources from Africa: https://www.youtube.com/watch?v=CvS3JQ7qGcc https://www.rockingtheplayroom.com/rocking-the-playroom/ https://www.mamalisa.com/?t=ec&c=69
- By playing music with a fast beat, children can experience the beat by running like a cheetah chasing a buck. Slow movements can be illustrated by moving as slowly as a tortoise or a snail, and can be experienced physically by walking to the beat of slow music.
- Appreciate and accept the contribution of every child in the group.

11.7 DRAMA AND IMAGINATIVE PLAY

Dramatic play is a form of symbolic play where a child pretends to take on the role of someone else, imitating actions and speech from earlier observed situations. It is a way of sorting out their relationship with the world. When another child becomes involved in the play, this it is called socio-dramatic play. Dramatic play is often the forerunner of drama, which is more structured and is the portrayal of fictional or non-fictional events through the performance of written dialogue. Examples include theatre, plays, television shows, etc.

In an ECCE setting, the focus is predominantly on socio-dramatic play but there will also be a place for drama, especially with the older children. Dramatic play is child initiated and spontaneous, whereas drama will usually be teacher guided. Drama often entails children acting out stories and playing various roles in informal settings. Children should not be expected to memorise lines and act given roles. Drama in the context of ECCE refers to role taking in which children are encouraged to create or recreate stories, rhymes or incidents with little emphasis on learning lines or practising their roles.

Imaginative play (socio-dramatic play in our context) and drama provide opportunities for children to practise and refine many skills and concepts. Both can enhance critical thinking and problem-solving processes. In addition, both contribute to children's ability to strengthen communication. Children are imagining, talking out loud and using vocabulary.

Through imaginary play, children have the opportunity to explore their feelings through interaction with other children and gauge the suitability of their communicative acts. It is through interactions that children begin to understand what an appropriate response is and what is unacceptable. Collaboration with peers becomes essential as rules are made and, as a result, self-regulatory behaviours are enhanced. Role play is a good way for children to express positive feelings openly and to develop ways of expressing uncomfortable feelings in acceptable ways. They can experiment with being someone else, for example a parent, a teacher, a powerful leader, a prince or a princess. They are in charge and in control. They can direct what happens and because they are playing at their own level, the risk of failure is minimised. In this way, children can begin to understand what it feels like to be someone other than a small child.

Various settings and activities encourage imaginative play. These include dressing up, a home corner, small world play, puppets and books.

Reflection

What fantasy stimuli would be appropriate for the children in your care, bearing in mind their cultural and social context?

Find out more

Observe children playing, for example 'shop, shop', in the fantasy corner. Through imaginative play, the young child gets opportunities to develop knowledge, skills and attitudes which will form an integral part of formal learning, for example turn taking, vocabulary development and early number concepts. Identify the skills, knowledge and attitudes they are forming through their imaginative play.

Did you consider that as children play shop, they are using numbers and counting in a way that resonates with the real world by putting, for example, five pieces of fruit in a bag for a customer? In home corners, they work out how many plates will be needed when setting a table; this is one-to-one correspondence. The use of symbols relates to almost every aspect of life. For example, the alphabet is a set of symbols that carry meaning. Children in symbolic play use one thing to represent another, for example a box for a bus, or a wooden block as a car.

Something to consider

'Small world play' creates a life scene that stimulates play. Use miniature items (such as furniture, animals or any other small toys) in the environment that you create for the children (Maes, 2014). This type of play can be on the carpet, in a sand tray or in a miniature dollhouse, spaza shop or farm setup. The goal is for the children to act out ideas from real life. They can also experience what it feels like to be someone else. Props need to be changed regularly to continuously stimulate their imagination. Books, stories, rhymes and poems also stimulate the imagination.

11.7.1 Books, stories, rhymes and poems

From a very young age, children should listen to stories and rhymes that fuel the imagination. When they do so, they create their own mental pictures of what they are hearing. This valuable stimulation of their fantasy world will benefit their creative development. They will be able to observe illustrations of fantasy worlds, of characters and images, depicted in artistic techniques and media. Some stories or rhymes can be selected and acted out using role play (see Figures 11.10 and 11.11). Enacting stories can embrace movement, dance and gestures. In addition, the story or rhyme can stimulate children's imagination for visual art projects as their fantasy world expands.

Figure 11.10   Riding a toy horse

Figure 11.11   Fantasy play: a fairy

11.7.2 Setting up drama and imaginative play activities to promote creative learning opportunities in early childhood

Children often play more freely when an adult is not directing the activity. The role of the teacher is to ensure that the children have the resources to stimulate their imagination. They should have access to a wide range of materials, equipment and props that will support this form of play. If these resources represent their own lives and communities, children can be supported in exploring their own backgrounds. This act of contextualisation will have a positive impact on their self-concept, which will in turn positively influence their emotional and social development.

Some children's play will reflect what they have learned or heard from the important adults in their lives, from the television or from older siblings. This may include stereotypical ideas, such as 'Girls can't be policemen' and 'Boys don't play in the home corner'. Such comments that display gender bias can limit play because they may stop some children from joining in certain activities. Comments such as these should be discouraged, and all children encouraged to participate in all the activities. Your choice of resources should promote an acceptance of difference. For example, terms such as 'police officer' and 'firefighter' should replace 'policeman' and 'fireman'. Non-discriminatory and unbiased ideas that recognise and value all individuals without prejudice should be promoted. Table 11.3 provides an overview of important considerations and some questions to ask when setting up fantasy play.

Table 11.3 Dramatic play: some considerations

Considerations for fantasy play	
Can the children access the different outfits and equipment on offer?	Make sure that the resources are displayed appropriately
Can the children put on the outfits by themselves or with a minimum of help?	Encouraging independence in this area will help children build their self-help skills. Make use of Velcro instead of buttons/zips where possible
Are the outfits and equipment safe, clean and in a good state of repair?	Play clothes and fantasy-corner equipment must be washed and checked on a regular basis for safety purposes. Remove broken equipment and have it repaired. Young children will often put 'pretend' food in their mouths or drink from 'pretend' cups
Are appropriate theme props provided (eg for a tuck shop/spaza shop/street vendor/hairdresser/hospital/post office)?	Hats, shoes, handbags, feathers, necklaces, sunglasses, scarves, different coloured cloths, hairdryer, kettle, medical equipment, empty grocery boxes, etc
Can the children admire themselves in a mirror?	An important part of dressing up is being able to see yourself in another role. Having a full-length safety mirror near the dressing-up clothes will allow this to happen. A full-length mirror is essential for the development of body image

➡

Considerations for fantasy play	
Do the outfits and equipment reflect the children's own culture and that of others?	Children need to be able to act out experiences in their own lives and to 'try out' the lives of others. This will encourage the development of respect and empathy (being able to understand another person's feelings). Provide applicable props and clothes for children of different cultural backgrounds
When the children use the area, do they seem to act out stereotypical roles; for example, do the boys dress up as construction workers and the girls as brides?	If this seems to be the case, you should be thinking about why this is happening. What choices of outfits are there for the children? Are you promoting stereotypes by providing only, for example, nurse and 'impi' outfits? These situations can provide teachable moments where you suggest that there are alternative views
Is there enough space for the children to play freely with the equipment?	If space is limited, set up the fantasy area outside
Does this area encourage child-initiated play?	Child-initiated play supports the child's voice and agency. Allow children to play without teacher interference, but maintain a watchful eye
Are there enough resources for the children to develop their own ideas?	You may notice that some children will share resources but still have completely different ideas about how the game is played. As they get older, they begin to play together, negotiating the boundaries of their game and developing their ideas. They learn to adapt their own ideas to take into account the ideas of others

The activities that follow illustrate the integrated nature of early learning. You will notice that many of the activities include elements of music and movement as well as literacy, drama and dramatic play, and games adults might play with children (such a peek-a-boo).

Infant: birth to 18 months

- Play games in which the child copies the adult.
- Chant and recite rhymes.
- Provide opportunities for babies to listen to a variety of rhymes and poems. Encourage careful listening with voice intonation, and gestures.
- Make babies aware of sounds in the environment – cars, aeroplanes and doorbells. Encourage them to copy the sounds.
- Read from age-appropriate storybooks and provide materials that enable children to enact the story.

Toddler: 18–36 months

- Offer toddlers opportunities to act out short poems with movements and gestures.
- Provide opportunities to listen to poems and stories from a variety of genres, and provide props to role play the story.
- Combine poems and stories with movement, facial expressions and gestures.
- Read from children's storybooks, show and discuss the illustrations, and provide props to enable the enactment of the stories.
- Encourage all children to assist in domestic activities, like sweeping the floor.

Young child: 3–4/5 years

- Provide opportunities for listening to poems and stories from other cultures and in different languages.
- Encourage imaginative play with dressing up and acting out specific characters. Ask children to suggest suitable props for their imaginative play.
- Tell stories using puppets.
- Encourage children to express various emotions using gestures and facial expressions. Ask them to suggest situations that could bring out these different emotions. Combine with movement and dance.
- Encourage all children to assist in domestic activities, like washing dishes Provide smaller versions of brooms, cloths, etc, in the fantasy corner.
- Read and discuss stories with children, and invite them to provide alternative endings Source: Department of Basic Education (2009:16–17).

11.8 VISUAL ART

All children show the potential for creativity in more than one way. There are strong links between holistic development, creative development and the arts. Visual art, which implies creating in 2D and 3D as well as visual literacy (see section 11.3.3), engages young children, and develops their imagination and aesthetic awareness. Their thinking patterns become enriched through opportunities to explore and learn from their experiences. Appropriate experiences heighten their awareness of shapes, objects and details in the world around them. Visual art requires logical/analytic thinking. In the process of innovating and making, problem solving occurs naturally through intuitive, aesthetic and metaphorical modes of knowing (Deans, 2008).

Just like walking and talking, mark making follows universal development patterns. Prominent authors who have formulated stage theories that are used as an introduction to visual art development are Kellogg (1967), Goodnow (1977), Gardner (1978), Lowenfeld and Britain (1982), Golomb (1983), Edwards (2002), and Wachowiak and Clemens (2007). At the same age that speech develops, toddlers will also begin to make graphic representations. They will begin their mark making in their saliva, porridge, in sand or any substance that they can manipulate.

The initial scribbles show very little resemblance to reality, but provide valuable insight into their total development. Their feelings and understanding of the world are expressed through their markings on paper. Drawing develops through the stages of scribbling (two to four years) and pre-schematic (four to six years), and so on, until they are able to draw recognisable images. Recent research has identified the same pattern of development that occurred in the 20th century in drawings made by 21st-century children in South Africa (Westraadt, 2018).

11.8.1 Scribbling stage

From about 18 months onward, as soon as toddlers can hold drawing tools such as crayons or use their fingers, they will start making random marks on a surface. This action pleases them and the results are not important. Gradually, they begin to realise the connection between their actions and the marks they make. They begin to control the haphazard marks and start scribbling. The scribbles toddlers make is their graphic communication. This is similar to how Deans and Wright (2018) describe dance as a semiotic language where expressive movements and gestures precede speech.

When children begin to scribble, there is no top or bottom of the page – they will use the entire surface. Initially, the movements are large and come from the shoulder, resulting in the scribbling going off the page. Very gradually, the scribbles will become more controlled and from the wrist (see Figure 11.12).

Something to consider

The controlled scribbling corresponds with progress in speech; for example, sounds become words at the same time as scribbles become circular. This process corresponds with the gradual mastery of objects and things in the environment. Some toddlers will begin to name their scribbles. Towards the end of this stage, isolated circles will emerge from the scribbles. With sufficient opportunity to draw, children will draw within the edges of the paper and begin to add smaller circles inside the bigger circles and attach lines to the circles.

Find out more

Observe young children in your care and identify aspects of their scribbling that correspond with the research we have discussed.

Remember, there are huge varieties in the ages that children reach the different stages. Their development depends on opportunities to explore with drawing media and their environment and experiences.

Figure 11.12 Children's early scribbles

11.8.2 Pre-schematic stage

Very gradually, circular scribbles become heads and the number of lines attached to the circle (head) decrease. In time, two of the lines will be drawn longer (legs), while the other two shorter lines (arms) come from the head. Inside the head, two circles for eyes will appear and, with time, a smiling mouth. The 'big-head' or 'hairpin' figure will be drawn repeatedly to represent humans and animals alike. Most toddlers will draw themselves and family members first, and they will draw themselves quite big.

In time, the longitudinal lines become bodies. Figures often float in the pictorial space. As they search for their own personal schema, which according to Lowenfeld and Britain (1982) is a unique but recognisable representation of the human figure, they will draw the human figure in many different ways. At some stage, they will begin to draw a neck; arms will come from the body, and not from the head anymore. They attach many fingers at the end of the arms and like to draw wildly scribbled hair. Faces will gradually be drawn with more detail, like ears, eyelashes and noses. Their people will face the front, with a smiling mouth (see Figure 11.13).

Clothing and characteristics that distinguish between male and females, humans and animals will gradually be noticed. The children's drawings are highly personalised, realistic representations, and proportion is not intended or a concern. There is great individuality and uniqueness in each drawing, which, to enable creative development, should be respected and encouraged.

Figure 11.13 Progression in drawing

There is freedom and flexibility as their drawings develop considerably during this stage. Children become aware of top and bottom, and begin to draw feet touching the bottom of the page. Toward the end of this stage, the youngster will repeatedly draw according to a schema depicting the human figure. It is a significant milestone in the development of the child to arrive at a personal schema for a person (usually the self) and to draw a a visual image (see Figure 11.14).

Figure 11.14 Visual images

During the gradual transition from scribbling stage to pre-schematic, youngsters will work on a flat surface of clay as in 2D, and make (draw) their human representation using small bits and rolled-out coils of clay. Through scaffolding, usually verbal, the teacher helps the children become aware that clay has 3D properties (Pianta, 2012). From this stage onwards, they should be encouraged to create 3D models (see Figure 11.15).

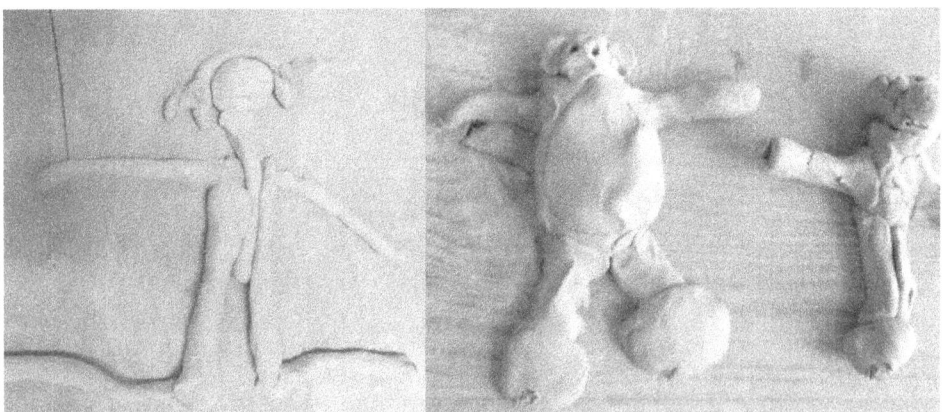

Figure 11.15 Creating 3D models

Towards their Grade R year, children will draw on the baseline, at the bottom of the paper showing they have attained the concept of ground and sky.

11.8.3 Setting up visual art activities to promote creative learning opportunities in early childhood

As already mentioned, drawing is a natural part of cognitive development and every child is born with the potential to create visual art. There should be numerous opportunities for drawing provided in the daily programme. A variety of media (see section 11.8.5) that encourage free expression and experimentation is the ideal, depending on the age and readiness of the children. Activities for visual art should include opportunities to create and make, as well as observe and appreciate visual images. The media and processes for early learning in and about art will be determined by, in part, the children's skill in the handling and application of art materials.

It is important not to interfere with their creative thinking or with their individual depiction of their worlds (see Figure 11.16). However, in agreement with Pramling et al (2009), there should be a clear purpose for the activity, and at some stage some discussion about the processes they apply. Children require carefully considered guidance to inspire and motivate them so that they can express themselves using their visual art skills. There should be a balance between free, creative exploration on the one hand and planned, sequenced skills-based teaching on the other. The teacher's art focus should link with the experiences and cultures of the children (Deans & Brown, 2008).

Figure 11.16 An individual depiction of a child's world

Recommended visual art activities that teachers can consider:

Infant: birth to 18 months

- Make babies aware of colours and shapes in the nursery.
- Vary the pictures in the nursery to make it stimulating.
- Point at shapes and colours, and name them.
- Name the colours on the toys they play with and objects outside, for instance a big white cloud, etc.
- Encourage stacking of building blocks into towers (see Figure 11.17).
- Show colourful pictures in children's storybooks.

Figure 11.17 Stacking building blocks

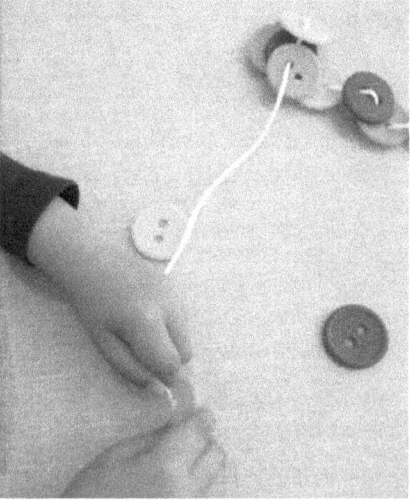

Figure 11.18 Stringing buttons in a sequence

Toddler: 18–36 months

- Make them aware of the colours and shapes of their building blocks.
- Give them large wooden beads in a variety of colours to thread. Encourage the older children to string the beads (or buttons) in a particular colour sequence (see Figure 11.18).
- Provide a drawing surface, for instance a drawing board on the wall, placed according to their height. Children can then draw on the board with chubby chalks in a variety of colours.
- Provide large sheets of paper and chubby crayons for their drawings.
- Gradually provide broad brushes and dyes, or ready-mixed paints and large sheets of paper.
- Combine media, such as crayons, with paint, and encourage them to apply colour to their drawings.
- Make them aware of thick and thin lines, and various textures.
- Provide ready-mixed paints in two primary colours plus white, and encourage the children to mix their own colours and use them in their drawings.

Further ideas for toddlers include the following:
- Children can begin to tear shapes out of magazine pages sorted into colour ranges, for instance blues. These shapes can be pasted with glue onto their drawings, arranged from dark to light.
- Introduce clay for coiling, rolling and shaping.
- Provide glue and spreaders as well as a variety of small boxes and card for constructions.
- Constructions can be painted and decorated with a variety of found and recycled materials.
- Show them colour photographs of appropriate masterworks, and point out the shapes and colours. Encourage them to speak about what they see in this work.
- Encourage children to talk about their work.
- Provide a variety of different surfaces on which they can draw with any available medium (see Figures 11.19 and 11.20).

Figure 11.19 Exploring with different media

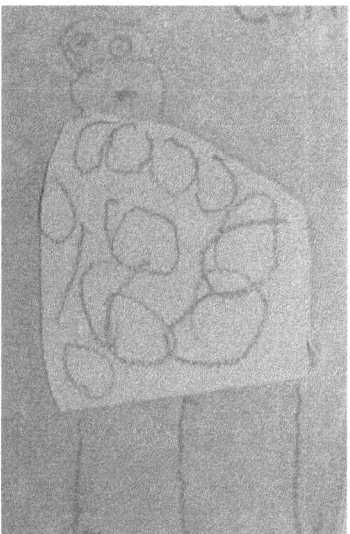

Figure 11.20 Exploring with different media

Young child: 3–4 years

- The activities we have discussed are also suitable for children aged three to four years. These children will gradually become able to add detail to their work. As their experiences of the world expand, their subject range will become wider. A variety of media, such as crayons, paint and collage, can be combined in one project.
- Other drawing instruments such as various types of crayons, pastels and felt-tipped pens can be introduced.
- Dyes and colourants in a variety of colours can be combined with crayon drawings.
- Make them aware of thick and thin lines, various textures, and light and dark in their application of the media.

- Expand their experience of mixing primary colours to arrive at a variety of hues and shades.
- The shapes they tear out of magazine pages for collage can begin to resemble things, such as leaves, petals, etc.
- Clay modelling (see Figure 11.22) can advance into joining pieces together and adding detail in an ever-expanding topic repertoire.
- Provide glue and spreaders as well as a variety of small boxes and card for constructions.
- Constructions can be painted and decorated with a variety of found and recycled materials.
- Other media and techniques such as weaving, threading, cutting and printing with objects can become part of the programme.

Further enriching activities
- Show them colour photographs of appropriate masterworks from around the world and let them point out the shapes and colours. Enlarge their 'visual vocabulary' by showing them 3D work and crafts.
- Encourage them to speak about what they see in the work they observe.
- Plan time for the children to comment about their own work and that of their peers (see Figure 11.21). This picture allows for many descriptive possibilities.

Figure 11.21 A catalyst for discussion

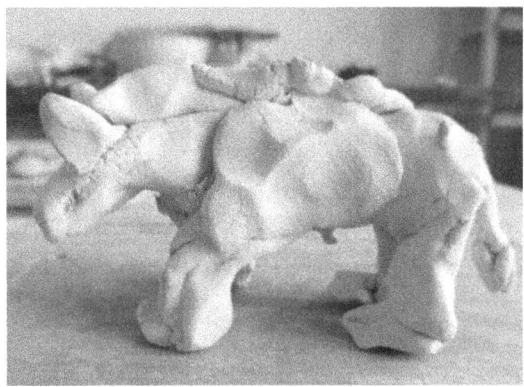

Figure 11.22 Creative clay modelling

Something to consider

During this phase, thinking becomes more sophisticated so that it is not only reliant on sensorimotor input. The development and use of language during this stage is immense. Youngsters portray an originality and inventiveness that is rarely equalled after the age of six.

11.8.4 Media suggestions for visual art projects

Edwards (2010) maintains that children deserve proper media and material for visual expression:

- Draw up and submit a budget to management for art materials.
- Locally manufactured media are more affordable. Obtain a catalogue online. Most suppliers will deliver. Compare prices.
- There is a large variety of drawing media, crayons and markers available. Start with the basics and gradually build up a stock.
- It is more cost effective to purchase powder paint and mix it according to daily needs.
- To start, you only need paint in the primary colours (red, yellow and blue), plus white. Buy more white and yellow than blue and red because the latter are stronger colours and you will therefore use less.
- Buy broad, short-handled brushes. Teach the children to wash and care for brushes and equipment after use. Never use brushes to spread glue.
- Construction glue is less expensive than glue sticks and it can be thinned with water.
- Use glue spreaders cut out of a shoebox to save money.
- Provide the glue to the children on a piece of paper. Left-over glue can be scooped back into the container.

- Food colouring costs far more than locally manufactured dyes. These are obtainable in a wide range of colours, for instance from DALA, and are child friendly and non-toxic. Their web address is https://www.dala.co.za
- Earthenware clay is much cheaper than play dough, and it can be recycled. There are various varieties available which do not require firing. We do not encourage the use of food (eg flour) as an ingredient for play dough. One kilogram of flour costs double the price of the same amount of clay, which can be sourced naturally.
- Ask parents to collect and bring to the ECCE centre newspapers and magazines, cleaned margarine containers, cereal and egg boxes, and other small boxes. Collect lids and bottle tops, coffee tins, wool and string, and any other materials that can be used for visual art.
- Be innovative with the use of recycled material: newspaper pages can become a surface for drawing. Glue four used A4 worksheets together to provide an A2 drawing surface, or two for an A3 size.
- The side of a large cereal package or cardboard box can provide a suitable surface for artwork.

Something to consider

Choosing creative art products for small children

- Art activities are common in ECCE centres, and teachers sometimes assume that all craft supplies are safe and appropriate for children. However, they must be aware that products bearing the CL (caution label) can contain toxic ingredients and are not appropriate to use with young children. Rather buy art accessories that have labels that indicate that they are non-toxic.
- Suggestions when choosing products for the ECCE programme
    - Instant papier maché can contain toxic substances that can be easily inhaled.
    - Avoid using permanent felt-tipped markers. Rather use water-based ones.
    - Use white glue (polyvinyl acetate), which is the safest for children. Avoid adhesives/glue that are not water based.
    - Do not use aerosol spray cans and products that can stain the skin or clothing, or chemicals such as acids and alkalis, such as bleach.
- Older materials are more likely to contain toxic substances, like lead or asbestos, which can be present in old papier maché and modelling materials.

Choosing creative art products for small children

- Safety precautions during art activities:
  - Children should not be allowed to eat or drink while using art and craft material.
  - Always clean the creative art area with soap and water – this clean-up area should not be used for food preparation.
  - Children's hands and art supplies like brushes must be washed after working with art materials.
  - If possible, keep art materials in the original packaging, which includes a list of the ingredients and safety information. Make sure that all art materials are marked and safely stored.
  - Always use non-toxic paint.
  - Do not use apparatus with sharp edges (children using scissors need careful supervision).
  - Continuous supervision is essential.

11.8.5 Suggestions for parents in relation to the creative development of their young children

- Let your children watch your face while you talk or sing to them.
- Sometimes carry babies at shoulder height so that they can look at their surroundings and observe different environments.
- Interesting mobiles overhanging babies' cribs, colourful pictures in the nursery and music playing during their wakeful periods increase opportunities for perceptual stimulation.
- Never interfere when toddlers are drawing, especially not to show them how to do something. Colouring-in books or photocopied sheets stifle their creativity. Rather let them apply colour to their own drawings.
- Read and tell stories. This enables children to form their own mental images of the story.
- Play music that allows discussion of the sounds of various instruments, the tune and rhythm.
- Limit screen time in early childhood. Encourage free, childlike and original play and experimentation without the influence and intrusion of technological devices.
- Consider that branded and labelled children's clothing, books, magazines and other media can encourage stereotyping; for instance, the concept of 'pretty' means being 'blonde, slim and blue-eyed'. Rather discourage consumerist ideas and guide children to be themselves without the pressure of conforming to the latest trends.

11.9 SUMMARY

The creative arts provide innumerable opportunities for holistic development, wellbeing and the general enrichment of a child's life. Drama, visual art, music and dance are a natural context for the enhancement of creativity and the fuelling of the imagination and innovation. The creative efforts of every child should be encouraged, supported and, where necessary, mediated appropriately. Creativity is an innate quality of childhood. It can be sparked through creative movement such as dance, a story or rhyme that lends itself to role play, music that can be responded to and visual arts using a range of media. A knowledgeable, flexible teacher is a major role player in the generation of opportunity for learning and development. On many occasions, a 'hands-off' approach by teachers as young children enact their fears, delights, interests and observations in child-initiated arts activities results in greater participation by children. A child's self-esteem and confidence can also be boosted in this context. The environment the teacher provides and the identification and use of teachable moments set a context for rich engagement in the creative arts.

Appendix 1: A brief explanation of some perceptual motor terms

Where applicable, these terms refer to all sensory perceptual skills. Remember that the very young child may only be beginning to develop the basis of some of these skills.

Discrimination

Discrimination refers to the ability to differentiate one object or sound from another, either through the sense of sight or hearing. For example, a toddler distinguishes between a blue and a red mug, or between a door slamming and a car starting.

Perceptual motor coordination

Perceptual motor coordination refers to the eyes and/or ears and muscles working together to enable a baby to play with a baby gym or a toddler to move to music, for example.

Memory/recall

This is the ability to store and recall information that is seen, heard, touched, tasted or smelt, for example remembering where an object has been placed, following a simple instruction, or rejecting a vegetable that has been tasted once and disliked.

Closure

Closure is the ability to complete objects, pictures or drawings from an incomplete visual picture or stimulus, or to complete a sound. Visual closure requires the child to recognise or identify the whole object even though the total picture/stimulus is not presented. Auditory closure/blending is the ability to blend sounds into a complete word, for example a child hears 'butter' and because he is in an outside environment, he 'closes' or completes the word to 'butterfly'.

Form constancy and form perception (recognition)

Form constancy is the ability to distinguish between forms and symbols in one's environment, regardless of their size or position. It is also the ability to observe certain characteristics of objects such as form or shape, colour and clarity, for example recognising a circle as a circle because of its unique shape or that a specific letter of the alphabet is the same whether it is a lower-case or capital letter. For example, the child recognises a triangle no matter which way it is facing.

Figure-ground perception

Figure-ground perception refers to the ability to distinguish an object or a sound from its surrounding background and to make a meaningful distinction between objects or sounds. Children must be able to distinguish between foreground and background. They must be able to concentrate on things in the foreground while ignoring the background. For example, they can hear a bell ring even though there is a lot of background noise, or see a specific shape in among many other shapes.

Sequencing

This is the ability to place a series of items in the order they were observed or heard. For example, give children pictures of each part of the daily programme and ask them to place the pictures in the correct order. The alphabet, numbers and the months of the year are learned as auditory sequences. This is best done in a singing context.

Auditory localisation

This refers to the ability to localise sounds in space in relation to oneself, for example hearing a car in the distance. To develop auditory localisation, let the children sit quietly or lie on the carpet with their eyes closed. Present a sound and ask them to identify where it is coming from, for example outside or by the door, etc. To make the listening more interesting, the teacher could cut out paper masks for the children to wear over their eyes and thus increase the challenge by eliminating peeping.

Tactile and kinaesthetic perception

Tactile and kinaesthetic perception go hand in hand. Tactile perception refers to the sense of touch, while kinaesthetic perception deals with the sense of body movements and muscle feelings. Together they provide information about body movements and their interrelationships, and therefore form an important part of perceptual motor learning.

Olfactory perception

This is the ability to recognise and interpret information sent to the brain through the sense of smell. To develop this sense, cover the children's eyes with a mask, and ask them to smell and identify certain fruit, such as bananas or pineapples, without touching them. Do the same with vegetables, herbs, etc. Draw the child's attention to specific smells – the smell of rain, newly cut grass, a flower in the garden, etc.

Gustatory perception

This is the ability to recognise and interpret information through the sense of taste. The tongue identifies five different tastes – sweet, sour, bitter, salty and *umami* – a strong savoury flavour that makes Marmite and sushi so hard for some to resist. The sense of smell plays a further role in identifying specific tastes.

REFERENCES

Anthony, M. 2019. *Activities that explore hearing for 0–2 year olds.* https://www.scholastic.com/parents/kids-activities-and-printables/activities-for-kids/activities-explore-hearing-0-2-year-olds.html (Accessed 12 February 2019).

Arya, R, Chansoria, M, Konanki, R & Dileep, K. 2012. Maternal music exposure during pregnancy influences neonatal behaviour. *International Journal of Paediatrics.* Creative Commons.

Ayres, AJ. 2005. *Sensory integration and the child.* Los Angeles: Western Psychological Services.

Ayres, AJ & Robbins, J. 2010. *Sensory integration and the child.* Los Angeles: Western Psychological Services.

Barrett, MS. 2016. Attending to 'culture in the small': A narrative analysis of the role of play, thought and music in young children's world-making. *Research Studies in Music Education*, 38(1): 41–54.

Beaver, M, Brewster, J, Neaum, S, Sheppard, H & Tallack, J. 2010. *Children's care, learning and development: Nvq 2 candidate handbook.* Cheltenham United Kingdom: Nelson Thornes Ltd.

Bronfenbrenner, U. 1979. *The ecology of human development.* Cambridge, MA: Harvard University Press.

Case, R., 1992. *Intellectual development from birth to adulthood: A neo-Piagetian interpretation.* New Jersey: Erlbaum.

Casper, V & Theilheimer, R. 2010. *Early childhood education. Learning together.* New York: McGraw-Hill.

Deans, J & Brown, R. 2008. Reflection, renewal and relationship building: An ongoing journey in early childhood arts education *Contemporary Issues in Early Childhood.* (9)4. http://www.wwwords.co.uk/CIEC (Accessed 31 July 2018).

Deans, J & Wright, S. 2018. *Dance-play and drawing-telling as semiotic tools for young children's learning.* New York : Routledge.

De Jager, M. 2011. *Baba gim.* Welgemoed, South Africa: Metz Press.

Department of Basic Education (DBE). 2015. *The South African National Curriculum Framework from birth to four.* Pretoria.

Department of Basic Education (DBE). 2009. *National early learning and development standards for children birth to four years (NELDS).* Pretoria.

Downs, R. 2015. 5 Amazing things preborn children can do inside the womb. *National Right to Life News,* 1 May.

Edwards, LC. 2010 *The creative arts. A process approach for teachers and children.* London: Pearson.

Eisner, E. 2004. *The arts and the creation of mind.* New York: Yale.

Estes, LS. 2010. *Essentials of childcare and early education.* London: Pearson.

Extension. 2015. Play activities to encourage motor development in childcare. http://articles.extension.org/pages/25802/play-activities-to-encourage-motor-development-in-child-care (Accessed 16 July 2018).

Extention. 2015. What childcare providers can expect in infants' physical development. http://articles.extension.org/pages/25651/what-child-care-providers-can-expect-in-infants-physical-development (Accessed 16 July 2018).

Fein, G. 1981. *Child development.* New Jersey: Prentice Hall.

Flemming, A. 2014. How a child's food preferences begin in the womb. *The Guardian Weekly.* https://www.theguardian.com/lifeandstyle/wordofmouth/2014/apr/08/child-food-preferences-womb-pregnancy-foetus-taste-flavours (Accessed 1 November 2019).

Gallahue, DL & Donnelly, PL. 2003. *Developmental physical education for all children.* Champaign, IL: Human Kinetics.

Gardner, 2006. *Multiple intelligences: New horizons in theory and practice.* Jackson, TN: Ingram Publishing Services.

Gordon, AM & Browne, KW. 2017. *Beginnings & beyond: Foundations in early childhood education.* Boston: USA: Cengage Learning.

Houlahan, M & Tacka, P. 2008. *Kodály today: A cognitive approach to elementary music education.* Oxford: Oxford University Press.

Kear, M & Callaway, G. 2000. *Improving teaching and learning in the arts.* NY: Falmer Press.

Koopman, C. 2005. Art as fulfilment: On the justification of education in the arts. *Journal of Philosophy of Education*, 39(1): 85–97. http://proquest.umi.com/ (Accessed 16 August 2016).

Kranowitz, CS. 1998. *The out-of-sync child.* New York: The Berkley Group.

Kemple, MK & Nissenberg, SA. 2000. Nurturing creativity in early childhood education: Families are part of it. *Early Childhood Education Journal*, 28(1): 67.

Krofliˇc, R. 2012. The role of artistic experiences in the comprehensive inductive educational approach. *Pastoral Care in Education: An International Journal of Personal, Social and Emotional Development.* 30(3): 263–280. http://dx.doi.org/10.1080/02643944.2012.671342 (Accessed 24 February 2015).

Krofliˇc, R & Smirtnik-Vitulic, H. 2012. The role of artistic experiences in the comprehensive inductive educational approach. *Pastoral Care in Education: An International Journal of Personal, Social and Emotional Development,* 30(3): 263–280. http://dx.doi.org/10.1080/02643944.2012.671342 (Accessed 24 February 2015).

Inverarity, L. 2018. *An overview of proprioception.* https://www.verywellhealth.com/proprioception-2696141 (Accessed 20 February 2019).

Isbell, RT & Raines, SC. 2013. *Creativity and the arts with young children.* Annapolis, MD: Linda Ganster.

Le Roux, A. 2017. *Music in early childhood development and the Foundation Phase (0–9 years).* Pretoria: Le Roux.

Loubser, A. 2015. Knowing the Grade R child, in Excell, L & Linington V (eds). *Teaching Grade R.* Cape Town: Juta & Co. 50–76.

Lowenfeld, V & Britain, WL. 1982. *Creative and mental growth.* London: Macmillan.

Maes, A. 2014. *A beginner's guide to small word play.* http://littleworldsbigadventures.com/a-beginners-guide-to-small-world-play/ (Accessed 20 February 2019).

Mascolo, MF. 2015. *Theories of cognitive development.* New York: Elsevier.

McPherson, GE (ed). 2015. *The child as musician: A handbook of musical development.* Oxford Scholarship Online. (Accessed 31 July 2018).

Matterson, E. 1991. *This little puffin.* London: Puffin Books.

Norton, A, Winner, E, Cronin, K, Lee, D & Schlaug, G. 2005. Are there pre-existing neural, cognitive, or motoric markers for musical ability? *Brain and Cognition*, 59(2): 124–134. doi:10.1016/j.bandc (Accessed 17 July 2018).

Ohgi, S, Takahashi, T, Nugent, JK, Arisawa, K & Akiyama, T. 2003. Neonatal behavioral characteristics and later behavioral problems. *Clinical Pediatrics*, 42: 679–686.

Oswalt, A. 2018. Early childhood physical development: Gross and fine motor development. https://www.gracepointwellness.org/462-child-development-parenting-early-3-7/article/12755-early-childhood-physical-development-gross-and-fine-motor-development (Accessed 16 July 2018).

Piaget, J. 1964. Cognitive development in children: Development and learning. *Journal of Research in Scientific Teaching*, 2: 176-186. https://onlinelibrary.wiley.com/doi/abs/10.1002/tea.3660020306 (Accessed 1 November 2019).

Pianta, RC (ed). 2012. *Handbook of early childhood education*. New York: The Guildford Press.

Phenix, S. 2019. *The vestibular system: Definition, anatomy & function*. https://study.com/academy/lesson/the-vestibular-system-definition-anatomy-function.html (Accessed 20 February 2019).

Samuelsson, IP, Carlsson, A, Olsson, B, Pramlinga, N & Wallerstedt, C. 2009. The art of teaching children the arts: Music, dance and poetry with children aged 2–8 years old. *International Journal of Early Years Education,* 17(2): 119–135. http://www.informaworld.com (Accessed 31 July 2018).

Prentice, R. 2000. Creativity a reaffirmation of its place in early childhood education. *The Curriculum Journal,* Summer, 11(2): 145.

Price, CJ & Hooven, C. 2018. Interoceptive awareness skills for emotion regulation: Theory and approach of mindful awareness in body-oriented therapy (MABT). *Frontiers in Psychology*, 9: 798. google.com/search?q=Price%2C+CJ.%26+Hooven&rlz=1C1CAFA_enZA657ZA657&oq=Price%2C+CJ.%26+Hooven&aqs=chrome..69i57j69i59.1628j0j7&sourceid=chrome&ie=UTF- (Accessed 1 November 2019).

Reimer, B. 2004. New brain research on emotion and feeling: Dramatic implications for music education. *Arts Education Policy Review*, 6(2): 21–27.

Santrock, JW. 2010. *Child development*. 7th ed. London: Brown & Benchmark.

Sigelman, CK. & Rider, EA. 2003. *Life-span human development*. Belmont, CA: Wadsworth.

Steinhoff, A. 2016. *The importance of music in early childhood development*. https://novakdjokovicfoundation.org/importance-music-early-childhood-development/ (Accessed 16 July 2018).

Swim, TJ. 2014. *Infants & toddlers curriculum and teaching.* 8th ed. Belmont, CA: Wadsworth Cengage Learning.

Tassoni, P, Bulman, K & Beith, K. 2009. *Children's care, learning and development candidate handbook.* Oxford: Heinemann.

Van As, AJ & Excell, L. 2018. Strengthening early childhood teacher education towards a play-based pedagogical approach through a music intervention programme. *South African Journal of Childhood Education* 8(1): a525. https://doi.org/10.4102/sajce.v8i1.525/

Vygotsky, L. 1978. *Mind in society. The development of higher mental processes.* Cambridge, MA: Harvard University Press.

Wendy, LH. 2018. The importance of service learning in the early years: Taking ownership of your own community. *Early Years Bulletin*, Summer, 5(4).

Westraadt, G. 2018. *The drawings of young children.* EASA Conference, Durban, South Africa.

Chapter 12

From babbles to books: literacy and the young child

Elsabe Wessels, Zelda Barends, Vivien Linington and Lorayne Excell

In this chapter, we consider

- what literacy is and how it relates to the young child
- the holistic nature of literacy development in young children
- strategies to promote early literacy development in young children
- early intervention if difficulties arise
- diversity and multilingualism.

12.1 INTRODUCTION

This chapter deals with the language development of the young child and how this early development contributes to communicative competence as well as later success in reading and writing. Literacy development begins very early in a child's life and lays the foundation for learning to read and write (Paulson, Moats & Nelson, 2010).

The National Association for the Education of Young Children (NAEYC) emphasises that the early childhood years – from birth through age eight – are the most important period for literacy development (NAEYC, 1998: 30). Snow, Burns and Griffin (1998), together with Paulson et al (2010), consider the early literacy development phase from birth to six years as particularly important. These crucial six years largely determine a child's overall literacy development, therefore during this time children should be exposed to as much language and literacy as possible so that they can eventually become skilled readers (Snow et al, 1998).

Whitehead (2010: 83) points out that 'babies and very young children entering group care and education settings are in the process of accomplishing their greatest intellectual and social feat of learning: they are, with very rare exceptions, learning to produce and understand a language or two'. Whitehead in fact argues that the most significant aspect of knowledge about language for the early childhood care and education (ECCE) teacher is the insight that language is about human potential. An important context for realising this potential is play, so much so that documentation for the early years in the UK acknowledges the importance of play and communication as the essential precursors to children's language and literacy development.

12.2 EXPLORING EARLY LITERACY

Literacy is no longer seen as a simple skill or competency but as a process. Literacy is defined as the ability to 'acquire the essential knowledge and skills that enable [individuals] to actively participate in all the activities for which reading and writing are needed (Ribeiro et al, 2006). It involves – in part – listening, speaking, reading and writing. Listening and reading are called the receptive skills, because information is received using these skills, while speaking and writing, also known as responsive or expressive skills, are used to provide information. Speaking is a natural act that develops as young children listen to adults who talk to them, read to them and tell stories to them. Moreover, speaking is further developed as adults use opportunities from their environment to make children aware of the world around them. However, learning to read and write usually requires formal education (Paulson et al, 2010).

Another definition of literacy is provided by Brewer (2007) who defines it as the ability to be able to read and write well enough to solve problems, learn new information and find pleasure in the written word. Literacy is indeed the ability to read and write, but it is also much more than that. In the 21st century, literacy encompasses a far wider range of skills.

Something to consider

The Organisation for Economic Co-operation and Development (OECD, 2009: 14) distinguishes between reading, mathematical and scientific literacy, which is shown in Table 12.1.

Table 12.1 Reading, mathematical and scientific literacy

Reading literacy	An individual's capacity to understand, use, reflect on and engage with written texts in order to achieve one's goals, to develop one's knowledge and potential, and to participate in society
Mathematical literacy	An individual's capacity to identify and understand the role that mathematics plays in the world, to make well-founded judgements and to use and engage with mathematics in ways that meet the needs of that individual's life as a constructive, concerned and reflective citizen
Scientific literacy	An individual's scientific knowledge and use of that knowledge to identify questions, to acquire new knowledge, to explain scientific phenomena, and to draw evidence-based conclusions

In addition, there is a multiliteracy perspective that embraces digital technologies, music, dance and visual representations as valuable tools to support knowledge construction (New London Group, 1996; Rowsell, 2013). Thus, people use a number of different literacies in their everyday lives, especially when confronted with problem solving and critical thinking.

The necessity of good early literacy practices cannot be overemphasised. Literacy at preschool level will, of course, differ considerably from literacy for Grade 1 and older learners. One of the main differences lies in the informal, play-based way literacy should be approached in relation to the young child as opposed to the more formal approach taken in school. Informal language development from birth lays the foundation for formal literacy instruction that will include reading and writing. Literacy for babies and young children reflects a developmental perspective and is often referred to as emergent literacy (Kennedy et al, 2012).

The concept of emergent literacy alludes to "the skills, knowledge and attitudes that are presumed to be the developmental precursors to conventional forms of reading and writing" (Kennedy et al, 2012: 45). Put simply, there are certain skills, knowledge and attitudes that should be developed from birth so that children acquire the necessary dispositions for success in formal literacy. However, the question remains: what are these knowledges, skills and attitudes, and how do young children acquire them? In addition, what is the role of the teacher in enhancing this acquisition? In order to answer these questions, it is essential to understand how literacy develops.

12.3 LITERACY DEVELOPMENT

Babies are born with an inherent ability to process language. From their earliest interactions with others, they become aware of spoken language. They internalise this language and respond to the tone of the words spoken by their parents and teachers. Language development is thus closely tied to individual relationships and early experiences of the child (Cunningham, Zibulsky & Callahan, 2009). Children cannot acquire language if they do not hear it, therefore it is important for parents to talk to their children, play word games with them and model appropriate language usage.

These initial language interactions continue throughout the preschool years and should be enriched by stories, rhymes and songs as they are an important step in the development of the child's oral language (Brewer, 2007; Cunningham et al, 2009; Paulson et al, 2010: 7). Reading, talking and singing with babies helps to build their understanding of language. The language they hear or receive becomes what is called their receptive language, which forms the base for speech or what is called expressive language. Reading to children helps them to understand how text works. It also helps to increase their vocabulary and gain other knowledge that forms part of language acquisition. This early phase, before children are conventional readers, is called as we have already noted the early or emergent literacy phase.

> **Something to consider**
>
> **Teachers and parents should remember:**
>
> The development of language is inextricably linked to early literacy. Early literacy development is embedded in everyday activities and interactions, and exposure to books and print further develops it.

Neuman (2014: 7–10) states that during the early literacy phase children acquire many important aspects of literacy:

- They build vocabulary.
- They learn how language works and use it to tell stories, share ideas and ask questions.
- They learn how to handle and use books, and about different types of books like stories, non-fiction (fact) books, poetry, cookbooks, etc.
- They engage in early forms of writing through making marks on paper, scribbling and drawing.
- They play with the sounds of language through traditional songs, rhymes as well as nonsense rhymes and tongue twisters. (It is important to remember that rhyme is not an important feature in African languages, although there are many songs that can be used in language play.)

- They build their knowledge of the world around them.
- They understand letter–sound connections.
- They develop a love of literacy and begin to understand its many uses.

Try this out

Share these games and rhymes with young children, and note their responses.

- I scream, you scream, we all scream for ice cream
- Cute cuddly kittens
- Six slimy snails slid slowly seaward
- Fuzzy Wuzzy was a bear
  Fuzzy Wuzzy had no hair
  Fuzzy Wuzzy wasn't very fuzzy, was he?
- Betty Botter bought some butter
  But, she said, the butter's bitter
  If I put it in my batter
  It will make my batter bitter.

For more ideas, go to the following websites:

http://gbyc.tripod.com/mindmeld/tonguetwisters/1.htm/

https://www.mykidstime.com/things-to-do/20-popular-tongue-twisters-for-kids-to-recite/

Find out more

Paulson et al (2010) argue that the foundations of early literacy are formed when children develop competency in oral language, gain awareness of the sound structure of language (phonological awareness) and find meaning in the symbols they see around them, for example a picture on their locker that identifies it as their space.

Play a game with children showing them pictures of their locker symbols, and ask them to identify which one is theirs and what it depicts, for example a dog, a car, etc.

A knowledge of literacy development enables teachers in ECCE to provide quality literacy-related teaching and learning opportunities for young children. It is important to re-emphasise that early literacy does not only mean early reading. Early reading usually demands formal instruction where children are taught models of literacy and this is not developmentally appropriate for the young child (Neuman & Roskos, 2005). Early literacy emphasises a developmental approach towards literacy where certain knowledge, skills and attitudes should unfold naturally through the enjoyment of language and books.

> **Something to consider**
>
> **Teachers and parents should remember:**
>
> Children should develop language and literacy skills before they begin formal reading instruction.

12.3.1 The holistic nature of early literacy development

Some research has suggested that literacy begins in utero, for example playing classical music to unborn babies may stimulate brain activity (Riley, nd). Classical music is thought to stimulate the development of the complex neural pathways (see Chapter 3) that allow the brain to process information, and in later life enhance creativity and improve children's ability to speak, see and hear.

Young babies communicate through crying, babbling and cooing. These sounds can be encouraged by parents and teachers through talking to babies, reading/telling them stories, singing songs and reciting rhymes. These activities help to establish a child's oral language (Brewer, 2007; Paulson et al, 2010). In addition, children's language is developed by the way their family and teachers speak to them before they even really understand what the sounds mean.

Children begin to understand how speech is constructed when they are in an environment that is emotionally safe, and when adults speak in timely and responsive ways. The best way to encourage the development of language is to provide consistent opportunities for children to hear and interact with language. Children's play is a primary source for language development. Young children need a variety of settings to learn language and practise communication skills.

Learning to read and write, as we have said, begins long before formal schooling as the biological, cognitive and social precursors are put in place. Adequate health and functional sensory and speech organs are important preconditions for the development of language since the window of opportunity for acquiring language skills is relatively brief (Snow et al, 1998).

The International Literacy Association (ILA, 2018) states young children are able to identify and interpret different symbols and develop the insight that specific kinds of print represent meanings. Initially, children use physical and visual cues, like logos in environmental print, to determine what something says. An example of this is when children recognise common labels and signs, such as logos like MacDonald's and road signs in their environment. Through this they realise that print is permanent and that it carries meaning.

After this phase, children develop an understanding that there is a predictable relationship between sounds and letters. The age at which children can understand this relationship is influenced by the extent of their literacy knowledge and the context in which the child grows. Although it may seem as though some children acquire these understandings magically or on their own, studies suggest that they are the beneficiaries of considerable, informal adult guidance through playful instruction (ILA, 2018: 2–3).

Recognising that early literacy is an emerging set of relationships between different language skills leads one to define the specific components of early literacy (see Table 12.2). The three critical components of early literacy are the ability to understand oral language, phonological awareness and print knowledge (Paulson et al, 2010). Hence, focusing on these three components will enhance learning to read and write in formal schooling.

Table 12.2 Essential components of early literacy development

Oral language	Phonological awareness	Print knowledge
Refers to children's ability to understand when spoken to; includes ability to listen Once children understand language, they develop the ability to speak	Refers to the awareness of the sound structure of the language (see Table 12.3 for activities)	Refers to knowing that spoken words are represented by written symbols

SOURCE: ADAPTED FROM PAULSON ET AL (2010: 7–8)

These essential components will now be briefly discussed.

12.3.1.1 Oral language

A good command of oral language during the preschool years is critical for later literacy achievement (Roskos, Tabors & Lenhart, 2009; Wong Fillmore & Snow, 2002). Moreover, children who do not develop strong oral language skills during this time find it difficult to keep up with their peers in later years as they start to fall behind even before they start school (Snow et al, 1998).

Roskos et al (2009: 1) have identified the following five primary areas of oral language, which young children need to acquire:

1.	Semantics:	Developing an understanding of the meaning of words children hear in their conversations with others
2.	Syntax:	Learning the rules of how words are linked together to form sentences
3.	Morphology:	Figuring out how words are formed
4.	Phonology:	Understanding the sound structure of language
5.	Pragmatics:	Understanding the social uses of language and basic social norms like saying 'hello', 'goodbye', 'please' and 'thank you', as well as taking turns in a conversation

Reflection

What are the social language norms in your particular context? For example, who greets whom first? Do differing ages play a role? If possible, compare them with another student's cultural norms.

Something to consider

Teachers and parents can engage children in daily activities to develop oral language and vocabulary. These include talking and singing as well as telling and reading stories. Children need to be provided with stimulating language-experience activities so that they have opportunities to learn new words and phrases to further develop their oral language proficiency (Brewer, 2007). Put simply, with the help of adults, children's oral language proficiency can develop to the point where it forms an oral language foundation for effective communication for life (Roskos et al, 2009: 2).

Teachers and parents need to intentionally plan language learning experiences that help children go beyond what they already know and can do (see Chapter 3 and Vygotsky's zone of proximal development). Children's oral language will be developed if opportunities are created for them to speak freely during everyday conversations and free play, and through teaching that includes guided participation, scaffolding and opportunities to use language effectively. If teachers and parents deliberately create environments for language learning that are rich, appropriate and enjoyable, all children benefit (Roskos et al, 2009). To achieve this, teachers and parents should plan purposeful and engaging play-based activities for interacting daily with young children. Moreover, adults' language exchanges and interactions with children should encourage, in a variety of different occasions, the use of new words, as well as the use of oral language skills (Roskos et al, 2009; Paulson et al, 2010).

Theme discussions with older children, which should be a common occurrence in a playroom, are an ideal way to build vocabulary. Songs, rhymes, word play, storytelling and dramatic play all encourage children to explore, learn and use oral language in the early years. Reading a book together with the child creates a warm, close context as well as fanning literacy.

In the early years, young children should have extensive opportunities to converse with adults and peers. The development of vocabulary as a building block of language is a prerequisite for fluent oral language. One needs to distinguish, as we have already pointed out, between receptive vocabulary (words that the child understands) and expressive vocabulary (words that the child uses to communicate). By the age of three, children should have built an expressive oral vocabulary of at least 1 000 words (Paulson et al, 2010). Vocabulary develops from both explicit instruction (sharing books, songs, rhymes, word play, storytelling and dramatic play) as well as children's everyday interactions with parents and teachers. Knowledge of the sounds of language is an essential component of early literacy, thus phonological awareness activities should be coupled with speaking as part of the everyday programme.

12.3.1.2 Phonological awareness

Phonological awareness is knowledge of the sounds of the language, and involves the ability to identify and manipulate larger parts of spoken words, particularly syllables. Children who are phonologically aware will know about rhyme and syllables, and will even display awareness of individual phonemes; for example, the word 'mommy' begins with the phoneme /m/.

Phonological awareness considers two important elements – the awareness of speech sounds and the ability to manipulate sound structures in words (Paulson et al, 2010). Paulson et al (2010) identify rhyming, alliteration, segmenting and blending as phonological skills. These terms are described in Table 12.2. The child's ability to hear, identify and manipulate individual sounds or phonemes in spoken words is called phonemic awareness, a subcategory of phonological awareness (Armbruster, Lehr & Osborn, 2001). A child who has phonemic awareness can identify the letter sounds in simple words such as 'cat' (/c/ /a/ /t/).

The activities in Table 12.3 are generally more suited to older children. The rhyming and alliteration are usually possible with four-year-olds but use your discretion with the blending and segmenting – some children might be ready for such a challenge.

Table 12.3 Phonological skills

Skill	Activity
Rhyming	Say nursery rhymes
	Identify what rhymes and what does not, eg Do house and mouse rhyme? (cat and hat; door and floor; tap and cap; ball and wall, etc)
	Odd-one-out rhymes, eg Which one does not rhyme?: floor; tap; door
	Make own oral rhymes, eg The boys play with toys
Alliteration	Match and produce words with the same beginning sounds, eg My name is Sarah, it begins with /s/. It matches with Sue
	Say words that start with the same sound: axe, at, ant, apple

Skill	Activity
Blending	Combine syllables and sounds to make words, eg If I add 'hair' and 'brush', I have 'hairbrush'
	(bulldog; cupcake; doorbell; handbag; lipstick; necklace; speedboat; spotlight; toothbrush)
Segmenting	Segment (break) sentences into words and count the words in a sentence, eg I have a black cat; Please drink your milk; Sue eats a pear
	Segment multisyllabic words and clap hands with each syllable (butterfly (- - -); elephant; helicopter (- - - -); ladybird; motorbike; umbrella)
	Delete syllables in compound words, eg Say 'toothbrush' without 'tooth'

Snow et al (1998: 151) state that phonological awareness skills in preschool children have been identified as a predictor of reading success in the early grades, thus children should be able to 'play with words'. They should be able to play with rhymes, syllables and speech sounds, as this will enable them to later learn the relationship between letters and sounds (Paulson et al, 2010: 53). Unlike vocabulary, phonological awareness skills are less likely to develop through incidental exposure. The development of phonological skills follows a hierarchy from larger word units (syllables, eg My name is Bren-dan) to smaller units (identifying beginning sounds, eg My name begins with /b/) and individual speech sounds (eg /b/ /e/ /d/) (Paulson et al, 2010).

Something to consider

Children need to develop oral language comprehension for listening and speaking, vocabulary for building background knowledge, phonological awareness and alphabet knowledge to attend to the structure and sounds of language, and print knowledge to develop concepts about books and printed words (Roskos et al, 2009: 3).

Children who experience problems with reading later on are often those who started school with fewer verbal skills. In other words, they have less vocabulary, less letter knowledge, less phonological awareness, less experience with books and the purposes and mechanics of reading. In order for all children to be ready to meet the challenges of reading instruction in the early grades of primary school, young children must be exposed to rich language environments in their homes as well as in their ECCE centre. Rich language environments would include language activities such as telling stories and reading books, songs and rhymes. These activities should start as early as possible, for example when changing a baby's nappy. When the baby is at the age of three months, the mother can say a simple rhyme, such as *This little piggy*.

Try this out

Use this rhyme with a young child and note how they respond. Do they smile, chuckle etc.? The words of the rhyme are:

This little piggy went to market
This little piggy stayed home
This little piggy had roast beef
This little piggy had none
And this little piggy went wee, wee, wee, wee all the way home.

The 'little piggies' refer to the child's toes. Each time the mother starts a new sentence she tickles another toe.

12.3.1.3 Print knowledge

Print knowledge in the early years involves the awareness of how print carries meaning. The teacher or parent should expose the young child to books and perhaps make older children aware of how they are read by pointing to the letters while reading. Developmentally appropriate activities to enhance print knowledge include making children aware of how to hold a book, the front and back of the book, and the direction in which words are read. Young children can sing alphabet songs and play with magnetic alphabet letters, which exposes them to early alphabet knowledge.

Reading and writing are inextricably linked. The awareness of being a writer starts when a young child makes his first scribbles. In the younger years, writing activities are closely related to art activities, and also gross motor development. The development of the larger muscles in the shoulders and arms is a prerequisite for the development of the smaller muscles of the hand and fingers. It is these muscles that enable a child to hold crayons and paintbrushes effectively. Creative art activities, where young children are exposed to crinkle paper, cutting and pasting, and drawing and painting, contribute to later development of writing skills. Teachers and parents should show interest in children's first attempts to draw and guide them to a stage where they realise that their pictures carry meaning that can also be expressed through words. Teachers and parents should ask children to tell them about their pictures and occasionally write a sentence or two on them to build their understanding that pictures and print are different but also similar as they both carry meaning. The sentence the teacher writes should convey the child's interpretation of what the drawing shows.

Figure 12.1 Exploring books together

12.4 STRATEGIES TO PROMOTE EARLY LITERACY DEVELOPMENT IN THE YOUNG CHILD

A relaxed environment where children feel safe, coupled with rich, play-based literacy experiences are essential for literacy development. Such an environment would include free access to a variety of books. In the playroom, the teacher should provide a book corner where young children can engage with books. Books made from cloth are suitable for babies. Books made from plastic and those with thicker pages or made from cardboard that is not easily torn are ideal for very young children. Skills on how to handle books should be taught from a young age. Older children might enjoy magazines that contain a variety of stimuli.

12.4.1 The role of picture books

Joyful interaction with picture books at a young age forms the basis for becoming a literate adult – an adult who enjoys reading and takes the time to read. The importance of picture books should not be underestimated and serves two purposes: firstly, to engage children with a story and, secondly, as a major resource in children's acquisition of literacy (Jalongo, 2004). To counter the prominent focus given to electronic media, the teacher should ensure that picture books and stories delight the young child. The teacher should ensure that the child is captivated by the story and, as a result, wants to explore the book further (see Figure 12.1). It is enjoyment that convinces the child to look at the book, then to talk about the pictures, then to listen to the story, probably several times, and ultimately to remember and retell a favourite tale. Older children will also make up their own story, based on the pictures they have seen, or perhaps change the ending to give a familiar story a new twist.

Find out more

Picture books can enhance the young child's love for language if introduced enthusiastically by the teacher, for example **PRIDDY picture books** by Roger Priddy. (Visit the PRIDDY picture books website at http://www.priddybooks.com/ for more information.) Compile a list of suitable books for babies and toddlers. Some of the books introduce different sensory stimuli such as touch and feel. You can, of course, also make your own books using a range of materials and other resources such as cotton wool or steel wire (scouring pads) to build illustrations.

When introducing a new book, the teacher should consider the child's developmental level as well as his interest, but the focus should be on enjoyment. Thus, the choice of picture books is an important factor which will determine whether the young child will love the book or not. Age-appropriate humour is an easy way to create emotional appeal and enjoyment when reading a book, for example the *Spot, the dog* series by Eric Hill. In addition, humour can capture the attention of the child. Remember, very young children do not necessarily have the same sense of humour as adults, and humour is always to a degree culturally based.

Something to consider

Baba et al (2017) analysed the characteristics of picture books based on the reactions of young children (aged birth to three years). Reactions that indicated their involvement included staring at pictures, pointing fingers, reaching for objects in the pictures and, in the case of infants, making gestures when they were not able to express themselves verbally. In addition, the young child would imitate objects or persons to enact the story of the picture. The child would also imagine herself to be in the picture book and become emotionally involved in the world depicted in the book. The research concluded that picture books that young children react to have a very simple style, contain scenes with repetitive gestures, show alignment between the pictures and the text, include a variety of characters, and contain a repetitive, rhythmical narration. Simple rhythm and repetition enable improved understanding of the story (Baba et al, 2017). Realistic pictures that are not too detailed and depict what is happening in the story are most suitable for young children.

12.4.1.1 Choosing books for young children

When choosing books for young children, one should also consider the type and length of the story. Children under the age of four enjoy reality stories based on their life experiences. The length of the story will be influenced by their age and their concentration span (see Chapter 3 on milestones of development).

Parents and teachers can use the checklist in Table 12.4 to guide their choices.

Table 12.4 Checklist for book choices

Does the topic of the book interest the child?	
Does the topic relate to the child's real-world experiences?	
Does the book have rhyme (if in English or Afrikaans) and/or repetition?	
Is the humour on the child's developmental level?	
Do the pictures support the child's understanding of the story?	
Does the child relate to the characters?	
Does the story have an interesting plot?	
Does the length of the story match the concentration span of the child?	
Does the story have a happy ending?	

Once a suitable book has been chosen, parents and teachers should take care that it is read or told in such a manner that the young child is actively engaged in it, for example by listening carefully. Wessels and Phatudi (2015: 248) suggest steps to utilise a storybook for learners in Grade R. These steps can be adjusted to be used for children from birth to age five years.

> **Try this out**
>
> Create a dialogic reading situation where you participate in a conversation with a four- to five-year-old child about the content and context of the story. The basis of this approach is asking simple questions and following up with expanded questions. Follow the steps below and reflect on the successes and challenges you encountered:
>
> - **Step one** involves a 'picture walk'. The pictures in the book are discussed and predictions made about the possible outcome of the story. This activity creates a purpose for listening because the children are curious about what is about to happen.
> - **Step two** involves the reading of the story. During this step, older children may be engaged in an interactive manner, such as dialogic reading. Dialogic reading means that the adult helps them to understand the story and deepen their language skills by asking simple questions about the text including the pictures. Through questioning the child becomes the teller of the story. When the teacher expands on the child's dialogue, the child may learn new vocabulary (semantics or word meanings), new syntax (the rules or patterns of language), the conventions associated with reading text (pragmatics), as well as the social skills of taking turns.

Try this out

Source suitable books for dialogic reading. Ask yourself if the book presents plenty of question and answer opportunities. For example, a good book for one- to two-year-olds is **Brown bear, brown bear, what do you see**? where each page ends with a question. Eric Carle's **The very hungry caterpillar** works well with two- to four-year-olds.

Something to consider

Once a young child indicates a preference for a specific story, this provides the opportunity to repeat it several times. Repetition aids memorisation and the re-telling of the story, provides for experience in fluent oral language. Multiple repetitions can be enriched by using puppets (which can be made from brown paper bags or socks), dramatisation or art activities. In fact, the parent and teacher can introduce any interesting activity to enhance the understanding of the child while having fun.

Find out more

Multimodality suggests that the teacher should engage in different kinds of activities to enhance young children's understanding and internalisation of a story. These include dramatisation, where young children act out the story with props and/or masks. In addition, if coloured copies of a few pages in the books are made and laminated, this will assist young children to remember the sequence of events. Children can be given the pictures, and sequence the pictures themselves. Begin with two or three pictures and increase gradually. Children could also draw their own interpretations or favourite part of the story. These drawings could be bound with string into a book with the teacher adding a sentence or two on each picture, recording what the child is saying about the picture. This could then be displayed as group book, which would encourage ownership by the children of the story.

Try this out

Working with young children of different ages, try some of the activities we have just discussed. Reflect on how the children responded to the activities. What could you add or change?

12.4.1.2 Story telling

Apart from reading picture books and acting out the stories, telling stories is part of all cultures in South Africa. Young children enjoy listening to stories being told because this allows for close interaction between them and the adult telling them, and they can relate certain parts of the story or provide repetitive choruses such as the refrain: 'Don't forget the bacon' in the book by Pat Hutchins. The adult can observe the reaction of the children, and adapt the story's length or even the story line and ending. When telling stories, the use of one's voice is an important tool. The adult should use body language and voice variation to depict the different characters; for instance, the dog will have a different voice from the cat.

Storytelling is considered a best practice for developing listening and speaking skills in young children (Roskos et al, 2004). As children listen to a story, they will be immersed in the sounds of the language and develop auditory memory. When young children retell a story (see Figure 12.2), they develop their sense of story structure and sequencing. The younger the child, the more adult support is needed, such as providing clues or prompts. Specifically, when children do not speak the language of learning and teaching, pictures or drawings are necessary to support understanding. In fact, visual aids not only enrich the story but facilitate understanding with all young children.

Figure 12.2 Sharing a story with an adult caregiver

When asking questions about the story, the adult should provide opportunities for both lower- and higher-order questions. Lower-order questions focus on what the child can remember about the details of the story, such as the names of the characters, the setting, etc. Higher-order questions are open ended, which encourages language development (Van Kleeck, 2006), critical thinking skills and later reading comprehension. Open-ended questions help generate discussion and stimulate more elaborate responses, for example: 'What would you do if you met a tortoise?'

When the teacher has modelled telling a number of stories, he can begin guiding the children to tell their own stories. This gives them agency and choice. The teacher models good storytelling, guides the children and supports them in their own storytelling. This helps develop their ability to sequence a narrative and give the *who, what, when* and *where* of an experience. Encourage young children to draw on their own experiences to make up stories.

Something to consider

What follows is a brief summary of points to consider when you read or tell a story, either at home or in a playroom. There is no one correct way to tell or read a story to young children; either at home or in a playroom. However, here are some suggestions on how to make story time an enjoyable experience:

- Ensure the books are in a good state of repair and handle them yourself with care. This helps children to learn to respect and value books.
- Stories must be interesting to the children.
- Stories should not leave children feeling anxious after they have been heard.
- Be enthusiastic when you read or tell a story. Make sure all children can hear you and read/or tell story in a clear, expressive voice.
- Use different voices for different characters to heighten both understanding and enjoyment.
- Where applicable, encourage children to join in a repetitive refrain.

In addition:

- Children's storybooks should contain clear, suitably sized pictures. Make sure children can see these pictures while you are reading the story or see the visual aids if you are telling it.
- Children should be comfortable. You can sit and read a book to a baby whom you are holding on your lap; you could sit in a big chair and read together with a toddler; older children could be sitting on the floor listening to a story.

- You could read a story outside with children sitting under a tree or lying on a rug.
- Engage in conversation around the story. Encourage children to share their own observations once the story is completed, and perhaps older children could suggest a different ending.
- Allow children to choose which books they would like to have read to them.
- Young children enjoy repetition, so you can read and reread the same book or tell the same story many times. Make sure, however, you also introduce children to new stories.

12.4.3 Activities to enhance early writing

Babies and toddlers need to be introduced to a variety of activities that form the basis for handwriting in primary school. These include both gross and fine motor activities such as outdoor play, playing with educational toys (see Chapter 7) and creative art. Activities such as painting on an easel or large sheets of paper pinned on a wall strengthen the muscles of the shoulder and neck. Other suitable activities include crunching and tearing paper, playing with play dough, finger paint and creative art activities involving cutting and pasting, rubbing, stamping and printing, as well as drawing and painting.

Beaty (2014) indicated that the first stage towards developing writing skills in children is making marks and scribbling (see Chapter 11). Children scribble anyhow with whatever object they have, which could be pencils, crayons and any other 'sharp' (within reason) objects that leave a mark. As they scribble, children begin to notice what they are doing. As their hands and fingers become stronger and they are better able to control their scribbling instrument, their scribbles begin to evolve into shapes – circles, ovals, squares and crosses, etc – which often overlap each other (see Chapter 11).

To encourage children to scribble, adults need to set out paper, pencils, crayons, koki pens, chalk, charcoal and other possible drawing tools such as sticks to make marks in sand. Children should be able to draw whatever they choose. Provide them with regular opportunities to express themselves on paper so that they can develop an understanding that writing has a real purpose (ILA, 2018: 4). Proper planning is essential to encourage a playful approach to the development of early writing skills in young children. To enhance the writing process, there should be planned and purposeful activities with appropriate resources, both indoors and outdoors (Hobart & Frankel, 2005). In short, creative art activities where young children can scribble, draw or paint freely will contribute not only towards prewriting skills but also towards the enrichment of their imagination and creativity.

12.5 TECHNOLOGY AND EARLY LITERACY

'Technology' is an umbrella term that covers all sorts of communicative devices ranging from the more conventional ones such as radio, telephone and television, to the contemporary computers, satellite systems, and other information-transmitting devices (Hennessy, Ruthven & Brindley, 2005), thus technology is a very broad term that is still evolving. The development of language and literacy in children has been remarkably influenced by the use of technology, but not always in the best possible way.

Young children are technologically aware, and from a young age many will have access to computer games, smartphones, television and digital technologies such as tablets (Zevenbergen, 2007; Lauricella, Wartella & Rideout, 2015). The development of modern toys should prompt parents and early childhood teachers to focus on the diverse ways in which information and knowledge is communicated. Technology plays a very crucial role in the expansion of language skills as it has become an indispensable way of learning (Chauhan, 2013). Although what we have just said can be true for a number of children, there are many more who do not have access to such sophisticated technologically related toys.

Burnett (2010) highlights the fact that technology can enhance the process of language and literacy learning in young children because it provides interaction with literacy as well as supporting meaning making through visual input. In addition, children's interactions with technology contribute to playfulness, agency, and creativity and problem solving as, for example, they experiment with how to move a fantasy figure in the game *Fortnite*. Fox (2014) as well as Korat and Segal-Drori (2016) note that the use of electronic devices increases intrinsic motivation in children because they tend to read and mimic words as they are pronounced by the characters featured through the technological device. However, parents and teachers should pay attention to the language being modelled through these devices. Young children will also mimic incorrect pronunciation. Care should be taken that extensive exposure to technology does not hamper the young child's holistic development.

Something to consider
Addiction to technology

Adults' beliefs about technology influence how young children relate to it (Lauricella et al, 2015; Plowman, 2015). Specifically, the use of technology in ECCE centres is influenced by teachers' access to information technology (IT) learning and resources available, as well as their beliefs about the role of technology and young children (Nuttall et al, 2013; Thorpe et al, 2015). Claims that play-based learning does not include technology make it difficult for teachers to accept technologies as valued learning activities for very young children (Edwards et al, 2017; Lindahl & Folkesson, 2012; Ruckenstein, 2010). Optimising the role technology plays in literacy development requires teachers to understand the impact of technology and the most constructive ways to include it in children's routine at home and in ECCE centres.

Children's home technology experiences may be richer than those experienced in the ECCE centres. Edwards et al (2017) indicated that technologies should be used in ECCE centres because they are often an important part of young children's lives and can enhance literacy learning. Again, it must be borne in mind that for many communities this will not be economically viable. A partnership between all community stakeholders (See chapter 5) is essential if technology is going to be available and used constructively to enhance the development of language and literacy in young children.

12.6 ASSESSMENT AND EARLY INTERVENTION

The purpose of assessment is to inform teaching and learning activities so that they facilitate the optimal development of each child. In addition, assessment methods should be ongoing and informal – the child should never be exposed to a 'test-like' experience. Teachers should have an in-depth understanding of the developmental continuum of the child's literacy skills (see Table 12.5).

Knowledge of milestones can help teachers to assess a child's progress in language development. Milestones also help them identify any difficulties that the children might be experiencing so that early intervention can be initiated. Several documents have informed the developmental continuum of literacy (Table 12.5). These are the National Educational Psychological Service (NEPS, 2016) and the National Early Learning Development Standards (NELDS) (DBE, 2009), which is a South African document. We drew on both these documents and hands-on experience to compile the developmental continuum of literacy. This continuum should be used only as a guide because the pace of development is influenced by a variety of factors (see Chapter 3). The purpose of this continuum is rather to indicate the research-based progression of literacy activities from birth to six years of age so that parents and teachers get an overview of the developmental process underpinning formal reading and writing.

It is important that teachers know what skills or components are being addressed when they engage with young children in language activities. The Curriculum and Assessment Policy Statement (CAPS, 2011) arranges the assessment standards of Grade R learners around listening and speaking, emergent reading as well as emergent writing, all of which, as we have said, have a strong foundation in ECCE. CAPS requirements are long-term goals but should nonetheless be borne in mind by teachers of young children.

The NELDS for children from birth to four years of age (DBE, 2009: 16) provide early learning standards that focus on the young child's holistic development. The standards for language development are addressed within this document (DBE, 2009: 24) and focus on learning to communicate effectively and use language. The NELDS arrange literacy developmental milestones around two topics. Firstly, children listen, understand and respond when communicating with others and, secondly, children respond to stories, songs, rhymes and books. The National Educational Psychological Service (NEPS, 2016) arranged developmental milestones around (1) early literacy concepts; (2) phonological awareness; (3) phonics or letter/sound relationships; (4) letter knowledge; (5) sight vocabulary/fluency; (6) writing and spelling; and (7) comprehension.

Table 12.5 provides a developmental continuum of literacy from birth to six years, and it is organised around the four language skills: listening, speaking, reading and writing, as well as comprehension. You may also wish to consult Chapter 3 where overall developmental milestones are discussed. There are specific milestones for visual and auditory perceptual skills, fine motor development as well as for speech, language and communication.

Table 12.5 Developmental continuum of literacy skills

Language skill		Developmental continuum of literacy skills: birth to six years
Listening and speaking	Birth – 2 years	Listens when spoken/sung to – makes eye contact, turns head towards sounds
		Imitates conversations by babbling
		Recognises and understands more words (receptive language) than they can speak (expressive language)
		First sentences are only two or three words, developing to full sentences by about 3–4 years of age
		Responds to action rhymes
		Can recite three nursery rhymes with correct words and rhythm
		Joins in songs and rhymes
	2–4 years	Recognises rhyming words – hears and says rhyming words
		Matches picture cards of objects with rhyming sounds (eg 'cat' and 'mat')
		Can select odd one out from three words looking at pictures
		For example, the teacher will present three pictures: a house, a mouse and a cake, saying the words loud and clear.
		Once the child can identify the one that does not rhyme with the others, the teacher will say the words: 'house', 'mouse' and 'cake', without presenting the pictures and the child should be able to identify, without any visual input, the word that does not rhyme
		Makes rhymes by thinking of words that end with the same sound
		Claps or counts the words in a three- to five-word sentence
		Claps or counts correct syllables* in own name
		Can hear and say the syllables in a word (eg but-ter-fly)
		Blends syllables together (eg pen-cil, pencil)
		Participates in discussions and take turns in conversations

Language skill		Developmental continuum of literacy skills: birth to six years
Listening and speaking	2–4 years	Listens to stories and joins in choruses at appropriate times For example, if the teacher reads Brown Bear, Brown Bear, what do you see? by Bill Martin Jr /Eric Carle, and asks: 'Brown Bear, Brown Bear, what do you see?', the child looks at the picture and responds: 'I see a red duck looking at me'. Describes characters in stories *Remember that linguistic terms such as 'syllable' will not be used with the young child. It is playing with the sounds that is important
	4–6 years	Can hear and say the first, middle and final sounds in a word (/c/ /a/ /r/; /b/ /a/ /t/) Identifies initial sounds in own name Matches pictures according to initial sound Can select the odd one out when given three words (two sharing the same initial sound) with pictures For example, the teacher presents pictures of a sun, a sock and a pen, saying the words out loud. The child identifies the one that does not begin with /s/ Knows some words sound the same at the beginning (run, race) Knows some words sound the same at the end (win, fun) Says a word without the first sound (chair–air = air) Says a word without the last sound (ant–t = an) Changes the first sound in a word to make a new word (not – hot) Changes the last sound in a word to make a new word (his – him) Hears and says the sound in the middle of a word (s-u-n) Listens attentively to announcements and responds appropriately

Language skill		Developmental continuum of literacy skills: birth to six years
'Reading'	Birth – 2 years	Points to pictures or objects Enjoys looking at pictures in books
	2–4 years	Looks carefully at pictures and can talk about what he sees in them and relate this to his own life Identifies the front of the book, and knows that a book should be read from the front to the back Indicates where the story begins and turns pages to read – points out the direction of reading Points to the first and the last word in a sentence Interprets pictures to make up own story Recognises high-frequency words in the community: road signs (eg STOP; shop names, eg MacDonald's)
	4–6 years	Has favourite books and retells stories in own words Finds specific images in a busy or detailed picture (figure ground visual perceptual skill – see Chapter 11) Recognises and reads own name Matches words to objects; matches labels to labelled items on an interest table Can identify the first and last letter in a word
'Writing' and art activities	Birth – 2 years	Makes large marks and then scribbles in sand, on walls (if appropriate) or on large pieces of paper (provide children with large pieces of paper on which to scribble) When painting, covers whole paper, called patch painting From about one year, the young child holds onto the pen with the entire fist (also called fisted grasp) and makes whole-arm movements Fumbles (messes up) paper: when exposed to (old) magazines or newspapers, young children will fumble paper and sometimes even tear it

Language skill		Developmental continuum of literacy skills: birth to six years
'Writing' and art activities	2–4 years	Gradually the scribbles develop into circles Draws 'stick figures' with little detail Patch painting continues Uses modified tripod grip of crayon or paintbrush Begins to form letters using finger painting, paint brushes, wax crayons Copies own name Tears paper Cuts with scissors on a line Rolls play dough into a ball and 'snake'
	4–6 years	More detail in pictures – starts drawing grass/ground for figures to stand on Draws pictures to convey a message such as own 'news' Holds the pencil correctly – tripod grip Writes own name independently – forms letters, sometimes with correct formation Knows that a name starts with a capital letter Illustrates stories with drawings or paintings Understands that writing and drawing are different: pretend writing represented using squiggles Recognises and names some letters of the alphabet, especially own name Cuts with scissors on curved line
Comprehension	Birth – 2 years	Toddler points to familiar objects when teacher says the name Typically names everyday objects (eg soap, cup, etc)

Language skill		Developmental continuum of literacy skills: birth to six years
Comprehension	2–4 years	Identifies the characters in a story by pointing to the picture in the book Makes simple predictions about a familiar story Retells story with prompts from adult Recalls information about the story (eg plot, character, beginning and ending)
	4–6 years	Recounts the storyline in chronological order Answers specific factual questions relating to the story Can make connections between own background knowledge and text; for example, if the story is about a cat, the child will be able to apply prior knowledge about cats to the story Can pick out the main idea of a story they have been told

SOURCE: ADAPTED FROM NATIONAL EDUCATIONAL PSYCHOLOGICAL SERVICE (NEPS, 2016); NATIONAL EARLY LEARNING DEVELOPMENT STANDARDS (DBE, 2009)

Something to consider

If a teacher, through observation based on the given developmental continuum, identifies that a young child is falling behind, bear in mind that if the child has not had sufficient exposure or practice in a specific skill, he may not meet the 'norm'. This lack of exposure or practise may be the reason for the delay; however, there may be other reasons. Teachers should then consider the holistic development of the child and pay attention to physical, emotional as well as social factors.

We will now consider some of these factors.

12.6.1 Physical factors

Physical factors that might adversely affect language development include problems with eyes, ears and/or speech organs, such as the mouth, lips, tongue. etc.

In relation to sight, babies from birth turn their head towards a light source. They watch a familiar face when being fed or talked to, and start to focus on the movements of their own hands. If a squint persists after about two months of age, have the child's sight checked.

Some of the earliest signs that a baby can hear is when he makes eye contact when listening to a voice and when he looks in the direction from which a sound comes. A simple way of determining if a child can hear is to make a sound behind his back and check for his reaction. Some babies may have had their hearing checked at birth, but this cannot be assumed. If a problem is suspected, refer the child for an appropriate hearing test. Ears can be negatively affected by prolonged infections of the middle ear. Medical attention should be given to such a situation, because to acquire vocabulary and speak clearly, a child needs to hear clearly.

Children should have a vocabulary of about 200 words by the age of two (see Table 3.4 on developmental milestones in Chapter 3). If the child has very little or no vocabulary by this age, further investigation should be initiated. Pronunciations can also be developmentally dependent. It is usually only by five to six years of age that speech is mostly clear and easy to understand. Even then, some immaturities might still be noted, for example with /r/ and /th/ sounds. We have already noted that gross and fine motor development can be enhanced through specific activities. Similarly, specific activities can strengthen the muscles involved in speech production such as the tongue, lips and cheeks. Suckling is a very good way for babies to strengthen these muscles that are necessary for later clear speech production. As part of a play-based approach, licking honey from a small plate provides play-based exercise to develop the muscles of the tongue.

12.6.2 Emotional factors

From an emotional perspective, a warm, supportive atmosphere as well as a responsive parent or teacher will assist the young child to be emotionally secure and confident. Security and confidence are prerequisites for all constructive learning, including language. Payne (2016) notes that children need to feel secure, happy, valued and listened to before they can learn. If these conditions are not met, literacy development might be affected.

Teachers who want to support young children with regard to language development should ensure that their home circumstances provide enough support and that their emotional needs are taken care of (see Chapter 10). Emotional and social development are closely linked. We will now consider social factors that might influence language development.

12.6.3 Social factors

Unfortunately, not all children are provided with the same opportunities for literacy development during their early years. Cunningham et al (2009: 488) emphasise that the physical and emotional wellbeing of families, as well as their ability to invest in material resources related to child development, have an impact on the quality of language interactions at home. Every child's language development differs. As children grow, they experience different levels of exposure to language. Some children may have been immersed in a rich language environment while others may have had limited opportunity to hear and therefore acquire language. There are also community-level inequalities in accessing a range of formal and informal literacy experiences. Quality libraries and the amount of environmental print children see in their neighbourhoods are enhancers of language and literacy development. Not all communities will enjoy the same number of facilities. The teacher can help to counter a limited exposure to literacy by planning extra language activities for children who may need extra support (Cunningham et al, 2009: 488).

12.7 LANGUAGE DIVERSITY AND MULTILINGUALISM

Considering the diversity in children's language development, it is important to recognise the implications this has for literacy acquisition. No one teaching method or approach is likely to be the most effective for all children. For effective literacy facilitation, teachers utilise a variety of teaching strategies to accommodate the great diversity of children in ECCE centres (see Chapter 8). Excellent facilitation for literacy will build on what children already know and can do, as well as provide them with the knowledge, skills and dispositions for lifelong learning (ILA, 2018).

Teachers and parents should remember that the core function of language is to make and gain meaning. Adults should therefore engage in code switching and translanguaging to ensure that the young child whose home language is not the dominant language spoken in the ECCE centre comprehends what is being said. Code switching means that the teacher alternates between two or more languages to enhance the young child's comprehension. Translanguaging is the planned and systematic use of the home language of children coupled with the language of the playroom in order to foster understanding. Childs (2016) indicates that translanguaging practices allow for fluid movement between the home and the centre language. Instead of being dehumanised by traditional language practices, teachers and children are encouraged to bring their languages to the playroom. This approach is in line with the additive approach to language learning advocated by the Department of Basic Education.

For more information on the acquisition of an additional language, go to https://yalebooksblog.co.uk/2019/02/18/multilingualism-marek-kohn/

This website should lead you to an article entitled 'Why multilingualism matters – a Q&A with Marek Kohn

Try this out

Read the following two case studies and reflect on what advice you would give to the teachers and parents in both these situations.

CASE STUDY

Case study 12.1

When Maria was 18 months old, she stayed with her grandmother in a village in rural North West. The community where they lived are Setswana speaking and the ECCE centre used Setswana to communicate with children. The mother of the child believed that it would be beneficial for her child to be educated in English. To ensure that Maria got some English exposure, the mother provided a tablet with numerous English songs and rhymes. When Maria returned from the ECCE centre, the grandmother played the English songs and rhymes, and Maria watched the accompanying videos while she listened to the songs and rhymes.

When Maria turned three, she started to attend an English-medium ECCE centre. The teacher requested a meeting with the mother and grandmother. At the meeting she shared her concerns about the fact that Maria spoke a 'funny' language. Though the teacher could understand what she wanted to communicate, Maria was often involved in conflict, because her friends did not understand what she was saying. This led to social problems, and Maria tended to be aggressive.

The mother agreed to take Maria to a speech therapist, who initially asked a doctor to check for possible physical problems particularly in relation to the ears and mouth. When the doctor could not find anything wrong, the next step of the assessment was to evaluate Maria's vocabulary and language development.

In the feedback, the speech therapist concluded that Maria was frustrated at the ECCE centre because she did not understand English, which was the medium of instruction. In addition, the English songs and rhymes that Maria had heard over the years were not pronounced properly, thus she could not pronounce the English words that she knew clearly. The result was that Maria mixed the Setswana words that she knew with her English vocabulary and was not able to make herself understood when she used English.

Reflect on:
- What advice would you give to parents who want to introduce their children to English as a second language at an early age?
- How would you provide support for Maria so that she is more readily able to interact with the other children?

The key to language development in young children is to provide the best stimulation possible for language enrichment. Besides stimulation, it should be borne in mind that children learn when they feel secure, happy, valued and listened to (Payne, 2016). This is central to any learning experience in a child's early years. Language acquisition, like every other developmental component, should be viewed holistically so that teachers and parents identify and use every spontaneously occurring opportunity to communicate with a child.

To find out more, we suggest you go to the following website:

https://learnenglishkids.britishcouncil.org/helping-your-child/how-young-children-learn-english-another-language

The information on this site focuses on acquiring English as an additional language. The insight provided is, however, relevant for the acquisition of any additional language.

Case study 12.2

Fillip is the youngest of three children in an Afrikaans family. Both his parents are teachers and he has been going to an ECCE centre since he was three months old. Though the ECCE centre is popular among parents, the owner does not adhere to the 1:6 adult:children ratio, which is a legal requirement.

On his second birthday, the teacher at the ECCE centre requested a meeting with the parents. The teacher's concern was that Fillip did not participate in playroom activities and often seemed to be 'in a world of his own'. She was also worried about Fillip's language development and said that he did not speak frequently and when he did, his pronunciation was not clear.

The mother agreed to take Fillip to a speech therapist, who initially asked a doctor to check for possible physical problems, particularly in relation to the ears and mouth. The doctor said that Fillip had a chronic middle ear infection, and prescribed medication to treat it. Once the ears were healed, his pronunciation improved, but he still did not participate in playroom activities. The next step in the assessment was to evaluate Fillip's vocabulary and language development.

In the feedback, the speech therapist concluded that Fillip's language and vocabulary development matched those of a two-year-old child, but he lacked confidence to speak. She suggested that the parents ensure that Fillip had enough time to speak, given that he was the youngest of three children and at an ECCE centre where 12 young children were in the care of one adult. The parents followed her advice and provided Fillip with ample time each night to tell them about his day at the ECCE centre. By encouraging him and providing him with ample time to speak, his expressive language soon improved.

For further insight into the process of language acquisition and articulation refer to the following websites

  https://www.healthline.com/health/language-delay

  https://kidshealth.org/en/parents/not-talk.html

12.8 SUMMARY

This chapter highlighted the importance of language/literacy development in the early childhood years and emphasised that during these years children should be exposed to as much language and literacy as possible. It has been argued that oral language, phonological awareness and concepts of print are the essential components of early literacy development. These essential components should be taught using a multimodal approach in a language-rich environment where children feel safe.

Assessment and the role of developmental milestones, and physical, emotional and social factors and their impact on development have also been explored. The importance of sensitivity to culture and diversity to support multilingualism has been highlighted. We conclude that play-based learning activities and a focus on story should provide optimal opportunities for literacy development in the young child as well as a solid foundation for the future learning of reading and writing skills.

REFERENCES

Armbruster, B, Lehr, F & Osborn, J. 2001. *Put reading first: The research building blocks for teaching children to read.* Washington, DC: National Institute for Literacy. Cambridge, MA: MIT Press.

Baba, M, Uehara, H, Kasamatsu, M, Utsuro, T & Zhao, C. 2017. *Analyzing characteristics of picture books based on an infant's developmental reactions in reviews on picture books.* ALLDATA, 66.

Beaty, JJ. 2014. *Early writing and scribbling.* London: Pearson Allyn Bacon Prentice Hall.

Brewer, J. 2007 *Introduction to early childhood education: Preschool through primary grades.* Boston: Pearson Education.

Burnett, C. 2010. Technology and literacy in early childhood educational settings: A review of research. *Journal of Early Childhood Literacy*, 10(3): 247–270.

Chauhan, AK. 2013. Role of ICTs and learning English language in different perspective. *Interdisciplinary Journal of Contemporary Research in Business,* 7(5): 406–419.

Childs, M. 2016. Reflecting on translanguaging in multilingual classrooms: Harnessing the power of poetry and photography. *Educational Research for Social Change (ERSC),* 5(1): 22–40.

Cunningham, AE, Zibulsky, J & Callahan, MD. 2009. Starting small: Building preschool teacher knowledge that supports early literacy development. *Reading Writing*, 22: 487–510.

Department of Basic Education. 2009. *National Early Learning and Development Standards for Children: Birth to Four Years (NELDS)*. Pretoria.

Department of Basic Education (DBE). 2011. *Curriculum and Assessment Policy Statement (CAPS)* Grades R-3, English home language. Pretoria: Government Printing Works.

Edwards, S, Henderson, M, Gronn, D, Scott, A & Mirkhil, M. 2017. Digital disconnect or digital difference? A socio-ecological perspective on young children's technology use in the home and the early childhood centre. *Technology, Pedagogy and Education*, 26(1): 1–17.

Fox, LCC. 2014. *Effects of technology on literacy skills and motivation to read and write*. The College at Brockport: State University of New York.

Hennessy, S, Ruthven, K & Brindley, S. 2005. Teacher perspectives on integrating ICT into subject teaching: Commitment, constraints, caution and change. *Journal of Curriculum Studies*, 37(2): 155–192.

Hillingdon NHS. 2010. *Getting ready for communication*. London: Borough of Hillingdon.

Hobart, C & Frankel, J. 2005. *A practical guide to activities for young children*. London: Nelson Thornes.

International Literacy Association (ILA). 2018. *Literacy leadership brief: What effective pre-k literacy instruction looks like*. Newark: Delaware.

Jalongo, MR. 2004. *Young children and picture books*. 2nd ed. Washington, DC: National Association for the Education of Young Children.

Kennedy, E, Dunphy, E, Dwyer, B, Hayes, G, McPhillips, T, Marsh, J, O'Connor, M & Shiel, G. 2012. *Literacy in early childhood and primary education (3–8 years)*. National Council for Curriculum and Assessment, 24. Research Report No 15. Dublin: National Council for Curriculum and Assessment. http://www.ncca.ie

Korat, O & Segal-Drori, O. 2016. Electronic (e-)books as a support for young children's language and early literacy, in Tremblay, RE, Boivin, M & Peters, D (eds). *Encyclopedia on early childhood development*. 9–24. http://www.child-encyclopedia.com/sites/default/files/dossiers-complets/en/technology-in-early-childhood-education.pdf (Accessed 1 November 2019).

Lauricella, AR, Wartella, E & Rideout, VJ. 2015. Young children's screen time: The complex role of parent and child factors. *Journal of Applied Developmental Psychology*, 36: 11–17.

Lindahl, MG & Folkesson, AM. 2012. ICT in preschool: Friend or foe? The significance of norms in a changing practice. *International Journal of Early Years Education,* 20(4): 422–436.

National Association for the Education of Young Children (NAEYC). 1996a. NAEYC position statement: Responding to linguistic and cultural diversity – Recommendations for effective early childhood education. *Young Children*, 51(2): 4–12.

National Association for the Education of Young Children (NAEYC). 1996b. NAEYC position statement: Technology and young children –Ages three through eight. *Young Children*, 51(6): 11–16.

National Association for the Education of Young Children (NAEYC). 1998. Learning to read and write: Developmentally appropriate practices for young children. A joint position statement of the International Reading Association and the National Association for the Education of Young Children. *Young Children*, 53(4): 30–46.

National Educational Psychological Service (NEPS). 2016. *A balanced approach to literacy development in the early years.* Literacy Working Group. Dublin: Department of Education and Science. http://www.child-encyclopedia.com/sites/default/files/dossiers-complets/en/technology-in-early-childhood-education.pdf (Accessed 1 November 2019).

Neuman, SB. 2014. Explaining and understanding early literacy. *Investigaciones Sobre Lectura,* (2): 7–14.

Neuman, SB & Roskos, K. 2005. Whatever happened to developmentally appropriate practice in early literacy? *Young Children*, 60(4): 22–26.

New London Group. 1996. A pedagogy of multiliteracies: Designing social futures, in Kalantzis, BCM (ed). *Multiliteracies: Literacy learning and the design of social futures* New York, NY: Routledge. 9–37.

Nuttall, J, Edwards, S, Lee, S, Mantilla, A & Wood, E. 2013. The implications of young children's digital consumerist play for changing the kindergarten curriculum. *Cultural Historical Psychology,* 2: 54–62.

Organisation for Economic Co-operation and Development (OECD). 2009. *PISA 2009 assessment framework: Key competencies in reading, mathematics and science.* Paris: Author.

Paulson, H Moats, LC. & Nelson, JR. 2010. *LETRS for early childhood educators.* Boston, MA: Cambium Learning.

Payne, LM. 2016. *Just because I am: A child's book of affirmation*. Golden Valley: Free Spirit Publishing.

Plowman, L. 2015. Researching young children's everyday uses of technology in the family home. *Interacting with Computers*, 27(1) 36–46.

Ribeiro, V & Gomes Batista, AA. 2005. Commitments and challenges towards a literate Brazil. *EFA Global Monitoring Report.* New York: UNESCO. EFA+Global+monitoring+Report+2006&oq=EFA&aqs=chrome.0.69i59j69i57j0l4.3284j0j7&sourceid=chrome&ie=UTF-8 (Accessed 1 November 2019).

Riley, L. nd. *Q and A: Should I play Mozart for my baby?* https://www.parents.com/pregnancy/my-baby/qa-should-i-play-mozart-for-my-baby

Roskos, KA, Tabors, PO & Lenhart, LA. 2009. *Oral language and early literacy in preschool: Talking, reading and writing.* Newark, DE: International Reading Association.

Rowsell, J. 2013. *Working with multimodality: Rethinking literacy in a digital age.* New York: Routledge.

Ruckenstein, M. 2010. Toying with the world: Children, virtual pets and the value of mobility. *Childhood,* 17(4): 500–513.

Snow, CE, Burns, SM & Griffin, P. 1998. *Preventing reading difficulties in young children.* Washington, DC: National Research Council.

Thorpe, K, Hansen, J, Danby, S, Zaki, FM, Grant, S, Houen, S, Davidson, C & Given, LM. 2015. Digital access to knowledge in the preschool classroom: Reports from Australia. *Early Childhood Research Quarterly.* 3: 174–182.

Van Kleeck, A. 2006. Fostering inferential language during book sharing with prereaders: A foundation for later text comprehension strategies, in Van Kleeck, A (ed). *Sharing books and stories to promote language and literacy.* San Diego, CA: Pleural. 269–317.

Wessels, E & Phatudi, N. 2015. Language diversity: Teaching a second language in Grade R, in Excell, L & Linington, V (eds). *Teaching in Grade R.* Cape Town: Juta. 235–259.

Whitehead, M. 2010. *Language and literacy in the early years, 0–7.* London: SAGE.

Wong Fillmore, L & Snow, CE. 2002. *What teachers need to know about language.* McHenry, IL: Center for Applied Linguistics and Delta Systems Co.

Zevenbergen, R. 2007. Digital natives come to preschool: Implications for early childhood practice. *Journal of Contemporary Issues in Early Childhood,* 8(1): 19–29.

Chapter 13

Opening the doors of learning: a playful approach to understanding the world and nurturing an inquisitive mind

Vivien Linington, Lorayne Excell, Elsabe Wessels and Penny Andrew

In this chapter, we consider

- why it is important to encourage young children to explore their world, and how different contexts and cultural backgrounds influence children's experiences of it
- the meaning of science, technology, engineering, art and mathematics (STEAM), and explore how to implement STEAM both at home and in the early childhood care and education (ECCE) setting
- how children explore and investigate their world from a STEAM as well as a historical and geographical perspective
- how to support these investigations through a playful pedagogical approach that considers the thoughtful introduction of appropriate open-ended resources
- the self-reflective teacher and how she accesses appropriate knowledge, skills and attitudes to competently encourage young children to explore their world
- how to model and support the enthusiasm and delight young children experience as they make their own discoveries.

13.1 INTRODUCTION

Through play, children learn and develop essential knowledge, skills and insights that enable them to understand their world. They find out about concepts, how to group and classify objects, how to make sense of things and events, and how to solve problems (see Chapter 3). Play requires a child to make choices, direct activities and make plans to reach a goal. This informal approach to learning will often involve exploration and discovery, trial and error, and problem-solving tasks requiring critical thinking. Through play, children acquire the basic concepts and skills that will later influence the learning of STEM as well as other subjects, such as history and geography and information and communication technology (ICT). The Lego Foundation, in a White Paper entitled 'Learning through play: a review of the evidence', makes the point that

> Neuroscience presents us with strong evidence for the profound influence of early experiences. In order to build healthy brain connections from the outset, young children need responsive and rich social interactions with caregivers, combined with sufficient nutrients and an environment free of toxins (CDC at Harvard University, 2016, in Zosh et al, 2017: 5).

Playful activities offer a unique context for these supportive and rich learning experiences in early childhood that enable children to make sense of and explore their world.

In this chapter, we unpack how children engage with:
- their surroundings (eg people, animals, vegetables and minerals of all kinds)
- the history of their own families and later on their neighbourhoods and broader community
- the geography of their surroundings (eg hills, rivers, flat spaces, rocks, weather and climate)
- the tools that they use such as pencils, scissors, cutlery and household and other equipment such as cameras, mobile phones, computers and tablets, which fall under the area of technology (DBE, 2015).

Current research focuses on STEM and STEAM, and best practice in relation to how the young child could explore these knowledge domains. In ECCE, STEM and STEAM are not explored as discrete subjects but are rather integrated into the whole of the daily programme. It is only later that they will become separate subject areas. In the ECCE stage, integration is key. It is through thoughtful interactions with other children and drawing on appropriate everyday activities that young children develop the basic concepts, skills, attitudes and values that open the doors to learning and promote the exploration of STEAM.

13.2 HOW TO SUPPORT CHILDREN'S INVESTIGATIONS THROUGH A PLAYFUL PEDAGOGICAL APPROACH

As we have already stressed, children are curious about the world. Unfortunately, we often hear the old saying: 'Curiosity killed the cat' being made to young children when they ask questions, but it is those questions that feed further curiosity, which is a crucial pre-requisite to discovery and learning. To optimise a child's engagement, the teacher needs to gain their attention and keep them interested. Having done so, the teacher should support them in utilising all of the appropriate senses so that information passes into their short-term memory. Successful learning requires hands-on experiences and making connections between prior and new knowledge. Repetition will assist the eventual storage of information in the long-term memory, which will enable the young child to retrieve information when needed. It is through playful pedagogy (see Chapter 6) that the teacher can meet the approaches to learning that have been discussed.

Something to consider

The challenge for teachers is to incorporate playful pedagogy into each element of the play continuum (see Chapter 6). This continuum ranges from high child control over the choice and types of interactions and activities to high teacher control, where children have little choice. In free play, children have wide choices. In collaborative and guided play, the teacher may suggest and generally facilitate to varying degrees. High teacher control is realised through instruction. It is the most prescriptive of the possible interactions, and involves the teacher telling and demonstrating. We are not saying there is no place for instruction; for example in toilet routines or certain teacher-guided activities. One of the aims of early education is movement towards becoming an autonomous self-directed learner. A teacher context that totally constrains voice and agency does not support this kind of development and learning. It is through playful learning that the acquisition of core concepts and skills occurs, and it is these that that lay the foundation for later formal study in subjects such as mathematics, science, technology, history, geography and ICT.

Find out more

Woodwork, gluing and box constructions are excellent problem-solving activities that cross many subject disciplines such as mathematics, technology and science. Children ask questions like: 'How do I stick these two pieces of wood together?', or 'How can I strengthen this joint?'

Present some of these activities to children, and observe how they attempt to solve the problem. Record your observations. Remember, the end result is not important – rather it is the thinking that children do while participating in the activities (Bruce, 2010). Early childhood learning is process, and not end product driven. The teacher's role is to support, suggest and encourage, but not to take over or complete the activity or to impose their own ideas or values on the children's constructions.

If they are to acquire new knowledge and skills, children should be given many opportunities to practise skills and explore concepts in a range of different contexts. For example, they can sort and classify different materials such as blocks, large buttons and sticks according to different criteria and as part of different activities. Providing varied opportunities and keeping a child engaged is essential to all learning, but especially for the learning of basic concepts in relation to STEM.

13.3 IMPLEMENTING STEM AND STEAM

STEM is an interdisciplinary and applied approach to the teaching of specific disciplines. In 2010, teachers realised the importance of integrating the creative arts into the teaching STEM concepts. This integrated approach is known as STEAM (Sharapan, 2012). To summarise, STEAM is an educational philosophy designed to integrate five key disciplines that support children's natural curiosity and excitement for exploration, while also building a foundation for later academic achievement (Barrett, 2017).

STEAM is also a way of thinking about how adults could help young children integrate knowledge across subjects and encourage them to think in a more connected and holistic way. This integration should happen in varied and natural play contexts, both inside and outside the ECCE playroom. For example, young children should go outside to explore nature. The value of this natural setting has also been noted by Bruns, Eichen and Gasteiger (2017); Gasteiger (2014) and Van Oers, (2010), who claim that high-quality early mathematics education occurs in natural learning settings, for example water or block play.

This aligns with our earlier assertion that learning is strengthened when children acquire the same skills, ideas and concepts in different contexts using different resources. Such occurrences can also enhance positive attitudes and values in relation to STEAM as children are guided, for example, into respecting their environment.

Find out more

The teacher's role is of utmost importance – an enthusiastic and positive attitude will support the young child's learning. In addition, the teacher should initially model the needed skills and 'think out loud' while solving problems. This includes interacting with children through sustained shared thinking and co-construction of knowledge (see Chapter 8).

Provide a practical example of how you could co-construct knowledge with young children in relation to an aspect of STEAM. Indicate the aspect, set a context and provide some of the questions you might ask and activities you could offer.

Something to consider

Mathematical and science experiences should be blended to make learning interdisciplinary using a STEAM approach. Curiosity and problem solving should be encouraged by asking thought-provoking questions (see Chapter 8) to encourage the young child to identify objects, make comparisons and predict. Additional activities include exploration of sizes, shapes, patterns and quantities. In this way, young children can learn concepts from different disciplines in different contexts, all in ways that are naturally engaging to them. It is important to remember that a very early exploration of the world sets the stage for later learning and attitudes towards STEAM and the environment in general.

Encourage children to communicate about how they solved problems they encountered. Young children can represent their reasoning through art or other creative activities (see Chapter 11). Lopes, Grando and D'Ambrosio (2017) explain the importance of a playroom rich in opportunities to solve problems. Their study with four and five-year-old children indicated that these children, in sharing their solutions with each other, constructed further knowledge. Lopes et al (2017) concluded that experience in problem solving provides children with the opportunity to take informed guesses, to discuss possibilities and to draw conclusions.

Play provides the ideal context where children use tools such as blocks to deepen their exploration of their surroundings. Appropriate, timely and effective adult guidance (Balfanz, Ginsburg & Greenes, 2003) can also deepen learning.

Reflection

To be successful, teachers should constantly reflect on their practice. They should ask themselves what they are hoping the children will achieve in a particular activity. Answers to this question should lead to purposeful, yet informal, learning activities.

13.4 EXPLORING EARLY MATHEMATICS

Insight into how to bring children into the world of mathematics is contained in two documents that focus on birth to four years of age stage – the National Early Learning Development Standards (NELDS) and the National Curriculum Framework (NCF). NELDS sets out two standards related to children's mathematical knowledge and skills. The first is to demonstrate and understand numbers, and the second, symbols, shapes, size and space. Section 3 of NELDS (DBE, 2009) states: 'Children's play and daily experiences provide opportunities for them to develop an understanding of many mathematical concepts. They do not need formal instruction but will benefit if adults talk to them about what they are experiencing'. In order for teachers to utilise all activities to enhance the young child's learning, a basic knowledge of the targeted concepts is essential. Appropriate mathematical knowledge will enable teachers to assess young children, and provide early support if need be.

The NCF presents six early learning development areas, one of which is mathematics.

> **Find out more**
>
> A mathematical thread with significant similarities runs throughout these two documents. ECCE teachers should familiarise themselves with these documents, noting how the ideas in NELDS and the NCF resonate with the more formal terminology of the Curriculum and Assessment Policy Statement (CAPS). These documents can all be accessed through the worldwide web (see Chapter 7).

A teacher of young children needs insight into the learning pathway that lies ahead of them in the years of formal schooling. An example of this would be knowledge of the CAPS documents (DBE, 2012). CAPS identifies five content areas of mathematics learning, namely numbers, operation and relationships; patterns, functions and algebra; space and shape (geometry); measurement; and data handling (DBE, 2012). You may think that CAPS is not relevant for ECCE, which is informed by the NELDS (DBE, 2009) and the NCF (DBE, 2015), but an overview is important because early learning should never be seen in isolation as it plays an important role in setting the foundation for successful schooling and lifelong learning.

It is also worthwhile to consider the work of Piaget (see Chapter 3), as he made a major contribution to our understanding of how children learn and develop. He describes four stages of cognitive development. The first two are relevant to children from birth to four years of age.

> **1. The sensorimotor stage (from birth to about two years old)**
>
> Children's learning takes place through their senses and bodies. The senses are sight, hearing, touch, smell and taste.
>
> **2. The preoperational stage (from about two to about seven years old)**
>
> Children's learning at this stage takes place through language and the exploration of objects. They are not yet able to think logically.

SOURCE: DONALD, LAZARUS & LOLWANA (2007)

Knowing Piaget's stages of development assists us in planning mathematical activities that involve the children using their senses and actively exploring mathematical concepts.

Though we will explore each mathematical content area individually, it should always be borne in mind that learning is a holistic process and that while children are counting, they are also exploring, for example, patterning and developing language. The NELDS document (DBE, 2009) acknowledges this holistic nature of learning. Desired result 5: 'Children are learning about mathematical concepts', states that this learning involves not only cognitive, but also social learning.

> **Try this out**
>
> Reread the early learning and development areas (ELDAs) for mathematics and creativity from the NCF. Can you begin to think of ways in which you could develop children's mathematical understanding though a creative playful approach? For example, you could take the toddler's hand and say a rhyme while doing the actions. Using your finger, you trace circles around the toddler's hand while saying, 'Roundabout, roundabout goes a wee wee mouse', then as your fingers 'walk' up the toddler's arm, you say, 'Up one stair, up two stairs and in a wee house'. As you say 'in a wee house', you tickle the toddler's armpit.
>
> Now think of your own activity drawing on your own cultural context. What mathematical concepts are you introducing to the toddler?

Likewise, similar connections between the CAPS document, NELDS and the NCF can be made for other subject disciplines such as science and technology, both of which have a place in ECCE. We will first explore early mathematics before going on to investigate other aspects of STEAM.

13.4.1 Learning about number concept

For babies and toddlers, number concept and counting are mentioned as desired competencies in the early years. This could be promoted by counting the fingers of one hand after changing a nappy, and could then be complemented by a finger rhyme, such as *The beehive*:

> **Try this out when changing a baby's nappy**
>
> *Here is the beehive* (make a fist)
> *Where are the bees?*
> *Hiding inside where nobody sees*
> *Watch them come creeping out of the hive*
> *One, two, three, four, five* (release one finger at a time from the fist)
> *BUZZ-ZZZ* (wiggle fingers)

A natural way of learning number concept is to make young children aware of their age throughout the year. A two-year-old, for example, could begin to take part in a number game such as, 'Show me two fingers, show me two toes, but, oh dear, there is only one nose'. You are not only dealing with number concept but also with body awareness, which is an example of integrated learning.

Other ways of reinforcing the concept of two could be to say, 'You have two shoes, I am giving you two pieces of bread and you will invite two friends which will make three children'.

Try this out

When children get older, counting backwards can be fun and enhanced by rhymes, such as *Five little ducks*:

Five little ducks went swimming one day (hold up five fingers)
Over the hill and far away (hold arm across body and tuck fingers behind shoulder on the opposite side of the body)
Mother Duck said, 'Quack, quack, quack' (use the other hand to make a mother duck beak and open and close hand to quack)
And four little ducks came swimming back (bring first hand back to the front with four fingers showing).

Continue until two little ducks went swimming and only one little duck came back, then:

One little duck went out one day
Over the hill and far away
Father Duck said, 'Quack, quack, quack' [loudly]
And five little ducks came swimming back.

Reflection

Think of some other ways in which you can build number concept into your daily interactions with young children.

Something to consider

Mathematical language is automatically used during routines in an ECCE centre. For example, you could ask the children who are wearing something red to go to the toilet first. Those wearing something green go second, etc. Here you are laying a seed for ordinal numbers.

The language of maths permeates every aspect of the ECCE day. For example, during snack time you might ask a child if he would like a whole or half a sandwich, or a quarter of an apple. Though children might not be aware of it, they are being introduced to fractions, which are an aspect of numbers, operations and relationships. Note how these introductions are incidental.

Number is just one of the five content areas. Patterns, functions and algebra, the second content area mentioned in CAPS, is not a specific focus in NELDS or the NCF. Nonetheless, the ECCE context presents many informal opportunities to explore the language and concepts in this content area in a spontaneous playful way.

13.4.2 Patterns, functions and algebra

ECCE teachers can build young children's early maths skills by helping them learn sequencing, seriation and patterning. Sequencing is the ability to identify and create patterns. For example, children may stack blocks in a pattern of red, blue; red, blue, etc. Seriation is arranging objects in order by size. You can ask children to arrange objects from shortest to tallest, or smallest to largest, etc. Children create patterns of their own and in so doing begin to recognise order in the world.

Playful ways to introduce sequencing to young children is through stories and action rhymes. Young children sequence activities in a specific rhyme, for example when singing *Head and shoulders, knees and toes*. Through repetition, the child remembers the sequence of movements that accompany the words. Another example is a story like *Goldilocks*, which involves not only a sequencing of events, but also classifying the plates, chairs and beds into 'the small one, the middle one and the large one'.

Threading beads in a sequence, such as big, small, big, small, does not only allow for patterning, but also involves sorting the beads based on size. A simple activity like this could introduce many other concepts to the young child, such as texture, for example rough and smooth, and shape, which we will now consider.

> **Try this out**
>
> Go on a nature walk with your children. Let them collect natural objects such as leaves and sticks. They can then sort and arrange them, for example by putting the sticks in a line from shortest to longest, or putting leaves of the same colour together.

13.4.3 Shape and space

Understanding of shape and space begins at birth. As the baby starts to move and begins throwing toys out of his cot, he starts to realise the concept of space. This continues when he starts crawling – underneath a table, over a carpet, through a doorway – or sits inside a box. The reflective knowledgeable teacher will know to emphasise the words 'under', 'over', 'through' and 'inside'. The naming of positional prepositions by the parent or teacher should continue as children tackle, at a later stage, things like obstacle courses. The regular use of prepositions, or 'position in space words', will help children to identify their position in space. This is the beginning of spatial awareness and orientation behaviours, which are important underpinning perceptual motor concepts for the later acquisition of more formal numeracy and literacy skills, for example place value. Encourage children to use full sentences to describe their position in space, for example 'I crawl under the table, I climb over the chair, I jump in the circle'.

Ask children to make different geometrical shapes with their bodies. Ask four children to make a square and six children to make a rectangular shape. How many children do you think you would need for them to lie down and make a circle? This is a good example of a kinaesthetic activity – exploring a concept through using the body.

Find out more

Babies and young children are so creative when you provide them with empty boxes. Larger boxes could be used as minibus taxis, cars, buses or houses, and smaller ones for construction. Smaller empty boxes also provide opportunities to sort according to sizes, which in turn involves estimation. Exploring 3D shapes is part of everyday activities. For example, playing with a ball, an empty plastic cooldrink bottle or an empty tin provides hands-on activities with a ball and cylinder. Provide the children in your care with different-sized boxes, and note how they use them. This is a good example of open-ended material, which allows children to use their imagination and create their own context.

Blocks are also an important 3D shape. A set of blocks of different sizes and shapes allows the child to explore, in a playful way, many of the principles that underlie geometry. If you are not able to afford a commercial set of blocks, make one using matchboxes and other small throwaway containers.

13.4.4 Measurement and data handling

As children play with the blocks, the adult can encourage them to compare blocks of different sizes. Encouraging young children to compare sizes is a good way to introduce the concept of measurement in the early years. Measurement is part of our daily lives. We measure mass – for example quantities of food ingredients; volume – the amount of liquid a container can hold; length – for example the length of your foot; temperature – how hot or cold something is; and time, which young children measure in a more concrete way such as number of sleeps until their birthday.

When you are discussing mass, volume, length and time with children, it is very important that you use the language of measurement, for example: 'My foot is longer than yours!' (length); 'My bag is heavier than yours!' (mass); 'This bottle holds more water than that bottle!' (volume); and 'When the sun sets, it is the evening and time to wash and go to bed' (time). In this way the children are learning the language of measurement correctly.

Activities such as comparing the size of the mother and the baby's hands, or the young boy comparing the size of his shoe to that of his father's are fun ways to engage with early measurement. When playing with sand or water, the teacher can introduce estimation by asking: 'How many cups do you think it will take to fill up that bucket?' This is yet another example of an integrated curriculum where mathematics content areas overlap. As in the previously mentioned activity, children are being asked to estimate as well as count. Engaging young children in cooking or baking activities provide for both estimation and measurement activities. Children as young as three are capable of baking, for example biscuits, following pictorial representations of the ingredients and how much of each they should include.

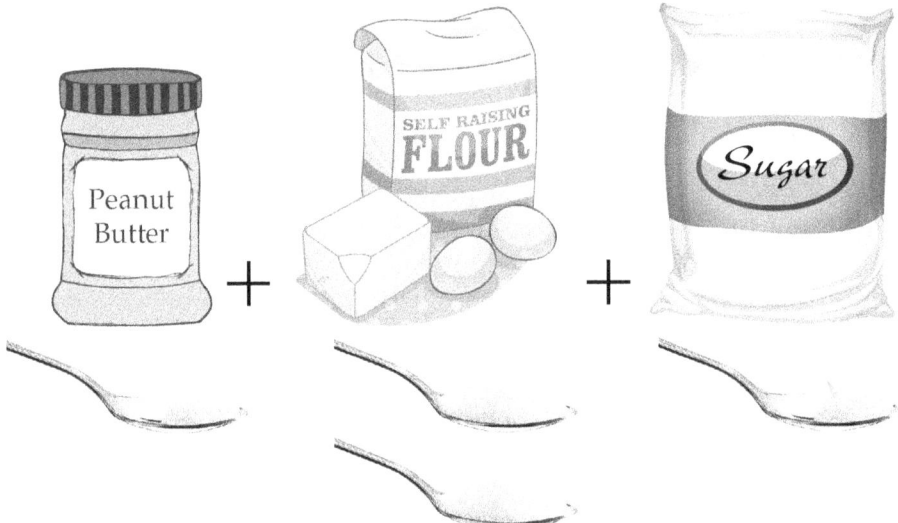

As children bake, they can observe water and steam, and also see, for example, how batter changes into a cake when baked. Observation of this kind is an early scientific skill and again an example of an integrated curriculum.

Observation is also enhanced if you take children on a walk in nature where they enjoy picking up stones, leaves, feathers and other objects found in nature. The material they have gathered is data, and when they unpack everything, count it, sort it and compare, for example, which they have the most of, this becomes data handling. Children could go on to create a collage with the data they have gathered and sorted. Collecting and organising objects is an early form of data handling and can be introduced early in the child's life. Even routines in the ECCE day such as tidy-up time can provide opportunities for sorting and counting.

13.4.5 Integrating mathematical activities into the young child's day

As children participate in the various activities we have discussed, they are constructing a deepening understanding of their world. As Charlesworth (2016) says,

Constructivism grows out of the theories of Piaget, Vygotsky and Bruner; children develop the basic concepts and skills of science, mathematics, technology and engineering. They move towards intellectual autonomy through independent activity, which serves as a vehicle for the construction of knowledge.

Reflection

Take each mathematical content area. Consider the ECCE programme (routines, teacher-guided activities and free play) as well as the various activities that will be offered to the children. Can you identify which and how mathematical concepts could be explored by the children during these aspects of the ECCE day? In other words, how can incidental and spontaneous mathematical learning occur during the day? Think about your role and how you could facilitate these learning opportunities and the questions you could ask to prompt mathematical thinking and language.

For example, let us see how much we have all grown during the holidays. Children could estimate who is now the tallest in the class and then find out if their estimations were correct by standing back to back and gradually eliminating the shorter of the two. The teacher would play quite an active role in this measurement process. If a child cannot take part because he is, for example, wheelchair bound, he could help the teacher with deciding who is the taller of the two. In a movement activity, children could be asked how many steps they need to take from one point to another.

Table 13.1 was compiled drawing on the authors' experience, 'Guidelines for Mathematics in the Early Years Foundation Stage', and the NELDS document. The purpose of the table is not only to enable teachers to engage in age-appropriate as well as culturally responsive activities, but also to provide an overview of activities and the progression of activities. When planning activities or engaging in spontaneous activities with young children, the teacher must bear their strengths, capabilities and interests in mind (Early mathematics: A guide for improving teaching and learning, 2016).

Table 13.1 Activities to enhance the development of mathematics (see Table 3.4 for additional ideas)

Age	Activity	Mathematical Concept
Birth – 6 months	Following a mobile, soft hand toys, blocks, rattles, activity centre, songs and rhymes.	Shape and space, patterns and number sense

Age	Activity	Mathematical Concept
6–12 months	Rolling noise making balls; plastic blocks, push-pull toys, listening to music, lying on their tummies and reaching for plastic blocks	Shape and space, number sense
1 year	Hammer toys, unpacking cupboards, posting box, counting when walking up the stairs.	Number sense, shape and space
2 years	Building towers with empty cooldrink tins and comparing the highest to the lowest one; counting the number of empty tins Number stories (visit https://www.education.com/stories/math/) Jumping with feet together and counting the jumps Following instructions such as 'crawl under the table', 'sit on the chair' and 'stand behind the table'	Shape and space, position, number sense, measurement
3–4 years	Number walk: draw numbers with chalk on a paved area/with a stick in the sand and let the child call the numbers as he walks Nature walk: collect natural objects (leaves, sticks) and sort according to a category. Measure sticks in terms of length and mass Make worms out of play dough and sort them with the children from largest to smallest/ longest to shortest Water play with different-sized cups and jugs.	Number sense, data handling and measurement

SOURCE: ADAPTED FROM DBE (2009; 2012)

Reflection

Based on your own context, identify at least two activities that you can introduce to babies, toddlers and young children to enhance their development of mathematics.

13.5 SCIENCE AND THE YOUNG CHILD

There is a growing understanding of the value of science in early learning (Worth, 2010). Firstly, there is increasing recognition of the power of children's early thinking and learning, especially when they are immersed in stimulating environments that are supported by skilful teachers. In addition, it is now acknowledged that early exposure to scientific learning not only builds a basis for future scientific understanding but also develops other important skills and attitudes for learning. These include working with one another, improved attention span and self-regulatory abilities, as well as refining basic large- and small-motor control, enhancing language and early mathematical understanding (Bowman, Donovan & Burns, 2001).

The overall aim of science is to understand the natural world through a process known as scientific enquiry. Scientific knowledge helps us explain the world around us, why the wind blows, the importance of insects, how is water polluted and where light comes from. Scientific knowledge can help us predict what might happen: a cyclone may hit the coast; there may be a measles epidemic. Scientific knowledge can also help solve problems such as water or air pollution, or the spread of diseases (Worth, 2010). Science can guide technological development to serve our needs and interests, such as high-speed travel and using digital devices. The actual knowledge falls into two categories, life sciences and physical science. Life sciences are concerned with the study of living organisms, including biology, botany, zoology, microbiology, physiology, biochemistry, and related subjects. Physical science is concerned with the study of inanimate natural objects, including physics, chemistry, astronomy, and related subjects. Both types of scientific knowledge form natural fields of inquiry for the curious young child.

The benefit of science for young children, however, is not about the acquisition of scientific knowledge. It is rather about the interplay between doing science, the nature of science, scientific concepts and scientific reasoning (Worth, 2010). In short, it is about an integrated experience that enhances holistic development.

As Worth (2010) notes, inquiry into life science is different from inquiry into physical science, the former being more observational and taking place slowly over time. Inquiry in physical science is more experimental, usually with immediate results. An example of life sciences is watching a silkworm spin itself into a cocoon and emerge later as a moth, which then lays eggs. This process provides many opportunities for observation. A physical science experiment to do with children could be making a 'volcano' and watching it erupt. Children can, under the guidance of a teacher, make a 'volcano' from simple ingredients including dishwashing liquid, baking soda and cold water. See the following link for a variety of ideas on science activities for young children.

http://www.sciencefun.org/kidszone/experiments/how-to-make-a-volcano/.

13.5.1 Playful science

Doing science is a natural and critical part of children's early learning. Children are inherently inquisitive and want to find out about their natural world. This curiosity is a powerful catalyst for generating play-based learning. With appropriate guidance, this natural drive to make sense of the world becomes the foundation for beginning to use the skills of inquiry to explore basic phenomena and the materials in their surroundings. The inquiry skills to which we have referred are the following:

- Exploring objects, materials, and events
- Raising questions
- Making predictions or hypotheses
- Observing carefully
- Using a variety of simple tools to extend observations
- Engaging in simple investigations and experiments.

Additional skills that are equally important include the following:

- Describing (including shape, size, number), comparing, sorting, classifying and ordering
- Recording observations using words, pictures, charts, and graphs
- Identifying patterns and relationships
- Developing tentative explanations and ideas
- Working collaboratively with others
- Sharing and discussing ideas and listening to new perspectives.

Obviously, the type of skills that are encouraged will depend on the children's age, competences and interest. For example, younger children will explore objects and materials, and possibly sort them in a variety of different ways. Recording observations using graphs or charts is more suitable for the older child.

Try this out

Let children sweep autumn leaves into a pile. Then bring a tray of them into the playroom and let the children look carefully at them and describe what they see. (You might have to give them some appropriate words.) Ask them why they think they found them on the ground. The leaves could then be scrunched, and children asked to describe the noise they make. They could then use the leaves to make a nature collage.

Something to consider

When teaching young children, remember that they have a short concentration span and excellent imagination. If they are not interested and engaged in the activity, they will not pay attention. Teachers should allow for participatory play and investigation, since exploration allows the young child to actively engage in activities and take the initiative in their own learning. In the same way that an adult cannot prepare a meal without ingredients, children cannot explore without appropriate opportunities and 'ingredients'. Teachers should be flexible and allow children to explore their immediate indoor and outdoor environment. For example, invite children to work together gathering autumn leaves until they have a big pile they can jump into.

13.5.2 Places and spaces for doing science

13.5.2.1 *Outdoor play spaces*

Outdoor play forms a natural part of a young child's world. The garden is an important part of the early learning environment. Encourage children to observe the weather, including the colour of the sky and how it changes; the clouds – the differing shapes and types – and what happens when it storms. After a hailstorm, let children collect hailstones and observe what happens to them and how long it takes them to melt. They can also observe:

- the grass after rain
- sand
- flowers
- trees
- leaves
- different weeds
- dew in the early morning
- frost in winter (depending on the area).

As children explore the outdoor environment and collect interesting items such as stones, sand, gravel, leaves and flowers, they can use the language of description. They can also sort and classify items according to size, texture and colour, etc. These items can be used later for creative art activities such as a nature collage. Children could also do leaf or bark rubbings.

Through outdoor play opportunities, children can also observe and investigate insects and other garden creatures (bearing safety in mind) and plants. These include bees, especially in spring and summer time, beetles and ants under rocks or stones, mole crickets, and spiders and their webs, etc. These opportunities become especially important for children living in the inner city. Plants of different textures, such as velvety, thick, spongy, furry, etc, are also exciting to explore, and help develop language through tactile experiences. The sense of smell can also be addressed through the introduction of different plants and flowers. Make sure poisonous plants are not accessible to children. The following websites provide some information about poisonous plants in South Africa:

https://www.google.com/search?q=poisonous+plants+in+south+africa&rlz=1C1GGRV_enZA780ZA780&oq=poisonous+plants+in+south+africa&aqs=chrome..69i57j0l5.14442j0j8&sourceid=chrome&ie=UTF-8

https://www.babyproof.co.za/common-poisonous-plants-in-south-africa/

If there is a pond nearby, children can explore the various forms of pondlife, such as whirligigs, dragonflies, tadpoles and even fresh-water fish. Provide some fishing nets and encourage children to try to catch something in the pond. Should they be successful, after a short observation their catch must be returned to the water. This is a wonderful way of teaching children to respect all living creatures. They can also explore why some plants grow underwater.

A vegetable garden offers countless opportunities for exploring science. Children can be introduced to herbs, observe how different plants grow – some are underground while others are climbers – and learn about the growing cycle. Children can also explore the value of vegetables as a source of compost, nutrients and a food supply. Children can assist in the making of soup and salads with the ingredients picked from the vegetable garden. As the food cooks, children can note and talk about the changes they see, and when cooked and eaten they can note the change in texture. Baking introduces children to various science-related activities and materials such as bicarbonate of soda, which causes dough to rise.

Find out more

Collect a series of child-friendly recipes that you can use with the children to explore scientific as well as mathematical concepts, such as pictorial representations of quantity.

As we have said before, an ECCE curriculum is integrated. This is illustrated through all the skills and knowledge that are linked to the preparation of food. For example, from a skills perspective, chopping, cutting and rolling are practised, while from a knowledge perspective, the celebration of festivals such as Diwali can involve parents wearing traditional clothes, possibly singing traditional songs and telling oral history. These activities will support the social sciences, language and intercultural knowledge.

Particularly in rural areas, children can learn about farm animals and their produce. They could, for example, investigate the souring of fresh milk. In any ECCE context, children can explore products that come from farm animals, such as milk from cows; cream and cheese from milk; and wool from sheep, etc. Think of some more examples.

Where possible, design seasonal tasks so that children become aware of changes that happen in nature in the course of a year.

13.5.2.2 Indoor scientific play

Discovery and nature tables that feature a wide range of age-appropriate natural items, such as a fallen bird's nest, different types of seed pods, the different textures and colours of sand and stones, and, if your context allows, different types of shells, provide a resource for exploration and discussion. Add a magnifying glass and for older children a child's microscope to stimulate further inquiry. Introduce children to a world of colour by providing paints that can be mixed to produce a range of hues, shades and different colours. Encourage them to link types of clothing with specific seasons; for example, we wear a jersey if it is cold, a hat and sunscreen when we go out to play in summer, etc. In all these activities you need to consider if the materials you are presenting are age appropriate (eg could the stones or seeds be swallowed?) and nontoxic.

Try this out

Use your scientific knowledge and imagination to think of everyday scientific concepts that could linked to the kitchen and the bathroom, for example a tin opener, which has a cog and a wheel; a boiling kettle, which illustrates some of the properties of water. In the bathroom we explore why soap lathers and how it removes dirt. The following websites might give you some ideas:

Getting clean: The science of soap – Live Science: https://www.livescience.com/57044-science-of-soap.html

https://tuttnauer.com/blog/autoclave-sterilization/basic-concepts-of-steam

[body]Write a list of everyday items and activities you find in the bathroom and kitchen and the scientific concepts that are part of these activities, for example water play at bath time with different sized containers or adding bubbles to the bath water.

In short, both the indoor and outdoor environments provide a wealth of incidental learning opportunities for young children to be introduced to the world of science. Do not underestimate the value of spontaneous exploration to enhance children's curiosity and enjoyment for learning. The maximisation of learning opportunities depends very much on the skills and knowledge of the teacher. It is she who can ignite a child's passion for ongoing learning. We will now consider the role of the teacher in expanding the horizons of the world of the child.

13.5.3 The role of the teacher

As Worth (2010: 11) notes, 'the teacher's role is critical to children's science learning, and it is a complex one that is informed by her knowledge of children, of teaching and learning, and of pedagogical science knowledge'. In addition, in planning opportunities for science learning the teacher must consider contextual relevance and cultural practices. Contextually, for example, the purification and availability of water may be different in a rural and an urban context. Snakes are perceived in different ways in different cultures. In Western culture, for instance, a toy or dead snake on a nature table may be fascinating for the children. In an African culture, it may be seen as entirely inappropriate and even intimidatory.

In planning indoor and outdoor environment, teachers should consider the scientific discovery that the environment can generate. They should make provision for informal as well as formal scientific discovery, and be alert to the incidental scientific learning opportunities that might present themselves throughout the day.

Find out more

Free play with sand and water could lead to close observation about the properties of these elements, such as how different types of sand can affect the stability of a sand construction.

A teacher watching children at water play could ask them to predict what will happen if they pour the water out of the jug from different heights. These spontaneous teachable moments are dependent on a teacher's awareness of what the children are doing and how unobtrusive questioning can spark estimation, prediction and problem solving.

The ability to identify a teachable moment and thereby enhance incidental learning is something that comes with experience. Knowing when to step in and when to step back requires both sensitivity and an awareness of possibilities. These informal incidental learning opportunities are very different from a planned teacher-guided activity or ring where the concept that will be explored has been identified in advance of the activity.

Worth (2010: 10) notes that 'while explicit teaching of the concept is not appropriate, the structure of the experiences and the teacher's facilitation is guided by her understanding of the concepts and how children learn them. Her questions, comments, and probes draw the children's attention to the concept'.

Both formal and informal scientific exploration are enriched by suitable resources, which do not have to be expensive commercial products. Our 'volcano' experiment, for example, used bicarbonate of soda, which is a common kitchen ingredient and relatively inexpensive.

Identify resources in your environment that you could use as a catalyst for scientific discovery.

A key resource is the creativity of teachers, which also comes through in their questioning techniques. Good questions help children to reflect on their knowledge, feelings or events. Good questions also encourage participatory learning because children are involved through discussion. By exploring possible answers, children are able to make sense of their world. Good questioning involves children in scientific inquiry. Children may guess, predict or hypothesise a possible outcome, and then discuss what actually happened. Through good questioning techniques children are:

- encouraged to organise, use and evaluate information, articulate and reason, co-construct knowledge with others, explore creative and innovative ideas
- develop a sense of curiosity and wonderment as they extend and enrich their imagination
- develop communication and language skills
- empathise with the feelings of others.

Good questioning leads to discussion and, as Worth (2010) emphasises, discussion is critical to science learning. It is an important part of the inquiry process, and promotes the development of science reasoning. Discussion, as Worth (2010: 11) argues, 'encourages children to think about what they have experienced, listen to the experiences of others, and reflect on their ideas'. Age is not a barrier to scientific discovery. For example, young babies can be taken outside to create an awareness of nature. Everyday activities, such as an outside walk where babies hear sounds like birds or look at the movement of leaves, encourage an observant mind.

Children's learning is enriched when they gain accurate information about their world and the people in it. Their understanding of caring for people and creatures in their environment increases. In addition, as already mentioned, children grow in confidence when they are encouraged to show their knowledge and skills in practical ways (NCF, 2015: 65).

13.6 TECHNOLOGY

Children are born into a technological world. Depending on the context, as they grow they will be exposed to technological devices such as computers, tablets, multitouch screens, interactive whiteboards, mobile devices, cameras, DVD and music players, audio recorders, electronic toys and games, as well as to older analogue devices, such as tape recorders, to support learning.

The National Association for the Education of Young Children (NAEYC, 2012) discourages the use of technology for children under the age of two years as they have a limited understanding of what they see and hear on a screen. Furthermore, the NAEYC (2012) recommends no more than one to two hours of total screen time (including television, videos, digital media, video games, mobile media, cell phones, and the internet) per day for children aged from two to five years. They stress that teachers should use professional judgement to evaluate technology and media before young children are exposed to it. In addition, the NAEYC (2012) recommends that active engagement in hands-on experiences should stay a priority to ensure the holistic development and learning of the young child. Technology and interactive media should never replace creative play, real-life exploration, physical activity, outdoor experiences, conversations and social interactions.

When choosing technology and interactive media, teachers should:
- consider its developmental appropriateness and potential for an interactive experience, especially for children under the age of two
- consider its ability to intentionally extend and support hands-on activities to enhance children's engagement with their real world and expand their ability to gain new information
- discourage the use of media in which children do not take an active part; this includes the passive use of television, videos, DVDs and other non-interactive media for children under two (NAEYC, in Gordon & Browne, 2017).

Carlsson-Paige (2012) argues that what children see or interact with on a screen can never provide as full an experience as interactions with the real world. Carlsson-Paige (2012) notes that it is of concern that play is being undermined by media saturation. In the last 25 years, children's play has become more imitative and less original and creative, especially when this play is initiated by interactive, technologically driven toys and products.

Something to consider

Deciding on the right technology tools is key to optimal usage and learning. A computer in the hands of a child can be a tool for experiencing the world. Discovery-oriented experiences with computers can both stimulate and soothe a young child. We say soothe because computers do not judge and tease. They wait patiently for the child to make a move.

Technology is more than a computer or smartphone in the centre. Video recorders can be used to document activities, and overhead projectors can show enlarged images of items on a wall, allowing exploration of the details or shadowing of the item.

> **Find out more**
>
> Because of the contested nature of the use of information technology (IT) in ECCE, we ask you to think about and present your point of view on how, why and in what context IT should be used in ECCE.

Context has particular relevance for South Africa. According to Barrett (2017), lack of access to appropriate IT constrains the development of technological skills and understanding. This is often a problem in the South African context where many children will have either no or limited access to IT. Likewise, many ECCE teachers will not have easy access that would enable them to create and use technology-linked teaching resources.

Technology is available and can be beneficial for learning. Care should be taken to maintain a balance between technology exposure and hands-on, real-world activities. It is this balance that teachers should always seek, and advise parents to do likewise.

> **Case Study**
>
> Read the following case study:
>
> > Hedrus is four years old and does not want to attend the ECCE centre. He cries daily and seems to be very unhappy. This behaviour has social implications and soon Hedrus has no friends, and he is lonely and miserable. All attempts by the teacher to engage Hedrus in creative art activities or construction are unsuccessful. He usually just sits next to the teacher and observes the other children playing. When the teacher talks to Hedrus, he says that he 'hates papers'. Through further enquiry, the teacher finds out that Hedrus enjoys taking equipment apart – things such as broken hairdryers, kettles, DVD players and computers. It turns out that he has a whole toolbox at home to help him take old, electrical equipment apart. His mom and teacher agree that he should bring his toolbox to school and the other parents are invited to bring their broken electrical items to be 'repaired'.
>
> > Hedrus soon becomes the centre of attention, taking electrical equipment apart with a screwdriver, and cutting wires with a small side cutter. The other children begin to sort the nuts, bolts, pieces of electric wire, etc, and soon Hedrus has taught the whole class about recycling and the different parts of a computer.
>
> > Hedrus's social problems became a thing of the past, and he was able to share his toolbox with other children. He started to take part in art activities and later in the year won a prize for his creative art.

13.7 EXPLORING THE SOCIAL SCIENCES

According to the NCF (DBE, 2015: 65), 'knowledge and understanding of the world refers to children's immediate and surrounding worlds'. Introducing the natural and life sciences to young children has been explored in a previous section. In this section, we will examine how we can introduce young children to the social sciences, specifically history and geography.

In ECCE, history has a particular focus. It is preferable to start with the children's immediate family and then widen the lens to explore their neighbourhoods and then the broader community as well as different cultural practices found within their community. As children come to know people's different ways of being in the world and the beliefs underpinning their particular lifestyle, their understanding of diversity is enhanced. This understanding is one of the foundations of democratic citizenship

Similarly, geography has a particular focus, which includes physical as well as human geography. Physical geography refers to an investigation of children's surroundings, such as hills, rivers, flat areas, rocks, weather and climate. Human geography includes an exploration of the tools people use, such as pencils, scissors, cutlery, and household and other equipment, such as cameras, mobile phones, computers and tablets (NCF, 2015).

13.7.1 Social studies content in ECCE

As we have already said, children begin exploring their world from birth in an attempt to make sense of their social and physical environments. They gradually learn more about their expanding community, and eventually come to see themselves as citizens within that community. What becomes relevant social studies content is dependent upon the age of children and stage of development, their interests as well as their home environment and ECCE setting.

As early as the 1930s, John Dewey, a progressive educationist, encouraged teachers to use social studies as the foundation for activity-based learning that builds on the children's interests and familiar experiences of daily life (Mindes, 2005). Dewey's argument is still valid today. In a rural farming community, for example, this may mean exploring how young boys go to the fields to herd cattle. In an urban community, it may mean exploring the support systems available in an urban context, for example the clinic, the hospital, the fire station, etc.

Social sciences should focus on exploring and answering 'big ideas' and questions that require critical thinking (Zarrillo, 2004).

> **Reflection**
>
> What 'big ideas' do you think are appropriate for a young child to explore?
>
> Did you think about the suitability of topics related to self, family and community, or our surroundings?
>
> Have you thought about why, for example, your family came to live in a particular place? Were there geographical aspects involved, for example new opportunities in industry, or weather conditions that made their original place of living unsuitable? As Mindes (2011) points out, suitable topics that are big ideas might include:
>
> - migration and immigration (how and why did/do people come South Africa?)
> - transportation (how do we move around in our community?)
> - the role of money in our life (why do people have stokvels or use a bank?; where did the idea of money begin, and how has its use and appearance changed over time?)
> - heritage (how did our ancestors live?; which of their practices inform how we live today?) This exploration could be linked to cultural festivals, heritage days and religious celebrations.

13.7.1.1 Social sciences: historical perspective

The US-based National Council for the Social Studies (NCSS) (1994) suggests that historically based explorations can be grouped under the following topic areas:

- Different cultures
- Time, continuity and change
- Individual development and identity
- Individuals, groups and institutions
- Power, authority and governance
- Global connections
- Civic ideals and practices.

Not all of the NCSS topic areas are necessarily appropriate for young children. Some, such as global connections, may only be introduced in primary school.

Find out more

How do you think you could approach the NCSS topics and use differentiation and adaptation to make them relevant for babies, toddlers and young children?

For example, a topic such as individual development and identity could include an exploration of the concept family. Family might be considered from a variety of perspectives that acknowledge cultural diversity and family varieties. The teacher could talk to babies and toddlers about their family members, and encourage them to look at photographs of themselves together with other family members as an introduction to the concept. Older children could be asked to gather information to share with peers about their specific family structure. Exploring family from a four-year-old perspective might allow the teacher to introduce the topic area 'time, continuity and change', which could include a study of grandparents and other elders in the community.

Under the topic area 'civic ideals and practices', the concept of democracy could also be introduced to children at an age-appropriate level. Activities with young children might focus on ECCE centre rules to keep order, how to be fair and to respect one another, all of which are an integral part of democratic practice. We might also discuss turn taking and collaboration during tidy-up time, and how as a group we need to work together to become a 'community of learners' who try to support each other and share resources (Mindes, 2011).

13.7.1.2 Social sciences: geographical perspective

Geographical content could include, as we have already pointed out, information about where children live and what happens in the local neighbourhood, the location of the ECCE centre and why it is located where it is.

Preschool children could, for example, explore:

- people, places and environments
- production, distribution and consumption
- science, technology and society.

Something to consider

Do not be overwhelmed by the broadness of these topics. What you need to do is find an element that relates to the baby, toddler or young child, and try it out. People, places and environment, for example, could look at the many different types of homes people live in. It could explore neighbourhood businesses, both formal and informal, and investigate environmental change such as the weather and the seasons. Product, distribution and consumption could look at where milk comes from, how maize and wheat are stored, and later ground into mielie meal and flour respectively.

Each topic should be based on the children's interests and cultural context. There should be an inherent and inextricable link between family, culture and community in the teaching and learning of social studies in the early years. You will also notice how closely topics in the social sciences overlap with those from the natural and life sciences, as well as with areas of holistic development such as social and emotional development because each child's social understandings about the world begins with self and family, expanding to the ECCE setting and later the broader community (Mindes, 2011).

In addition, the child's social understandings will always be, to some extent, culturally determined. The primary purpose of social studies is to 'help young people develop the ability to make informed and reasoned decisions for the public good as citizens of a culturally diverse, democratic society in an interdependent world' (NCSS, 1993: 3). The NCSS might be America based but its aims are as relevant to South Africa as to the US.

13.7.2 Embracing playful pedagogy: a useful approach to introducing the social sciences

Bruner (1960) argued that children are active learners who construct their own knowledge. He maintained that the purpose of education is not to impart knowledge but to facilitate a child's thinking and problem-solving skills that can then be transferred to a range of situations. His argument therefore supports a hands-on learning approach drawing on inquiry-based teaching and learning, which fosters curiosity, problem-solving skills and an appreciation of investigation. Other education theorists also support this type of teaching and learning (see chapters 2 and 3), which is an important element in playful pedagogy (see Chapter 6).

The notion of investigation is a useful starting point as children participate in the resolution of simple playroom and ECCE issues, such as how five children can share two red pencils in a fair way. This form of social inquiry that facilitates personal interactions and forms part of self-development enhances the child's understanding of the social world of the playroom, the ECCE setting and the type of issues that can arise. In developing these social inquiries, teachers first focus on what children know and are able to do. They then scaffold additional learning as they help children deepen their understandings of the world around them and how to negotiate their way in this world.

Teachers should model acceptable behaviour patterns and reinforce them in babies, toddlers and young children. Acceptable behaviours form part of ethical considerations and will include decisions about honesty, fairness, courtesy and respect for others. For example, toddlers in an ECCE centre are taught that they cannot grab a sandwich off a friend's plate but must wait their turn to be offered one. Young children should be encouraged to take turns doing tasks that keep the playroom tidy and running smoothly; in other words, tidy-up time.

Such tasks can be accompanied by the use of song and rhyme, for example sung to the tune of *I hear thunder*:

Time to tidy, time to tidy
Let's all help, let's all help
All of us together, all of us together
I take this, you take that

Try this out for yourself in your playroom or home setting.

Teachers (and parents) enhance the child's self-development by providing a safe, respectful environment that offers sufficient appealing resources and toys to foster curiosity and inquiry. Infants and toddlers play alone, side by side and with others to construct their social understandings of themselves and others but still need, as we have stressed throughout, nurturance and respect from teachers and families. A sensitive, respectful approach to the child and his family sets the tone for each child's broader social learning experience.

Find out more

In these early years, playful pedagogies include rhymes and songs, telling as well as reading stories from various viewpoints and cultures, displaying pictures that reflect families in the community, and modelling an appreciation for all cultures and backgrounds. Inviting parents and other community members to share, for example, their cultural practices with the children or share information about their occupation or hobby are other ways to encourage children to become curious about their local communities. It also helps to develop respect for others, and provides opportunities to learn about various cultural practices. Knowledge fuels understanding.

Try this out

Can you find five books and several rhymes or songs that are suitable for young children? They could serve as a link to a particular theme such as food, homes and shelter, clothing and transportation to name a few.

Teachers can encourage young children to hypothesise (say what they think might happen), find out about the theme (perhaps through a discussion or a teacher-facilitated inquiry) and share their findings (which they could capture in a drawing). In this way, even young children are becoming 'social scientists' as they investigate a topic and come to some conclusions.

Young children can be taken on outings (where possible), shown relevant books and pictures, or view short relevant TV or DVD clips or a downloaded excerpt from the internet to extend their knowledge. However, use technology cautiously and not too often, as we know young children require hands-on interactive learning experiences.

An interest or topic table that displays relevant learning material is an essential learning resource. Remember children should have easy access to interest and discovery tables to support hands-on, interactive learning. The tables should be at the children's height and contain materials that they can safely touch and explore. Families should also be encouraged to contribute relevant items for the table.

Posters, which are both pictorial and have the theme name written on them in child-friendly print, should be placed above the theme table. Relevant pictures that are both clear and large enough for young children to see easily should also be placed on the wall near to the table.

> **Find out more**
>
> Try to find out through the internet or other sources what type of print is considered suitable for young children. (Hint: in Google or another search engine, type in the words 'Foundation Phase font.) Choose a social studies theme. Collect two pictures, possibly from magazines or old calendars, which could be displayed on a theme poster. Make this poster to use in your playroom.

13.8 SOME CONCLUDING THOUGHTS ABOUT SOCIAL STUDIES

If teachers view social studies as both content (organised around the children's interests and questions) and process (action-oriented strategies that reflect playful pedagogies), the social studies curriculum will become an integral part of the daily programme. Both emergent literacy and numeracy can be enhanced through accessing and using social studies content. Social development and understanding of the world are also fostered through explorations of concepts and ideas that form the various foci of social sciences.

CASE STUDY

Read the following case study: Lebo, aged three, stays with her grandmother, who is very responsive to her needs and encourages her to take part in everyday activities in the home. For instance, if Gogo prepares bread, she asks Lebo to count the cups of flour that she puts into the bowl. She also allows Lebo to feel the temperature of the lukewarm water and explains to her why the water should not be too hot or too cold when baking bread. Once the dough is ready, she gives a small piece to Lebo and allows her to mould it.

Later in the morning when they go outside, Gogo makes Lebo aware of the weather, and they pick up leaves or stones and count them. When Lebo rests in the afternoon, Gogo tells her stories and sings songs. When it is time for supper, she prepares the food with Gogo noticing how water turns into steam. Once the food is made they count the number of people who will be eating together and take out the corresponding number of plates and spoons. At night, when Lebo washes before she goes to bed, Gogo fills up the basin. Lebo plays in it with empty yoghurt cups and plastic containers, while Gogo observes and talks about what Lebo is doing. 'The plastic container floats, the cup is full, now the cup is empty', or 'It takes two small cups to fill up the large one'.

List the knowledge, skills, attitudes and values that Gogo is promoting in her interactions with Lebo. Draw on all the learning areas we have looked at in this chapter to inform your answers. Can you identify how Lebo's learning is integrated? No specific learning area is explored in isolation.

Something to consider

A birthday ring is a good example of an integrated activity. Often in an ECCE centre this is a special ring. The child chooses some special friends to sit next to her and her favourite songs to sing, and there may be a birthday cake to share with her peer-group classmates. If possible, her parents also attend, and the birthday child is made to feel very important, which enhances her self-esteem. These are all elements of personal and social development. In addition, the children are learning mathematics (number and time – how age changes over time). Social and natural sciences are also explored. Children can talk about what other family members do to celebrate their birthdays, and they can explore the calendar and elements of season and weather – Sipho's birthday is in winter – July – and Annie's birthday is in spring – September. The children can also be asked to draw the birthday child a special birthday picture, which can be made into a birthday book. In this way both the visual arts and aspects of early literacy are being explored.

13.9 SUMMARY

This chapter focused on the many different ways in which children can interact with and learn about their world. Using STEAM and the social sciences as a frame, it has considered how the teacher can facilitate learning through making appropriate choices and seeing potential in the simplest of materials, for example a broken alarm clock. It has also shown how playful pedagogies and the creative arts can provide a form of expression and exploration that fosters young children's holistic development, learning and wellbeing.

REFERENCES

Balfanz, R, Ginsburg, HP & Greenes, C. 2003. The Big Math for Little Kids early childhood mathematics program. *Teaching Children Mathematics*, 9(5). Texas: National Council of Teachers of Mathematics, Inc.

Barrett, D. 2017. STEAM *Framework Feasibility Study*. https://child360.org/wp-content/uploads/2017/06/LAUP_CA_FULLREPORT_STEAMFFS_rev20170619.pdf (Accessed 1 November 2019).

Berry, CF & Mindes, G. 1993. *Planning a theme-based curriculum: Goals, themes, activities, and planning guides for 4s and 5s.* Glenview, IL: Goodyear.

Bowman, B, Donovan, M & Burns, M. 2001. *Eager to learn: Educating our preschoolers.* Washington, DC: National Academic Press.

Bruce, T. 2010. *Early childhood: A guide for students.* London: SAGE.

Bruner, J. 1960. *The process of education*, Cambridge, MA: Harvard University Press.

Bruns, J, Eichen, L & Gasteiger, H. 2017. Mathematics-related competence of early childhood teachers visiting a continuous professional development course: An intervention study. *Mathematics Teacher Education and Development*, 19(3): 76–93.

Carlsson-Paige, N. 2012. Media and technology in early childhood education. *Connections: The Journal of the California Association for the Education of Young Children*, 25–28.

Department of Basic Education (DBE). 2015. *The National Curriculum Framework from birth to four*. Pretoria.

Donald, D, Lazarus, S & Lolwana, P. 2007. *Educational psychology in social context.* Cape Town: Oxford University Press Southern Africa.

Early mathematics: A guide for improving teaching and learning. 2016. Education Review Office: New Zealand government. https://www.ero.govt.nz/publications/early-mathematics-a-guide-for-improving-teaching-and-learning/ (Accessed_12 May 2019).

Gasteiger, H. 2014. Professionalization of early childhood educators with a focus on natural learning situations and individual development of mathematical competencies: Results from an evaluation study, in Kortenkamp, U, Brandt, B, Benz, C, Krummheuer, G, Ladel, S & Vogel, R. (eds). *Early mathematics learning.* Berlin: Springer. 275–290.

Ginsburg, HP. 2016. Helping early childhood educators to understand and assess young children's mathematical minds. *ZDM Mathematics Education*, 48: 941–946.

Gordon, AM & Browne, KW. 2017. *Beginnings and beyond. Foundations in early childhood education.* 10th ed. Boston: Cengage Learning.

Lopes, CE, Grando, RC & D'Ambrosio, BS. 2017. Experiences situating mathematical problem solving at the core of early childhood classrooms. *Early Childhood Education Journal,* 45: 251–259.

Mindes, G. 2005. Social studies in today's early childhood curricula. *Young Children*, September.

Mindes, G. 2011. *Assessing young children.* 4th ed. Upper Saddle River, NJ: Pearson Education.

National Association for the Education of Young Children (NAEYC). 2012. *Position Paper: Technology and interactive media as tools in early childhood programs serving children through birth to age 8.* http://www.naeyc.org (Accessed 31 July 2019).

NCSS. 1993. Definition approved. *The Social Studies Professional.* 114 (January/February): 3.

The National Council for the Social Studies. https://www.socialstudies.org

Sharapan, H. 2012. From STEM to STEAM: How early childhood educators can apply Fred Rogers' approach. *Young Children*, 67(1): 36.

Van Oers, B. 2010. Emergent mathematical thinking in the context of play. *Educational Studies in Mathematics,* 74(1): 23–37.

Worth, K. 2010. *Science in early childhood classrooms: Content and process.* Newton, Massachusetts: Center for Science Education Development, Inc.

Zarrillo, JJ. 2004. *Teaching elementary social studies: Principles and applications.* 2nd ed. Upper Saddle River, NJ: Prentice Hall.

Zosh, JM, Hopkins, EJ, Jensen, H, Liu, C, Neale, D, Hirsh-Pasek, K, Solis, SL & Whitebread, D. 2017. *Learning through play: A review of the evidence.* The LEGO Foundation, DK.

Chapter 14

Responsive spaces: observation and assessment in a democratic context

Lorayne Excell, Vivien Linington, Nontokozo Mashiya, Lara Schoenfeld and Susan Greyling

In this chapter, we consider:

- theoretical principles that underpin the assessment of young children
- developmentally appropriate and culturally responsive strategies for assessing young children
- the implementation of assessment strategies, including the recording of data and reflection on findings
- intersectoral collaboration and strategic partnerships for effective assessment practices
- an inclusive professional and ethical approach to assessment
- indicators of possible difficulties that may require intervention.

14.1 INTRODUCTION

Young children learn in ways that may seem unfamiliar to adults. For instance, children's development is fluid and multifaceted. As teachers, therefore, we need to be open to accommodating a wide range of variation within normal development and different behavioural patterns. We also need to be open to the existence of possible difficulty. Early childhood care and education (ECCE) teachers should bear this in mind as they plan their assessment strategies.

This chapter will focus on how to observe and assess young children, and the principles that underpin such assessments. An inclusive approach that is culturally and contextually relevant is a major informing principle. By recognising diversity in the playroom, we are able to plan and accept difference, which allows us to embrace one another in our diversity. By recognising that people differ in many ways – in race, culture, language, religion, age and gender, to mention but a few – we are able to create responsive spaces. Such spaces promote a conducive atmosphere for children to develop and learn. Responsive spaces allow teachers to respond to children in a positive way, as well as to assess their progress holistically.

This chapter will raise awareness of difficulties that children may have which need to be addressed. In addition, the chapter will highlight the importance of including parents and other relevant stakeholders in the assessment process being followed, and the results that emanate from it.

14.2 WHAT IS ASSESSMENT?

Assessment is an integral part of teaching and learning. The National Curriculum and Assessment Policy (2011: 66), defines assessment as:

> a continuous planned process of identifying, gathering and interpreting information about the performance of learners, using various forms of assessment. It involves four steps: generating and collecting evidence of achievement; evaluating this evidence; recording the findings and using this information to understand and thereby assist the learner's development in order to improve the process of learning and teaching.

In young children, assessment is a process that takes place over a period of time. The child should be observed in a number of different contexts using a variety of strategies before any definitive conclusions are made about the child's progress. At all times during this process, evidence should be gathered in a systematic and planned way. For the assessment to be authentic and reliable, clear criteria need to have been applied.

Find out more

The terms 'assessment' and 'evaluation' are often used interchangeably. In education, however, it is useful to make a distinction between them. Table 14.1 makes the distinction clear.

Table 14.1 Distinguishing between assessment and evaluation

Evaluation	When judgements are made about the curriculum, the teaching and learning environment or the teaching methods, this is called evaluation. It is the programme and not the child that is being evaluated (Brewer, 2014: 4; Gordon & Browne, 2017). Evaluation is a cyclical process. The teacher observes the children, and the findings from these observations inform the curriculum, the teaching and learning environment, and the teaching methods. The whole process is therefore involved in the creation of responsive spaces for learning
Formative or informal or daily assessment	Informal or daily assessment is the process of collecting information about the young child's progress through observations, discussions and other informal interactions. Informal assessment could include documenting children's activities and noting their participation. It provides an opportunity to give all the stakeholders, children, parents and others feedback on how the children are doing. The teacher may use an observation book or a checklist with all the children's names to record their progression (Brewer, 2014; Gordon & Browne, 2017; Excell & Linington, 2015)
Summative assessment	The term 'summative' describes assessment processes that 'sum up' what a child has learned by reviewing documentation gathered over time from a range of sources. These processes bring together information about what the child knows, understands and can do in relation to specified benchmarks (developmental milestones and competencies). This is not the preferred form of assessment in the early years, but it does on occasions have a place (National Quality Standard Professional Learning Programme, 2012; Brewer, 2014)

As we have already said, assessment is important because it provides us with valuable feedback about how we teach, the efficacy of this teaching and how children progress in their development and learning on a daily basis. However, the way in which teachers assess children from birth to four years of age needs to be carefully considered. They should be clear about what they want to achieve and how they are going to do so (Brewer, 2014). In order to do this, they need to have a sound knowledge of the field, which includes various assessment methods and the instruments that support each one (Brewer, 2014; Gordon & Browne, 2017).

Something to consider

The main goals of assessment are:
- to enhance the young child's personal growth and development
- to monitor the progress of the child
- to facilitate learning
- to inform the teacher about the effectiveness of the teaching-learning process

Find out more

There are comprehensive guidelines provided for assessment, both at national and provincial levels. Valid assessment consists of a number of stages:
1. Collecting evidence
2. Recording assessment evidence
3. Evaluating the evidence
4. Using this evidence to inform the teaching and learning process
5. Using all the evidence gathered to provide a detailed report of the child's holistic development, learning and wellbeing to parents and other stakeholders (Brewer, 2014; Gordon & Browne, 2017; Excell & Linington, 2015).

14.3 COLLECTING EVIDENCE: ASSESSMENT STRATEGIES

14.3.1 Observation

Observation is possibly the best way to gather a multiplicity of information about the progress of the young child. It is used to gather a broad range of insights about children and thus provides a window into their progress and current competence levels. It will also inform planning of the learning environment and the curriculum.

Observation in relation to the young child is a multisensory activity that requires teachers to use their five senses. Hygiene, for instance, requires a sense of smell, for example when a baby requires a nappy change. A distinct sign of possible fever is that a child is hot to the touch. A way of testing if the food is too hot might be through the sense of taste. Close looking and listening are also obviously important observation tools. In short, observation is to take notice, watch attentively, and focus on particular aspects of the child, sometimes with a specific reason in mind. Observation also allows one to reflect on the appropriateness of provision for individual children as well as groups (Davin & Van Staden, 2005; Gordon & Browne, 2017). Teacher observation occurs continually as a natural part of the learning and teaching process as children participate in both planned and spontaneous activities.

To observe successfully teachers need to:
- know when and what they want to observe
- set aside sufficient time
- make use of a variety of observation strategies
- record all observations – this could be done using a notebook, a checklist or by taking photographs or even a video recording
- reflect carefully on what they have observed
- share findings, when appropriate, with other caregivers, parents and stakeholders.

Try this out
Select a child in your care and, using the above guidelines, observe and record a particular behavioural aspect, for example the child's interaction with other children.

Something to consider
When doing intentional observation, each activity used for assessment should be carefully planned so that it assesses a number of the child's skills, behaviours and attitudes (Mindes, 2011). Remember that excellent observation moments can arise spontaneously. This is called anecdotal observation. Always be prepared to note down such occasions. You could, for example, carry a small notebook and pen in a pocket. Often, exchanges between children in the fantasy corner can provide rich data about their holistic development, including their perceptions of gender roles and other diversity related issues.

It is important to observe children in a variety of situations throughout the day. Meaningful occasions for observation include those listed in Table 14.2.

Table 14.2 Meaningful occasions for observation

Transition periods	Arriving, moving from the presence of the parent to the teacher
	Leaving, reaction to seeing parents, behaviour when tired
	Change over from one activity to next
	Moving from indoor to outdoor play

	Arriving, moving from the presence of the parent to the teacher
	Leaving, reaction to seeing parents, behaviour when tired
	Change over from one activity to next
	Moving from indoor to outdoor play
Other routine periods	Sleep/nap time, for example the child is fretful or settles down quickly
	Feeding, for example enjoys snack time, eats well, finishes/refuses bottle
	Toileting – number of nappies soiled, attitude to potty training, independence in toileting
Play activities	Spontaneous indoor and outdoor play
	Choice of play activities and play interests
	Play characteristics – alone, parallel cooperative play, shares, takes turns, shares resources
	Making choices – wanders aimlessly, plays, enthusiastically
	Vocalisations/language
Teacher-guided activities	Pays attention
	Cooperates, answers questions
	Participates
	Restless, engaged in activity

SOURCE: ADAPTED FROM BRUCE, LOUIS & MCCALL (2015)

Find out more

In order to strengthen observation practices, Davin and Van Staden (2005) suggest the teacher makes use of the tools outlined in Table 14.3. These three methods are both easy to use and to interpret, and if used correctly, valid and reliable. There are other methods, but we have found these to be the most useful.

Table 14.3 Observation tools

Descriptive records	Descriptive records:
	- are a particular way of recording information about the young child in the ECCE centre. They could be diaries, anecdotes or running records (these note a particular continuous behaviour sequence of the child)
	- are based on all information gained through a variety of observation techniques (eg watching and listening to young children)
	- are often continuous written records of everything said or done during the observation period
	- allow for the use of Stick-it labels or Post-it notes as useful ways of recording data
	- are often a spontaneous form of observation
Developmental checklists	A developmental checklist:
	- is a prepared list of important age- and stage-appropriate developmental milestones (eg the ability to hop on one leg – see Chapter 3)
	- indicates what kind of behaviour can be anticipated from the young child
	- enables the teacher to easily record whether or not a specific milestone has been reached or the identified behaviour displayed
	- is not a test, but merely a way of tracking a young child's emerging competencies and noting strengths or difficulties, and unique aspects
	- provides a reliable basis for progress reports and feedback sessions with parents and other stakeholders
	- allows the teacher to decide in advance what to observe
	- gives no detail about the context or about how children reacted in a specific situation

➨

Participation charts	Participation charts: • capture all possible play spaces, both indoor and outdoor • allow a teacher to record individual children's play preferences and time spent in each play area and with whom • may sound time consuming, but in fact only involve looking around every 10–15 minutes and noting down where the young child(ren) being observed that day is/are playing (see Appendix 1 for an example of a participation chart)

SOURCE: DAVIN & VAN STADEN (2005)

Try this out

Use Table 14.3 to draw up your own observation tools and use them to observe a child over a period of two days, both indoors and outdoors. Interpret your data and compile a progress report for parents.

14.3.1.1 Sampling and rating techniques

These are two additional observational tools. Though they are of limited value, they can be of assistance to busy teachers to help with the gathering of evidence. However, they should not replace descriptive or narrative records. These techniques include the following:

- Time sampling – this enables the teacher to note what specific children are doing at specific times or what is happening in a particular play area, for example the block corner or the fantasy corner.
- Event sampling – the teacher chooses an event, for example a quarrel, and when two children begin to argue, notes this specific event. Like a checklist, event sampling leaves out interesting information.

These rating techniques do not capture the causes or contexts, and give little information to use for forward planning (Bruce et al, 2015).

Reflection

Reflect on the observation activity you have completed (see the previously mentioned 'Try this out') and list the skills you used. Did you, in drawing up your observation schedule, consider the following six questions?

Why?	Decide on the general reason for the observation
What?	Decide on what to observe and the outcome or behaviour that needs to be observed
Who?	Select the children to be observed
Where?	Choose the place/activity
How?	Select the methods of observation
When and how long?	Decide on the time and length of the observation

SOURCE: DAVIN & VAN STADEN (2005)

When you carried out your observation, you should have made use of a number of observational skills. These include:

- looking
- listening
- writing
- thinking
- questioning.

These skills are an integral part of strengthening any observation. Systematic gathering and recording of evidence require preparation. This does not necessarily mean that all aspects of the process of observation need to be anticipated, but that the approach taken is deliberate rather than haphazard. It is necessary, at least, to know in advance what kinds of learning outcomes are anticipated and how evidence will be recorded. Adequate records are essential for good assessment (Gordon & Browne, 2017).

Today, of course, electronic recording also forms part of gathering data and record keeping. They have some advantages such as:

- the same photograph can be used in the portfolio of different children all sharing the same educational experience
- similar notes that feature a number of children can be used in several portfolios
- there can be a section for parents to insert comments
- they are easy to access, and examples of children's drawings, etc, can be scanned into the report.

However, there are disadvantages. These include:

- teachers and parents may not have access to electronic media, and they may not feel comfortable enough to use it

- teachers must be sure that they use the media in a helpful and informative way, and that the gathering of assessment data is not adversely affected by the use of electronic data – in other words, observation must not be compromised (Bruce et al, 2015).

All observations should be recorded in writing or through another means of documentation such as audio recordings or photographs. Keep updated assessment records and use these for feedback and planning for the next steps in the learning and teaching process. Teachers are required to analyse their recorded observations so that they might respond appropriately to what has been observed and report these observations to parents and other stakeholders (see section 14.7).

In addition, talking to and with children, interacting with them, watching what they are doing and initiating particular activities to enable observation of specific behaviours add further enrichment to the observation process. These help teachers plan for interactive learning experiences, reflect on the effectiveness of their teaching strategies and, if necessary, initiate interventions to meet the educational needs of children (see section 14.4). Through ongoing observation over the course of a year, a full picture of each child, complete with challenges and strengths, emerges. This allows for challenges to be addressed, if appropriate, and strengths to be maximised.

In summary, observation helps teachers get to know young children as individuals with unique personalities, provides a basis for making educational decisions and generates the data needed to help parents see and understand their children's progress (Gordon & Browne, 2017; Excell & Linington, 2015; Mindes, 2011; Davin & Van Staden, 2005). The creeping worksheet culture has no place in an ECCE centre. Worksheets cannot provide valid and reliable data on children of this age. Children need to play in an experiential hands-on context. We would do well to heed the words of Maria Montessori – remember to teach less and observe much. This is especially apt when working with children between birth to four years.

14.3.2 Other assessment strategies: portfolio

Though observation remains, in most cases, the assessment tool of choice, other forms of assessment such as a portfolio should also be considered. A portfolio is a meaningful collection of a child's activities and engagement with many aspects of the daily programme. It is another way of documenting a child's interests and participation in learning and other events throughout the year. It is therefore a selection of significant moments representing growth, development and learning, and provides a snapshot of a child's experiences and changing interests over the whole year. It provides ongoing evidence of children's participation, thinking and imagination. Both the child (if age allows) and the teacher should decide what goes into the portfolio.

A portfolio used during parent–teacher interviews allows parents to enter the 'school' world of their child and see for themselves his current competencies and achievements. Parents should be encouraged to value the importance of the portfolio and take time to reflect on the portfolio with their child.

A portfolio also provides evidence of teacher accountability. The items in the portfolios provide a record of what the child has done.

Among the items the teacher and child can select are the following:
- Drawings or paintings
- Photos of the child playing with a variety of resources, for example puzzles, sorting beads (if age appropriate), Duplo, blocks and other constructions, and play, often with others, in the fantasy corner
- Photos or videos of the young child playing outdoors, for example climbing on outdoor equipment, catching or throwing a ball, or experimenting in the sandpit
- A description of books the young child has listened to and stories he has told
- Notes about the child's social and emotional growth
- Narratives of observations about the child's increasing independence with routine activities such as toileting.

A portfolio is child centred, focuses on what the child can do and should provide a complete picture of the child's learning. The teacher could create age-appropriate sections of the portfolio to correspond with each early learning development area, namely wellbeing; identity and belonging; communication; exploring mathematics; creativity; knowledge and understanding of the world (NCF, 2015).

The value of a portfolio cannot be underestimated. It complements process learning and captures the approaches to playful pedagogy that should be part of any quality ECCE day. For babies and toddlers, portfolios provide pictorial evidence of an important part of their world.

By employing various assessment tools, the teacher starts to know the individual child better. Good use of assessment tools allows the teacher to gain in-depth insight into the young child's abilities, interests and level of development. Through good assessment techniques, children with special needs can be identified and interventions put in place to address specific problems.

14.4 IDENTIFICATION, ASSESSMENT, INTERVENTION AND REFERRAL OF YOUNG CHILDREN WITH DIVERSE NEEDS

As we have mentioned previously, all playrooms should be inclusive. Specifically, an inclusive playroom considers four aspects. According to the European Agency (2012) these are as follows:

1. Early identification and assessment of children with special needs
2. Early intervention
3. Early support
4. Planning for transition.

As we have repeatedly said, all children have their own strengths and weaknesses. Their development progresses according to certain sequences, but the pace may vary. A child with special needs is one who requires some form of special care due to physical, social, emotional, mental or other health reasons.

14.4.1 Early identification and assessment

The ECCE teacher should be in a position to detect, identify and assess children who have possible special educational needs so that necessary support and resources are provided. Normal growth is one of the best indicators of good health in babies and toddlers (Haymond et al, 2013). If ECCE teachers suspect delayed growth, early detection and intervention are essential to ensure optimal management of underlying medical conditions and to ensure that additional resources and support are made available for these children.

As teachers we must have detailed knowledge about holistic development and insight into children's particular contexts. Within the South African context, we must also be aware of the many and varied socioeconomic challenges facing families. Poverty, inadequate housing and living conditions, poor access to health services and the absence of one or both parents are well-described contexts for many young children (Viviers, Biersteker & Moruane, 2013)). Sometimes inadequate nutrition, lack of sleep or conditions related to poor personal and environmental hygiene (see Chapter 9) are the reasons for developmental and learning difficulties. These ought to be addressed in conjunction with families and other appropriate stakeholders.

In addition, we also need to be aware of possible development lags and certain behaviours that might alert us to a possible learning difficulty in young children. Section 14.5.2 on red flags provides an overview of possible developmental and behavioural challenges that could alert us to referring children for further assessments which might lead to early intervention and support.

14.4.1.1 Early intervention and support

Early support is a recognised form of best practice as it aims to improve the delivery of services for children with special educational needs and their families. Early intervention refers to the support given to children who are at high risk for developmental delays or disabilities, as well as for those who may be victims of child abuse and/or neglect (McWilliam, 2010). Early intervention requires a comprehensive, collaborative approach between all the stakeholders. It includes services or provision for very young children and their families. This support is usually provided at the request of families at a certain time in a child's life. The support refers to any action taken to provide support for the identified special needs. It may also include enhancing a child's personal development, strengthening the family's own competences, and promoting the social inclusion of the family and the child (European Agency, 2010).

In ECCE centres, support should be provided through the day. The early learning environment should be one that is respectful and embraces diversity. The early childhood curriculum is flexible and adaptable (see Chapter 7) and should provide for all children's interests and needs. A playful pedagogical approach (see Chapter 6) supports differentiation and actively encourages all children to participate in all activities. By adopting a variety of teaching and learning strategies (see Chapter 8), teachers are able to respond thoughtfully to individual children's learning and developmental needs. An inclusive environment will also 'read' children and help them with special needs to adapt when necessary to a new learning environment.

14.4.1.2 Planning transition

Transitions happen whenever children move from one situation to another. This could be from parent to teacher, from one place to another, or from one activity to another. Proper planning for any transition is essential as different places and spaces have their own purposes, expectations and ways of doing things (Child Professional Support Coordinator, 2012). Good planning by ECCE centres supports and encourages the entry of children with special educational needs (Conn-Powers, Ross-Allen & Holburn, 1990) into the next phase, age group or grade. Transition may cause stress to children and it is important to note that each child responds differently to stress (Dunlop & Fabian, 2006).

Stakeholders including parents and teachers involved in the transition planning phase should ensure that children, where possible, have an active role in preparing for transitions to enable them to understand the reasons for the transition and what their role in this is. Stakeholders should also talk to the children about what is expected of them as they move to the next stage (Child Professional Support Coordinator, 2012).

14.4.2 Red flags for development from birth to four years

There is such a variation in when children reach milestones, and many parents wait anxiously to see if their child walks or talks when they are supposed to. Some parents and caregivers also compare their children to others, causing unnecessary anxiety. Children are all so different and so it is not helpful to use milestones as a list against which a child's achievements are measured. In fact, half of all children do not necessarily reach individual milestones at the exact anticipated age they are meant to (Dosman, Andrews & Goulden, 2012).

However, it is important to be mindful of some of the signs of delay and the importance of getting help early as this can result in a different learning journey altogether for the child. There are many examples of children who saw occupational therapists, speech or physiotherapists as young children and have reached high levels of achievement. Indeed, one such individual now works for the National Aeronautics and Space Administration (NASA), launching rockets into space.

So what should one be aware of? Let us consider each age in turn. Research has identified the oldest age by which a skill should be achieved (Dosman et al, 2012). If there are two or more areas of concern, the child should be assessed.

By 4 months	Gross motor: baby lifts head when placed on tummy. Should not be floppy or stiff (eg arching back)
	Fine motor: baby brings hands together in the midline. Reaches for and grasps an object
	Social-emotional: baby calms when spoken to, enjoys making eye contact and can express joy, sadness, distress, anger and surprise using facial expressions
	Cognitive: baby looks to find caregiver, watches own hands and explores the environment visually
	Language: baby coos and by two months should have smiled and gurgled

By 6 months	Gross motor: baby can pull up into sitting position when hands are held. Can sit supported; has good head control. Should play with feet when lying on back
	Fine motor: baby can shake a rattle. Hands should not be clenched, and baby should explore objects using hands, mouth and eyes. Can hold a block using two hands, as well as a block in each hand. Grasps using the palm and first, fourth and fifth fingers, then the palm and first and second fingers
	My Finger Names 1 thumb 2 index 3 middle 4 ring 5 little 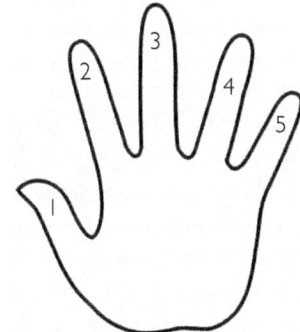
	Social-emotional: baby likes to get attention by smiling, and responds to being smiled at. Anticipates a predictable schedule. Shows interest in other babies but prefers familiar people
	Cognitive: baby will drop an object and look for it. Bangs blocks together. When trying something new, will try different ways to problem solve
	Language: baby will look at a person when spoken to and make sounds in answer (called babbling). Laughs

➡

By 9 months	Gross motor: baby must be able to get into and out of a sitting position, sit well and roll both ways (front to back, and then back to front). If baby moves out of his centre of balance, reflexes should allow him to regain balance (eg putting arms out to the side or backwards). Must take weight on legs when held in the standing position
	Fine motor: baby takes objects into hand and can use the thumb and first and second fingers to hold the object. The palm of the hand is not involved. Baby should be able to eat solids
	Social-emotional: baby is attached to consistent caregivers. Baby shares enjoyment
	Cognitive: baby realises that a hidden object still exists (also known as object permanence)
	Language: will make sounds to initiate conversation. Baby will look at a familiar object if named by caregiver. Uses gestures
By 12 months	Gross motor: baby can get into sitting position, can crawl, and pull up to stand. Can walk with support
	Fine motor: baby can use pincer grasp and can let go of an object at will
	Social-emotional: baby can play a game like peekaboo. Shows empathy to another baby. Engages in joint attention (ie will observe caregiver focusing on an object and then will look from caregiver to the object and also focus on it)
	Cognitive: baby will try and find a hidden object. Will use cause-and-effect toys (eg when a button is pushed, something pops up)
	Language: baby responds to name and can request or refuse using gestures and babbles. Can imitate clapping and wave bye-bye

➡

By 18 months	Gross motor: toddler should be able to stand independently and walk. Can also walk up and down stairs using a railing
	Fine motor: toddler should be able to stack two to three blocks. Can feed self using fingers. Can scribble holding a crayon using the whole fist
	Social-emotional: toddler can copy friend's behaviour; points to, comments on or seeks more information (another example of joint attention). Can self-calm using a dummy, blanket or soft toy. Shows emotions, such as frustration, by a temper tantrum
	Cognitive: toddler likes to sweep or mop to imitate
	Language: can follow a single instruction and point to six body parts. Generally uses 15 words and combines requests with gestures, such as taking caregiver's hand to lead to an object. Shakes head for 'no' and claps with excitement
By 2 years	Gross motor: toddler likes to run, jump and kick, and can throw a ball overhand. Can come down stairs using the railing
	Fine motor: can stack six blocks. Can copy a vertical line. Can dress self with assistance and feed self with a spoon
	Social-emotional: engages in playing next to others but does not try to interact (parallel play). Will look to caregiver to see emotions and then decide how to respond (social referencing). Can show empathy to others by comforting them
	Cognitive: engages in simple pretend play such as feeding a doll with a toy cup, but still using the object as the object
	Language: uses 50 words and two-word phrases

➡

By 3 years	Gross motor: can pedal a tricycle, if available. Can walk down stairs without using the railing
	Fine motor: can copy a drawing of a horizontal line and a circle. Can stack 10 blocks. Can use a spoon well, and drink from an open cup. Removes socks and shoes, and undresses. Tells caregiver if nappy is soiled
	Social-emotional: separates from attachment figure easily. Initiates playing with others and can share if prompted. Engages in role play (eg 'house house' and 'doctor doctor' games)
	Cognitive: symbolic pretend play has emerged and now child can use another object to represent the real object (eg feed the doll with a stick instead of a spoon). Can name one colour, count two objects, sort shapes, finish a three- to four-piece puzzle, and can use the term 'bigger' correctly when comparing objects
	Language: follows two instructions at a time and uses three- to four-word sentences
By 4 years	Gross motor: child can hop and walk backwards in a straight line
	Fine motor: can copy a drawing of a cross; can draw a two- to four-part person; can cut a piece of paper in half. Can dress self but not undo/do buttons
	Social-emotional: makes up elaborate fantasy play with roles, and rules for the role. Has a preferred friend
	Cognitive: counts four objects and understands opposites. Self-talks when problem solving. Theory of mind has developed where child understands that we can believe something different to someone else
	Language: follows a sequence of three instructions, uses complex sentences, creates imaginary scenarios, and likes playing with words and jokes

As we have already said, if you notice two or more red flags you should seek further advice and possibly refer the child for further assessment. In Table 14.4, a list of common childhood conditions is given and the specific skills that could be affected are outlined. In addition, referral suggestions are given.

Table 14.4 Common childhood conditions and the skills that are mostly affected

Condition	Gross motor	Fine motor	Social-emotional	Cognitive	Language	Who should see the child?
Cerebral palsy: damage to the immature brain causing movement difficulties	X	X		X	X	Paediatrician, speech therapist, physiotherapist, occupational therapist
Intellectual disability: a condition affecting cognitive development, from mild to severe impairments	X Will have delayed milestones Often floppy posture	X Will have delayed milestones	X Will have delayed milestones	X Will have delayed milestones	X Will have delayed milestones	Paediatrician, speech therapist, physiotherapist, occupational therapist
Autism: difficulty in social interaction and communication. Limited interests. Can be high functioning to severe. Sensory-processing difficulties	X Displays motor movements that are not typical (eg hand flapping or rocking repetitively)		X Could be withdrawn In severe cases, little or no interaction with others	X Can impact cognitive functioning	X	Paediatrician, developmental psychologist, speech therapist, occupational therapist

➡

Condition	Gross motor	Fine motor	Social-emotional	Cognitive	Language	Who should see the child?
Social emotional difficulties. Anytime a child shows a change in behaviour that persists or cannot perform due to excessive anxiety, depression or stress			X			Psychologist, Social worker
Learning difficulty: difficulty in attention, concentration, (in older children difficulties in maths or reading, writing			X	X		Developmental psychologist, occupational therapist, paediatrician, neurologist
Communication skills					X	Speech – language therapist, audiologist
Coordination and movement: difficulty in using groups of muscles together to perform tasks	X	X			X If mouth muscles affected	Occupational therapist, physiotherapist

➡

Condition	Gross motor	Fine motor	Social-emotional	Cognitive	Language	Who should see the child?
Vision* impairment	X	X	X	X		Ophthalmologist, developmental optometrist
Hearing* impairment			X	X	X	Audiologist, speech therapist
Sensory processing difficulty: under- or oversensitive to touch, sound, taste, smell, position and balance sense	X	X	X	X	X	Occupational therapist

* Deficient performance in any area may require a vision or hearing screening.

If children are going to be given the best possible chance in life, it is essential to recognise potential difficulties and, if appropriate, refer the child and family for further assessment. One way to make sure that no wrong conclusions have been drawn about a child's possible developmental and learning difficulties is to reflect thoughtfully on all assessments made before recommending that parents seek further advice. The teacher's goal is to offer parents a considered opinion.

14.5 REFLECTING ON ASSESSMENT

In order to accurately interpret data, teachers should reflect on their impressions of what happened during the observations. These reflections should include what was actually observed as well as the thoughts and questions that occurred to them while doing the observations. They should also reflect on the conclusions they have reached. Are they accurate and unbiased, and do they actually represent what was observed? Given what you know, what would an appropriate plan of action be for the young child? What should be done? What would be helpful? How do you share this information with the parents and if necessary other stakeholders? (Davin & Van Staden, 2005; Bruce et al, 2015).

14.6 REPORTING ASSESSMENT DATA

The accountability of teachers to children and parents takes place through reporting. Once assessment has taken place, it should be recorded and reported to the relevant stakeholders who include parents, administrators and others who make decisions about children. The teacher shares assessment data with colleagues and the principal of the centre. In addition, reporting to parents should be done on a regular basis to encourage parental involvement and to ensure the optimal development and learning of the child. Parents are considered to be the child's first or primary educators, hence there should be a close sharing of all observed information with parents.

The sharing of assessment data can take many forms. Apart from written reports, oral reports or examples of children's work in the display of labelled photographs, the compilation of a portfolio can be considered. Assessment findings can also be reported through parent meetings, short narrative reports, telephone calls, casual conversations, newsletters and videotapes.

However, it is advisable for teachers to compile a formal report at three- to four-monthly intervals. Where the ECCE centre follows school terms, this report could be shared with parents at the end of each term. Formal reports should be written on a specially compiled report form that displays the centre's name and logo on the front cover. All reports should be dated, have the child's name written in full, as well as the child's birth date and the exact age in years and months.

The format of the report should cover aspects relating to the child's day, the child's participation in routine activities, the child's play interests, how he interacts with other children as well as commentary on his holistic development. Children's written reports should include constructive feedback and suggestions for appropriate activities that parents could do with their child. If there are any areas of concern, it is useful to include suggestions for parents on how to deal with this issue.

However, if a more serious developmental or learning problem is suspected, teachers should always invite parents for a face-to-face contact session before putting it in writing. During such sessions, teachers can explain their concerns more fully and offer appropriate support and advice. If the teacher deems it necessary, she can refer the parents to an appropriate expert for further assessment of their child. Should this happen, it is likely that the person to whom the child has been referred will also require a copy of the child's recent reports.

When discussing assessment findings with parents, it is a good idea to share the various contexts in which the assessment occurred. To help parents understand the process of assessment in an ECCE centre, photographs of daily activities in the playroom can be displayed in the playroom, in hallways and in the entrance to the centre. Labels in the playroom describing the value of what children learn in the various activity areas (eg the fantasy area) also help adults gain deeper insight into the nature and importance of early learning. Posters explaining the value of specific activities can also be used to support parental understandings of the assessment process.

Such visual representations provide graphic evidence to parents, administrators and other teachers of children learning in a rich, exciting and inclusive context. Teachers can also send home parent newsletters that explain the activities children are doing in the playroom and the teachers' goals and objectives. When parents understand the value of developmentally appropriate activities, they will feel confident that their children are learning and growing, and that play is the best context for this.

14.7 SUMMARY

The word 'assessment' is used when decisions are made about young children's development and learning. Continuous assessment in the playroom comprises ongoing observation that considers the whole child. This means that the child is observed in a variety of different contexts, using a range of observation tools and recordings that are carefully and consistently complied. An important principle underpinning all professional practice is inclusion, and this applies as much to assessment as to the curriculum and learning environment. For assessment to be inclusive, all aspects of a child's life world need to be taken into account. A child, for example, should not be seen as developmentally delayed when he has not had an opportunity to practise a specific skill such as cutting. On the other hand, the notion of red flags, which has been discussed, should alert the teacher to areas of possible concern and the need for referral.

REFERENCES

Brewer, JA. 2014. *Early childhood education, preschool through primary grades.* Boston: Pearson.

Bruce, T, Louis, S & McCall, G. 2015. *Observing young children.* London: SAGE.

Child Professional Support Coordinator. 2012. Plan effective transitions for children in education and care services. *Child Australia.* Western Australia.

Conn-Powers, MC, Ross-Allen, J & Holburn, S. 1990. Transition of young children into the elementary education mainstream. *Topics in Early Childhood Special Education,* 9(4): 91–105.

Couper, J. 2016. *The precious years: A guide to early child development – birth to three years.* Pretoria: Struik.

Davin, R & Van Staden, C. 2005. *The Reception Year. Learning through play.* 2nd ed. Johannesburg: Heinemann.

Department of Basic Education (DBE). 2011. *National Curriculum and Assessment Policy Statements (CAPS).* Pretoria. http://www.education.gov.za (Accessed 13 May 2019).

Department of Basic Education (DBE). 2015. *National Curriculum Framework from birth to four.* Pretoria.

Dosman, CF, Andrews, D & Goulden, KJ. 2012. Evidence-based milestone ages as a framework for developmental surveillance. *Paediatrics & Child Health,* 17(10): December: 561–568. https://doi.org/10.1093/pch/17.10.561

Dunlop, AW & Fabian, H. 2006. *Informing transitions in the early years.* England: McGraw-Hill International.

Early years learning framework practice-based resources – Developmental Milestones. Community Child Care Co-operative Ltd. https://www.acecqa.gov.au/sites/default/files/2018-02/DevelopmentalMilestonesEYLFandNQS.pdf

Emirbayer, M & Mische, A. 1998. What is agency? *American Journal of Sociology,* 103: 962–1023.

European Agency for Development in Special Needs Education. 2012. *Young views on inclusive education.* Odense, Denmark: European Agency for Development in Special Needs Education.

Excell, L & Linington, V. 2015. *Teaching Grade R.* Cape Town: Juta.

Gordon, AM & Browne, KW. 2017. *Beginnings & beyond. Foundations in early childhood education.* 10th ed. Boston: Cengage Learning.

Haymond, M, Kappelgaard, AM, Czernichow, P, Biller, BMK, Takano, K & Kiess, W. 2013. Early recognition of growth abnormalities permitting early intervention. *Acta Paediatr*, 102(8): 787–796.

McWilliam, RA. 2010. *Routines-based early intervention.* Baltimore: Brookes Publishing Co.

Mindes, G. 2011. *Assessing young children.* 4th ed. Upper Saddle River, NJ: Pearson Education.

National Quality Standard Professional Learning Programme. 2012. *E-Newsletter no 40.* http://www.imagineeducation.com.au/files/CHC30113/Summative_20Assessment_NQS_PLP_Newsletter_No40.pdf

Red flags. 2016. *Early identification guide for children aged birth to five years, Child Development Program.* Brisbane North Primary Health Network. https://www.childrens.health.qld.gov.au/wp-content/uploads/PDF/red-flags.pdf (Accessed 16 June 2019).

Viviers, A, Biersteker, L & Moruane, S. 2013. Strengthening ECD service delivery: Addressing systemic challenges. *Child Gauge.* Cape Town: Children's Institute, University of Cape Town.

Chapter 15
ECD policy in practice

Linda Biersteker

In this chapter we consider:

- the legislative and policy framework governing early childhood care and education (ECCE) in South Africa
- the different roles and mandates of national, provincial and municipal government
- the implications for providers and teachers registering ECCE services of different kinds
- key management and administration functions for an ECCE centre
- ECCE services as a key point for broader early childhood development (ECD) (family support, documents, health, nutrition and social service referrals)
- future policy directions

15.1 INTRODUCTION

The legislative and policy framework for ECCE in South Africa – in other words, the laws, policies and plans that govern the provision of ECD services in South Africa – are grounded in the 1996 Constitution of the Republic of South Africa. They are also grounded in the international and regional obligations to young children which the government of South Africa has ratified, including the Convention on the Rights of the Child, the African Charter on the Rights and Welfare of the Child and, most recently, the Sustainable Development Goals (SDGs).

In this chapter, we discuss some sector-specific policies that have bearing on ECCE and the roles of different departments and levels of government. We further investigate policy and legislative requirements for ECCE service providers and teachers, and specifically outline ECCE centre registration requirements.

15.2 THE LEGISLATIVE AND POLICY FRAMEWORK FOR ECCE IN SOUTH AFRICA

ECD covers the broad range of developmental domains including emotional, cognitive, sensory, spiritual, moral, physical, social and communication, and as such involves multiple sectors and stakeholders. While a range of sector-specific polices and laws have a bearing on the delivery of ECCE services, the following are particularly important:

- National Development Plan Vision 2030 (2012)
- Children's Act 38 of 2005 as amended (including related regulations and norms and standards)
- National Integrated Early Childhood Development Policy (2015)
- National Early Learning and Development Standards (NELDS) (2009)
- National Curriculum Framework birth to four years (2015).

15.2.1 National Development Plan 2030

This has identified ECD as a top priority among measures to improve educational quality and children's future prospects. The recommendations are to:

- design and implement a nutrition programme for pregnant women and for children under three, followed by a care and development programme
- increase state funding and support for universal access to two years of ECD exposure prior to Grade 1 (National Planning Commission, 2012: 70)

15.2.2 Children's Act 38 of 2005

The Children's Act 38 of 2005 came into effect in 2010 and provides the legal framework to guide anyone involved in the care, development and protection of children for the promotion of their rights and wellbeing. As part of this, the Act regulates the provision of programmes and services for young children up to school-going age. There is a specific chapter on ECD which recognises that ECD programmes can be offered in a variety of settings. The Department of Social Development is responsible for ensuring that ECD centres meet required standards through a compulsory registration process that also involves local government clearance for health and safety, and land use. Section 92 of the Act states that the national Minister for Social Development must include a comprehensive national strategy aimed at securing a properly resourced, coordinated and managed ECD system. However, the Act does not oblige the state to provide or fund ECD services, and this is left to the discretion of provincial government. The Act requires that ECD services be prioritised in communities where families lack the means of providing proper shelter, food and other basic necessities of life to their children; and for children with disabilities and chronic illnesses.

15.2.3 National Integrated Early Childhood Development (NIECD) Policy, 2015

The 2015 NIECD policy is the primary policy that aims to ensure the provision of comprehensive, universally available and equitable ECD services. It is the country's first national policy that provides an overarching, multisectoral framework for ECD services. Service delivery covers health and nutrition, social protection programmes, parent support, opportunities for learning, communications, housing, water, sanitation, refuse removal and safe affordable energy, food security and play facilities, sport and culture.

The policy presents several strategic shifts to tackle the root causes of disadvantaged and compromised development during early childhood. These include the following:

- Locating ECD service provision as a state-led responsibility and public good (the term 'public good' recognises that ECD services contribute not only to the development of the child but also to the growth and development of society as a whole)
- Identifying and prioritising the developmental period from conception to two years (the first 1 000 days) as most critical for investment, intervention and support to enable the greatest long-term gains
- Using a rights-based approach to define an essential and comprehensive package of services and support, which should be publicly available, and identifying programmatic priorities to specifically address the current gaps in services.

The NIECD long-term policy goal is that, by 2030, a fully comprehensive, quality ECD programme that is developmentally age and stage appropriate will be available and accessible to all infants and their caregivers. To achieve this, it is proposed that, by 2024, the essential components of this programme will be in place. To date there has been a focus on establishing the necessary legal framework(s), the organisational and institutional arrangements, planning, and putting in place financing mechanisms necessary to support and realise the policy.

The policy recognises that there is a role for both public and non-governmental (for-profit and non-profit) provision of services in meeting ECD commitments. Government, however, is responsible for ensuring that all services are compliant with legal requirements and guidelines.

15.2.4 National Early Learning and Development Standards (NELDS) for children from birth to four years (2009)

This specifies desired results or developmental expectations to be reached by children from birth to four years. Age categories are: Babies birth–18 months, Toddlers 18–36 months and Young children 3–4 years. The NELDS were age and content validated, and can be used for supporting curriculum and programme development, including training, monitoring progress in learning programmes, and developing school readiness tools. The desired results are aimed at ensuring children learn in an integrated way, and enabling parents, teachers and others to provide appropriate programmes and strategies to support children's learning activities. The desired results are as follows:

- Children are learning how to think critically, solve problems and form concepts.
- Children are becoming more aware of themselves as individuals, developing a positive self-image and learning how to manage their own behaviour.
- Children are demonstrating a growing awareness of diversity and the need to respect and care for others.
- Children are learning to communicate effectively and use language confidently.
- Children are learning about mathematical concepts.
- Children are beginning to demonstrate physical and motor abilities, and an understanding of a healthy lifestyle.

15.2.5 National Curriculum Framework (NCF) birth to four years (2015)

Based on the NELDS and in line with Children's Act norms and standards for ECD programmes, the NCF provides guidelines for the design of early learning programmes. It takes an affirmative view of young children as competent and active learners, promotes cultural sensitivity, honours diversity and recognises the need for strong connections with adults. It is organised around six early learning and development areas, linked to age guidelines in the NELDS. The competency of children in each learning and development area is explored from an age-phase perspective. See Figure 15.1.

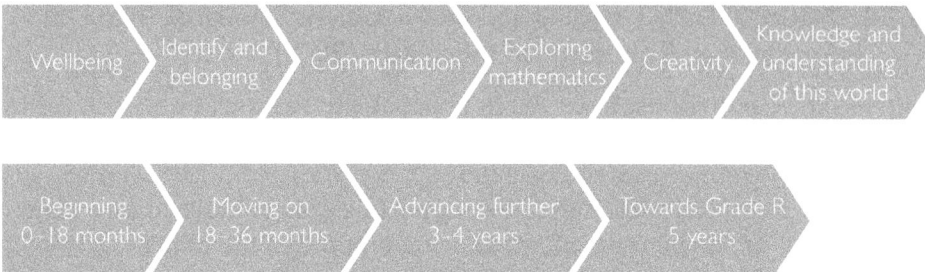

Figure 15.1 The early learning development areas and age phases

Early Learning and Development Area: Exploring Mathematics Aim 2. Children sort, classify, make comparisons and solve problems Advancing Further: Approximately 3–4 years	
Developmental guidelines	Examples of activities for adults/older children to offer younger children
Young children: • attempt to solve number problems • separate objects in different ways • count objects in a group	• Encourage interaction during activities such as storytelling, rhymes • Ask children to talk about how they solved a problem • Use pictures and objects as stories and rhymes are told • Encourage children to sort objects according to their preferences (likes and dislikes), size, shape and colour. Ask them to count on their own. Model counting behaviours to help them • Use role play and stories to demonstrate language such as 'few', 'less', 'more than', 'same as'

15.3 ROLES OF DIFFERENT DEPARTMENTS AND LEVELS OF GOVERNMENT

The role of national government in relation to ECD is developing laws, policies and norms and standards for ECD programmes and services, setting high-level access and quality targets, and monitoring and evaluating progress towards meeting them. Delivery of health, basic education and social services is a provincial responsibility and includes funding, registration and monitoring of compliance and either providing these services through the public sector or contracting private or non-profit organisations to deliver them on behalf of government. Municipalities have particular responsibilities for infrastructure, zoning/land allocation, and environmental health and safety, and can also be assigned responsibility for registration.

Table 15.1 National integrated ECD policy programming responsibilities

Department	Responsibility
Health	**Provision of health and nutrition programmes** for pregnant women, infants and children, parenting support programmes, opportunities for learning and play through health facilities, and home visits for children at risk of poor development outcomes. Focus on children from birth to two years old
Social Development	**Ensuring universal availability and adequate quality** of, and equitable access to, inclusive learning opportunities Development, delivery, regulation, registration, quality monitoring, improvement and evaluation of ECD programmes
Education	Continuity and synergy between **early learning and Grade R Training**, implementation and monitoring relating to curriculum delivery for children from birth to four years old
Municipality	Provision of basic services including water and sanitation Development of policies and by-laws governing childcare facilities, including childminder services Municipal planning and spatial development including providing and regulating land used for childcare facilities and for safe and adequate play and recreation facilities

15.4 POLICY AND LEGISLATIVE REQUIREMENTS FOR ECCE SERVICE PROVIDERS AND TEACHERS

ECCE professionals and others working with young children are required to perform their duties and responsibilities according to the Children's Act. The Act distinguishes between an ECD service and an ECD programme:

- An **ECD service** is one intended to promote the development of children from birth to school-going age, which is provided regularly by a person who is not the child's parent or caregiver. This applies where there are more than six children. This therefore applies to ECD centres, preschools and crèches.

- An **ECD programme** is a programme planned within an ECD service to provide learning and support suitable to the child's level of development. It is a planned schedule of activities designed to promote development and learning. This schedule of activities is sometimes called the learning programme or curriculum. All ECD services must offer an ECD programme, but programmes may be offered in other settings such as through home visits, toy libraries or community playgroups. Home visits with an early learning focus, playgroups and toy libraries are mostly offered by non-governmental organisations. Home visits for health or social support to vulnerable families are not classified as ECD programmes and do not have to register, though their programmes may include information on early learning stimulation. Similarly, therapeutic toy libraries offered by provincial hospitals, or toy and book libraries available from municipal or provincial library services, are not considered to be ECD programmes.

15.4.1 Registration requirements

In South Africa there is virtually no public provision of ECCE centres for this age group (birth to four years). ECCE centres are either offered on a private for-profit basis or as a non-profit community service. However, for anyone setting up an ECCE centre, preschool or crèche, including privately as a business, it is a legal requirement to undergo two registration processes:

1. Partial care registration
2. ECD programme registration.

Partial care registration focuses mostly on the place where the programme is happening to ensure that it is safe and conducive to development and learning. Programme registration is intended to ensure the quality of the early learning stimulation and applies to programmes in ECD services and other types of non-centre-based programmes.

The process of **partial care registration** involves a number of steps. ECD services that meet all the norms and standards receive a registration certificate from the Department of Social Development that is valid for five years. Because meeting all the norms and standards is very challenging for many ECCE centres, those meeting basic standards may be granted conditional registration while they upgrade their facilities toward full registration. This lasts for a shorter period and requires an upgrading plan that indicates what will be done to meet the outstanding requirements (eg building improvements, training of staff).

To register an ECCE centre, the application must be submitted to the provincial head of social development, together with a report from a social services worker and supporting documentation, including a business plan, a centre constitution, a copy of the building plans, an emergency plan, clearance certificates certifying that the applicant and staff members are not listed on the National Register for Sex Offenders or Part B of the National Child Protection Register, and a health certificate issued from the environmental health practitioner at the local municipality. Zoning permission from the local authority may also be required or in tribal areas land use permission from the tribal authority. The nearest social development office or municipal office should be contacted for help with the registration process.

> **Summary of the partial care facility registration process**
>
> 1. **Meet the social worker**
>   - Consult a social worker at the nearest Department of Social Development (DSD) office, where you will be given Form 11 to complete.
>
> 2. **Approach the municipality/local authority**
>   - Enquire about land use or a zoning certificate.
>   - Apply for health clearance – the environmental health practitioner will assess the physical condition of the site.
>
> 3. **Supporting documentation for the application**
>   - A business plan (business hours of the partial care facility, fee structure, daily routine, staff composition, disciplinary policy)
>   - A title deed, lease agreement or a permission to occupy (PTO) document.
>   - The constitution of the centre
>   - A copy of the approved building plan
>   - Emergency plan
>   - A clearance certificate (a clearance issued by the Department of Justice and Constitutional Development to ensure that your name and those of staff members do not appear in Part B of the National Child Protection Register or the National Register for Sex Offenders)
>   - A health certificate from the local municipality.
>
> 4. **Site visits and inspections**
>   - The social worker will determine compliance with norms and standards.
>   - If all conditions are met, the DSD will issue a registration or conditional registration certificate valid for five years.

The specific norms and standards and the forms that require completion can be found in the Children's Act and associated regulations (see http://www.justice.gov.za/legislation/acts/2005-038%20childrensact.pdf/) and are summarised in Table 15.2.

Table 15.2 Summary of the key areas assessed for partial care registration

Safe environment for children
Proper care for sick children or those that become ill
Adequate space and ventilation
Safe drinking water
Hygienic, and equipped with toilet facilities and adequate refuse disposal
Safe storage of anything that may be harmful to children
Hygienic area for the preparation of food for children
Measures for the separation of children of different age groups to be followed if possible (and appropriate adult-to-child ratios)
Action plans for emergencies
Policies and procedures regarding health care at the facility
Compliance with by-laws such as traffic requirements (eg parking bays, transport safety for transport organised by the facility)

To register an **ECD programme**, staff need clearance to prove that they do not appear in the National Register for Sex Offenders or in Part B of the Child Protection Register. An overview of the programme and implementation plan must be provided, as well as information on staff composition and qualifications. This is to determine whether the programme can meet the developmental needs of the children who will be enrolled. ECD programmes are assessed and monitored every two years. While registration is with the provincial DSD, provinces generally require the ECD programme to align with the National Curriculum Framework for Children birth to four years. In several provinces, education department staff assist with compliance with this requirement.

Table 15.3 Summary of early learning programme areas assessed for programme registration

Provide appropriate developmental opportunities
Help children reach their full potential
Care constructively for and provide support and security which includes having appropriately trained staff and the following staff-to-child ratios • For children between the ages of one month and 18 months 1:6 • For children between the ages of 18 months and three years 1:12 • For children between the ages of three and four years 1:20 • For children between the ages of five and six years 1:30 Plus an assistant for each of these staff
Ensure development of positive social behaviour
Respect and nurture the culture, spirit, dignity, individuality, language and development of the child
Meet the emotional, cognitive, sensory, spiritual, moral, physical, social and communication development needs of children

Current norms and standards for programme registration are most suitable for ECD centre programmes as they contain a number of provisions around care, hygiene, safety and nutrition, and need revision to allow flexibility for other forms of ECE service delivery, such as toy libraries, home visiting, and parent-and-child playgroups.

Registration requirements, especially the provisions for partial care registration, present a number of challenges, especially for the informal childcare sector, which is prevalent in poor communities.

Some of the challenges that registration may present are shown in the following case studies

Case Study

ECCE Centre 1

ECCE Centre 1 is a community-based centre that has been operating in a small town in the Western Cape for 27 years. It employs a principal, three teachers, a cook and a general assistant. It receives a subsidy from the provincial DSD, and parents pay between R300 and R350 per month. The new registration policy requires that centres have to re-register and comply with all the new requirements. Compliance is more difficult because of the recent municipal requirements, and is extremely costly. Firstly, the centre has never had building plans in the past and these are now required. They cannot afford the R8 000 to have these drawn up and then pay to register them. They also need an electrical compliance certificate and to fit fireproof doors. The centre has a beautiful children's toilet and washroom container donated by an NGO but the septic tank is too small and the centre cannot afford to connect to municipal sewerage. How do you think the centre could begin to negotiate a way forward? For example, what should they prioritise and how could they raise money to support the upgrade?

ECCE Centre 2

ECCE Centre 2 is located in a poor rural village in KwaZulu-Natal. It was set up by community members to help prepare their young children for schooling. It is a service for which few parents can afford to pay, and the staff are volunteers. Because it is in a traditional area, the local chief had to grant a PTO document to the site, which was provided free, and there are no land-use problems. In order to register, forms must be collected from the closest DSD offices, which are some 50 kilometres from the village. Getting there is costly and time consuming for each visit as there is only one taxi to the area each day and the centre has very little income. Making copies of the required forms and getting to the police station for sworn affidavits and certified identity documents relating to child protection clearance is also expensive and difficult. The principal and committee members have low education levels and have needed help to complete the different registration forms. The local social workers are overloaded as they have many responsibilities other than ECD, and so completing the forms has taken several visits and it has been difficult for social workers to go and check on the centre. After two years this centre has still not been registered, and the principal and committee are very discouraged.

ECCE Centre 3

The requirement for the separation, where possible, of children of different age groups is informed by safety and different adult-to-child ratios. This has become a problem for curricula such as Montessori, which promote mixed age/family style grouping to allow for older children to scaffold the learning of younger children. It all depends, of course, on how rigidly officials in some districts and provinces apply this requirement.

Something to consider

Why do you think registration is important for partial care and learning programmes?

Once the ECCE centre is registered, this is valid for five years, but the centre will have to reregister if the service moves to another building or site, makes changes to the structure to accommodate more children, or if there is a change in ownership.

The local authority and department of social development (or institution contracted to them for this purpose) will undertake site visits and inspections to check compliance with the norms and standards, and general operations.

15.4.2 Legal requirements for ECCE services operating on a for-profit and non-profit basis

Private ECCE services operating as small businesses need to register as a business and decide on the way they will operate (eg as a sole proprietor, cooperative, close corporation or partnership).

Non-profit ECCE centres that wish to be exempt from income tax and to apply for donor funding must register with the DSD as a non-profit organisation (NPO) (DSD, nd). To do this, they need a constitution or other founding document, and to complete an application. There are different kinds of legal entities for NPOs including Section 21 companies, voluntary associations and trusts. Many small ECCE services choose to form voluntary associations because they do not deal with a lot of money, equipment or valuable property.

In addition, ECCE services should register as a taxpayer with the South African Revenue Services (SARS) in order to submit annual returns and apply for tax benefits.

15.4.3 Funding for ECD services and programmes

Provincial social development departments pay the ECCE centre subsidies per child per day for children whose parents or caregivers qualify in terms of an income-based means test and who attend registered non-profit ECCE centres. The number of eligible children receiving the subsidy depends on amount of budget allocated by the province. The subsidy is intended to be used towards the provision of food and materials, and staff costs. It is not expected to cover all costs and ECCE centres undertake fundraising and usually charge fees to supplement the subsidy. The means test and subsidy amounts vary across provinces, but the proposal is to standardise this using the receipt of the child support grant as the eligibility criterion.

Some provincial DSDs also fund non-centre-based ECD programmes, such as home visiting, community playgroups and mobile ECCE units run by NPOs. These kinds of programmes are prioritised in the policy in order to rapidly expand access to ECCE services, especially for poor and vulnerable children.

15.5 MANAGING AN ECCE CENTRE

For those who will set up and manage ECCE centres, there is a range of considerations in addition to keeping up with compliance with registration and other legal requirements. These involve management systems, including policy, staff management, financial management and administration, advertising and marketing of the service. It is now widely accepted and demonstrated in studies that leadership and quality systems at organisational level are crucial to help sustain high-quality interactions and learning environments in ECCE centres (Biersteker et al, 2016). A local example of this comes from a study of the quality of ECD centres in the Western Cape, which found that the management and administration score was the key predictor of classroom quality for centres with similar fees and income (Talan & Bloom, 2011). Quite apart from the resourcing needs of ECCE services – including staffing, learning materials and infrastructure – keeping staff updated and motivated through reasonable working conditions, good communication and opportunities for continuing professional development are important for providing good-quality learning programmes.

According to Talan and Bloom (2011), key areas that an ECCE centre manager will need to consider include the following:

- Centre policies and operations
- Personnel and human resource development
- Financial management
- Programme planning and evaluation
- Marketing and public relations
- Family partnerships.

15.5.1 Centre policies and operations

Operational management includes the facilities and infrastructure, such as routine cleaning and maintenance, fire and safety, insurance, emergency plans and internal communications, use of technology, and control of supplies.

Making policy is one of the most important functions of management. It means developing guidelines/rules for the effective management of the organisation, and is usually done in consultation with parents or the management committee.

Policies and records required by the DSD include:

- up-to-date registration forms
- an admission policy including policy regarding HIV-affected and -infected children, and those with disabilities
- staff job descriptions.

Management will also need to develop a range of other guidelines for day-to-day operations, for example an outings procedure, transport policy, accident register and complaints procedures. Templates are available in the Bhalisa Inkhulisa guide at: http://ilifalabantwana.co.za/resources/

15.5.2 Personnel and human resource development

The principal or centre manager with support from the management committee or board is responsible for staff recruitment and hiring, organising orientation for new staff, job descriptions and contracts. There should be a written salary scale differentiated by role, qualifications and experience, and information of what benefits (eg annual, family and medical leave; pension; medical benefits; etc) are available to staff. Payslips should be issued. Formal disciplinary and grievance procedures should be available and explained. All of this protects management and staff, and should be guided by the Basic Conditions of Employment Act of 1997. Individual staff records should be on file and kept strictly confidential for use only by management.

To ensure good performance, there should be supportive supervision and performance appraisals recorded in writing. A staff development plan for continuing professional development (onsite and/or external) should be in place. Regular staff meetings should be held, and minutes kept.

Managers can promote teamwork among staff by cultivating an atmosphere of trust and respect, making each member of the team feel that they have an important role to play in the programme and involving staff in making decisions about programme activities. A positive working environment depends to a considerable extent on whether staff members are happy. Managers also need to work to keep morale high by making staff members feel valued and respected for the work they do and the commitment they show to ECD.

Something to consider

What are some things the centre manager could do to build and maintain staff morale?

15.5.3 Financial and asset management

The centre manager will have to plan and regularly monitor the budget including operating expenses and provision for large maintenance projects, equipment replacement and capital improvements. Some of the financial functions include drawing up income and expenditure reports, the authorisation of expenditure, banking, receipt and monitoring of fee payments, and preparing for an annual independent audit. Fundraising is another key role, including grant and subsidy applications if the centre is eligible for these and enrols children from families within the designated income group.

15.5.4 Programme planning and evaluation

Each ECCE service should have a written a vision statement which explains what the service ultimately seeks to achieve (eg creative, well-prepared lifelong learners) and a mission statement which briefly describes the way the particular service will work to realise the vision. There should also be a business or strategic plan that includes an assessment of needs and goals, and strategies for achieving these. These can be used as the basis for evaluating progress towards programme goals. Programme evaluation should draw on multiple sources of information including staff and parent evaluations, and there is a growing trend to solicit and include feedback from the children. Information gathered in the programme evaluation process should feed back into planning and programme implementation, and provision should be made for further feedback to staff and parents on progress.

> **Something to consider**
>
> Why would it be important to feed back to parents and staff about how the issues they have raised are being addressed or not? What would be some ways to do this?

15.5.5 Marketing and public relations

Attracting and retaining take-up of the ECCE service requires the use of different channels of communication for both prospective and current admissions. This may include written material, signage, a website, regular newsletters sent out or posted on a social networking page, as well as open days. Staff need to be trained to respond to enquiries about the programme, and there should be an efficient process for following up on them.

In addition, the service will benefit from building a network with other local community organisations including faith-based organisations, service organisations and local businesses that will be able to offer support and promote the ECCE centre. In turn, many ECCE centres also offer some outreach services to the broader community, such as making their premises available after hours for community meetings or for a health campaign. This strengthens their profile in the community and helps to mobilise support for the programme as well as improving conditions for young children in the area.

15.5.6 Family partnerships

South African ECD policy recognises parents and primary caregivers as the most important contributors to the early development of their children and that the state role is to support and capacitate them to provide an environment in which children can thrive. Ensuring a seamless transition from home to the early learning service requires that the centre manager orientates new families to how the centre operates. This includes information about fees, events, health requirements and discipline approach. Similarly, parents and caregivers are encouraged to share with the centre information about their children's health, developmental history and any special circumstances such as a death in the family. Once the child is enrolled, there should be ongoing messaging for day-to-day management and also regular conferences to discuss children's learning and development. These meetings will have to be scheduled to meet the needs of working parents. Centre managers will need to consider how best to communicate with different families, especially those whose home language is not the language generally spoken by staff.

Centres should address different ways of being family friendly, for example additional care arrangements, building the school community through functions, a recycling service and involving parents in the early learning programme in different ways. There needs to be provision for families to be involved in decision making as members of the governing body or an advisory structure.

Something to consider

What are some ways an early education programme could involve and engage families?

What would be ways of demonstrating sensitivity to different language and cultural groups, and different family structures?

15.6 ECCE SERVICES AS HUBS FOR SUPPORTING BROADER EARLY CHILDHOOD DEVELOPMENT NEEDS

While the main focus of ECCE professionals is on delivery of the early development learning programme, ECD policy recognises that the child's broader environment and especially the family play a critical role in their ability to benefit from an educational programme. The importance of good health and nutrition is obvious, and ECCE professionals need to ensure that snacks and meals provided at ECCE facilities are nutritious. They should also ensure that the programme includes sufficient rest and active play.

In addition to this, it is important to ensure that children are up to date with immunisations, and are not growth faltering or showing signs of ill health, abuse and neglect or developmental delay. Children also need birth certificates, and eligible parents might need to be assisted with applications for child support grants if they do not have them.

To do this, ECCE programmes need to develop an understanding of what local health and social services exist so that they can refer parents to such facilities. If possible, support services should be made available for caregivers are well as the children as reducing caregiver stress is important for their ability to provide positive parenting and responsive care. A good relationship with district or local-level health and social services will be invaluable for the speedy resolution of problems.

Table 15.4 Template for a referral directory

Service (eg)	Government facility or NGO	Physical address	Phone number	Contact person
Health services				
Occupational therapy Developmental assessment				
Nutrition services Growth monitoring Dietician				
SA Social Security Agency				
Department of Home Affairs				
Community safety				
Child protection				
Family counselling				
Libraries				
Parent support organisations				

Parent understanding of early learning, the kinds of activities they do with their children, what play materials are available in the home and family, and family reading practices are all significantly related to children's cognitive outcomes. Supportive and responsive relationships within the family, which are the building blocks for social and emotional development, are also crucial to enhance children's later learning. ECCE programmes should therefore support parents in preparing children for school by providing information on the importance of affectional care, the importance of play and limited screen time, early stimulation activities to do at home and how to make or access learning materials.

15.7 FUTURE POLICY DIRECTIONS

At the time of writing, a number of policy and legislation changes were in the pipeline. Firstly, the Children's Act ECD provisions are under review in order to align them with the National Integrated ECD Policy. The National Development Plan provides for the introduction of a second pre-primary year (a year prior to Grade R) and planning for this has begun, including a study of possible options for its institutional location. It will not necessarily be offered at primary schools.

A resolution taken at the 54th National Conference of the African National Conference in December 2017 was for the systematic relocation of the responsibility for ECD from the DSD to the Department of Basic Education. In the 2019 State of the Nation address, it was announced that responsibility for ECD centres (birth to four years) would be migrated from Social Development to Basic Education, and there would be a process towards two years of compulsory ECD for all children before they enter Grade 1. This process is still under review. It is not clear what the implications of this relocation of responsibility will be, but there is a strong focus on coordination from different ministries to provide a comprehensive ECD service package.

What is clear is that there will be a stronger focus on early learning and school preparedness in the years up to 2030, and government will simultaneously work to improve health, nutrition, and parent support for ECD as the National Integrated ECD Policy and National Development Plan are implemented.

15.8 SUMMARY

In this chapter, we considered the policies, rules and regulations that have a bearing on ECCE. We also set out in detail the requirements for opening an ECCE centre and meeting the registration process. This process is extremely complex, and we have noted that some centres may need considerable support to meet registration requirements. The multifaceted role of the principal and the management of the ECCE centre were also addressed. Leadership and management, including motivation of staff, is crucial for the continuing quality of ECCE services. We also considered the role of parent–centre partnerships. We concluded by exploring possible future directions for ECCE policy and practice.

REFERENCES

African National Congress. 2018. *54th National conference: Report and resolutions*. Johannesburg: African National Conference.

African Union. 1990. *African charter on the rights and welfare of the child*. https://au.int/en/treaties/african-charter-rights-and-welfare-child

Berry, L, Jamieson, L & James, M. 2011. *Children's Act guide for early childhood development practitioners*. Cape Town: Children's Institute, University of Cape Town and LETCEE.

Biersteker, L, Dawes, A, Hendricks, L & Tredoux, C. 2016. Predictors of centre-based early childhood care and education program quality: A South African study. *Early Childhood Research Quarterly*, 36: 334–344.

Carroll, C. 2017. *Social worker toolkit to support the partial care registration process*. Cape Town: Ilifa Labantwana.

Department of Basic Education (DBE). 2009. *National Early Learning and Development Standards (NELDS) for children from birth to four years*. Pretoria: Department of Basic Education.

Department of Basic Education (DBE). 2015. *The South African National Curriculum Framework from birth to four*. Pretoria: Department of Basic Education.

Department of Social Development (DSD). 2010. *Children's Act and Regulations*. Pretoria: Department of Social Development.

Department of Social Development (DSD). nd. *Building a caring society together. Non-profit organisations.* http://www.dsd.gov.za/index.php/2-uncategorised/6-non-profit-organisations (Accessed 4 November 2019).

Hamadani, J, Tofail, F, Hilaly, A, Huda, S, Engle, P & Grantham-McGregor, S. 2010. Use of family care indicators and their relationship with child development in Bangladesh. *Journal of Health Population Nutrition*, 28(1): 23–33.

Ilifa Labantwana & Network Action Group (NAG). 2017. *Bhalisa inkulisa:*

Information for Centres Applying for Partial Care Registration. Cape Town: Ilifa Labantwana.

Meier, C & Marais, P. 2017, *Management in early childhood education*. 3rd ed. Pretoria: Van Schaik.

National Planning Commission. 2012. *National Development Plan: Vision 2030*. Pretoria: National Planning Commission, Office of the President.

OECD. 2012. *Starting strong 111: A quality toolbox for early childhood education and care*. Paris, France: OECD.

Republic of South Africa. 2015. *National Integrated Early Childhood Development Policy 2015*. Pretoria: Department of Social Development.

Talan, N & Bloom, PJ. 2011. *Programme administration scale: Measuring early childhood leadership and management*. 2nd ed. New York: Teachers College Press.

UNICEF.1989. *Convention on the Rights of the Child*. New York: UNICEF.

United Nations. 2015. *Transforming our world: The 2030 agenda for sustainable development*. https://sustainabledevelopment.un.org/focussdgs.html

Wachs, T & Rahman, A. 2013. The nature and impact of risk and protective influences on children's development in low income countries, in Britto, P, Engle, P & Super, C (eds). *Handbook of early childhood development research and its impact on global policy*. New York: Oxford University Press. 85–122.

Glossary

A

Accommodation – changing cognitive structures to accommodate or make room for new information if assimilation is unsuccessful and confusion arises

Aesthetic – concerned with something that is artistic, appealing or pleasing in appearance

Agency – the active participation of individuals to bring about change as they shape and influence their daily life

Albinism – a genetic condition where children are born without the usual pigment (colour) in their bodies, known as melanin, which is responsible for eye, skin and hair colour

Anti-bias – an active approach to the identification and challenging of prejudicial and discriminatory practices in relationships between people (children are not born with bias – it is a learned behaviour)

Antibodies – special substances in the blood that help us to fight off infectious diseases

Assessment – a process that involves gathering information about what children know, understand and can do, and using this information to further enhance learning

Assimilation – the process of fitting environmental experiences and stimuli into one's current cognitive structures, sometimes referred to a 'mental maps'; in other words, the child applies what they already know to try and understand to a new experience or concept

C

Catalyst – a substance that causes a change in another substance without undergoing any permanent chemical change itself

Classify – to arrange (a group of people or things) in classes or categories according to shared qualities or characteristics

Competing discourses – discussions based on differing interpretations of ideas

Concept – an idea or thought

Conception – the beginning of a new life, when the ovum (egg) is fertilised by the sperm (male seed)

Conception – the forming of a plan or an idea

Concrete learning experiences – physically manipulating objects

Creative – relates to a resourceful and imaginative act or child

Crèche – a centre which provides full day care for babies, toddlers and young children of working parents

Chronic disease – a long-lasting disease, often persisting for more than three months (eg tuberculosis, HIV/AIDS, hypertension (high blood pressure) and diabetes)

Communicable illnesses – an infectious disease (a disease caused by an infectious organism such as a bacteria or virus) that is spread from one person or animal or indirect object to another person

Co-construction – teacher and child building new knowledge together

Cross-contamination – unintended transfer of bacteria or other infectious organisms from one surface, substance, etc, to another especially because of unsanitary handling procedures

Culture – the ideas, customs and social behaviour of a particular people or society

Curriculum – an organised framework that informs teaching and learning

D

Decolonisation – the meaningful and active resistance to the forces of colonialism, which leads to the realisation of indigenous knowledge and practices

Developmental approach – an approach that understands and builds on the 'normal' sequence of development

Dialogic reading – a reading practice using picture books to enhance and improve literacy and language skills through questioning

Differentiation – interaction aimed at a particular child that may well differ from the interaction with another child (activities can also be presented at a different level)

Discrimination – unfairness, intolerance or prejudice

Documentation – record keeping through a variety of media

E

Environment – the physical, natural and social world around us

Equilibrium – a state of cognitive balance between assimilation and accommodation – the process to achieve this balance is what Piaget called equilibration: the 'engine' that drives a child's construction of knowledge

Ethics – the standards of good and bad distinguished by a certain community

Emergent curriculum – one that is responsive to children's interests, strengths, needs and lived realities

Enculturation – the gradual acceptance by a person or group of the standards and practices of another person or culture

Experiential learning opportunities – the process of learning though experience, often known as learning through reflection on doing

Emotional intelligence (EQ) – the ability to identify and manage one's own emotions as well as those of others

Empower – to make someone stronger and more confident

F

Facilitate – to make possible; clear the way for

G

Gastrointestinal – refers to the stomach and the intestines; symptoms of a gastrointestinal infection include diarrhoea, vomiting and abdominal pain

Gravity – the natural force that causes objects to fall toward the earth

H

Holistic development – the total development of a child, which includes physical, social, emotional, cognitive, language, perceptual-motor, creative, moral and spiritual development, as well as the child's history, present status and relationships with others

Hypothesise – to give a possible but not yet proved explanation for something

I

Immune system – the processes of the body that provide resistance to infection and toxins (poisons)

Immunisation – the action of making a person immune (resistant) to getting an infectious disease (babies and young children are immunised (vaccinated) against a number of diseases such as polio, tetanus and tuberculosis)

Inclusion – recognising the right of all children to feel welcomed into a supportive educational environment

Inclusion – an approach that is inclusive of all children and marginalises no one

Inclusive learning opportunities – learning experiences that are provided and adapted to ensure participation of all who wish to take part

Intrinsic motivation – performing and action or behaviour for its own sake and personal rewards

Indigenous knowledge – local knowledge that refers to the understandings, skills and philosophies developed by societies with long histories of interaction with their natural surroundings (UNESCO, nd)

Indigenous knowledge – knowledge systems embedded in the cultural traditions of regional, indigenous or local communities

Intentional teaching – an active process and way of relating to children that embraces and builds on their strengths

Interactive – people communicating with each other, for example interactive teaching

Interdependent – mutually supportive

L

Language – a socially and culturally constructed system of communication

Learning environment – the space where teaching and learning takes place

Literacy – the ability, confidence and willingness to engage with language to acquire, construct and communicate meaning

M

Mediation – the use of, for example, language (a psychological tool) to bring about qualitative changes in thinking

Mediation – the guidance, support and collaboration with others to solve a problem

Metacognition – an awareness and understanding of one's own thought processes

Midline – an imaginary line that runs vertically down the centre of the body, dividing it into two equal halves, or horizontally, dividing it into an upper and lower section,

Multilingualism – the ability of an individual speaker or a community of speakers to communicate effectively in three or more languages

Multiliteracies – the ability to identify, interpret, create and communicate meaning across a variety of visual, oral, corporal, musical and alphabetical forms of communication.

N

Neurogenesis – the process by which new neurons are formed in the brain, which is crucial when an embryo is developing, but also continues in certain brain regions after birth and throughout our lifespan

Neuroscience – the study of the brain and the nervous system; in babies and young children this explores the development of the brain and the many influences on brain development, including a child's relationships, experiences and environment

Neural pathways – a series of connected nerves along which impulses travel though the body to the brain and back to initiate an appropriate response

Neurochemical synapsis – a process in which a nerve cell passes an impulse from one neurone to another by means of a chemical transmitter

Notifiable disease – any disease that is required by law (in South Africa by the Health Act) to be reported to government authorities, usually the medical officer of health of the local authority where the disease occurs

O

Octave – a series of eight musical notes

Oral–faecal transmission – a particular route of the transmission of a disease wherein pathogens (infectious organisms) in faecal (the body's solid waste) particles pass from one person to the mouth of another person

Organism – a living thing, for example a plant, animal, bacterium, virus

Orthodontics – corrections to irregularities of the teeth and jaw

P

Participatory learning opportunities – first-hand experiences and interactions with people and objects in which children should be encouraged to actively take part in their own learning

Pedagogical content knowledge (PCK) – the integration of subject expertise and skilled teaching of that particular subject (ie a combination of content and pedagogy). In an ECCE context it is an integrated approach informed by what and how

Philosophy of education – a set of beliefs about the purpose and practice of education

Pedagogy – the method and practice of teaching

Power – the capacity of an individual to influence the behaviour of others

Perspective – a particular view on an issue

Phoneme – the smallest unit of sound in a word; for example, the word 'cat' has three phonemes: /c/ /a/ /t/

Playful pedagogy – teaching and learning opportunities that allow children to make sense of their world as they actively engage (play) with people, nature and objects.

Post-structural approaches – considering different meanings as opposed to one fixed idea; a range of different meanings

Preschool, nursery school or pre-primary school – offers an early education programme, usually half-day and most often for children from three years, often including a Grade R class. These programmes tend to have qualified staff and may offer aftercare

Professional – working and behaving in such a way that demonstrates the ability to adapt, communicate, empathise, understand and take responsibility for the teaching and learning of children in your care

Psychology – the study of the human mind and of human and animal behaviour

Predict – to say or estimate that a specified thing will happen in the future or will be a consequence of something

Progressive education – a pedagogical movement introduced by John Dewey in the late 19th century, which values experiential learning over the more formal 'chalk and talk' approach

R

Racism – prejudice against or dislike for people who belong to other races

Receptive language – the words and sentences that a child can understand (expressive language refers to the child's spoken words)

Reflection – a form of personal response to experiences, situations, events or new information that should deepen your learning. Reflective practice is an important part of professional development

Reggio Emilia – an educational programme, child centred in nature, that originated in northern Italy.

Reliable – when used for assessment findings, describes those that make sense and that are consistent and dependable

Responsive teaching – teaching that helps to both support children and build positive relationships with them

Responsive curriculum – a learning and teaching framework that is sensitive to the unique needs of each child and their particular family context

S

Scaffold – offering support through suggestion in small helpful steps

Social justice – a view that everyone should have an opportunity to enjoy the same economic, political and social rights regardless of race, socioeconomic status, gender or other characteristics

Self-concept – an idea of the self, determined from the beliefs one holds about oneself and the responses of others

Self-esteem – confidence in one's own worth or abilities; self-respect

Self-image – how one views oneself; the idea one has of one's abilities, appearance and personality

Sensiopathic – sensory activities, frequently tactile, that offer the child an opportunity to release pent-up emotions

Seriation – the arrangement of objects by size

STEM – an acronym for science, technology, engineering and mathematics, an interdisciplinary and applied approach to the teaching of these specific disciplines

STEAM – a strengthening of STEM by the inclusion of the arts

Stokvel – a South African term referring to a savings or investment society to which members regularly contribute an agreed amount and from which they receive a lump sum payment from time to time

Socialisation – the process beginning during childhood by which individuals acquire the values, habits, and attitudes of a society

Society – a large social group sharing the same spacial or social territory

Sociology – the study of the social behaviour of humans, which also explores the meaning that they make from their lives

Sociocultural approach – an approach that considers the influence of cultural and social environments on children's development

Social construct – an understanding that society has created

Socio-dramatic play – a form of play where children create imaginary worlds, characters and scenarios that often relate to the real world

T

Teacher transmission model – an approach where the teacher instructs the children and allows very little child input, interaction and free choice

Toxic residue – poisonous remains; often refers to pesticides (poisonous chemicals) which are left on food after they have been applied to food crops to destroy possible harmful organisms

Transgender – people who have a gender identity or gender expression that differs from their assigned sex (ie a female who has a male identity, and vice versa)

Trustworthy – dependable, honest and truthful

V

Validity – refers to the fact that the assessment covered what it was intended to cover

Voice – a concept which, when used with regard to children, indicates that they are knowledgeable and competent, and what they say can and should be highly valued and respected

X

Xenophobia – racial intolerance and a fear of foreigners

Index

Page numbers that refer to figures and tables are in *italics*.

A

Abecedarian Project 19
acceptable behaviours 272, 273, 403
accommodation 51, 52, 148, 291, 455, 456
active listening 209, 297–298, 313
activity plans
    language ring *196–198*
    mathematics *389–390*
    musical appreciation *317–318*
adaptation 148
adult–child interactions 180–181
aesthetic
    definition 455
    perception *308*
affective development 36, 37, 57–58, 259, 269–270
African perspective 27, 32–34, 53
Age of Reason 28
age phases *438*
age-appropriate developmental milestones
    by 2 years 82–87, *425*
    by 2½ years 87–91
    by 3 months 63–64
    by 3 years 91–95, *426*
    by 4 months *422*
    by 4 years 95–99, *426*
    by 5 years 100–104
    by 6 months 65–67, *423*
    by 9 months 67–70, *424*
    by 12 months 71–74, *424*
    by 15 months 74–78
    by 18 months 78–82, *425*
    newborn babies 59
agency
    of children 2, 31–32, 146, *323*, 369
    of educators 115, 118
    meaning 31, 115, 455
    parents 127
agent of change 118, 222
aggressive behaviour 47, 99, 274
Ainsworth 37
air transmission of germs 226
albinism 455
alertness and responsiveness of newborn baby 59
algebra 386
alliteration 352
anger 261–262, 278, 287
antenatal services 106
anti-bias 455
antibiotics 253
antibodies 455
anxiety 262, 263–264, 268, 269, 278
arts
    creative development 304–305
    description 304

developmental continuum of literacy skills *367–368*
foundation for learning and development *305*
asphyxia *241*, *245*
assessment
basic care needs *6–7*
definition *455*
distinguished from evaluation *411*
early identification and *420–421*
early support *421*
evidence *412–419*
holistic development *420*, *431*
inclusive *431*
observation *412–418*
ongoing and informal *363*, *411*, *431*
planning transitions *421*
portfolio *418–419*
purpose of *363*
recordkeeping *417–418*
red flags for development *422–430*
referral suggestions *427–429*
reflections on *430*
reporting *430–431*
responsibilities of teachers *6–7*
standards *364*
summative *411*
what is *410–412*
asset management *447*
assimilation *51*, *52*, *148*, *291*, *455*, *456*
assistants *137–138*
associative play *156*, *267*
attachment theory *37*, *50*, *268*, *287*
attention
benefits of music *308*
auditory discrimination *298–299*
auditory localisation *338*
auditory perception *297–299*
Australian early childhood curriculum *39*
autism *427*
axons *54–55*

B
babies
introducing solids *237–238*
newborn see newborn babies (neonates)
shoe-protection policy for play areas *233*
Bandura, Albert *35*, *46*, *47*
baracas *316*
bathrooms *249*
beat (music) *309*
becoming child *39*, *40*
behavioural problems *281–284*
behaviourist theory *35*, *46*, *47*, *178*
behaviour(s)
acceptable *272*, *273*, *403*
discriminatory *284–285*
disruptive *278–281*
meaning of *272*
modification of *278–281*
orientation *295*
self-regulatory *287*
sensory motor *295–303*
sexual *285–286*
social *272–273*
being child *39*
'being in' family *31–32*
belonging child *39–40*
Bill of Rights *5*
biological determinism *34*
birthday
food for celebrations *239*
ring *406*
biting *246*, *262*, *283*
blending *353*
blood transmission *226*
bodily awareness *264–265*
books
drama and imaginative play *320*
role of picture *355–361*

selecting 356–358
story telling 359–361
bottle feeding 236–237
boundaries 269, 273
Bowlby, John (1907–1990) 268
Brazelton 37
breast milk 236
breastfeeding 106, 236
British Infant School 8
Bronfenbrenner 38, 104
bullying 282
burns 245

C

care and nurturing
    meaning 7
    relationship between growth, development and learning and 7–8, 15
caregiver
    inconsistent relationship with 268
    loving relationship 268
catalyst 455
centre policies and operations 446–447
cephalo–caudal development 44, 57
cerebral palsy 427
chickenpox (varicella) 253
child labour 28, 29
child-centred pedagogy 117, 150
child-centredness 164
childhood
    African perspective 27, 32–34, 53
    constructions of 27
    developmental perspective 27, 35–39, 41, 43, 278, 346
    historical perspective 27–29
    multifaceted (complex) understanding of 26
    shifts in understanding 25–26
    social construction 25, 27
    sociocultural contexts 30–31
    sociological perspective 26, 27, 30–32, 177
    sociology of 26, 29, 31, 34, 176
    universal child see universal child
child-initiated activities see free play
childminders 18, 439
children
    as active participants 31–32
    agency of 2, 31–32, 146, *323*, 369
    being, belonging and becoming 39–40
    best interests 122, 138, 225
    collaboration with teacher 163
    community of see community: of children
    as competent beings 171
    curriculum and 172–175
    differences in 119
    with disabilities 8, 14, 118, 119, 213, 222, 421, 435, 446
    diversity 118
    interdependent relationships 30
    knowledge and abilities 153
    lower-income 19
    moulding (shaping) 27
    multifaceted (complex) understanding of 26
    right to be heard 2
    rights of 5
    shifts in understanding 25–26
    with special needs 420–421
    vulnerable 6, 15, 16, 34, 445
    who become sick during day 251–252
Children's Act 38 of 2005 *12*, 14, 18, 19, 106, 225, 244, 285, 435, 437, 439, 441, 451
choking hazards 238, 246
chronic diseases 455
classify 455
clean water 233

cleaning 227–228, *228–230*
climbing equipment 248
closed questions 214
closure 338
co-construction
    of knowledge 151, 162, 217–218, 284, 381
    meaning 456
code of ethics for ECCE professional educators 117–118
cognitive development 52, 53, 57, 59, 86, 217, 261, 292, 329, 383
cognitive disequilibrium 51
collaboration
    during play 146, 163
    between stakeholders 8, 113, 119, 132, 138, 163
    between teacher and child 163
collegiality 116
communicable diseases 226, 227, *253–254, 254–255*, 456
communication
    adult–child interactions 181
    difficulties *428*
    early learning development area 174
    factors to consider 132–134
    of ideas during play 146
    ways to keep parents informed 133
community
    -based informal childcare 18
    of children 135–137
    definition 126, 131
    involvement 126, 131–132
    playgroups 16, 17, 18, 440, 443, 445
    sense of 135, 261
competing discourses 455
comprehension
    developmental continuum of literacy skills *368–369*
concentration
    benefits of music 308

concept 455
conception 455
concrete learning experiences 28, 155, 455
concrete operational stage *52*
conflict management 273–276
conjunctivitis (pink eyes) 253
Constitution of the Republic of South Africa, 1996 170
construction play 158–159
constructivism 36, 50–52, 149, 217, 389
content knowledge 146, 175, 179, 203, 218, 256, 459
cooperative play 156, 157, *414*
coordination
    benefits of music 307
    difficulties *428*
cot toys 249
cots 240, *249*
cradles 249
creative
    definition of 455
creative arts 304, 305–310, 325
creative development 289–290, 292, 304–305, 320, 327, 336
creative learning
    collaborative learning and 291
    importance of 291
creative solutions 146
creativity
    arts 304–305
    benefits of music *307, 308*
    coordinating gross and fine motor skills 293–294
    creative potential 290
    dance activities *317–318*
    development domains 292
    dramatic play 319–325
    encouragement of 181
    imaginative play 319–325
    learning development area 175

meaning of 290–291
music 305–316, *317–318*
not limited to arts 290
nurturing of 290–291
perceptual motor development 294–295
physical development 292
role in learning and development 291–304
stimulation 291
suggestions for parents 336
visual arts 325–336
crèches see also ECD centres or crèches
   definition 455
   home-based 18
critical thinking 146
cross-contamination 456
cultural diversity 191, 213, 270, 402
cultural factors
   growth, development and learning 107
   influencing well-being 107
cultural practices 53, 222, 396, 400, 404
cultural transmission / directive approach to play 153–154
culture 456
curiosity 188, 207, 290, 379–380, 382, 392, 395, 397, 403, 404
curriculum
   Australian early childhood curriculum 39
   caring teaching 183
   child and 172–175
   children as competent beings 171–173
   content knowledge 179–180
   contents of 176–177
   creating playful learning spaces 184–186
   culturally responsive, inclusive and integrated 182
   definition 456
   early learning development areas (ELDAs) 171–172, 174, 176, 184, 304
   emergent 150, 152, 164, 208, 209, 456
   flexibility 6
   good adult–child interactions 180–181
   growth, development and learning 171
   guiding principles 181–183
   hidden 177
   holistic development 182
   importance of learning and development 173
   language 182–183
   learning areas 171–172
   learning through play 183
   necessity of specialised for young children 171
   philosophy of education 170
   realising 184–186
   responsive teaching 183, 460
   social and emotional environment 186
   strong connections with adults 173
   understanding learning 178–179
   values 170
   well-being 182
   what is a 169, 170–177
Curriculum and Assessment Policy Statement (CAPS) 383, 384, 385

D

daily programmes *103*, 187–188, 193, *194–196*, 211, 213, 270, 329, 338
dancing 304, 312–313, *317–318*
dark play 164, 165
data handling 387–388
day-mother care 16, 18
decolonisation 34, 456

democracy
    education for 108
    morals and values 4
    role of ECCE in 4–5
    social sciences 402
demonstrating tasks 201–202
dendrites 54–55
Department of Basic Education (DBE) 11, *12*, 16, 371, 451
Department of Health *13*
Department of Home Affairs *13*
Department of Social Development 8, 11, *12*, 16, *139*, 435, 440, 441, 451
description as teaching strategy 202–203
descriptive records *415*
design
    environmental 227
development
    affective 259, 269, 270
    areas *438*
    cephalo–caudal 44, 57
    cognitive see cognitive development
    cumulative 45
    emotional 47, 57, 155, 187, 260, 261–264, 266, 268, 403, 451
    from general to specific 45
    language 57, *139*, 346, 347–355, 360, 363, 364, 369, 370, 371, 372–373
    milestones 29, 32, *38*, 40, 44, 45, 46, 58, *59–104*, 175, 289, 363, 364, 370, 374, *411*, *415–416*, 422–426
    perceptual motor see perceptual motor development
    personal 260, 264–266, 268, 269
    physical 56–57, 175, 292
    proximal–distal 44, 57
    rate of 45
    red flags for 422–430
    similar same pattern of 45
    from simple to complex 45
    social 57, 149, 155, 187, 260–261, 266, 370, 403, 405, 406, *439*, 451
    theories *35–38*, 44–56 see also behaviourist theory; constructivism; maturation theory; psychodynamic theory; psychosexual theory of development; psychosocial development theory; sociocultural theory
developmental approach 456
developmental checklists *415*
developmental continuum of literacy 363–364, *365–369*
developmental domains 35, 43, 56–104, 171, 172, 173, 174, 175
developmental milestones see age-appropriate developmental milestones
developmental perspective 35–39
developmental stages 274, 304
developmental theories
    description *35–38*
    implications of 44–56
    maturation theory 35, *38*, 44–46
Dewey, John 400, 459
Diagnostic Review 14–15
dialogic reading 357, 456
diarrhoea 232, 235, 253, 457
differentiation 191, 456
direct contact with infected skin or objects 227
disabilities 8, 14, 118, 119, 213, 222, 421, 435, 446
discrimination
    gender 284
    perceptual motor term 337
discriminatory behaviours and language 284

diseases
  chronic 455
  common childhood 253–254
  communicable 226, 227, 253–254, 254–255, 456
  notifiable 458
disinfectant solution 228
disinfecting 227–228
disruptive behaviours 278–281
diversity
  language 371–373
  valuing of in children 118
documentation 219–220, 456
'doing' family 31–32
donor funding 445
dramatic play
  books, stories, rhymes and poems 320
  description 304, 319
  setting up 321–324
drowning 244
drums 316
dustbins 228, 230, 234
dynamics (music) 310

E

early childhood care and education (ECCE)
  benefits 4
  changing landscape 2
  crucial for human development 4
  different settings 16–19
  economic, social and political support for 1
  government support 8
  historical development of 8–10
  importance of 4–5
  prior to democracy 8–9
  programmes see ECD programmes
  quality opportunities 6
  role of in democratic society 4–5
  services see ECCE services
  shift from early childhood development (ECD) 14–16
early childhood development (ECD)
  changing focus 10
  compulsory 16
  definition 9–10
  departments involved 12, 13
  difficulties with implementing policies 13
  focus areas 3
  government department responsible for 11
  historical development of 9–10
  introduction of 1
  National Integrated ECD Policy 12, 106, 439, 451
  shift to early childhood care and education (ECCE) 14–16
  stakeholders 12, 13
  what is 1–2, 3–4
early learning development areas (ELDAs) 171–172, 174, 176, 184, 304
Early Learning Resource Unit (ELRU) 140
ECCE centres
  family partnerships 448–449
  financial and asset management 447
  health and safety policies 227–240
  health certificate 225, 441
  helping children settle into 270–271
  leadership 446
  management of 446–449
  marketing 448
  non-profit 445
  personnel and human resource development 447
  policies and operations 446–447
  for-profit 445
  programme planning and evaluation 448
  public relations 448
  quality management 446
  registration requirements 440–445

Index **469**

regulation of 225
standards for 225
ECCE professional educators see also teachers
  characteristics of 112–113, 122
  code of ethics for 117–118
  emotional intelligence 113–114
  identification of difficulties 139
  leadership 112–113
  management 112–113
  professional ethics 115
  role of reflection 121
  who is inclusive ECCE teacher 118–121
ECCE programmes see ECD programmes
ECCE services
  description 7, 439
  funding 445
  health 449
  importance of quality 7–8
  legal requirements for 445
  nutrition 449
  referral directory 450
  support services for caregivers 449–450
  supporting broader early childhood development needs 449–451
ECD centres or crèches 7, 16, 18, 19, 20, 91, 435, 439, 446, 451
ECD programmes
  areas assessed for registration 443
  description 440
  funding 445
  planning and evaluation 448
  positive effects of high quality 19
  registration requirements 440–445
ecological theory 38, 104
economic factors 106
education
  health 256–257
  national integrated ECD policy programming responsibilities 439
  progressive 459
  right to 5
Education Act of 1967 9
Education Manifesto of Nationalist government 9
educational psychologists 140
educators
  agency of 115, 118
effortful control 287
electrical appliances 249
electronic recording 417–418
emergent curriculum 150, 152, 164, 208, 209, 456
emergent literacy 155, 297, 346, 347, 405
emergent responsive approach 152, 153, 154, 165
emotional development 47, 57, 155, 187, 260, 261–264, 266, 268, 403, 451
emotional factors influencing language development 370
emotional intelligence (EQ) 113–114, 456
emotions
  benefits of music 307
empathy 54, 57, 114, 323
empower 456
empowerment 220–222
encouragement 203–204
enculturation 456
enlightenment 28
entrapment 241, 245
environment 456
environmental design 227
environmental factors 31
  growth, development and learning 106
  well-being 106

environmental hygiene 227–230
equality 117
equilibrium 51, 456
equity 117
Erikson, Erik 37, 48–49, 149, 268
ethics 115–118, 456
evaluation distinguished from assessment 411
evaluation of data 146
event sampling 416
experiential learning opportunities 456
expression (emotions)
    benefits of music 307

F

facilitate 456
facilitating 205
fair play 116
falls 245
family
    importance of 172
    partnerships 448–449
fantasy play 160, *322–323* see also socio-dramatic play
fear(s) 262, 263–264, 278
feedback 204–205
feeding
    bottle 236–237
    breastfeeding 236
    introducing solids to babies 237–238
    problems 240
    toddlers and young children 238–239
fever 252, 253, 254, 412
figure-ground perception 338
financial management 447
fine motor development
    activities to enhance 186, 238, 361, 364
    coordinating gross motor skills and 293–294
    development domain 182
    developmental milestones 58, 61, 63, 65, 68, 75, 79, 84, 88, 92–93, 96, 101, 191, 342, 364, 422–426
    influence of common childhood diseases on 427–429
    occupational therapy 139
    physical development 56–57, 292
    play 153
floor sleeping mattresses 240
floor surfaces 248
flowers and plants 248
food
    for birthday celebrations 239
    hygiene requirements 234–236
    poisoning 236
    regulations 225
    reheated 236
    servers 235
    storage 234
form constancy 338
form perception (recognition) 338
formal operational stage 52
for-profit ECCE centres 445
Foucault, Michel 27
foundation phase 10, 169
Fourth Industrial Revolution 296
free play 45, 162, 191–192, *194–196*
Freud, Sigmund 36, 47–48, 149
Freudian stages of psychosexual development 48
friendships 276
Froebel, Friedrick (1782–1852) 8, 28, 29, 149, 150
functional play 77, 158
functions (mathematics) 386
fungal infection 253

G

games with rules 157, 161, 184, 267
Gardner, Howard 114, 120, 290
gastrointestinal 457
gender discrimination 284
geography 174, 379, 380, 400, 402–403
germ transmission 226–227
German measles 253
Gesell 35, *38*
gloves 232
Goleman, Daniel 113–114
government's role 438–439
Grade R 10–11, 15, 169, 293, 328, 364
gravity 457
grief 276–277
gross motor development / skills
    activities 186, 198, 205, 354, 361, 370
    coordinating fine motor skills and 293–294
    development domain 182
    developmental milestones 198, 422–426
    influence of common childhood diseases on 427–429
    physical development 57, 292
group sessions see community playgroups; playgroups
grouping 212–213
growth, development and learning see *also* well-being
    connections and relationship between 2
    cultural factors 107
    curriculum 171
    environmental, biological, social and cultural influences 2
    environmental factors 106
    factors influencing 104–107, *105*
    nutrition 239–240
    physical factors 106–107
    psychosocial factors 107
    relationship between care and nurturing and 7–8, 15
gustatory perception (taste) 300–301, 339

H

hand, foot & mouth disease (HFMD) 253
hand hygiene 231–232
handwashing 226, 227, 231–232, 234, 235, 256
head lice 253
head to toe development 44, 57
health
    breast milk and breastfeeding 236
    certificate 225, 441
    children who become sick during day 251–252
    conditions not requiring exclusion from group childcare 252
    conditions requiring exclusion from group childcare 252–253
    ECCE services 449
    education 256–257
    ensuring 181
    germ transmission 226–227
    key legislation 224–226
    medication administration 255
    national integrated ECD policy programming responsibilities *439*
    nutrition, food and feeding practices 233–240
    occupational 225
    personal hygiene 231–233
    policies 227–240
    preventative care 250–255
    promotion 256
    rationale for 225–226
    rest and sleep 240–241
    services 106, 256, 420, *450*
    stakeholders 256

hearing
    developmental milestones 60, 62, 64, 67, 69, 72
    impairment 429
    language development and 370
heat exhaustion 247
heating 249
height 240
herpes zoster 253
historical child 27–29
history 400, 401–402
Hogares Comunitarios (Community Day Care Programme) 18
holistic development
    appreciation of 290
    assessment 420, 431
    creative activities 304
    creative arts 304, 305–310, 325
    curriculum 171, 175, 182
    importance of 420
    meaning 3, 4, 457
    role of music 305–310
    science and 391
    self-regulatory behaviours 175
    sensory motor integration and 303
    social sciences 403
    standards 364
    technology 362, 398
    visual art and 325
    well-being and 175, 181, 261
home language 73, 182, 266, 270, 371, 449
home visiting 16–17, 19, 440, 443, 445
home-based ECD centres or crèches 18
human geography 400
human resource development 447
human rights 4, 15, 39
Hundred Languages of Children 151
hygiene
    environmental 227–230
    food 234–236
    hand 231–232
    personal 231–233
hypothesise 457

I

identification
    assessment and early 420–421
identity
    and belonging 174
    crisis 202
    development 265–266
illnesses 45, 140, 226, 252, 435, 456 see *also* diseases
imagination 289, 290, 291, 320, 321, 325, 337, 387
imaginative play see *also* socio-dramatic play
    books, stories, rhymes and poems 320
    description 319
    setting up 321–324
imitation 34, 47, 243, 267, 284
immune system 457
immunisation 106, 140, 226, 251, 255, 457
impetigo (infectious skin disease) 253
inclusion
    core value of 118
    definitions 457
    of subject disciplines 175
    teachers 116, 118, 120
inclusive learning opportunities 457
income tax 445
independence
    developmental milestones 62, 67, 70, 74, 78, 82, 87, 91, 95, 99, 104
    personal development 260
indigenous knowledge 2, 34, 182, 191, 456, 457
indoor learning environment 184–185, 248–249
indoor scientific play 395

Industrial Revolution 28
inequality 4, 164, 165, 220
infants
    dramatic and imaginative play 324
    equipment safety list 249
    music and dance activities 317
    visual arts 330
informal groups 213
informal language development 346
injuries
    prevention of unintentional 241–242, 244–245
instructing 207–208
integrity 116
intellectual disability 427
intellectual environment 186
intentional teaching 183, 200, 211, 457
interactive 457
interdependent 457
International Literacy Association 349
interoception sense 302, 303
intervention
    assessment and 363
    planning transitions 421
    red flags for development 422–430
    support and early 421
intrinsic motivation 362, 457

J
John Bowlby (1907–1990) 37, 268
joint decision making 128, 129, 138, 281
junior primary phase 10

K
kinaesthetic perception 339
kindergarten 8, 28, 150
kitchen areas 234
knowledge
    co-construction of 151, 162, 217–218, 284, 381
    and understanding of world 174
Kohlberg 37

L
language
    acquisition 45, 183, 191, 216, 347, 373
    definition 457
    development 57, *139*, 346, 347–355, 360, 363, 364, 369, 370, 371, 372–373
    discriminatory 284–285
    diversity in 371–373
    emotional factors influencing development 370–371
    home 73, 182, 266, 270, 371, 449
    influence of childhood conditions on 427–429
    milestones 422–426
    oral 350–352
    physical factors influencing development 369–370
    receptive 86, 347, 365, 459
    ring 196–198
    as tool for learning 182–183
large groups 212
leadership 112–113, 446
learning
    builds on everyday lives 178
    conditions for 178–179
    difficulties 428
    dispositions (characteristics) 49, 108, 202, 260
    must be authentic 178
    participatory opportunities 458
    programmes see ECD programmes
    rewarding or satisfying 178–179
    through play 162, 183, 379
    understanding 178–179
learning environment
    community of children and 135–137

description 136, 457
social organisation of 211
learning spaces
　creating 184–186
　indoor learning environment 184–185
　outdoor learning environment 185–186
legislation 435–438
Lego Foundation 379
life science 391, 403
listening
　description 208–209
　developmental continuum of literacy skills 365–366
　to music 311–312
literacy
　assessment 363–371
　benefits of music 306
　components of development 350–353
　definition 345, 457
　development 347–353
　developmental continuum 363–364, 365–369
　early intervention 363–371
　early phase 347–348
　early writing activities 361
　emergent 155, 297, 346, 347, 405
　exploring early 345–346
　holistic nature of early development 349–353
　informal language development 346
　mathematical 346
　multiliteracy perspective 346
　oral language 350–352
　phonological awareness 350, 352–354
　picture books 355–361
　print knowledge 350, 354
　reading 346
　scientific 346
　strategies for developing early 355–361
　technology and 362–363
Locke, John (1632–1714) 27, 46

M

make-believe play see socio-dramatic play
Malaguzzi, Loris (1920–1994) 149, 150, 151
malnutrition 4, 15, 107
management
　conflict 273–276
　ECCE centres 446–447
　ECCE professional educators 112–113
　financial and asset management 447
　quality 446
　of sick children 251–252
manipulative play 159
marketing 448
Maslow 38
mathematical literacy 346
mathematics
　activity plans 388–389, *389–390*
　developmental guidelines *438*
　early learning development area 174–175
　exploring early 382–390
　measurement and data handling 387–388
　number concept 384–385
　patterns, functions and algebra 386
　shape and space 386–387
maturation theory 35, *38*, 44–46
measles *253, 254*
measurement 387–388
media
　influence on well-being of child 106
mediation 458
medical doctors *140*
medication administration 255

meetings between parent and teacher 133
melody 310
memory / recall 337
message book 134
metacognition 458
middle ear infection 45, 67, 370, 373
midline 458
midline outwards development 44, 57
mixed culture and gender grouping 213
modelling 209, 210, 284
Montessori, Maria (1870–1952) 149, 150, 418
mops 228, 232
moral development 3, *37*, 291
moro reflex 59
morphology 350
motivation 114, 362, 457
motor control 57 see *also* fine motor development / skills; gross motor development / skills
movement
    dancing 312–313
    difficulties *428*
multi-age groups 212–213
multilingualism 371–373, 458
multiliteracies 458
multiple intelligences 114, 120, 290
mumps *254*
municipalities
    responsibilities of 438, *439*
music
    activities *317–318*
    beat 309
    benefits of *306–308*
    description 304
    dynamics 310
    holistic development 305–310
    implementation 311–316
    listening to 311–312
    making 315
    melody 310
    moving to (dancing) 312–313
    percussion instruments *315–316*
    pitch 309
    rhythm 309
    singing 314
    tempo 310
    texture 310
    timing *309*

N

name calling 284
nappy changing 184, 187, 188, 226, 227, 232–233
National Association for the Education of Young Children (NAEYC) 117, 118, 344, 397–398
National Child Protection Register 244, 441, 442
National Curriculum Framework 106, 143, 164, 171–177, 304, 382, 383, 385, 437–438
National Development Plan 2030 10, 20, 435, 451
National Early Learning Development Standards (NELDS) 45, 106, 171, 304, 314, 363, 364, 382, 383, 384, 385, 389, 435, 437
National Educational Psychological Service 363, 364
National Environmental Health Norms and Standards for Premises and Acceptable Monitoring Standards for Environmental Health Practitioners 225
national government 438–439
National Integrated Early Childhood Development (NIECD) Policy, 2015 12, 106, 240, 436, *439*, 451
National Register for Sex Offender 244, 441, 442

negative reinforcement 46
negative resolution 49
neural pathways 458
neural plasticity 14, 55
neurochemical synapsis 458
neurogenesis 14, 54, 458
neurones 14, 54–55, 458
neuroscience 54–56, 379, 458
newborn babies (neonates)
    alertness and responsiveness 59
    developmental milestones 59
    hearing and vision 60
    posture and large movement 59
    primitive reflexes 59–60
    social interaction 60
newsletters 133, 257, 430, 431, 448
non-governmental organisations (NGOs) 9, 110, 440
non-profit ECCE centres 445
non-profit organisations (NPOs) 9, 132, 256, 436, 440, 445
non-social reinforcers 46
non-verbal encouragement 204
normative theory 35, *38*
notifiable diseases 458
number concept 384–385
numeracy
    benefits of music *308*
nursery schools 8, 19, 29, 459
nursing support *139*
nurturing see care and nurturing
nutrition 239–240, 449

O

observation
    anecdotal 413
    assessment 412–418
    electronic recording 417–418
    intentional 413
    meaningful occasions for *413–414*
    measurement and data handling *388*
    sampling and rating techniques 416–418
    skills 417
    tools *415*
occupational therapists 138, *139*, 422, 427–429
octave 458
olfactory perception (smell) 300–301
open-air nursery school 8
open-ended questions 214–215, 216
operational management of ECCE centres 446–447
oral language 350–352
oral–faecal contamination 226–227, 232, 458
organism 458
orientation behaviours 295
orthodontics 458
othering 284
outdoor learning environment 185–186, *248*, 393–395

P

palmar grasp (middle of the hand) 44, 59
parallel play 87, 156, 267, *414*, 425
parent evenings 134
parents involvement and partnerships
    benefits of involvement 127–128, 133
    description 125–126
    on home front 128
    joint responsibility 127
    meetings 133
    mutuality 127
    parental participation 127
    parent–centre partnerships 128
    principles to encourage involvement 128–129

range of activities 126
reciprocity 127
shared decision making 127
workshops 129
parents
agency 127
definition 127
roles and responsibilities 3
ways to keep informed 133, 134
partial care
facilities see ECCE centres
key areas assessed for registration 442
registration requirements 440–445
participation charts 416
participatory learning opportunities 458
partnerships with parents / teachers 117
patterns 386
pedagogical content knowledge (PCK) see content knowledge
pedagogy see also child-centred pedagogy, playful pedagogies; playful teaching and learning
meaning 459
perceptual motor coordination 337
perceptual motor development 57, 134, 293, 294–304, 337–339
percussion instruments 315–316
performing arts 304
perimeter fence 248
Perry Preschool Project 19
personal care items 233
personal development 260, 264–266, 268, 269
personal hygiene 231–233
personal professional development 119
personality development 128
personnel and human resource development 447
perspective
meaning 459

pertussis (whooping cough) 254
pest control 230
Pestalozzi (1746–1827) 28, 149, 150
philosophy of education 170, 459
phoneme 297, 459
phonological awareness 350, 352–354
phonological skills 352–353
phonology 350
physical development 56–57, 175, 292
physical factors
growth, development and learning 106–107
influencing language development 369–370
influencing well-being 106–107
physical geography 400
physical outbursts 278
physical science 391, 403
physical space 211
physiotherapists 139, 422
Piaget, Jean (1896–1980) 26, 36, 50, 51, 52, 148, 156, 157, 177, 217, 291, 383
picture books 355–361
pincer grasp (thumb and forefinger) 44, 45
pink eyes 253
pitch (music) 309
places and spaces for doing science 393–395
planning transitions 421
play
active engagement 146
associative 156, 267
characteristics (behaviours) 144–146
classification of 156–157
collaboration between teacher and child 163
commonalities 155
construction 158–159

cooperative 156, 157, *414*
cultural transmission / directive approach 153–154
developmental milestones 64, 67, 70, 73, 77, 81, 86–87, 90, 94, 98–99, 103
emergent responsive approach 152, 153, 154, 165
emotional and social development 155
fair 116
free choice 164
free play 191–192
functional 77, 158
games with rules 157, 161, 184, 267
importance of 4, 144–147
joyful experience 146
learning through 162, 183, 379
manipulative 159
meaningful 146
meeting ELDA 1 (wellbeing) 176
one month old baby 62
parallel 87, 156, 267, *414*, 425
problematising 164–165
process oriented 155
repetition 146
risk-taking 165
role of teachers 162–164
sensory-motor / practice 156–157
social interaction 146
socio-dramatic 47, 52, 54, 160, 185, 264, 303, 319, 460
solitary 156
as source of inequality 164
spectator 156
spontaneous 155
stimulating free 45
structure or series of steps to explore 162
symbolic (make believe, fantasy or pretend) 157
teacher-guided / directed activities 163

theories 148–154
types of 157–164
underpinnings and characteristics 155
universal activity 155
voluntary 155
what is 147–148
playful pedagogies 149, 151–154, 165, 287, 404, 405, 459 see *also* playful teaching and learning
playful teaching and learning
co-construction of knowledge 217–218
demonstrating 201–202
description 200, 202–203
documentation 219–220
empowerment 220–222
encouragement 203–204
facilitating and suggesting 205–206
feedback 204
grouping 212–213
importance of 2
listening 208–209
modelling 209, 210, 284
positioning of people and equipment 211–212
praise 204
promotion of 201–216
questioning 214–215
scaffolding 216–217
science 391–397
social sciences 400–405
supervision 213
supporting children's investigations 379–381
technology 397–399
telling and instructing 207–208
playgrounds 248
playgroups 13, 16, 17, 18, 440, 443, 445
playroom
assistants 137–138
layout and maintenance 248

poems 320
poisoning
    food 236
    risks 245
police clearance 137, 244
Policy on Minimum Requirements for Programmes Leading to Qualifications in Higher Education for Early Childhood Development Educators 11
policy(ies)
    ECCE centres 446–447
    framework 435–438
    future directions 451
    programming responsibilities 439
portfolio as assessment strategy 418–419
positioning of people and equipment 211–212
positive reinforcement 46, 210
positive resolution 49
post-structural approaches 27, 459
posture and large movement
    developmental milestones 61, 63, 66, 67, 71, 74, 78–79, 82–83, 87–88, 91–100
    meeting ELDA 1 (wellbeing) 176
    newborn baby (neonate) 59
potty training 128, 184, 246
poverty 4, 15, 29, 106, 107, 139, 420
power
    meaning 459
pragmatics 350, 357
praise 204–205
pre- and postnatal experiences 107
predict
    meaning 459
predictable sequence of development 44–45
Pre-Grade R 15, 20, 451
preoperational stage 52, 383

pre-primary education
    provincial competence 9, 438
    shift to early childhood development 9–10
    training 9
pre-primary schools 9, 18, 459
pre-schematic stage 326–328
preschool
    meaning 459
    movement 8
pretend play see socio-dramatic play
PRIDDY picture books 356
principals 139
principled practice 115–116
print knowledge 350, 354
private speech 54
problem solving 96, 158, 213, 290, 319, 325, 346, 362, 380, 382, 403, 426
professional
    meaning 459
professional ethics 115–118
professionalism
    meaning 2
programmes
    daily 103, 187–188, 193, 194–196, 211, 213, 270, 329, 338
    ECD see ECD programmes
    planning and evaluation 448
progressive education 459
protective surfaces under equipment 248
provincial government 9, 438
proximal–distal development 44, 57
psychodynamic theory 47–48
psychological perspective 26, 35–39
psychology
    meaning 459
psychosexual theory of development 36, 47–48
psychosocial behaviours 107

psychosocial development theory 37, 48–50, 149, 268
psychosocial factors
    growth, development and learning 107
    influencing well-being 107
public ECD centres 19
public relations 448

Q
questioning 214–215, 397

R
rash 139, 232, 252, 253
rating techniques 416–418
rattles 316
reading
    developmental continuum of literacy skills 367
    dialogic 357, 456
    literacy 346
reception year see Grade R
receptive language 86, 347, 365, 459
receptive skills 345
recognition 338
recordkeeping of assessment 417–418
referral directory 450
referrals to services 138–140
reflection
    in becoming a professional 121–122
    meaning 365
reflexes of newborn babies 59–60
refuse removal 230
Reggio Emilia approach 137, 149, 150, 219, 291, 459
reliable
    meaning 365
repetition 35, 55, 56, 146, 156, 205, 314, 356, 358, 361, 380, 386
repetitive play 205

respectful treatment of children and family 269
respiratory syncytial virus (RSV) 254
responsive curriculum 460
responsive spaces 409–410
responsive teaching 183, 459
rest and sleep 240–241
rhymes 216, 320
rhyming 352
rhythm
    musical term 309
    sticks 316
right to be heard 2
rings or circle time see teacher-guided activities
ringworm (fungal infection) 253
risk-taking play 165
Road to Health booklet 225–226, 240
role modelling 264, 274, 284
role play 90, 319, 320, 337, 438
rooting reflex 59
roseola (baby measles) 254
Rousseau, Jean Jacques (1712–1778) 28
routines 187–188, 263, 269
rubella (German measles) 253
rubeola (measles) 253

S
sadness 277
safe sleep policy for babies 241
safety
    advanced planning 241
    checklist 247, 248–249
    checklist responsibilities 250
    education 242
    occupational 225
    policy guidelines 241
    prevention of unintentional injury 241–242, 244–245
    quality supervision 242

risks *244–245*
staff concerns 243
sampling 416–418
scabies 253
scaffolding 53, 162, 200, 213, 216–217, 292, 328, 351, 460
school admission age 10
school preparedness 451
science
    aim of 391
    holistic development and 391
    indoor scientific play 395
    life 391, 403
    outdoor play spaces 393–395
    physical 391, 403
    places and spaces for doing 393–395
    playful 392–393
    questioning techniques 397
    role of teachers 396–397
    value of 391
science, technology, engineering and mathematics (STEM) see STEM
science, technology, engineering, art and mathematics (STEAM) see STEAM
scientific literacy 346
scribbling stage 325–326
segmenting 353
selfactualisation 38
self-awareness 114, 260
self-care
    developmental milestones 62, 67, 70, 74, 78, 82, 87, 91, 95, 99, 104
    personal development 260
self-concept 40, 57, 265, 266, 321, 460
self-confidence 147, 260
self-development 403, 404
self-discipline 287
self-esteem 260, 460
self-image 57, 147, 460

self-reflection 284
self-reflective teachers 278
self-regulation 54, 57, *103*, 114, 119, 163, 175, 206, 287
self-regulatory behaviours 287
self-respect 260
semantics 350, 357
sense of loss 277
senses 302
sensiopathic 264, 275, 303, 460
sensorimotor stage *51*, 383
sensory development 51
sensory motor behaviours 295–303
sensory motor integration 138, 303–304
sensory processing difficulties 429
sensory-motor / practice play 156–157
separation fears / anxiety 130–131, 268, 269, 278, *428*
sequencing 338
seriation 386, 460
services see also ECCE services 138–140
sexual behaviour 285–286
shaken-baby syndrome 246
shape and space 386–387
shared thinking 54, 151, 162, 180, 189, 284, 381
sharing 267
Sheridan, Mary 35, *38*
shingles (herpes zoster) 253
shoe-protection policy 233
sick children
    common childhood communicable diseases 253–254
    conditions requiring exclusion from group childcare 252
    conditions not requirng exclusion from group childcare 252–253
    management of 251–252

sight 369
singing 216, 314
Skinner 35, 46
sleep and rest 240–241
sleigh bells *315*
small groups 212
smell 300–301
social and emotional environment 186
social behaviour
    developmental milestones *62, 64, 67, 70, 73, 77, 81, 86–87, 90, 94, 98–99, 103*
    learning about 272–273
    meeting ELDA 1 (wellbeing) *176*
social cognition 260, 271
social construct 27, 34, 460
social constructivism 36, 149, 217
social development 57, 149, 155, 187, 260–261, 266, 370, 403, 405, 406, *439, 451*
social emotional difficulties *428*
social factors influencing language development 370–371
social interaction 30, 53, *60, 103*, 146, 272, 379, 398
social justice 2, 220, 222, 460
social learning theory 35, 47, 284
social organisation of learning environment 211
social referencing 77, 265, 267, 273, 425
social reform 2, 29
social reinforcers 46, 47
social relationships 266–267
social rules 272, 273
social sciences
    contents of 400–401
    embracing playful pedagogy 403–405
    exploring 400–405

    geographical perspective 402–403
    historical perspective 401–402
    holistic development 403
social skills 114, 127, 266, 276, *307*
social workers *139*, 444
social world
    understanding and managing 271–286
socialisation 26, 27, 33, 47, 112, 287, 460
society
    meaning 460
sociocultural approach 30–31, 460
sociocultural theory 30–31, 53–54
socio-dramatic play 47, 52, 54, 160, 185, 264, 303, 319, 460 see *also* imaginative play
socioeconomic factors 106
sociological child 30–32
sociology
    of childhood 26, 29, 31, 34, 176
    meaning 30, 460
solitary play 156
South African Council of Educators (SACE) 11, 118
South African National Curriculum Framework 106, 143, 164, 171–177
South African Schools Act 84 of 1996 9, 10
space(s)
    for doing science 393–395
    physical 211
    responsive 409–410
    shape and 386–387
    sufficient 136, 191, 205, 211, 227
spatial awareness 295, *308*
spatial orientation 57, 295
speaking 345, *365–366*
special needs 45, 420–421
spectator play 156

speech, language and communication
    developmental milestones 62, 64, 69, 72, 76, 80, 85–86, 89, 93–94, 97–98, 102
speech and hearing therapists 139
stakeholders
    collaboration between 8, 113, 119, 132, 138, 163
    early childhood development 12, 13
    health 256
standards
    assessments 364
    ECCE centres 225
    holistic development 364
    National Early Learning Development Standards (NELDS) 45, 106, 171, 304, 314, 363, 364, 382, 383, 384, 385, 389, 435, 437
    National Environmental Health Norms and Standards for Premises and Acceptable Monitoring Standards for Environmental Health Practitioners 225
STEAM 379, 381–382, 384, 407, 460
STEM 379, 381–382, 460
stiff neck 252, 253
stokvels 460
storage of equipment 249
story telling 207, 264, 359–361
stress 107, 130, 146, 262, 263, 421, 428
subsidies 445
sudden infant death syndrome (SIDS) 241, 246
suffocation 241, 245
suggesting 205–206
sun damage 246
sun-safe policy 246–247
supervision 213, 242
supervisors 139

support
    early 421
    referrals to services 138–140
    services for caregivers 449–450
swearing 98, 283–284
swings 248
symbolic (make believe, fantasy or pretend) play 157
synaptic connections 55
syntax 350, 357

T

tabula rasa 27, 46
tactile perception (touch) 300, 339
tambourines 316
tantrums 86, 90, 262, 281, 425
taste 300–301, 339
taxation 445
teacher transmission model 201, 460
teacher-guided activities 187, 188–190, 196–198, 203, 212, 216, *414*
teachers
    career opportunities 20
    collaboration and teamwork 119
    collaboration with children 163
    content knowledge 179–180
    good adult–child interactions 180–181
    inclusive ECCE teacher 118–121
    management strategies in inclusive context 119
    personal professional development 119
    Policy on Minimum Requirements for Programmes Leading to Qualifications in Higher Education for Early Childhood Development Educators 11
    professionalisation 11
    qualifications 11, 15, 20, 110, 122
    referrals for support 139
    role during free play 192

role in play 162–164
roles and responsibilities 3
science 396–397
self-reflection 278
special needs *139*
who are 110–122
teaching
    caring 183
    intentional 183, 200, 211, 457
    playful *see* playful teaching and learning
    responsive 183, 459
    understanding 179–181
teamwork 119
technology
    and early literacy 362–363
    holistic development 362, 398
    meaning 362
    playful teaching and learning 397–399
telling 207–208
temper tantrums 281, 425
tempo (music) 310
temporal awareness 295, *308*
temporal environment 187–189
texture (music) 310
The Essential Package 15
theory(ies)
    of action 121
    of child development and learning 35–38
    of needs 38
third teacher 150
time
    constraints 211
    sampling 416
timeframe for teaching 170
tippy tap 231
toddlers (18–36 months)
    dramatic and imaginative play 324
    music and dance activities *317–318*

visual arts 331
toilet areas 232–233
touch *60*, 300
toxic residue 228, 460
toy(s)
    libraries 13, 16, 18, 20, 106, *140*, 440, 443
    wheeled 244
Training and Resources in Early Education (TREE) *140*
transgender 284, 461
transitional objects 121, 130
translanguaging 371
transport-related risks 244
triangles *315*
trust
    meaning *117*
    partnership principles 138
    relationship 263, 269
trustworthy 461
tuberculosis *254*
Turkish Early Education Project 17

U

Ubuntu 132, 134, 141
ulnar grasp (little finger) 44
undesirable behaviour 46, 282
United Nations Convention of the Rights of the Child 143
universal child 25, 26, 29, 40, 46, 172

V

validity 461
value-based practice 115–116
values and professional ethics 116, 117–118
varicella *253*
ventilation *249*
verbal encouragement 203–204
vision impairment 429

Index **485**

visual acuity 297
visual art
    activity planning 329–334
    art products 334–336
    description 304, 325
    holistic development and 325
    media suggestions for projects 334–336
    pre-schematic stage 326–328
    scribbling stage 325–326
visual literacy 304, 325
visual perception
    description 296
    developmental milestones 61, 63, 66, 68, 75, 79, 84, 88, 92–93, 96, 101,
vocabulary development 351, 370
vocalisations of babies 69
voice 461
voluntary associations 445
volunteers 137–138
vomiting 247, 253, 457
vulnerable children 6, 15, 16, 34, 445
vulnerable families 440
Vygotsky, Lev (1896–1934) 31, 36, 53–54, 85, 149, 160, 178, 217, 292, 389

W

walking
    average age of 45
    risks 244
wandering unsupervised 245
water supply 233
waterproof gloves 232
Watson 35, 46
weight 240
well-being see *also* growth, development and learning
    early learning development area 174, 175
    factors influencing 104–107, *105*
    holistic development and 175, 182, 261
wheeled toys 244
whole hand grasp 45
whooping cough 254
writing
    developmental continuum of literacy skills *367–368*
    early activities to enhance 361

X

xenophobia 284, 461

Y

young chilren (3–4 years)
    developmental milestones *91–99, 426*
    dramatic and imaginative play 324
    music and dance activities *318*
    visual arts 332–334

Z

zone of proximal development (ZPD) 53, 178, 216

www.ingramcontent.com/pod-product-compliance
Lightning Source LLC
Chambersburg PA
CBHW081201170426
43197CB00018B/2887